CASP+
Advanced Security
Practitioner Practice Tests
Second Edition

CASP+

Advanced Security Practitioner Practice Tests

Exam CAS-004

Second Edition

Nadean H. Tanner

73c99f3c5cb19301ed9de1524c40a1b8

Acknowledgments

To my husband, no one I'd rather quarantine with.
    To my children, who will never read this book.
    To Kenyon Brown, for trusting me to do this again.
    To Kelly Talbot, for gently reminding me of deadlines.
    To Ryan Hendricks, your turn!

—Nadean H. Tanner

About the Author

Nadean H. Tanner is the manager of Consulting – Education Services at FireEye/Mandiant, working most recently on building real-world cyber-range engagements to practice threat hunting and incident response. She has been in IT for more than 20 years and specifically in cybersecurity for over a decade. She holds over 30 industry certifications, including CompTIA CASP+, Security+, and (ISC)² CISSP.

Tanner has trained and consulted for Fortune 500 companies and the U.S. Department of Defense in cybersecurity, forensics, analysis, red/blue teaming, vulnerability management, and security awareness.

She is the author of *Cybersecurity Blue Team Toolkit*, published by Wiley in 2019, and *CASP+ Practice Tests: Exam CAS-003*, published by Sybex in 2020. She also was the technical editor for *CompTIA Security+ Study Guide: Exam SY0-601* (Sybex, 2021) and *CompTIA PenTest+ Study Guide: Exam PT0-002* (Sybex, 2021), both written by Mike Chapple and David Seidl.

In her spare time, Tanner enjoys speaking at technical conferences such as Black Hat, Wild West Hacking Fest, and OWASP events.

About the Technical Editor

Ryan Hendricks (CISSP, CEH, CASP+, Security+) has more than 16 years of cybersecurity and intelligence experience. His first venture started while working intelligence operations for the U.S. Navy and then continued in the government and private sector as an educator, facilitator, consultant, and adviser on a multitude of information technology and cybersecurity principles.

Hendricks holds many certifications covering hardware, networking, operating systems, and cybersecurity. He worked as a trainer for the U.S. Department of Defense, educating hundreds of students on everything from military communication systems to the CompTIA CASP+ and (ISC)[2] CISSP certifications.

Hendricks is a staff architect and manager at VMware. He currently supports all technical content creation for the VMware Carbon Black portfolio and additional VMware Security products. Additional responsibilities include developing labs, updating materials, piloting and expanding the certification programs, mentoring and managing the security technical content team, and educating anyone who is willing to learn. When not working, Hendricks tries to balance spending his time learning new security tools and attack techniques to feed his need for knowledge and playing video games with his kids.

Contents at a Glance

Contents

Introduction

CASP+ Advanced Security Practitioner Practice Tests is a companion volume to *CASP+ Study Guide*. If you're looking to test your knowledge before you take the CASP+ exam, this book will help you by providing a combination of 1,000 questions that cover the four CASP+ domains and by including easy-to-understand explanations of both right and wrong answers.

If you're just starting to prepare for the CASP+ exam, we highly recommend that you use *CASP+ Study Guide: Exam CAS-004* by Jeff T. Parker to help you learn about each of the domains covered by the CASP+ exam. Once you're ready to test your knowledge, use this book to help find places where you might need to read a chapter again and study more.

Because this is a companion to the CASP+ Study Guide, this book is designed to be similar to taking the CASP+ exam. It contains multipart scenarios as well as standard multiple-choice questions similar to those you will encounter on the certification exam.

How to Contact the Publisher

If you believe you've found a mistake in this book, please bring it to our attention. At John Wiley & Sons, we understand how important it is to provide our customers with accurate content, but even with our best efforts an error may occur.

To submit your possible errata, please email it to our Customer Service Team at wileysupport@wiley.com with the subject line "Possible Book Errata Submission."

Chapter

1

Security Architecture

THE CASP+ EXAM TOPICS COVERED IN THIS CHAPTER INCLUDE:

✓ **Domain 1: Security Architecture**

- 1.1 Given a scenario, analyze the security requirements and objectives to ensure an appropriate, secure network architecture for a new or existing network.

  - Services

  - Load balancer

  - Intrusion detection system (IDS)/network intrusion detection system (NIDS)/wireless intrusion detection system (WIDS)

  - Intrusion prevention system (IPS)/network intrusion prevention system (NIPS)/wireless intrusion prevention system (WIPS)

  - Web application firewall (WAF)

  - Network access control (NAC)

  - Virtual private network (VPN)

  - Domain Name System Security Extensions (DNSSEC)

  - Firewall/unified threat management (UTM)/next-generation firewall (NGFW)

  - Network address translation (NAT) gateway

  - Internet gateway

  - Forward/transparent proxy

  - Reverse proxy

  - Distributed denial-of-service (DDoS) protection

  - Routers

  - Mail security

  - Application programming interface (API) gateway/Extensible Markup Language (XML) gateway

- Traffic mirroring
- Switched port analyzer (SPAN) ports
- Port mirroring
- Virtual private cloud (VPC)
- Network tap
- Sensors
- Security information and event management (SIEM)
- File integrity monitoring (FIM)
- Simple Network Management Protocol (SNMP) traps
- NetFlow
- Data loss prevention (DLP)
- Antivirus
- Segmentation
  - Microsegmentation
  - Local area network (LAN)/virtual local area network (VLAN)
  - Jump box
  - Screened subnet
  - Data zones
  - Staging environments
  - Guest environments
  - VPC/virtual network (VNET)
  - Availability zone
  - NAC lists
  - Policies/security groups
  - Regions
  - Access control lists (ACLs)
  - Peer-to-peer
  - Air gap

- Deperimeterization/zero trust
  - Cloud
  - Remote work
  - Mobile
  - Outsourcing and contracting
  - Wireless/radio frequency (RF) networks
- Merging of networks from various organizations
  - Peering
  - Cloud to on premises
  - Data sensitivity levels
  - Mergers and acquisitions
  - Cross-domain
  - Federation
  - Directory services
- Software-defined networking (SDN)
  - Open SDN
  - Hybrid SDN
  - SDN overlay
- 1.2 Given a scenario, analyze the organizational requirements to determine the proper infrastructure security design.
  - Scalability
    - Vertically
    - Horizontally
  - Resiliency
    - High availability
    - Diversity/heterogeneity
    - Course of action orchestration
    - Distributed allocation
    - Redundancy
    - Replication
    - Clustering

- Automation
  - Autoscaling
  - Security Orchestration, Automation and Response (SOAR)
  - Bootstrapping
- Performance
- Containerization
- Virtualization
- Content delivery network
- Caching
- 1.3 Given a scenario, integrate software applications securely into an enterprise architecture.
  - Baseline and templates
    - Secure design patterns/types of web technologies
    - Storage design patterns
    - Container APIs
    - Secure coding standards
    - Application vetting processes
    - API management
    - Middleware
  - Software assurance
    - Sandboxing/development environment
    - Validating third-party libraries
    - Defined DevOps pipeline
    - Code signing
    - Interactive application security testing (IAST) vs. dynamic application security testing (DAST) vs. static application security testing (SAST)
  - Considerations of integrating enterprise applications
    - Customer relationship management (CRM)

- Enterprise resource planning (ERP)
- Configuration management database (CMDB)
- Content management system (CMS)
- Integration enablers
- Directory services
- Domain name system (DNS)
- Service-oriented architecture (SOA)
- Enterprise service bus (ESB)
- Integrating security into development life cycle
  - Formal methods
  - Requirements
  - Fielding
  - Insertions and upgrades
  - Disposal and reuse
  - Testing
  - Regression
  - Unit testing
  - Integration testing
  - Development approaches
  - SecDevOps
  - Agile
  - Waterfall
  - Spiral
  - Versioning
  - Continuous integration/continuous delivery (CI/CD) pipelines
  - Best practices
  - Open Web Application Security Project (OWASP)
  - Proper Hypertext Transfer Protocol (HTTP) headers

- 1.4 Given a scenario, implement data security techniques for securing enterprise architecture.

  - Data loss prevention
    - Blocking use of external media
    - Print blocking
    - Remote Desktop Protocol (RDP) blocking
    - Clipboard privacy controls
    - Restricted virtual desktop infrastructure (VDI) implementation
    - Data classification blocking
  - Data loss detection
    - Watermarking
    - Digital rights management (DRM)
    - Network traffic decryption/deep packet inspection
    - Network traffic analysis
  - Data classification, labeling, and tagging
    - Metadata/attributes
  - Obfuscation
    - Tokenization
    - Scrubbing
    - Masking
  - Anonymization
  - Encrypted vs. unencrypted
  - Data life cycle
    - Create
    - Use
    - Share
    - Store
    - Archive
    - Destroy

- Data inventory and mapping
- Data integrity management
- Data storage, backup, and recovery
  - Redundant array of inexpensive disks (RAID)
- 1.5 Given a scenario, analyze the security requirements and objectives to provide the appropriate authentication and authorization controls.
  - Credential management
    - Password repository application
    - End-user password storage
    - On premises vs. cloud repository
    - Hardware key manager
    - Privileged access management
  - Password policies
    - Complexity
    - Length
    - Character classes
    - History
    - Maximum/minimum age
    - Auditing
    - Reversable encryption
  - Federation
    - Transitive trust
    - OpenID
    - Security Assertion Markup Language (SAML)
    - Shibboleth
  - Access control
    - Mandatory access control (MAC)
    - Discretionary access control (DAC)
    - Role-based access control

- Application virtualization
- VDI
- Provisioning and deprovisioning
- Middleware
- Metadata and tags
- Deployment models and considerations
  - Business directives
  - Cost
  - Scalability
  - Resources
  - Location
  - Data protection
  - Cloud deployment models
  - Private
  - Public
  - Hybrid
  - Community
- Hosting models
  - Multitenant
  - Single-tenant
- Service models
  - Software as a service (SaaS)
  - Platform as a service (PaaS)
  - Infrastructure as a service (IaaS)
- Cloud provider limitations
  - Internet Protocol (IP) address scheme
  - VPC peering
- Extending appropriate on-premises controls

- Storage models
  - Object storage/file-based storage
  - Database storage
  - Block storage
  - Blob storage
  - Key-value pairs
- 1.7 Explain how cryptography and public key infrastructure (PKI) support security objectives and requirements.
  - Privacy and confidentiality requirements
  - Integrity requirements
  - Non-repudiation
  - Compliance and policy requirements
  - Common cryptography use cases
    - Data at rest
    - Data in transit
    - Data in process/data in use
    - Protection of web services
    - Embedded systems
    - Key escrow/management
    - Mobile security
    - Secure authentication
    - Smart card
  - Common PKI use cases
    - Web services
    - Email
    - Code signing
    - Federation
    - Trust models
    - VPN
    - Enterprise and security automation/orchestration

- **1.8 Explain the impact of emerging technologies on enterprise security and privacy.**
    - Artificial intelligence
    - Machine learning
    - Quantum computing
    - Blockchain
    - Homomorphic encryption
        - Private information retrieval
        - Secure function evaluation
        - Private function evaluation
    - Secure multiparty computation
    - Distributed consensus
    - Big Data
    - Virtual/augmented reality
    - 3D printing
    - Passwordless authentication
    - Nano technology
    - Deep learning
        - Natural language processing
        - Deep fakes
    - Biometric impersonation

1. Your organization experienced a security event that led to the loss and disruption of services. You were chosen to investigate the disruption to prevent the risk of it happening again. What is this process called?

   A. Incident management

   B. Forensic tasks

   C. Mandatory vacation

   D. Job rotation

2. Brett is a new CISO, and he is evaluating different controls for availability. Which set of controls should he choose?

   A. RAID 1, classification of data, and load balancing

   B. Digital signatures, encryption, and hashes

   C. Steganography, ACLs, and vulnerability management

   D. Checksums, DOS attacks, and RAID 0

3. Charles has received final documentation from a compliance audit. The report suggested his organization should implement a complementary security tool to work with the firewall to detect any attempt at scanning. Which device does Charles choose?

   A. RAS

   B. PBX

   C. IDS

   D. DDT

4. Nicole is the security administrator for a large governmental agency. She has implemented port security, restricted network traffic, and installed NIDS, firewalls, and spam filters. She thinks the network is secure. Now she wants to focus on endpoint security. What is the most comprehensive plan for her to follow?

   A. Antimalware/virus/spyware, host-based firewall, and MFA

   B. Antivirus/spam, host-based IDS, and TFA

   C. Antimalware/virus, host-based IDS, and biometrics

   D. Antivirus/spam, host-based IDS, and SSO

5. Sally's CISO asked her to recommend an intrusion system to recognize intrusions traversing the network and send email alerts to the IT staff when one is detected. What type of intrusion system does the CISO want?

   A. HIDS

   B. NIDS

   C. HIPS

   D. NIPS

6. Kenneth is the CISO of an engineering organization. He asked the security department to recommend a system to be placed on business-critical servers to detect and stop intrusions. Which of the following will meet the CISO's requirement?

    A. HIPS

    B. NIDS

    C. HIDS

    D. NIPS

7. Paul's company has discovered that some of his organization's employees are using personal devices, including cell phones, within highly secure areas. The CISO wants to know which employees are violating this policy. Which of the following devices can inform the CISO who is violating this policy?

    A. DLP

    B. WIDS

    C. NIPS

    D. Firewall

8. Suzette's company discovered that some of her organization's employees are copying corporate documents to Microsoft blob cloud drives outside the control of the company. She has been instructed to stop this practice from occurring. Which of the following can stop this practice from happening?

    A. DLP

    B. NIDS

    C. NIPS

    D. Firewall

9. Troy must decide about his organization's file integrity monitoring (FIM) monitoring. Stand-alone FIM generally means file analysis only. Another option is to integrate it with the host so that Troy can detect threats in other areas, such a system memory or an I/O. For the integration, which of the following does Troy need to use?

    A. HIDS

    B. ADVFIM

    C. NIDS

    D. Change management

10. Lisa is building a network intrusion detection system (NIDS). What can an NIDS do with encrypted network traffic?

    A. Look for viruses

    B. Examine contents of email

    C. Bypass VPN

    D. Nothing

11. What system is used to collect and analyze data logs from various network devices and to report detected security events?

    A. Syslog server

    B. NIPS

    C. WIPS

    D. SIEM system

12. The IT department decided to implement a security appliance in front of their web servers to inspect HTTP/HTTPS/SOAP traffic for malicious activity. Which of the following is the *best* solution to use?

    A. Screened host firewall

    B. Packet filter firewall

    C. DMZ

    D. WAF

13. A security audit was conducted for your organization. It found that a computer plugged into any Ethernet port in its shipping facility was able to access network resources without authentication. You are directed to fix this security issue. Which standard, if implemented, could resolve this issue?

    A. 802.1x

    B. 802.3

    C. 802.1q

    D. 802.11

14. Your CISO is concerned with unauthorized network access to the corporate wireless network. You want to set a mechanism in place that not only authenticates the wireless devices but also requires them to meet a predefined corporate policy before allowing them on the network. What technology *best* performs this function?

    A. HIDS

    B. NAC

    C. Software agent

    D. NIPS

15. David's security team is implementing NAC for authentication as well as corporate policy enforcement. The team wants to install software on the devices to perform these tasks. In the context of NAC, what is this software called?

    A. Program

    B. Process

    C. Agent

    D. Thread

16. Grace is investigating the encryption of data at rest and data in transit and trying to determine which algorithm is best in each situation. Which of the following does not contain data at rest?

    A. SAN

    B. NAS

    C. SSD

    D. VPN

17. Your employees need internal access while traveling to remote locations. You need a service that enables them to securely connect back to a private corporate network from a public network to log into a centralized portal. You want the traffic to be encrypted. Which of the following is the *best* tool?

    A. Wi-Fi

    B. VPN

    C. RDP

    D. NIC

18. Robert's employees complain that when they connect to the network through the VPN, they cannot view their social media posts and pictures. What mostly likely has been implemented?

    A. Split tunnels

    B. DNS tunneling

    C. ARP cache

    D. Full tunnels

19. Robin's company is merging with another healthcare organization. The stakeholders are discussing the security aspects of combining digital communications. The main agreed-upon criterion for compliance and security is protecting the sharing of the business's domains. What is the best option for this organization?

    A. DNSSEC

    B. TLS

    C. SSL 2.0

    D. Keeping both entities separate

20. You are a network security administrator for a SOHO. Your staff tends to work from coffee shops without understanding the need for a VPN. You must show them why this can be dangerous. What network traffic packets are commonly captured and used in a replay attack?

    A. Packet headers

    B. Authentication

    C. FTP

    D. DNS

21. Sally needs to implement a network security device at the border of her corporate network and the Internet. This device filters network traffic based on source and destination IP addresses, source and destination port numbers, and protocols. Which network security device *best* suits her needs?

    A. Packet filter firewall

    B. Proxy server

    C. HSM

    D. DMZ

22. The IT security department was tasked with recommending a single security device that can perform various security functions. The security functions include antivirus protection, antispyware, a firewall, and an IDP. What device should the IT security department recommend?

    A. Next-generation firewall

    B. Unified threat management system

    C. Quantum proxy

    D. Next-generation IDP

23. One of your network administrators reports that they cannot connect to a device on the local network using its IP address. The device is up and running with an IP address of 10.0.0.5. Other hosts can communicate with the device. The default gateway is 10.0.0.1, and your local IP address is 10.0.0.3. What is the *best* type of scan to run to find the MAC of the offending machine?

    A. ARP

    B. NAT gateway

    C. IPConfig

    D. IFConfig

24. Ronald has architected his network to hide the source of a network connection. What device has he most probably used?

    A. Proxy firewall

    B. Internet gateway

    C. Layer 3 switch

    D. Bastion host

25. The IT group within your organization wants to filter requests between clients and their servers. They want to place a device in front of the servers that acts as a go-between for the clients and the servers. This device receives the request from the clients and forwards the request to the servers. The server will reply to the request by sending the reply to the device; then the device will forward the reply to the clients. What device best meets this description?

    A. Firewall

    B. NIDS

    C. Reverse proxy

    D. Proxy

26. Many users within your organization clicked on emails that, while looking legitimate, are malicious. Malicious code executes once the email is opened, infecting the user's system with malware. What could be implemented on the email server to help prevent such emails from reaching the end user?

   A.   Firewall

   B.   Spam filters

   C.   WAF

   D.   Forward proxy

27. Your network administrator, George, reaches out to you to investigate why your e-commerce site went down twice in the past three days. Everything looks good on your network, so you reach out to your ISP. You suspect an attacker set up botnets that flood your DNS server with invalid requests. You find this out by examining your external logging service. What is this type of attack called?

   A.   DDoS

   B.   Spamming

   C.   IP spoofing

   D.   Containerization

28. Aaron's end users are having difficulty signing into the network. The investigation of the situation leads him to believe it is which type of attack?

   A.   Port scanning

   B.   DDoS

   C.   Pass-the-hash

   D.   Trojan

29. A network engineer must configure a router on the network remotely. What protocol should be used to ensure a secure connection?

   A.   Telnet

   B.   FTP

   C.   HTTP

   D.   SSH

30. Ian has joined a company that licenses a third party's software and email service that is delivered to end users through a browser. What type of organization does Ian work for?

   A.   IaaS

   B.   SaaS

   C.   PaaS

   D.   BaaS

31. You are a security analyst with an enterprise global financial organization. The company just experienced an advanced persistent threat (APT) type of attack that was traced to ransomware delivered to end users via a phishing campaign. One of your IT analysts forwarded the email to the `phishing@mycompany.com` address. You want to rip open the ransomware to see what it does and what asset it touches. What do you build?

  A. Cloud sandbox

  B. A container

  C. SLA

  D. A hypervisor

32. Cody configured the application programming interface (API) connection between your web application that manages retail transactions and your bank. This connection must be as secure as possible. Because the API connection will handle financial transactions, what is the *best* choice for securing the API if it is well designed?

  A. SOAP

  B. HTTPS

  C. REST

  D. XML

33. Aniket is looking for a web server to process requests sent by XML. What is the *best* technology to use for this?

  A. REST

  B. SOAP

  C. Ajax

  D. XSS

34. The Cisco switch port you are using for traffic analysis and troubleshooting has a dedicated SPAN port that is in an "error-disabled state"; what is the procedure to reenable it after you enter privilege exec mode?

  A. Issue the `no shutdown` command on the error-disabled interface.

  B. Issue the `shutdown` and then the `no shutdown` command on the error-disabled interface.

  C. Issue the `no error` command on the error-disabled interface.

  D. Issue the `no error-disable` command on the error-disabled interface.

35. You were asked to recommend a solution to intercept and mirror network traffic and analyze its content for malicious activity while not interacting with the host computer. Of the following, which is the *best* solution?

  A. System scanner

  B. Application scanner

  C. Active vulnerability scanner

  D. Passive vulnerability scanner

36. One of Robert's objectives and key results (OKRs) for the upcoming year is to modernize the IT strategy by adopting a virtual cloud and taking advantage of new features and storage. He understands that once intellectual property is in the cloud, he could have less visibility and control as a consumer. What else is a major security concern for important data stored in the public cloud versus a private cloud?

   A. Cost effectiveness

   B. Elastic use

   C. Being on demand

   D. Data remnants

37. Your news organization is dealing with a recent defacement of your website and secure web server. The server was compromised around a three-day holiday weekend while most of the IT staff was not at work. The network diagram, in the order from the outside in, consists of the Internet, firewall, IDS, SSL accelerator, web server farm, internal firewall, and internal network. You attempt a forensic analysis, but all the web server logs have been deleted, and the internal firewall logs show no activity. As the security administrator, what do you do?

   A. Review sensor placement and examine the external firewall logs to find the attack.

   B. Review the IDS logs to determine the source of the attack.

   C. Correlate all the logs from all the devices to find where the organization was compromised.

   D. Reconfigure the network and put the IDS between the SSL accelerator and server farm to better determine the cause of future attacks.

38. After merging with a newly acquired company, Gavin comes to work Monday morning to find a metamorphic worm from the newly acquired network spreading through the parent organization. The security administrator isolated the worm using a network traffic access point (TAP) mirroring all the new network traffic and found it spreading on TCP port 445. What does Gavin advise the administrator to do to immediately to minimize the attack?

   A. Run Wireshark to watch for traffic on TCP port 445.

   B. Update antivirus software and scan the entire enterprise.

   C. Check the SIEM for alerts for any asset with TCP port 445 open.

   D. Deploy an ACL to all HIPS: DENY-TCP-ANY-ANY-445.

39. Jonathan is a senior architect who has submitted budget requests to the CISO to upgrade their security landscape. One item to purchase in the new year is a security information and event management (SIEM) system. What is the primary function of a SIEM tool?

   A. Blocking malicious users and traffic

   B. Monitoring the network

   C. Automating DNS servers

   D. Monitoring servers

40. Janet has critical files and intellectual property on several filesystems and needs to be alerted if these files are altered by either trusted insiders abusing their privilege or malware. What should she implement?

    A. FIM

    B. PCI

    C. DNS

    D. TCP

41. You are configuring SNMP on a Windows server. You have found that you are currently running SNMPv2c. Why would you want to upgrade to SNMPv3?

    A. Cryptographic security system

    B. Party-based security system

    C. Easier to set up

    D. Supports UDP

42. Victor is employed in a high-risk geographically diverse environment heavily using Cisco IOS. Which of these are not key service advantages of NetFlow?

    A. Peer-to-peer tunneling encryption

    B. Network traffic accounting and usage-based billing

    C. Network planning and security

    D. DoS monitoring capabilities

43. One of your managers asked you to research data loss prevention techniques to protect data so that cyber attackers cannot monetize the stolen data. What DLP do you recommend?

    A. Encryption and tokenization

    B. HIPAA and PCI

    C. I&AM management

    D. NIST frameworks

44. Eddie is looking for an antivirus detection tool that uses a rule or weight-based system to determine how much danger a program function could be. What type of antivirus does he need?

    A. Behavioral

    B. Signature based

    C. Heuristic

    D. Automated

45. Simon's organization has endpoints that are considered low-priority systems. Even though they are considered low priority, they still must be protected from malicious code capable of destroying data and corrupting systems. Malicious code is capable of infecting files but generally needs help moving from one system to another. What type of security product protects systems from this type of malicious code only?

    A. Antimalware

    B. Antispyware

    C. Antivirus

    D. Anti-adware

46. An employee downloads a video of someone stealing a package off their porch from their smart doorbell. How do you mitigate the risk of storing that type of data on your business network?

    A. Implementing a security policy and awareness

    B. Performing audits

    C. Monitoring networks for certain file types

    D. Using third-party threat intelligence reports

47. You conduct a security assessment and find legacy systems with vital business processes using standard Telnet protocols. What should you do to mitigate the risk?

    A. Migrate from IPv4 to IPv6.

    B. Install PuTTY.

    C. Move the system to a secure VLAN.

    D. Unplug the system until a replacement can be ordered.

48. Your hospital just merged with another hospital in another state that falls under a different legal jurisdiction. You are tasked with improving network security. Your CISO suggests data isolation by blocking communication between the two hospitals. How do you accomplish this?

    A. Implementing HIDS

    B. Building gateway firewalls

    C. Configuring ERP

    D. Creating network microsegmentation

49. Your company grew to a point where a screened host firewall solution is no longer viable. IT wants to move to a screened subnet solution. Which of the following is considered a type of screened subnet?

    A. LAN

    B. DMZ

    C. Egress

    D. WAN

50. Your CISO asked you to implement a solution on the jump servers in your DMZ that can detect and stop malicious activity. Which solution accomplishes this task?

    A. HIDS

    B. NIDS

    C. HIPS

    D. NIPS

51. Matthew's company just learned that an attacker obtained highly classified information by querying the external DNS server. He is told to never let this happen again. Which of the following is the best option?

    A. Implement a split DNS. Create an internal and external zone to resolve all domain queries.

    B. Implement a split DNS. Create an internal zone for an internal DNS for resolution and an external zone to be used by the Internet.

    C. Create DNS parking for round-robin DNSBL.

    D. Create DNS parking for cloud users.

52. Peyton is an IT administrator needing visibility into his staging network. He believes he has all the tools and controls in place, but he has no way to look for attackers who are currently exploiting the network. What tool can Peyton choose to help with seeing the dark spots in his environment?

    A. Fuzzer

    B. HTTP interceptor

    C. Port scanner

    D. SIEM

53. You want to replace an access point's removable antenna with a better one based on the results gathered by a wireless site survey. You want to be able to focus more energy in one direction and less in another to better distinguish between networks. What type of antenna should you purchase?

    A. Directional

    B. Omnidirectional

    C. Parabolic dish

    D. Radio

54. Which of the following is a protocol that provides a graphical interface to a Windows system over a network?

    A. RDP

    B. VNC

    C. VDI

    D. DLP

55. An attacker scanned your network and discovered a host system running a vulnerable version of VNC. Which of the following can an attacker perform if they can access VNC on the host?

   A. Remotely access the BIOS of the host system.

   B. Remotely view and control the desktop of the host system.

   C. Remotely view critical failures, causing a stop error or the blue screen of death on the host system.

   D. All of the above.

56. Levi's corporate public cloud network is configured such that all network devices reach each other without going through a routing device. The CISO wants the network reconfigured so that the network is segmented based on geography. In addition, the servers must be on their own subnetwork. What is a benefit of subdividing the network in this way?

   A. No benefit at all.

   B. By subdividing the network, the port numbers can be better distributed among assets.

   C. By subdividing the network, rules can be placed to control the flow of traffic from one subnetwork to another.

   D. Ease of deployment.

57. Your security team implemented NAC lists for authentication as well as corporate policy enforcement. Originally, the team installed software on the devices to perform these tasks. However, the security team decided this method is no longer desirable. They want to implement a solution that performs the same function but doesn't require software be installed on the devices. In the context of NAC, what is this configuration called?

   A. Agent

   B. Agentless

   C. Volatile

   D. Persistent

58. Jason's organization recently deployed some standard Linux systems in its network. The system admin for these Linux systems wants to secure these systems by using SELinux, which is required by their security policy. Which of the following is a benefit of using SELinux?

   A. Moves from a discretionary access control system to a system where the file creator controls the permissions of the file

   B. Moves from a discretionary access control system to a mandatory access control system

   C. Moves from a mandatory access control system to a system where the file creator controls the permissions of the file

   D. Moves from a mandatory access control system to a discretionary access control system

59. Bobby is a security risk manager with a global organization. The organization recently evaluated the risk of flash floods on its operations in several regions and determined that the cost of responding is expensive. The organization chooses to take no action currently. What was the risk management strategy deployed?

   A. Risk mitigation

   B. Risk acceptance

   C. Risk avoidance

   D. Risk transference

60. Randolf is a newly hired CISO, and he is evaluating controls for the confidentiality portion of the CIA triad. Which set of controls should he choose to concentrate on for confidentiality?

   A. RAID 1, classification of data, and load balancing

   B. Digital signatures, encryption, and hashes

   C. Steganography, ACL, and vulnerability management

   D. Checksum, DOS attacks, and RAID 0

61. You are tasked with deploying a system so that it operates at a single classification level. All the users who access this system have the same clearance, classification, and need to know. What is this operating mode?

   A. High mode

   B. Dedicated

   C. Peer to peer

   D. Multilevel

62. You work as an independent security consultant for a small town in the Midwest that was just breached by a foreign country. When it came time for payment to a town vendor, someone changed the transfers of monies from a physical check to an electronic payment. In response, what is the first security practice suggestion you make to prevent this from recurring?

   A. Incorporation

   B. Investigation

   C. Zero trust

   D. Data diddling

63. A hospital database is hosting PHI data with high volatility. Data changes constantly and is used by doctors, nurses, and surgeons, as well as the finance department for billing. The database is located in a secure air-gapped network where there is limited access. What is the most likely threat?

   A. Internal user fraud

   B. Manipulated key-value pairs

   C. Compliance

   D. Inappropriate admin access

64. Jeremiah works for a global construction company and has found cloud computing meets 90 percent of his IT needs. Which of these is of least importance when considering cloud computing?

    A. Data classification

    B. Encryption methodology

    C. Incident response and disaster recovery

    D. Physical location of data center

65. Your company hired a new IT manager who will be working remotely. Their first order of business is to perform a risk assessment on a new mobile device that is to be given to all employees. The device is commercially available and runs a popular operating system. What are the most important security factors that you should consider while conducting this risk assessment?

    A. Remote wipe and controls, encryption, and vendor track record

    B. Encryption, IPV6, cost, and color

    C. Remote wipe, maintenance, and inventory management

    D. Remote monitoring, cost, SSD, and vendor track record

66. Your CEO purchased the latest and greatest mobile device (BYOD) and now wants you to connect it to the company's intranet. You have been told to research this process according to change management and security policy. What *best* security recommendation do you recommend making the biggest impact on risk?

    A. Making this a new corporate policy available for everyone

    B. Adding a PIN to access the device

    C. Encrypting nonvolatile memory

    D. Auditing requirements

67. Brian's new insurance company is working with an ISP, and he wants to find out technical details, such as system numbers, port numbers, IP addressing, and the protocols used. What document will he find this information in?

    A. Memorandum of understanding

    B. Disclosure of assets

    C. Operation level agreement

    D. Interconnection security agreement

68. Your IT staff is seeking a wireless solution to transmit data in a manufacturing area with lots of electrical motors. The technology must transmit approximately 1 Mbps of data approximately 1 meter using line of sight. No obstacles are between the devices using this technology. Because of the environment, using RF is not a viable solution. What technology is *best* suited for this situation?

    A. Wi-Fi

    B. Bluetooth

    C. IrDA

    D. RF

69. Your company underwent a merger, and you are attempting to consolidate domains. What tool do you use to find out who the owner of a domain is, when it expires, and contract details?

    A. Netstat

    B. Whois

    C. SSH

    D. TCPDump

70. Your department is looking for a new storage solution that enables a yet undetermined number of systems to connect using file-based protocols (such as NFS and SMB) for peering. This solution will also be used for file-sharing services such as data storage, access, and management services to network clients. What is the *best* storage solution for your organization?

    A. SAN

    B. NAS

    C. DAG

    D. DAS

71. Your CISO asks you to develop deployment solutions for internally developed software that offers the best customization as well as control over the product. Cost is not an issue. What is the *best* solution for you to choose?

    A. Hosted deployment solution with a lower up-front cost but that requires maintaining the hardware on which the software is residing

    B. Cloud-based deployment solutions that require a monthly fee only

    C. Elastic virtual hosting based on need

    D. An on-premises traditional deployment solution

72. Fletcher is a security engineer for a government agency attempting to determine the control of highly classified customer information. Who should advise him on coordinating control of this sensitive data?

    A. Sales

    B. HR

    C. Board of directors

    D. Legal counsel

73. Two CISOs brought their IT leadership together to discuss the BIA and DRP for a merger between two automobile manufacturers. Their first priority is to communicate securely using encryption. What is the *best* recommendation?

    A. DNSSEC on both domains

    B. TLS on both domains

    C. Use SMime in select email transmissions

    D. Push all communication to the cloud

74. Your newly formed IT team is investigating cloud computing models. You would like to use a cloud computing model that is subscription based for common services and where the vendor oversees developing and managing as well as maintaining the pool of computer resources shared between multiple tenants across the network. Which of the following is the *best* choice for this situation?

   A. Public

   B. Private

   C. Agnostic

   D. Hybrid

75. Alice and Bob are discussing federated identity and the differences between 2FA and MFA. Bob says it is the same thing, and Alice is explaining to him that it isn't. Which is the *best* statement that describes the difference?

   A. Multifactor authentication (MFA) requires users to verify their identity by providing multiple pieces of evidence that can include something they know, something they have, or something they are. Two-factor authentication (2FA) is a user providing two authentication methods like a password and a fingerprint.

   B. 2FA and MFA have the same process with the caveat that 2FA must be two separate types of authentication methods. MFA could be two or more of the same methods.

   C. 2FA is safer and easier for end users than MFA.

   D. Multifactor authentication (MFA) requires users to verify their identity by providing at least two pieces of evidence that can include something they know, something they have, or something they are. Two-factor authentication (2FA) is a user providing two or more authentication methods like a password and a fingerprint.

76. For security reasons, Ted is moving from LDAP to LDAPS for standards-based specification for interacting with directory data. LDAPS provides for security by using which of the following?

   A. SSL

   B. SSH

   C. PGP

   D. AES

77. The corporate network has grown to a point where the management of individual routers and switches is problematic. Your CISO wants to move to a solution where the control function of the routers and switches are centralized, leaving the routers and switches to perform the basic forwarding of traffic. Which technology *best* performs this function?

   A. CDC

   B. NAS

   C. SAN

   D. SDN

78. A security engineer is concerned that logs may be lost on their hybrid SDN network if the devices should fail or become compromised by an attacker. What solution ensures that logs are not lost on these devices?

    A. Configuring a firewall on the local machine

    B. Archiving the logs on the local machine

    C. Sending the logs to a syslog

    D. Installing a NIPS

79. Your CISO watched the news about the latest supply chain breach and is genuinely concerned about this type of attacks affecting major organizations. He asks you, as a security analyst, to gather information about controls to put into place on your SDN network to stop these attacks from affecting your organization. How do you begin this process?

    A. Get the latest IOCs from OSINT sources

    B. Research best practices

    C. Use AI and SIEM

    D. Perform a sweep of your network using threat modeling

80. Cameron is a newly promoted network security administrator. His manager told him to start building his physical and SDN topology map with a concentration on finding out what ports are open on which assets across the entire enterprise. What tool will accomplish the task?

    A. Netcat

    B. Nmap

    C. BurpSuite

    D. IPConfig

81. Your organization has opted into a hybrid cloud solution for all your strategic organizations with multiple verticals with different IT requirements. Which one of these is an advantage?

    A. Flexible, scalable, reliable, and improved security posture

    B. Strong compatibility and integration requirements

    C. Complexity as the organization evolves

    D. Can be very expensive

82. While performing unit testing on software requested by your department, you found that privilege escalation is possible. Privilege escalation means that an attacker can elevate their privilege on a system from a lower level to an administrator level. What two performance unit testing techniques do you need to use?

    A. Vertical and horizontal

    B. Left and right

    C. North to south

    D. Ring 1 to 3

83. Phillip's financial company experienced a natural disaster, used a hot site for three months, and now is returning to the primary site. What processes should be restored first at the primary site?

    A. Finance department

    B. External communication

    C. Mission critical

    D. Least business critical

84. You work in law enforcement supporting a network with HA. High availability is mandatory, as you also support emergency 911 services. Which of the following would hinder your HA ecosystem?

    A. Clustered servers

    B. Primary firewall

    C. Switched networks

    D. Redundant communication links

85. Mark has been tasked with building a computer system that can scale well and that includes built-in logic for interfacing with many types of devices, including SATA, PCI, and USB, as well as GPU, network processors, and AV encoders/decoders. What type of system should he build?

    A. Matrix

    B. Heterogeneous

    C. LLC

    D. Meshed network

86. Not having complete control over networks and servers is a real concern in your organization, and upper management asks you if the company's data is genuinely secure now that you have migrated to the cloud. They have asked you to present industry research at the next board of directors meeting to answer questions regarding cloud security and your company's cyber-resilience. What research would be of most interest to the board of directors?

    A. Processor power consumption

    B. Encryption models

    C. COCOA

    D. CACAO

87. While investigating threats specific to your industry, you found information collected and analyzed by several companies with substantive expertise and access to source information. Which of these is the *least* beneficial item to your organization after subscribing to threat intelligence information?

    A. Determining acceptable business risks

    B. Developing controls and budgets

    C. Making equipment and staffing decisions

    D. Creating a marketing plan for your product

88. Andrew has evaluated several unified communications (UC) vendors. He has a need for one with their own data center facility hosting their own instance of the platform with built-in redundant power, remote backup, and secured entry as well as 24/7 staffing. Why would a UC vendor have minimal data center security?

    A. Cost savings

    B. Compliance requirements

    C. Ease of setup and use

    D. Perfect forward secrecy

89. Your organization slowly evolved from simply locking doors to RFID-enabled cards issued to employees to secure the physical environment. You want to protect these cards from cloning, because some parts of your organization host sensitive information. What should you implement?

    A. Encryption

    B. IDR

    C. HIDS

    D. NIPS

90. Damien is a security architect for a large enterprise bank that recently merged with a smaller local bank. The acquired bank has a legacy virtual cluster, and all these virtual machines use the same NIC to connect to the LAN. Some of the VMs are used for hosting databases for HR, and some are used to process mortgage applications. What is the biggest security risk?

    A. Shared NICs negatively impacting the integrity of packets

    B. Bridging of networks impacting availability

    C. Availability between VMs impacting integrity

    D. Visibility between VMs impacting confidentiality

91. One of the biggest issues your CISO has with migrating to more cloud environments is the process of acquiring and releasing resources. Technical as well as operational issues are associated with these processes. What type of procedure documentation should you create to help with this?

    A. How to authenticate and authorize

    B. How to dynamically provision and deprovision

    C. How to use SaaS, IaaS, and PaaS

    D. How to build a Type 2 hypervisor

92. You have received an RFQ response from a software company, which makes a tool that will allow you to record all changes in a single change management tool. This tool will track scheduling change, implementing change, the cost of change, and reporting. What type of software is this called?

    A. Vulnerability management

    B. Change control

    C. Security information and event management

    D. Automation

93. You are investigating a new tool that helps identify, analyze, and report on threats in real time based mostly on logs. What is the *best* solution?

    A. SOAR

    B. Antivirus

    C. XSS

    D. Port scanner

94. Steve is a software developer for a large retail organization. His CISO returned from a large conference and asked him to clarify exactly what the benefit of a container in software development is over virtual machines. Which of these is the *best* succinct answer?

    A. In a VM, hardware is virtualized to run multiple OS instances. Containers virtualize an OS to run multiple workloads on a single OS instance using a container engine.

    B. In a container, hardware is virtualized to run a single OS, where a VM can run multiple applications across multiple assets with a single OS.

    C. A VM is virtualized technology, but a container is not.

    D. A container is the same thing as a virtual machine, just smaller in size.

95. As a leader in your organization in DevOps, you want to convince your CISO to move toward containerization. Which of these is not an advantage to using containers over VMs?

    A. Reduced and simplified security updates

    B. Less code to transfer, migrate, and upload

    C. Quicker spinning up applications

    D. Large file size of snapshots

96. At the latest IT department meeting, a discussion on the best virtual methodology centered around using VMs versus containers. Which of these statements *best* aligns with those two models?

    A. VMs are better for lightweight native performance, whereas containers are better for heavyweight limited performance.

    B. VMs are for running applications that need all the OS has to offer, whereas containers are better when maximizing number of applications on minimal resources.

    C. VMs share the host OS, whereas containers run on their own OS.

    D. Containers are fully isolated and more secure, whereas VMs use process-level isolation.

97. Ross is a security manager looking to improve security and performance of his unified communications (UC) server. Which of the following options might help with decreasing the attack surface?

    A. Adding more users

    B. Adding more devices

    C. Turning off unused services

    D. Ease of setup

98. After analyzing traffic flows on the network, your department noticed that many internal users access the same resources on the Internet. This activity utilizes a lot of Internet bandwidth. Your department decides to implement a solution that can cache this type of traffic the first time it is requested and serve it to the internal users as requested, thereby reducing the Internet bandwidth used for accessing this traffic. Which solution *best* accomplishes this task?

   A. Proxy

   B. Packet filter firewall

   C. WAF

   D. IPS

99. You were asked to recommend a technology that will lessen the impact of a DDoS attack on your CDN. Which of the following is the *best* technology?

   A. HIDS

   B. Packet filter firewall

   C. Proxy

   D. Load balancing

100. Luke's company started upgrading the computers in your organization. As a security professional, you recommend creating a standard image for all computers with a set level of security configured. What is this process called?

   A. Configuration baselining

   B. Imaging

   C. Duplication

   D. Ghosting

101. Lydia is a security administrator, and her hospital's security policy states that wearable technology and IoT devices are not allowed in secure areas where patient information is discussed. Wearable devices are designed to be worn by one individual, but some are quite powerful with artificial intelligence. Why is this a concern?

   A. Danger of eavesdropping and compliance violations

   B. Insurance premiums going up

   C. Malpractice and litigation

   D. Chain of custody of evidence

102. Mark is evaluating cloud storage providers and gives each a product evaluation form. Which of these is not the best practice for a cloud service provider?

   A. Strict initial registration and validation

   B. System event and network traffic monitoring

   C. Utilization of weak encryption algorithms

   D. Incident response processes that help BCP

103. Containerization provides many benefits in flexibility and faster application development. Which of the following statements is false?

   A. Containers share the host OS's kernel during runtime.

   B. Containers do not need to fully emulate an OS to work.

   C. One physical server running five containers needs only one OS.

   D. Containers are pure sandboxes just like VMs are.

104. Hector has a team that replaced version 1.2 of software with 2.0. The newest version has a completely different interface in addition to updates. What is this called?

   A. Versioning

   B. Coding integration

   C. Secure coding

   D. Vulnerability assessment

105. Greg is a security researcher for a cybersecurity company. He is currently examining a third-party vendor and finds a way to use SQLi to deface their web server due to a missing patch in the company's web application. What is the threat of doing business with this organization?

   A. Web defacement

   B. Unpatched applications

   C. Attackers

   D. Education awareness

106. Your CISO decided to implement an overarching enterprise mobility management (EMM) strategy. She wants to ensure that sensitive corporate data is not compromised by the employees' apps on their mobile devices. Which of these will implement that *best*?

   A. App config through IDC

   B. App wrapping through SDK

   C. Open source through API

   D. Platform DevOps

107. You are a web developer who needs to secure API keys in a client-side JavaScript application created for your hospital. What is the *best* way to accomplish this task quickly and efficiently?

   A. Disable API access and use a hash of the key.

   B. Set API access and a secret key pair.

   C. Curl a request with an -H -o option.

   D. Set a RESTful request with access pairs.

108. Mitchell wants to enhance his overall security and compliance to protect his company more carefully. He engages his security team to examine enterprise application integration, data integration, message-oriented middleware (MOM), object request brokers (ORBs), and the enterprise service bus (ESB). He also wants to prioritize which web applications should be secured first and how they will be tested. What do you need to sit down with your IT security team and build?

A. Web application security plan

B. Web application–level attack list

C. Business logic justifications

D. Container security

109. Edwin's board of directors want to perform quarterly security testing. As CISO of a financial institution, he must form a plan specifically for the development of this test that includes software assurance. This test must have a low risk of impacting system stability because the company is in production. The suggestion was made to outsource this to a third party. The board of directors argue that a third party will not be as knowledgeable as the development team. What will satisfy the board of directors?

A. Gray-box testing by a major consulting firm

B. Black-box testing by a major external consulting firm

C. Gray-box testing by the development and security assurance teams

D. White-box testing by the development and security assurance teams

110. Trent is a security analyst for a financial organization and conducting a review of data management policies. After a complete review, he found settings disabled permitting developers to download supporting but trusted software. You submitted the recommendation that developers have a separate process to manually download software that should be vetted before its use. What process will support this recommendation?

A. NIPS

B. Digitally signed applications

C. Sandboxing

D. PCI compliance

111. Tiffany runs an organization that is blending its development team with the operations team because of the speed applications are being rolled out. Applications change with new services required in production, so she has undertaken the challenge of eliminating those silos of development and operations. What is this called?

A. Incremental

B. DevOps

C. Agile

D. Waterfall

112. Shelby is working for a software developer developing web applications for an international financial enterprise. She has also been tasked with building the rule set that governs the interaction between an end user and the web application linking authentication and access. What type of rule set is this?

    A. Session management

    B. Secure cookies

    C. Java flags

    D. Stateless firewall

113. Your software developer has a custom ROM for Android and wants to further customize it for mobile device use in your healthcare network. Android is an open source operating system, but your developer experiences difficulties uploading the new ROM to a test device even using validated third-party libraries for development. What does he need to unlock before uploading the new ROM?

    A. Bootloader

    B. BIOS

    C. FIFO

    D. TPM

114. Angel needs to provide software code for users to download. You want the users to be able to verify that the software has not changed or become corrupted. How might you provide this verification?

    A. Code signing.

    B. Script signing.

    C. The user can attempt to install and run the program. If it installs and operates properly, it hasn't been altered.

    D. Have the user authenticate first. If the user is authenticated, the software they download must be genuine.

115. You are creating a web application security plan and need to do white-box security testing on source code to find vulnerabilities earlier in the SDLC. If you can find vulnerabilities earlier in the process, they are cheaper to fix. What type of testing do you need to do?

    A. SAST

    B. CAST

    C. DAST

    D. FAST

116. You are creating a web application security plan and need to do black-box security testing on a running application. What type of testing do you need to do?

    A. SAST

    B. CAST

    C. DAST

    D. IAST

117. You had your internal team do an analysis on compiled binaries to find errors in mobile and desktop applications. You would like an external agency to test them as well. Which of these tests *best* suits this need?

    A. DAST

    B. VAST

    C. IAST

    D. SAST

118. Craig's newly formed IT team is investigating cloud computing models. He wants to use a cloud computing model that is orchestrated as an integrated infrastructure environment. Apps and data can share resources based on business and technical policies. Which of the following is the *best* choice for this situation?

    A. Public

    B. Private

    C. Agnostic

    D. Hybrid

119. You have been newly hired as a CISO for a governmental contractor. One of your first conversations with the CEO is to review requirements for recovery time and recovery point objectives, and enterprise resource planning (ERP). Who should you bring to the round table to discuss metrics surrounding your RTO/RPO?

    A. Board of directors

    B. Chief financial officer

    C. Data owners and custodians

    D. Business unit managers and directors

120. Which of the following is a use case for configuration management software?

    A. Incident remediation

    B. Continuance

    C. Asset management

    D. Collaboration

121. You have been analyzing the backup schedule for a CMDB. Your CIO has said the company has an RPO of 48 hours. What is the minimum backup schedule for the CMDB?

    A. 24 hours

    B. 6 hours

    C. 48 hours

    D. 12 hours

122. Your company is looking at a new CRM model to reach customers that includes social media. The marketing director, Tucker, would like to share news, updates, and promotions on all social websites. What are the major security risks?

   A. Malware, phishing, and social engineering

   B. DDOS, brute force, and SQLi

   C. Mergers and data ownership

   D. Regulatory requirements and environmental changes

123. In the last 5 years, your manufacturing group merged twice with competitors and acquired three startups, which led to more than 60 unique customer web applications. To reduce cost and improve workflows, you are put in charge of a project to implement centralized security. You need to ensure a model to enable integration and accurate identity information and authentication as well as repeatability. Which is the *best* solution?

   A. Implementation of web access control and relay proxies

   B. Automated provisioning of identity management

   C. Self-service single sign-on using Kerberos

   D. Building an organizational wide granular access control model in a centralized location

124. You are tasked with creating a single sign-on solution for your security organization. Which of these would you not deploy in an enterprise environment?

   A. Directory services

   B. Kerberos

   C. SAML 2.0

   D. Workgroup

125. The Domain Name System (DNS) maintains an index of every domain name and corresponding IP address. Before someone visits a website on your corporate network, DNS will resolve your domain name to its IP address. Which of the following is a weakness of DNS?

   A. Spoofing

   B. Latency

   C. Authentication

   D. Inconsistency

126. Your database team would like to use a service-oriented architecture (SOA). The CISO suggested you investigate the risk for adopting this type of architecture. What is the biggest security risk to adopting an SOA?

   A. SOA is available only over the enterprise network.

   B. Lack of understanding from stakeholders.

   C. Risk of legacy networks and system vulnerabilities.

   D. Source code.

127. A large enterprise social media organization underwent several mergers, divestitures, and acquisitions over the past three years. Because of this, the internal networks and software have extremely complex dependencies. Better integration is mandatory. Which of the following integration platforms is *best* for security and standards-based software architecture?

   A. IDE

   B. DNS

   C. SOA

   D. ESB

128. The retail division of your organization purchased touchscreen tablets and wireless mice and keyboards for all their representatives to increase productivity. You communicated the risk of nonstandard devices and wireless devices, but the deployment continued. What is the *best* method for evaluating and presenting potential threats to upper management?

   A. Conducting a vulnerability assessment

   B. Developing a standard image for these assets

   C. Making new recommendations for security policies

   D. Working with the management team to understand the processes these devices will interface with, and to classify the risk connected with the hardware/software deployment life cycle

129. You are selected to manage a software development and implementation project. Your manager suggests that you follow the phases in the SDLC. In which of these phases do you determine the controls needed to ensure that the system complies with standards?

   A. Testing

   B. Initiation

   C. Accreditation

   D. Acceptance

130. You were selected to manage a software development project. Your supervisor asked you to follow the proper phases in the systems development life cycle. Where does the SDLC begin?

   A. Requirement analysis

   B. System design specifications

   C. Initiation

   D. Implementation

131. You have turned a software project over to the fielding phase, delivering the working system to the customer. Which phase is this otherwise known as?

   A. Deployment

   B. Licensing

   C. Development

   D. Evaluation

132. Your vulnerability manager contacted you because of an operating system software issue. There are a few security-related issues due to patches and upgrades needed for an application on the systems in question. When is the *best* time to complete this task?

A. As quickly as possible after testing

B. After experiencing the issue that the vulnerability manager described

C. After other organizations have tested the patch or upgrade

D. During the usual monthly maintenance

133. Arnold has developed an application and want to prevent the reuse of information in memory when a user quits the program. Which of these is his *best* option to accomplish this task?

A. Garbage collection

B. Data validation

C. SDLC

D. OOP

134. Simon is a security engineer. While testing an application during a regular assessment to make sure it is configured securely, he sees a REQUEST containing method, resources, and headers, and a RESPONSE containing status code and headers. What technique did he most likely use to generate that type of output?

A. Fingerprinting

B. Fuzzing

C. Vulnerability scanning

D. HTTP intercepting

135. You have been asked to make a change to software code. What type of testing do you complete to make sure program inputs and outputs are correct and everything functions as it's supposed to?

A. White box

B. Black hat

C. Code review

D. Regression

136. You are conducting a unit test on a new piece of software. By looking at an individual program, how do you ensure that each module behaves as it should?

A. Input/output

B. BIOS

C. Processes running

D. Services running

137. Christopher is a software developer, and as part of the testing phase in the SDLC, he will need to ensure that an application is handling errors correctly. What is the *best* tool for him to use in this situation?

    A. Fuzzer

    B. Compliance

    C. Access control

    D. Integration testing

138. Your IT group is modernizing and adopting a DevSecOps approach, making everyone responsible for security. Traditionally, storage and security were separate disciplines inside IT as a whole. As a security analyst, what is your primary concern of data at rest?

    A. Encryption

    B. Authentication

    C. Infrastructure

    D. Authorization

139. As a software developer, Brian is extremely frustrated with a customer who keeps calling him on the phone and leaving messages to make changes to the software. What approach should Brian take with this customer to make the development process easier?

    A. Change control

    B. Increase security

    C. Appraise senior management

    D. Provide detailed documentation

140. Jackie is a software engineer and inherently prefers to use a flexible framework that enables software development to evolve with teamwork and feedback. What type of software development model would this be called?

    A. Prototyping

    B. Ceremony

    C. Agile

    D. Radical

141. You are working on a high-risk software development project that is large, the releases are to be frequent, and the requirements are complex. The waterfall and agile models are too simple. What software development model would you opt for?

    A. Functional

    B. Cost estimation

    C. Continuous delivery

    D. Spiral

142. You are a software engineer and need to use a software development process that follows an extremely strict predetermined path through a set of phases. What type of method is this called?

    A. Agile

    B. Waterfall

    C. Adaptable

    D. Verifiable

143. The SDLC phases are part of a bigger process known as the system life cycle (SLC). The SLC has two phases after the implementation phase of the SDLC that address postinstallation and future changes. What are they called?

    A. Operations, maintenance, revisions, and replacement

    B. Replacement, crepitation, evaluation, and versioning

    C. Validation, verification, authentication, and monitoring

    D. Revisions, discovery, compliance, and functionality

144. You are using continuous integration/continuous delivery methodology involving different members of your team while developing a new application. You meet every day after lunch to review, which can mean multiple integrations every day. What are the security implications of using CI/CD?

    A. There are no security issues.

    B. Errors will not need to be fixed because the next integration will fix them.

    C. Encryption will be impossible because of timing.

    D. Errors can be handled as soon as possible.

145. IT security is a rapidly evolving field. As a software engineer, you need to stay current on industry trends and potential impact on an enterprise. Many of these changes will lead to you adopting which of the following?

    A. Best practices

    B. Digital threats

    C. Antivirus programs

    D. NIST

146. You perform a security audit to find out whether any IoT devices on your network are publicly accessible. What website would you use to find this type of information?

    A. Shodan

    B. OWASP

    C. VirusTotal

    D. Maltego

147. During a web application security assessment, Kevin needs to grab the basic architecture to identify the framework used. He grabbed the HTTP header banner using Netcat, which gives you the application name, software version, and web server information. What activity did he just perform?

    A. Fingerprinting

    B. Authentication

    C. Authorization

    D. Code review

148. Many of your corporate users are using mobile laptop computers to perform their work remotely. Security is concerned that confidential data residing on these laptops may be disclosed and leaked to the public. What methodology *best* helps prevent the loss of such data?

    A. DLP

    B. HIPS

    C. NIDS

    D. NIPS

149. Your CISO, Karen, is concerned that all employees can use personal USB storage devices on the company's computers. She is concerned about malware introduction to the corporate environment and that data loss is possible if this practice continues. She wants to manage who can use USB storage devices on the company's computers. Which of the following actions should be used to implement this constraint?

    A. Replacing all computers with those that do not have USB ports

    B. Placing glue in the computers' USB ports

    C. Cutting the computers' USB cables

    D. Configuring a Group Policy within Microsoft Active Directory to manage USB storage device use on those computers

150. Many organizations prepare for highly technical attacks and forget about the simple low-tech means of gathering information. Dumpster diving can be useful in gaining access to unauthorized information. Which of these is the easiest to implement for reducing your company's dumpster-diving risk?

    A. Data classification and printer restrictions of intellectual property.

    B. Purchase shredders for the copy rooms.

    C. Create policies and procedures for document shredding.

    D. Employ an intern to shred all printed documentation.

151. Your organization decided to move away from dedicated computers on the desktop and move to a virtual desktop environment. The desktop image resides on a server within a virtual machine and is accessed via a desktop client over the network. Which of the following is being described?

    A. VPN

    B. VDI

    C. VNC

    D. RDP

152. Using Microsoft Network Monitor, you have captured traffic on TCP port 3389. Your security policy states that port 3389 is not to be used. What client-server protocol is probably running over this port?

  A. SNMP

  B. RDP

  C. PuTTY

  D. FTP

153. Your organization is pressured by both the company board and employees to allow personal devices on the network. They asked for email and calendar items to be synced between the company ecosystem and their BYOD. Which of the following *best* balances security and usability?

  A. Allowing access for the management team only because they have a need for convenient access

  B. Not allowing any access between a BYOD device and the corporate network, only cloud applications

  C. Only allowing certain types of devices that can be centrally managed

  D. Reviewing security policy and performing a risk evaluation focused on central management, including the remote wipe and encryption of sensitive data and training users on privacy

154. Nathan is tasked with writing the security viewpoint of a new program that his organization is starting. Which of the following techniques make this a repeatable process and can be used for creating the best security architecture?

  A. Data classification, CIA triad, minimum security required, and risk analysis

  B. Historical documentation, continuous monitoring, and mitigation of high risks

  C. Implementation of proper controls, performance of qualitative analysis, and continuous monitoring

  D. Risk analysis; avoidance of critical risks, threats, and vulnerabilities; and the transference of medium risk

155. You deployed more than half of your enterprise into the cloud, but you still have concerns about data loss, unauthorized access, and encryption. What continues to be the vulnerability in cloud infrastructure that leads to the most breaches?

  A. Misconfiguration

  B. SIEM

  C. SaaS

  D. Machine learning

156. Your company generates documents intended for public viewing. While your company wants to make these document public, it stills wants to prove the documents originated from the company. How can these documents be marked in such a way that information about their origin is maintained while not distorting the visual contents of the documents?

    A. Blowfish

    B. Steganographic watermarking

    C. Digital signatures

    D. PKI

157. Charlie works for a publisher and has been tasked with protecting the electronic media they produce. This will help ensure they receive the revenue for the product they produce. What is Charlie going to implement?

    A. Single point-of-failure

    B. Digital rights management

    C. Separate of duties

    D. Mandatory vacations

158. As a security analyst, Ben is searching for a method that can examine network traffic and filter its payload based on rules. What is this method called?

    A. Network flow

    B. DLP

    C. Data flow enforcement

    D. Deep packet inspection

159. You are a security administrator reviewing network logs. You notice a UDP trend where traffic increased more than 30 percent in the past 48 hours. You use Wireshark to capture the packets and see the following: UDP `192.168.1.1:123->46.110.10.5:123`. What attack scenario is most likely occurring?

    A. You are being attacked via the NTP client side and successfully exploited on 192.168.1.1.

    B. You are being attacked via the NTP server side and unsuccessfully exploited on 192.168.1.1.

    C. You are being attacked via the DNS client side and successfully exploited on 192.168.1.1.

    D. You are being attacked via the DNS server side and successfully exploited on 192.168.1.1.

160. René is working with upper management to classify data to be shared in his collaboration tool, which will create extra security controls limiting the likelihood of a data breach. What principle of information security is he trying to enforce?

    A. Confidentiality

    B. Integrity

    C. Accountability

    D. Availability

161. A new objective for your department is to establish data provenance or historical data records. Moving forward, you must now document the data's source and all manipulations performed on it. Every data item will have detailed information about its origin and the ways it was influenced. Why is this crucial to the security of the data?

    A. Unauthorized changes in metadata can lead you to the wrong datasets.

    B. Authorized changes to the data warehouse can lead you to the wrong datasets.

    C. Traceable data sources make it difficult to find security breaches.

    D. Traceable data sources make it difficult to find fake data generation.

162. Your CTO believes in the adage "Security through obscurity." Which of the following types of obfuscation makes a program obscure to other computers?

    A. Prevention

    B. Saturation

    C. Control flow

    D. Data

163. Lynn uses a process that substitutes a sensitive data element with something that is not sensitive. She uses this process to map back to the sensitive data. What is this called?

    A. Masking

    B. Encryption

    C. Tokenization

    D. Authorization

164. Which of the following storage techniques should you deploy if you want the option to selectively provide availability to some hosts and to restrict availability to others by using a masking process?

    A. NAS

    B. SAN

    C. iSCSI

    D. LUN

165. Ashton's end users are using mobile devices to access confidential information on the corporate network. He needs to ensure that the information from all databases is kept secure as it is transmitted to these mobile devices. Encryption is a requirement. Of the following options, which one *best* describes a major concern with PII on mobile devices?

    A. Mobile devices have more processing power than other computing devices.

    B. Mobile devices typically have less processing power than other computing devices.

    C. Mobile devices often have increased complexities.

    D. Mobile devices often have difficulties to obfuscate personal data.

166. Bob needs your professional opinion on encryption capabilities. You explained to him that cryptography supports all the core principles of information security, with one exception. What is that exception?

    A. Anonymity

    B. Integrity

    C. Confidentiality

    D. Availability

167. Your app developers focus on the speed of app development more than security. Because of this, they use easy-to-implement encryption algorithms with known vulnerabilities. What is the result of using this type of encryption algorithm?

    A. Malware infection

    B. Modification

    C. Attacker cracking the passwords

    D. Remote code execution

168. After a meeting with the board of directors, your CEO is looking for a way to boost profits. He identified a need to implement cost savings on non-core-related business activities, and the suggestion was made to move the corporate email system to the cloud. You are the compliance officer tasked with making sure security and data issues are handled properly. What *best* describes your process?

    A. End-to-end encryption, creation, and the destruction of mail accounts

    B. Vendor selection and RFP/RFQ

    C. Securing all virtual environments that handle email

    D. Data provisioning and processing while in transit and at rest

169. Evan's cyber-company has officially grown out of its startup phase, and his team is tasked with creating a pre-disaster preparation plan that will sustain the business should a disaster, natural or human-made, occur. Which of the following is the most important?

    A. Offsite backups

    B. Copies of the BDR

    C. Maintaining a warm site

    D. Chain of command

170. Christopher is a web developer. He built a web form for customers to fill out and respond to the company via a web page. What is the first thing that a developer should do to prevent this page from becoming a security risk?

    A. SQLi

    B. Input validation

    C. Cross-site request forgery

    D. Fuzzing

171. Marketing has put in a request for web-based meeting software with a third-party vendor. The software programs that you, a security analyst, have reviewed requires user registration and installation, and that user has to share their data as well as their desktop. To ensure that information is secure, which of the following controls is *best*?

A. Disallow the software; avoid the risk.

B. Hire a third-party organization to perform the risk analysis, and based on outcomes, allow or disallow the software.

C. Log and record every single web-based meeting.

D. After evaluating several providers, ensure acceptable risk and that the read-write desktop mode can be prevented.

172. With the rise of malware spread with removable media, your company wrote an amendment to include a ban of all flashcards and memory drives. They pose a threat due to all but which of the following?

A. Physical size

B. Transportability

C. Storage capacity

D. Being cheap and easy to use

173. A server holding sensitive financial records is running out of room. You are the information security manager and data storage falls under your purview. What is the *best* option?

A. Use first in, first out (FIFO).

B. Compress and archive the oldest data.

C. Move the data to the cloud.

D. Add disk space in a RAID configuration.

174. A situation that affects the CIA triad of an IT asset can include an internal and external risk source. A breach of physical security and theft of data can be instigated by_____.

A. untrusted insiders or trusted outsiders

B. trusted insiders or untrusted outsiders

C. hidden costs

D. service deterioration

175. During what phase of eDiscovery will you determine what digital data and documents should be collected for possible analysis and review?

A. Processing

B. Identification

C. Collection

D. Curation

176. You are a small company administrator hosting multiple virtualized client servers on a single host. You are told to add a new host to create a cluster. The new hardware and OS will be different, but the underlying technology will be compatible. Both hosts will be sharing the same storage. What goal are you trying to accomplish?

   A. Increased availability

   B. Increased confidentiality

   C. Increased integrity

   D. Increased certification

177. Good data management includes which of the following?

   A. Data quality procedures, verification and validation, adherence to agreed-upon data management, and an ongoing data audit to monitor the use and integrity of existing data

   B. Cost, due care and due diligence, privacy, liability, and existing law

   C. Determining the impact the information has on the mission of the organization, understanding the cost of information, and determining who in the organization or outside of it has a need for the information

   D. Ensuring the longevity of data and their reuse for multiple purposes, facilitating the interoperability of datasets, and increasing data sharing

178. Bob is implementing a new RAID configuration needed for redundancy in the event of disk failure. What security goal is Bob trying to accomplish?

   A. Availability

   B. Integrity

   C. Confidentiality

   D. Disclosure

179. You are monitoring your IT environment to detect techniques like credential dumping. Credential dumping is extracting usernames and passwords from a computer to then pass those credentials to other machines on a network. Where are the credentials stored on a Windows machine?

   A. In the SAM

   B. In PSEXEC

   C. In Documents and Settings

   D. In WUTemp

180. Jennie and her team are developing security policies, and they are currently working on a policy regarding password management. Which of these is not important?

   A. Account lockout

   B. Training users to create complex easy-to-remember passwords and not use the same password over again

   C. Preventing users from using personal information in a password, such as their birthday or their spouse's name

   D. Storing passwords securely in a password manager application

181. Keith's organization wants to move a vital company process to the cloud. He is tasked with conducting a risk analysis to minimize the risk of hosting email in the cloud. What is the best path forward?

    A. All logins must be done over an encrypted channel and obtain an NDA and SLA from the cloud provider.

    B. Remind all users not to write down their passwords.

    C. Make sure that the OLA covers more than just operations.

    D. Require data classification.

182. What is a major security concern associated with IoT?

    A. Lack of encryption

    B. Use of hard-coded passwords

    C. Lack of firmware support

    D. All of the above

183. Your company is recovering from a data breach. The breach was not deep but raised the security awareness profile of upper management. Realizing they have gaps in access control, upper management approved the purchase of password manager software for the organization. What else do you suggest they institute for end users?

    A. 2FA

    B. Password isolation

    C. Disaster recovery

    D. IDR

184. Which of the following access control principles should you implement to create a system of checks and balances on employees with heightened privileged access?

    A. Rotation of duties

    B. Need to know

    C. Mandatory access control

    D. Separation of duties

185. Your penetration testers' report shows that they obtained the credentials of specific user accounts through social engineering and phishing campaigns. Once on the organization's network, the penetration testers used these credentials to bypass access controls and to gain access to remote systems. In one case, they were able to switch from a user-level account to an administrator-level account. What is this type of attack called?

    A. XSRF

    B. Password mitigation

    C. Token theft

    D. Privilege escalation

186. You have an application that performs authentication, which makes checking for session management, brute forcing, and password complexity appropriate. What else might you check for?

    A. SQLi

    B. Ransomware

    C. Privilege escalation

    D. Static analysis

187. As the senior security architect, you create a security policy and standards that instruct employees to use strong passwords. You find that employees are still using weak passwords. Revising the procedures for creating strong passwords, which of these are you *least* likely to require for employees?

    A. Change your password every 90 days.

    B. Use a combination of numbers, letters, uppercase and lowercase letters, and special characters.

    C. Use a minimum number of characters.

    D. Use a Merriam-Webster dictionary.

188. You just accepted a CISO position for a small customer service business, and your first priority is to increase security and accessibility for current software-as-a-service (SaaS) applications. The applications are configured to use passwords. What do you implement first?

    A. Deploy password managers for all employees.

    B. Deploy password managers for only the employees who use the SaaS tool.

    C. Create a VPN between your organization and the SaaS provider.

    D. Implement a system for time-based, one-time passwords.

189. The collaboration tool that your company uses follows a username and password login model. If one of your employee's credentials are compromised, it could give attackers access to financial information, intellectual property, or client information. How would you mitigate this type of risk with a collaboration tool?

    A. Strict password guidelines

    B. Only use HTTPS

    C. Restrict usage to VPN

    D. Disable SSO

190. Wayne is a security manager for a small organization. He has evaluated several different types of access controls. Which of these are easiest for an attacker to bypass?

    A. Fingerprint

    B. Password

    C. Iris scan

    D. CAC card

191. What is FIM when it comes to obtaining access to networks?

    A. Fighting insidious malware

    B. Federated identity management

    C. Forest integration modules

    D. Fact investigative modifications

192. If Domain A trusts Domain B and Domain B trusts Domain C, what is it called when Domain A trusts Domain C because of the previously stated relationships?

    A. Transitive tort

    B. Transitive trust

    C. Transitive trade

    D. Transitive theory

193. You visit a website that requires credentials to log in. Besides providing the option of a username and password, you are also given the option to log in using your Facebook credentials. What type of authentication scheme is used?

    A. SAML

    B. OAuth

    C. ClosedID

    D. OpenID

194. You need to find a web-based language that is used to exchange security information with single sign-on (SSO). Which of the following is the *best* language to use?

    A. SOAP

    B. Kerberos

    C. SAML/Shibboleth

    D. API

195. Your IT manager wants to move from a centralized access control methodology to a decentralized access control methodology. You need a router that authenticates users from a locally stored database. This requires subjects to be added individually to the local database for access, which creates a security domain, or sphere of trust. What *best* describes this type of administration?

    A. Decentralized access control requires more administrative work.

    B. Decentralized access control creates a bottleneck.

    C. Decentralized access control requires a single authorization server.

    D. Decentralized access control stores all the users in the same administrative location using RADIUS.

196. The CISO is researching ways to reduce risk associated with the separation of duties. In the case where one person is not available, another needs to be able to perform all the duties of their co-workers. What should the CISO implement to reduce risk?

    A. Mandatory requirement of a shared account for administrative purposes

    B. Audit of all ongoing administration activities

    C. Separation of duties to ensure no single administrator has access

    D. Role-based security on the primary role and provisional access to the secondary role on a case-by-case basis

197. You implement mandatory access control for your secure data storage system. You change default passwords and enforce the use of strong passwords. What else should you do to make this storage system even more secure?

    A. Multifactor authentication

    B. Multifactor authorization

    C. Identification

    D. Verification

198. Your data owner must assign classifications to information assets and ensure regulation compliance. Which of these other criteria is determined by a data owner?

    A. Authorization

    B. Authentication

    C. Verification

    D. Validation

199. As a security specialist for your organization, you are increasingly concerned about strong endpoint controls of developers' workstations as well as access control of servers running developer tools. Which of these is *not* a benefit of an attribute-based access control (ABAC) scheme?

    A. Helping meet security goals and standards

    B. Ensuring only authorized users have access to code repositories

    C. Having runtime self-protection controls

    D. Safeguarding system integrity

200. As a security administrator at a high-security governmental agency, you rely on some assets running high-end customized legacy software. What type of access control do you implement to protect your organization?

    A. DAC

    B. RBAC

    C. MAC

    D. ABAC

201. Your organization needs an AAA server to support the users accessing the corporate network via a VPN. Which of the following will be used to provide AAA services?

A. RADIUS

B. L2TP

C. LDAP

D. AD

202. Your network administrator wants to use an authentication protocol to encrypt usernames and passwords on all Cisco devices. What is the *best* option for them to use?

A. RADIUS

B. DIAMETER

C. CHAP

D. TACACS+

203. Your company currently uses Kerberos authentication protocols and tickets to prove identity. You are looking for another means of authentication because Kerberos has several potential vulnerabilities, the biggest being which of the following?

A. Single point of failure

B. Dynamic passwords

C. Limited read/write cycles

D. Consensus

204. You need an authorization framework that gives a third-party application access to resources without providing the owners' credentials to the application. Which of these is your *best* option?

A. MAC

B. EAP

C. SAML

D. OAuth

205. You need develop a security logging process for your mission-critical servers to hold users accountable for their actions on a system after they log in. What is this called?

A. Authorization

B. Authentication

C. 2 -step verification

D. Accountability

206. Your credit card company identified that customers' top transaction on the web portal is resetting passwords. Many users forget their secret questions, so customers are calling to talk to tech support. You want to develop single-factor authentication to cut down on the overhead of the current solution. What solution do you suggest?

   A. Push notification

   B. In-band certificate or token

   C. Login with third-party social media accounts

   D. SMS message to a customer's mobile number with an expiring OTP

207. Your CISO wants to implement a solution within the organization where employees are required to authenticate once and then permitted to access the various computer systems they are authorized to access. The organization uses primarily Microsoft products. Which solution is *best* suited for this organization?

   A. Kerberos

   B. SSL

   C. HOTP

   D. TOTP

208. Your organization is upgrading computers. The new computers include a chipset on the motherboard that is used to store encryption keys. What is this chipset called?

   A. EKC

   B. TPM

   C. ESM

   D. RSA

209. You are logged into a website. While performing activities within the website, you access a third-party application. The application asks you if it can access your profile data as part of its process. What technology is this process describing?

   A. Attestation

   B. OAuth

   C. JWT

   D. Cookies

210. You are setting up a new virtual machine. What type of virtualization should you use to coordinate instructions directly to the CPU?

   A. Type B.

   B. Type 1.

   C. Type 2.

   D. No VM directly sends instructions to the CPU.

211. Your organization must perform vast amounts of computations of big data overnight. To minimize TCO, you rely on elastic cloud services. The virtual machines and containers are created and destroyed nightly. What is the biggest risk to confidentiality?

  A. Data center distribution

  B. Encryption

  C. Physical loss of control of assets

  D. Data scraping

212. Your DevOps team decided to use containers because they allow running applications on any hardware. What is the first thing your team should do to have a secure container environment?

  A. Install IPS.

  B. Lock down Kubernetes and monitor registries.

  C. Configure antimalware and traffic filtering.

  D. Disable services that are not required and install monitoring tools.

213. You work in information security for a stock trading organization. You have been tasked with reducing cost and managing employee workstations. One of the biggest concerns is how to prevent employees from copying data to any external storage. Which of the following *best* manages this situation?

  A. Move all operations to the cloud and disable VPN.

  B. Implement server virtualization and move critical applications to the server.

  C. Use VDI and disable hardware and storage mapping from a thin client.

  D. Encrypt all sensitive data at rest and in transit.

214. You are exploring the best option for your team to read data that was written onto storage material by a device you do not have access to, and the backup device has been broken. Which of the following is the *best* option for this?

  A. Type 1 hypervisor

  B. Type 2 hypervisor

  C. Emulation

  D. PaaS

215. You are a security architect building out a new hardware-based VM. Which of the following would *least* likely threaten your new virtualized environment?

  A. Patching and maintenance

  B. VM sprawl

  C. Oversight and responsibility

  D. Faster provisioning and disaster recovery

216. GPS is built into cell phones and cameras, enabling coordinated longitude and latitude to be embedded in a machine-readable format as part of a picture or in apps and games. Besides physical coordinates of longitude and latitude, which of these will not be embedded in the metadata of a photo taken with a cell phone?

    A. Names of businesses that are near your location

    B. Elevation

    C. Bearing

    D. Phone number

217. Your CISO asked you to help review data protection, system configurations, and hardening guides that were developed for cloud deployment. He would like you to make a list of goals for security improvement based on your current deployment. What is the *best* source of information to help you build this list?

    A. Pentesting reports

    B. CVE database

    C. Implementation guides

    D. Security assessment reports

218. Management of your hosted application environment requires end-to-end visibility and a high-end performance connection while monitoring for security issues. What should you consider for the most control and visibility?

    A. You should consider a provider with connections from your location directly into the applications cloud resources.

    B. You should have a private T1 line installed for this access.

    C. You should secure a VPN concentrator for this task.

    D. You should use HTTPS.

219. As the IT director of a nonprofit agency, you have been challenged at a local conference to provide technical cloud infrastructure that will be shared between several organizations like yours. Which is the *best* cloud partnership to form?

    A. Private cloud

    B. Public cloud

    C. Hybrid cloud

    D. Community cloud

220. Your objectives and key results (OKRs) being measured for this quarter include realizing the benefits of a single-tenancy cloud architecture. Which one of these results is a benefit of a single-tenancy cloud service?

    A. Security and cost

    B. Reliability and scaling

    C. Ease of restoration

    D. Maintenance

221. With 80 percent of your enterprise in a VPC model, which of the following is *not* a key enabling technology?

A. Fast WAN and automatic IP addressing

B. High-performance hardware

C. Inexpensive servers

D. Complete control over process

222. You have a new security policy that requires backing up critical data offsite. This data must be backed up hourly. Cost is important. What method are you most likely to deploy?

A. File storage

B. Electronic vaulting

C. Block storage

D. Object storage

223. Your current data storage solution has too many vulnerabilities that are proprietary to the manufacturer who created your storage devices. This, combined with a lack of encryption, is leading you to choose cloud storage for your database over on-premises storage. By choosing cloud storage, you will gain encryption of the data, but you will also bring in which attribute to your architecture?

A. Identity

B. Infrastructure

C. Complexity

D. Confidentiality

224. You want to implement a technology that will verify an email originated from a particular user and that the contents of the email were not altered. Of the answers provided, which technology provides such a function?

A. Digital signature

B. Symmetric encryption

C. Asymmetric encryption

D. Nonrepudiation

225. Which of the following protocols could be used for exchanging information while implementing a variety of web services in your organization?

A. SOAP

B. HTTP

C. SNMP

D. ASP

226. Your CISO is concerned with the secure management of cryptographic keys used within the organization. She wants to use a system where the keys are broken into parts, and each part is encrypted and stored separately by contracted third parties. What is this process called?

    A. Key objectives

    B. Key revenue

    C. Key escrow

    D. Key isolation

227. Your VPN needs the strongest authentication possible. Your network consists of Microsoft servers. Which of the following protocols provide the most secure authentication?

    A. EAP-TLS with smart cards

    B. SPAP

    C. CHAP

    D. LEAP

228. You own a small training business with two classrooms. Your network consists of a firewall, an enterprise-class router, a 48-port switch, 1 printer, and 18 laptops in each classroom. The laptops are reimaged once a month with a golden patched image with up-to-date antivirus and antimalware. User authentication is two-factor with passwords and smart cards. The network is configured to use IPv4. You also have a wireless hotspot for students to connect their personal mobile devices. What could you improve on for a more resilient technical security posture?

    A. Enhanced TLS controls

    B. Stronger user authentication

    C. Sufficient physical controls

    D. IPv6

229. You are a network defender and are finding it difficult to keep up with the volume of network attacks. What can you leverage to help with early detection and response to these threats, especially new ones?

    A. Machine learning

    B. SIEM

    C. DevSecOps

    D. Security as Code

230. You need an encryption algorithm that offers easier key exchange and key management than symmetric offers. Which of the following is your *best* option?

    A. Asymmetric

    B. Quantum

    C. Hashing

    D. Scytale

231. Your company wants to begin using biometrics for authentication. Which of the following are not biometrics that can be verified by a system to give an individual access?

    A. Facial recognition

    B. Iris recognition

    C. Retina recognition

    D. PIN recognition

232. Laura is a proponent of using a distributed ledger to secure transactions. She wants to make it difficult to tamper with a single record because an attacker would need to change the block containing that record as well as those linked to it to avoid detection. Participants will have a private key assigned to their transactions that acts as a personal digital signature. What type of cryptographic system does Laura need to implement?

    A. Homomorphic encryption

    B. Secure multiparty computation

    C. Blockchain

    D. Distributed consensus

233. Felipe wants to use a protocol that allows a client to retrieve an element of a database without the owner of that database knowing which element was selected. If implemented securely, the client will only learn about the element they are querying for and nothing else preserving privacy. Which of the following provides the *best* solution?

    A. Strong private information retrieval

    B. Secure function evaluation

    C. Private function evaluation

    D. Big data

234. Augmented reality (AR) advances are exciting, and cybersecurity is now dealing with a vast amount of complexity. The adoption of AR brings an expanding landscape of new cybersecurity vulnerabilities. Consumers and businesses are grappling with big data breaches, and implementing effective cybersecurity measures is a necessity for modern businesses. Which of these is not an urgent or relevant cybersecurity issue involving AR?

    A. Cloud structure

    B. Innovation outpacing secure development

    C. Wearable exposure

    D. Micro/nano technology

235. Three-dimensional printers include computers and run software that could be vulnerable to security issues that bad actors can take advantage of. To mitigate this issue, 3D printing vendors need to make secure coding and design a core part of their development process. Printer owners should also consider doing which of these first?

    A. Securely downloading plans for 3D printers

    B. Hardening their devices when possible and considering the security of the 3D production

    C. Encrypting SD cards used to hold all printing plans

    D. Cleaning the laser that melts the powdered material into objects layer by layer

236. Naomi wants to use passwordless authentication in her corporate network. Which of the following statements is not true?

A. Linux supports passwordless SSH logins.

B. Microsoft supports passwordless sign-in on Windows products and networks running Microsoft Active Directory.

C. Passwordless authentication can be used only on mobile devices.

D. Microsoft LDAP supports passwordless authentication through FIDO2 keys.

237. You want your organization to benefit from artificial intelligence, but some in the application development department are confused about what AI actually is. Which statement is true?

A. Artificial intelligence and machine learning are the same.

B. Machine learning and deep learning are the same.

C. Machine learning leads to deep learning, which leads to artificial intelligence.

D. Artificial intelligence parses big data to make decisions.

238. Terry is heading a project to implement a chatbot on the homepage of your insurance company to move away from live agents. What technology will he most likely employ?

A. Natural language processing

B. Biometrics

C. Virtual reality

D. Deep fake

Chapter

2

Security Operations

THE CASP+ EXAM TOPICS COVERED IN THIS CHAPTER INCLUDE:

✓ **Domain 2: Security Operations**

- 2.1 Given a scenario, perform threat management activities.
  - Intelligence types
    - Tactical
    - Commodity malware
    - Strategic
    - Targeted attacks
    - Operational
    - Threat hunting
    - Threat emulation
  - Actor types
    - Advanced persistent threat (APT)/nation-state
    - Insider threat
    - Competitor
    - Hacktivist
    - Script kiddie
    - Organized crime
  - Threat actor properties
    - Resource
    - Time
    - Money
    - Supply chain access
    - Create vulnerabilities
    - Capabilities/sophistication
    - Identifying techniques

- Intelligence collection methods
  - Intelligence feeds
  - Deep web
  - Proprietary
  - Open-source intelligence (OSINT)
  - Human intelligence (HUMINT)
- Frameworks
  - MITRE Adversarial Tactics, Techniques, & Common knowledge (ATT&CK)
  - ATT&CK for industrial control system (ICS)
  - Diamond Model of Intrusion Analysis
  - Cyber Kill Chain
- 2.2 Given a scenario, analyze indicators of compromise and formulate an appropriate response.
  - Indicators of compromise
    - Packet capture (PCAP)
    - Logs
    - Network logs
    - Vulnerability logs
    - Operating system logs
    - Access logs
    - NetFlow logs
    - Notifications
    - FIM alerts
    - SIEM alerts
    - DLP alerts
    - IDS/IPS alerts
    - Antivirus alerts
    - Notification severity/priorities
    - Unusual process activity

- Response
  - Firewall rules
  - IPS/IDS rules
  - ACL rules
  - Signature rules
  - Behavior rules
  - DLP rules
  - Scripts/regular expressions
- 2.3 Given a scenario, perform vulnerability management activities.
  - Vulnerability scans
    - Credentialed vs. non-credentialed
    - Agent-based/server-based
    - Criticality ranking
    - Active vs. passive
  - Security Content Automation Protocol (SCAP)
    - Extensible Configuration Checklist Description Format (XCCDF)
    - Open Vulnerability and Assessment Language (OVAL)
    - Common Platform Enumeration (CPE)
    - Common Vulnerabilities and Exposures (CVE)
    - Common Vulnerability Scoring System (CVSS)
    - Common Configuration Enumeration (CCE)
    - Asset Reporting Format (ARF)
  - Self-assessment vs. third party vendor assessment
  - Patch management
  - Information sources
    - Advisories
    - Bulletins
    - Vendor websites

- Information Sharing and Analysis Centers (ISACs)
- News reports

- 2.4 Given a scenario, use the appropriate vulnerability assessment and penetration testing methods and tools.

  - Methods
    - Static analysis
    - Dynamic analysis
    - Side-channel analysis
    - Reverse engineering
    - Software
    - Hardware
    - Wireless vulnerability scan
    - Software composition analysis
    - Fuzz testing
    - Pivoting
    - Post-exploitation
    - Persistence
  - Tools
    - SCAP scanner
    - Network traffic analyzer
    - Vulnerability scanner
    - Protocol analyzer
    - Port scanner
    - HTTP interceptor
    - Exploit framework
    - Password cracker
  - Dependency management
  - Requirements
    - Scope of work

- Rules of engagement
- Invasive vs. non-invasive
- Asset inventory
- Permissions and access
- Corporate policy considerations
- Facility considerations
- Physical security considerations
- Rescan for corrections/changes
- 2.5 Given a scenario, analyze vulnerabilities and recommend risk mitigations.
  - Vulnerabilities
  - Race conditions
  - Overflows
  - Buffer
  - Integer
  - Broken authentication
  - Unsecure references
  - Poor exception handling
  - Security misconfiguration
  - Improper headers
  - Information disclosure
  - Certificate errors
  - Weak cryptography implementations
  - Weak ciphers
  - Weak cipher suite implementations
  - Software composition analysis
  - Use of vulnerable frameworks and software modules
  - Use of unsafe functions
  - Third-party libraries

- Dependencies
- Code injections/malicious changes
- End of support/end of life
- Regression issues
- Inherently vulnerable system/application
  - Client-side processing vs. server-side processing
  - JSON/representational state transfer (REST)
  - Browser extensions
  - Flash
  - ActiveX
  - Hypertext Markup Language 5 (HTML5)
  - Asynchronous JavaScript and XML (AJAX)
  - Simple Object Access Protocol (SOAP)
  - Machine code vs. bytecode or interpreted vs. emulated
- Attacks
  - Directory traversal
  - Cross-site scripting (XSS)
  - Cross-site request forgery (CSRF)
  - Injection
  - XML
  - LDAP
  - Structured Query Language (SQL)
  - Command
  - Process
  - Sandbox escape
  - Virtual machine (VM) hopping
  - VM escape
  - Border Gateway Protocol (BGP)/route hijacking
  - Interception attacks

- Denial-of-service (DoS)/DDoS
- Authentication bypass
- Social engineering
- VLAN hopping
- 2.6 Given a scenario, use processes to reduce risk.
  - Proactive and detection
    - Hunts
    - Developing countermeasures
    - Deceptive technologies
    - Honeynet
    - Honeypot
    - Decoy files
    - Simulators
    - Dynamic network configurations
  - Security data analytics
    - Processing pipelines
    - Data
    - Stream
    - Indexing and search
    - Log collection and curation
    - Database activity monitoring
  - Preventive
    - Antivirus
    - Immutable systems
    - Hardening
    - Sandbox detonation
  - Application control
    - License technologies
    - Allow list vs. block list

- Time of check vs. time of use
- Atomic execution
- Security automation
  - Cron/scheduled tasks
  - Bash
  - PowerShell
  - Python
- Physical security
  - Review of lighting
  - Review of visitor logs
  - Camera reviews
  - Open spaces vs. confined spaces
- 2.7 Given an incident, implement the appropriate response.
  - Event classifications
    - False positive
    - False negative
    - True positive
    - True negative
  - Triage event
  - Preescalation tasks
  - Incident response process
    - Preparation
    - Detection
    - Analysis
    - Containment
    - Recovery
    - Lessons learned
  - Specific response playbooks/processes
    - Scenarios
    - Ransomware

- Data exfiltration
- Social engineering
- Non-automated response methods
- Automated response methods
- Runbooks
- SOAR
- Communication plan
- Stakeholder management
- 2.8 Explain the importance of forensic concepts.
  - Legal vs. internal corporate purposes
  - Forensic process
    - Identification
    - Evidence collection
    - Chain of custody
    - Order of volatility
    - Memory snapshots
    - Images
    - Cloning
    - Evidence preservation
    - Secure storage
    - Backups
    - Analysis
    - Forensics tools
    - Verification
    - Presentation
  - Integrity preservation
    - Hashing
  - Cryptanalysis
  - Steganalysis

- 2.9 Given a scenario, use forensic analysis tools.
  - File carving tools
    - Foremost
    - Strings
  - Binary analysis tools
    - Hex dump
    - Binwalk
    - Ghidra
    - GNU Project debugger (GDB)
    - OllyDbg
    - readelf
    - objdump
    - strace
    - ldd
    - file
  - Analysis tools
    - ExifTool
    - Nmap
    - Aircrack-ng
    - Volatility
    - The Sleuth Kit
    - Dynamically vs. statically linked
  - Imaging tools
    - Forensic Toolkit (FTK) Imager
    - dd
  - Hashing utilities
    - sha256sum
    - ssdeep

- Live collection vs. post-mortem tools
  - netstat
  - ps
  - vmstat
  - ldd
  - lsof
  - netcat
  - tcpdump
  - conntrack
  - Wireshark

1. As a senior security architect, you know that one of the most important principles of enterprise security is the rapid detection of a data breach. Many organizations that experience a breach will not learn about it for weeks or even months because they have invested heavily in the perimeter of the organization and are not actively threat hunting. Which of these will *not* help detect an actual breach before it causes widespread harm to your organization?

   A. Modern breach detection tools

   B. Periodic logging

   C. Security expertise on the team

   D. Global threat intelligence

2. One of your users clicked a link in an email and downloaded commodity malware. This malware ran successfully, and you need to measure how widespread it has become. It was contained to just one machine, so what is the scope is considered to be?

   A. Epic

   B. Intermediate

   C. Maximum

   D. Minimal

3. A publicly traded financial company's security policies and procedures were reevaluated recently after they experienced a breach six months ago. After reviewing the incident report, they have decided to make changes to communication procedures regarding strategic intelligence so that the organization can be more agile and have a faster recovery in the future. Why is this so important to an organization?

   A. By communicating intelligence that is actionable, informed decisions can be made to ensure that risks are managed, and people are safe.

   B. The capability to respond to an event quickly is the most important way to deal with an incident.

   C. Improving responses to events is a challenge that no leaders want to face.

   D. The ability to process incident feedback from stakeholders is important to improving the guidelines in incident detection.

4. Matthew's enterprise network is dealing with an increase of malicious activity that is being traced back to insiders. Much of the activity seems to target privileged users, but Matthew does not believe much of this activity is from the actual employees on the network. What will most likely deter these attacks?

   A. Role-based training and best practices

   B. More frequent vulnerability scans

   C. Full disk encryption

   D. Tightening security policy for least privilege and separation of duties

5. Charles is reading threat intelligence reports focusing on advanced persistent nation-state threat actors and their capabilities as well as tactics and techniques. He is trying to make an informed decision regarding this intelligence and how to optimally use it in his enterprise. Which of these is *not* a type of assessment made with cyberthreat intelligence?

   A. Arbitrary

   B. Strategic

   C. Operational

   D. Tactical

6. Darryl was tasked to lead a project setting up a security operations center (SOC). One of the tools leveraged for compliance that his company already owns could also be used in the SOC because of the threat intelligence and data mining capabilities. Which tool can be used for both compliance and SOC?

   A. Protocol analyzers

   B. SIEM

   C. Wired scanner

   D. Password crackers

7. A white-hat penetration test showed your organization to be susceptible to social engineering attacks. A victim in your organization was phished successfully, clicked a link in an email, and downloaded commodity malware. What processes could you take to prevent the spread of malware or ransomware in your environment in the future?

   A. IPSec on critical systems

   B. Use threat emulation

   C. Encryption

   D. Establish KPIs

8. Your organization has increasingly turned to using cloud access security broker (CASB) vendors to address cloud service risks, enforce security policies, protect from insider threat, and comply with regulations. Which of these is *not* one of the pillars of CASB?

   A. Visibility

   B. Data security

   C. Database normalization

   D. Threat protection

9. Your CISO wants you to conduct a risk assessment for a vital new healthcare system that needs to be in place as quickly as possible. As you conduct the assessment, you find a review from a competitor who is using the software that mentions a vulnerability with a low likelihood of exploitation. Why might your CISO still have reservations deploying this system?

   A. The CISO is concerned about government regulations and compliance.

   B. The CISO feels rushed to decide.

   C. Other competitors have elected not to use this system.

   D. Even one attack would be devastating to the organization, both financially and to its reputation.

10. A large pharmaceutical company uses social media for press releases. A hacktivist organization believes this pharmaceutical company makes too much money for the drugs they sell. After the company tweets a press release about a new drug treatment approved by the government, traffic on social media becomes viral, with lots of attention on one specific negative comment. This comment is immediately retweeted by thousands of social media users. What type of attack is this?

    A. Click farming

    B. Retweet storm

    C. Spray and pray

    D. Watering hole

11. Carolina is an IT administrator who has been alerted that there are connection requests across a large range of ports from a single host. She suspects that a script kiddie is attempting to do reconnaissance and identify systems. What is this attacker most likely doing?

    A. Vulnerability scan

    B. Port scan

    C. Scap scan

    D. Host-to-host scan

12. Julia was contacted by senior management to conduct a threat hunt type of investigation. Management know malicious activities are taking place but does not know if it is organized crime or internal personnel. They want to know if it is intentional or unintentional. After investigating, Julia believes it is an unintentional activity from internal personnel and that the most likely cause is which of the following?

    A. Fraud

    B. Espionage

    C. Embezzlement

    D. Social engineering

13. Which of the following *best* defines risk in IT?

    A. You have a vulnerability with a known active threat.

    B. You have a threat with a known vulnerability.

    C. You have a risk with a known threat.

    D. You have a threat with a known exploit.

14. Alex works for a financial institution that decided to purchase costly custom computer systems and software. In the supply chain, one of the vendors supplying the custom computer software is experiencing a delay without any type of explanation to the customer. What should Alex be wary of to limit exposure?

    A. SLA

    B. Penalty clause

    C. Supply chain attack

    D. Proof of insurance in the RFP

15. The CIO of your company, Benjamin, created a quarterly goal for the security team to reduce vulnerabilities. He wants to remove some of these vulnerabilities that are not high profile. Many of these vulnerabilities have compensating controls in place for security reasons. At this point in time, the budget has been exhausted. What is the *best* risk strategy to use?

    A. Accepting risk

    B. Mitigating risk

    C. Transferring risk

    D. Avoiding risk

16. A security engineer is concerned that a sophisticated attacker could bypass OS authentication on a computer if the attacker has physical access to the device. The concern is that the attacker could access the BIOS and have the computer boot from a removable drive. How could you prevent this from happening?

    A. Install a HIDS on the system.

    B. Disable all removable drives using Group Policy.

    C. Password-protect the BIOS.

    D. Install antimalware on the system.

17. Marie is the senior security analyst for a large online news organization. She was briefed that the organization fell victim to an XSS attack that executed malicious web-scripting code on a trusted web page. How can she prevent this from happening in the future?

    A. Make sure the web application can validate and sanitize input.

    B. Implement patch management immediately.

    C. Request an external penetration test.

    D. Marie cannot prevent this from happening on a public-facing web server.

18. Your company planned to develop custom IDS/IPS rules this quarter to be proactive and stay ahead of new rules released by IDS/IPS manufacturers. How should you prepare for this shift in methodology?

    A. Penetration test results

    B. Network monitoring

    C. OSINT and threat databases

    D. Vulnerability scans

19. Duane, a pentester, is conducting the type of reconnaissance that is concerned with being as untraceable as possible. What type of reconnaissance is he performing?

    A. Active reconnaissance

    B. Passive reconnaissance

    C. OSINT

    D. HUMINT

20. Nikolas been tasked with finding information in a database regarding governmental and legal resources. The only way to search for this information is using a browser on a specific part of the Internet. What part of the Internet is Nikolas searching?

    A. Dark web

    B. Deep web

    C. Proprietary

    D. Clearnet

21. As part of your security operations center, you have assembled a team of cyber analysts who are actively seeking out threats on your network. They purposefully seek out anomalies and attempt to find patterns in data to stay ahead of criminals. What would help this team attribute the indicators of compromise with the proper advanced persistent threat?

    A. Black box

    B. Gray box

    C. Intelligence feeds

    D. Data analytics

22. Budi has been tasked with using a framework in threat hunting. The aim of this framework is to improve post-compromise detection of adversaries in enterprises by illustrating the actions an attacker may have taken. What is the name of this framework that threat hunters will be using?

    A. NIST 800-53

    B. ISO 27001

    C. MITRE ATT&CK

    D. PCI DSS

23. You want to implement best practices for ICS and have identified other departments or people who have experience with their implementation. Where else might you look for guidance on ICS best practices?

    A. ATT&CK ICS

    B. ADA

    C. FBI

    D. GLBA

24. Gerard has been tasked by his SOC manager to do intrusion analysis, specifically analysis based on four core features: adversary, infrastructure, capability, and victim. What analysis is he performing?

    A. Gap analysis model

    B. Disaster recovery model

    C. Intrusion detection systems

    D. Diamond model

25. You are tasked with helping your organization better anticipate and recognize insider threats, social engineering, advanced ransomware, and other innovative attacks. What model could you use?

    A. Software development life cycle

    B. Systems development life cycle

    C. Cyber kill chain

    D. Indicators of compromise

26. Alice was tasked with testing network traffic and firewall rule sets for vulnerabilities and intrusions. Which of these tools is *best* to use for this task?

    A. Nmap

    B. Wireshark

    C. Traceroute

    D. Packet Tracer

27. Your CIO is upset that the security compliance audit failed due to the lack of data logging and analysis. You were chosen to lead a team to stand up a logging tool for proactively and reactively mitigating risk. What tool do you implement to lead this team to becoming compliant?

    A. SIEM

    B. VM

    C. DNS

    D. LASE

28. You disconnected a computer from the network because of a suspected breach. Which of the following should you do next?

    A. Back up all security and audit logs on that computer.

    B. Update the security policy.

    C. Reimage the machine.

    D. Deploy new countermeasures.

29. You recorded data that includes security logs, object access, vulnerability logs, and other activities that your SIEM tool often uses to detect unwanted activity. Which of the following *best* describes this collection of data?

    A. Due diligence

    B. Syslog

    C. IDS

    D. Audit trail

30. A newly certified administrator makes a change to Group Policy for 12,000 users. The box is checked on the operating systems to not allow the overwriting of operating system security logs. After 48 hours, no users can log into their domain accounts because the logs have filled up. What change control process was initially skipped in this scenario?

    A. Approval

    B. Testing

    C. Implementation

    D. Deployment

31. Ajay is examining Apache logs on an individual web server. He is concentrating on logs that contain information about requests coming into the web server such as pages people are viewing, status of requests, and how long a request took to respond. It looks like this:

    ```
    10.18.28.1 - - [31/Jan/2021:19:12:06 +0000] 808840 "GET
    /inventoryService/inventory/purchaseItem?userId=20253471&itemId=23434300
    HTTP/1.1" 500 17 "-" "Apache-HttpClient/4.2.6 (java 1.5)
    ```

    What type of log is Ajay reviewing?

    A. Error

    B. Operating system

    C. Vulnerability

    D. Access

32. While Dave was doing network traffic analysis, the CISO asked if he could provide detailed insight into bandwidth usage. Dave told him no because they were using SNMP for network traffic analysis for monitoring and capacity planning. What protocol would Dave have to switch to in order to answer the CISO's question?

    A. SMB

    B. FTP

    C. OSPF

    D. NetFlow

33. You reached out to your legal department to determine whether there are repercussions after a data breach, including notification of customers whose personal information might have been lost. Every state and federal definition of a data breach is based on the unlawful acquisition of personal information. What is the "safe harbor" for organizations?

    A. Encryption

    B. Divestiture

    C. Confidentiality

    D. Investigation

34. After merging two disparate networks, a security incident led you to the discovery of an attacker gaining access to the network, overwriting files, and installing backdoor software. What should you use to detect attacks like this in the future?

 A. Containerization

 B. Firewalls

 C. VM patch management

 D. FIM

35. You need to use a protocol that is utilized to synchronize the time on your network devices, phones, and workstations so that your SIEM tool processes log files consistently and alert properly. What protocol should be used in this situation?

 A. VoIP

 B. NMP

 C. NTP

 D. TFTP

36. As a security architect, you implemented dual firewalls, an IPS, and ACLs. All the files on this network are copied to a tape backup every 24 hours according to your DLP policy. This backup solution addresses which security tenet?

 A. Availability

 B. Distribution

 C. Integrity

 D. Confidentiality

37. You are a security administrator, and you were notified by your IPS that there is an issue. You quickly solve the problem. What needs to be done once the problem has been fixed?

 A. After-action report

 B. MOA

 C. Encryption

 D. Update to security policy

38. You're installing an antivirus product on computers within your corporate domain so that you can be alerted of any virus detection. Installing the product manually on each computer will take a long time to complete. Your company uses Microsoft Active Directory in your environment. Which of the following techniques is more efficient?

 A. Providing a copy of the antivirus product to the end users and allowing them to install the product themselves

 B. Using Group Policy to push out the antivirus product to all computers

 C. Creating a master image of the computers with the antivirus product installed and then reimaging all the computers

 D. Contracting out the installation of the antivirus product to a third party that manually installs the product on all the computers

39. You need to find the true severity of an incident and accurately measure based on certain factors like scope and impact as well as how you should have prioritized the incident. Which of the following is *not* a factor for measuring the severity of an incident for your organization?

    A. Cost

    B. Downtime

    C. Disclosure

    D. Legal ramifications

40. You are analyzing TCP and UDP connections open on a system. You need to look at statistics of sent, received, and possible errors and do a deeper dive on the ID of the processes making unusual connections to determine if they're legitimate. What tool helps with this?

    A. Netstat

    B. Ping

    C. Rarp

    D. Traceroute

41. A firewall administrator added new rules to the corporate border firewall. What should the firewall administrator do next to ensure that the rules are functioning properly?

    A. All firewall rules should be tested with traffic matching the rules.

    B. Only the new firewall rules should be tested with traffic matching the rules.

    C. No testing is required. Firewalls rules are checked for validity within the firewall.

    D. Because of time constraints, only firewall rules considered to be the most important should be tested.

42. A network engineer configures a router to block inbound traffic from a computer with IP address 192.168.1.25 on Ethernet port 0. Which ACL performs the action of blocking this computer?

    A.
```
!interface ethernet0
ip access-group 1 in
!
access-list 1 permit any
access-list 1 deny host 192.168.1.25
```

    B.
```
!
interface ethernet0
ip access-group 1 in
!
access-list 1 deny host 192.168.1.25
access-list 1 permit any
```

    C.
```
!
interface ethernet0
ip access-group 1 in
!
```

D. !
```
interface ethernet0
ip access-group 1 in
!
access-list 1 deny any
access-list 1 deny host 192.168.1.25
access-list 1 permit any
```

43. Unnecessary services are disabled on the container host, and monitoring tools are installed. You want to monitor the inner container traffic so that attackers cannot move laterally through the environment. What should you install on the host?

    A. Malwarebytes

    B. IPS

    C. SIEM

    D. TPM

44. A system administrator has a Bash script that does not need many commands. For security reasons, the admin wants to run the Bash script in restricted mode. Which of the following commands does *not* provide a restricted shell?

    A. bash /r

    B. rbash

    C. bash --restricted

    D. bash -r

45. As an information security professional, Jurgen is tasked with ensuring that data remains available after an incident like a system failure or natural disaster. This falls under which of the following?

    A. Data recovery

    B. Data protection

    C. Data security

    D. Data reliability

46. One of the biggest tasks for security professionals is identifying vulnerabilities. What is the difference between a vulnerability and a threat?

    A. A vulnerability is a weakness in system design, procedure, or code. A threat is the circumstance or likelihood of a vulnerability being exploited.

    B. A vulnerability is the driving force behind the activity. A threat is the probability of an attack.

    C. A vulnerability is the value to an institution, whereas a threat is the source of the risk, internal or external.

    D. A vulnerability is the probability of the realization of a threat. A threat is the driving force behind the activity.

47. Angel works for a large enterprise that is expanding through the acquisition of a second corporation. What should be done before connecting the networks?

A. Credentialed vulnerability scan

B. Implementation of a firewall system

C. Development of a risk analysis for the two networks

D. Complete review of the new corporation

48. Cody is the head of security for an insurance company. An internal security audit of his organization shows that some of his machines are not being scanned for vulnerabilities because employees are taking their laptops home at night when the scan is taking place. How can he scan the machines that have missed their vulnerability scan?

A. Agents

B. Compliance reports

C. Audit logs continuously

D. Scan computers against the baseline

49. Your manufacturing organization implemented a new vulnerability management tool. As the security analyst, you are tasked with creating a successful process for vulnerability assessment. What do you have to fully understand before assuming this task?

A. Threat definitions and identification

B. CVE and CVSS

C. Risk assessments and threat identification

D. Vulnerability appraisal and access review

50. Your CIO is reviewing a request for proposal (RFP) with a software vendor providing network vulnerability scanning. He has asked specifically for an approach that will help his enterprise's IT staff identify weaknesses throughout its network—such as ports that could be accessed by unauthorized users and software lacking the latest security patches—which will help ensure network compliance. What kind of network vulnerability scanning is your CIO looking for?

A. Passive

B. Active

C. Credentialed

D. Noncredentialed

51. You are working for the federal government as a vulnerability management supervisor. You are attempting to enable automated measurement and policy compliance because of FISMA. What protocol are you most likely to use?

A. XCDDF

B. SCAP

C. OVAL

D. CPE

52. You requested help from your network engineers with a compliance audit that is in the very near future. They supplied you with the following host statistics: guest accounts disabled: 60 percent compliant; local firewall enabled: 90 percent compliant. Which of the following protocols can provide that type of data?

    A. HTTPS

    B. ARF

    C. CCE

    D. SCAP

53. Several servers went offline since an update was pushed out. Other servers without that patch are still operational but vulnerable to attack. As the security administrator, you must ensure that critical servers are patched while minimizing downtime. What is the *best* strategy to minimize risk?

    A. Test all updates in a lab before deployment.

    B. Patch all systems in production automatically.

    C. Patch production servers only when updates are released.

    D. Test all updates after they are installed in a live environment.

54. Edward is a security analyst who is implementing a new vulnerability scanning tool. Previously, his company used third-party vendors to assess his network. While examining the scan results of the new scanner, he notices the report says various servers are missing patches. He decides to look for an automated process of installing patches on those systems. Which of the following automates this process?

    A. Security assessment

    B. Vulnerability management

    C. Vulnerability scanner

    D. Patch management system

55. Your CISO has received advisories and bulletins alerting him to the dangers of zero-day exploits. He did more research, and according to news reports and vendor websites, one organization offered $1.5 million for a single submission. He has tasked you with mitigating zero-day exploits. Which of these is the *best* way to protect your organization from a zero-day exploit?

    A. Update and patch on a cycle.

    B. Use vulnerability assessments.

    C. Do not use software that has a zero-day vulnerability.

    D. Harden a system for only the required functions.

56. Your organization is a member of an ISAC. While researching how your retail organization should regulate social media use and access, you found that cybercriminals can use social media botnets to disseminate malicious links and collect intelligence on high-profile targets.

A common attack you need to watch for includes leveraging a hashtag for a specific organization and distributing malicious links that appear in your newsfeeds. What is this social media attack called?

- **A.** Hashtag hijacking
- **B.** Trend-jacking
- **C.** Retweet storm
- **D.** Spray and pray

57. You are tasked with conducting a black-box vulnerability assessment on an application your company has created. The application needs to be running to find vulnerabilities that an attacker could exploit. What is this assessment called?

- **A.** Reverse engineering
- **B.** Side-channel analysis
- **C.** SAST
- **D.** DAST

58. Your role as an IT administrator includes providing new hardware to different departments within your organization. The company decided that all servers need dual NICs, so you are compiling a summary from public requests for proposal. Upper management wants to select the lowest bidder, but you have never heard of this overseas manufacturer. What do you recommend in this decision-making process?

- **A.** Requiring well-known and trusted hardware manufacturers
- **B.** Going with the lowest bidder if it makes upper management happy
- **C.** Requesting samples from all the bidders and vetting the hardware yourself
- **D.** Buying all new servers because there aren't that many new ones

59. Your company hired a third party to conduct an application assessment. The tool they use can provide results with little effort and remain running for weeks. However, it might not find all the bugs depending on how it is configured. What type of tool do they use?

- **A.** Vulnerability scanner
- **B.** Fuzzer
- **C.** Data validator
- **D.** HIPS

60. As a security analyst, you are tasked with analyzing the logs from your web server. You have been given access to the SIEM software. What kind of analysis is this?

- **A.** Network analysis
- **B.** Hardware analysis
- **C.** Software analysis
- **D.** Software composition analysis

81. You are part of a legal team participating in creating a disclosure plan after an incident. Data breach disclosure varies from state to state and from country to country. Even if you are not legally obligated to declare the incident, your company's reputation suffers if someone else discloses the attack. Who handles the hack's disclosure to concerned parties?

    A. Public relations

    B. Infrastructure

    C. Legal

    D. Data owner

82. You have implemented a Simple Certificate Enrollment Protocol (SCEP) in your organizations. SCEP is designed to support the issuing of certificates in a scalable way. How does SCEP work in an enterprise environment?

    A. The SCEP server CA issues and approves the certificate.

    B. The SCEP server RA issues pending certificates automatically, and the IAM admin approves them.

    C. A certificate is requested from the SCEP server and is issued automatically.

    D. The SCEP issues the certificate; the CA approves and issues the certificate.

83. Employees at Olivia's entertainment company want Bluetooth enabled for their mobile devices. What is her primary security concern?

    A. Bluetooth can be overused.

    B. Bluetooth sends data as clear text.

    C. Bluetooth uses weak encryption.

    D. Bluetooth is a lower-power wireless technology.

84. You have an application that requires data to be encrypted on legacy equipment with minimum hardware resources. Which type of cipher is *best* suited for this situation?

    A. Stream cipher

    B. Serial cipher

    C. Block cipher

    D. Parallel cipher

85. Jess is investigating a breach and traces it back to the unified communications tool. The malicious user attacked the UC network using a phishing email and spoofed a MAC address to register an employee's soft phone and made international calls through your UC network. Which one of the following options will *not* have affected this attack?

    A. Vulnerabilities in the UC platform

    B. Weak firewall configurations

    C. Social engineering

    D. Cipher lock on the server room door

86. You are doing a peer review of software and walking through each line of code, examining each object, method, and routine. You are inspecting code granularly to find any possible errors or areas for improvement and to see if all security concerns are met. What is the main disadvantage to doing a peer review?

A. Money

B. Damage

C. Time

D. Reproducibility

87. Your auditor informs you that vulnerability scans for some compliance requirements will be ran quarterly. Your organization's roadmap states the organization will begin weekly patch management. How often should you be scanning for vulnerabilities?

A. Monthly

B. Annually

C. Weekly

D. Biweekly

88. Identifying all potential threats is a huge responsibility. Threats can be categorized into all of the following *except* which one?

A. Human error

B. Unsafe functions

C. Malicious software

D. Financial loss

89. As a security architect, you have created a blended Windows and Linux environment. What is the technology you want to use that will virtualize an instance on top of either operating system's kernel?

A. Hypervisor 1

B. Hypervisor 2

C. Containerization

D. Automation

90. VoIP is dependent on continuous reliable packet flow. It is an issue in the face of attacks. High levels of packet loss raise questions about VoIP reliability. Which of these attacks could be called the "busy signal" of VoIP?

A. DDoS

B. SQLi

C. MiTM

D. Bluejacking

91. To protect your company's web applications, you first must determine any highly problematic area of the application. You have applications that enable users to use large amounts of data like blog posts. When these blog posts are done through HTML, they are at a high risk of what type of attack?

   A. NGINX

   B. Injection

   C. Arbitrary

   D. Recursive

92. You work for a SOHO and replace servers whenever there is money readily available for expenditure. Over the past few tech-refresh cycles, you have received many servers and workstations from several different vendors. What is the challenge and risk to this style of asset management?

   A. OS and asset EOL issues and updates

   B. OS complexities and OS patch version dependencies

   C. Failure rate of legacy equipment, replacement parts, and firmware updates and management

   D. Poor security posture, inability to manage performance on old OS

93. A senior security architect for a hospital is creating a hardened version of the newest GUI OS. The testing will focus on the CIA triad as well as on compliance and reporting. Which of these is the *best* life cycle for the architect to deploy in the final image?

   A. Employing proper disposal protocols for existing equipment and ensuring compliance with corporate data retention policies

   B. Updating whole-disk encryption and testing operational models

   C. Employing interoperability, integrity of the data at rest, network availability, and compliance with all government regulations

   D. Creating a plan to decommission the existing OS infrastructure, implementing test and operational procedures for the new components in advance, and ensuring compliance with applicable regulations

94. A vendor of software deployed across your corporate network announced that an update is needed for a specific vulnerability. Your CIO wants to know the vulnerability time (Vt). When can you give them that information?

   A. After the patch is downloaded and installed in the affected system or device

   B. After the patch is released and available to the public

   C. After the patch is created by the vendor

   D. After an inherent vulnerability is discovered

95. After a vulnerability scan, you found critical vulnerabilities in some installed services on a Windows server. These could lead to a server-side attack. Which one of the following mitigation techniques is the *least* effective?

A. Patching

B. System hardening

C. Firewalls

D. Identity management

96. Matthew needs a tool that will allow you to build a connection using JSON between two software packages, extending the functionality of both. What is this called?

A. API

B. RFP

C. IBM

D. AES

97. You have an employee, Jace, who has downloaded a health app in their browser. The browser extension is tracking all physical location and accessing photos and videos, as well as browser activity. What is this called?

A. Worm

B. Trojan

C. Virus

D. Ransomware

98. Your end users utilize Microsoft Office. A few users have reached out for approval to install ActiveX. How do you advise those end users to use ActiveX securely?

A. If you are browsing the web and a site wants you to install an ActiveX control, decline it.

B. If you are browsing the web and a site wants you to install an ActiveX control, accept it.

C. Request the vetting of the software to be downloaded.

D. You cannot use ActiveX securely. You must use Flash.

99. Legacy applications in your environment are running a Java applet written in Pascal. This applet was created as a supplemental tool that displays data in 3D. Because Java applets were phased out in 2017 according to JEP 289 in the OpenJDK, what should you consider doing in the near future?

A. Coding business logic in Java and rendering in HTML5

B. Building the program in Silverfrost

C. Requesting an extension to maintain Java SE10—the last Java to use Java applets

D. No need to deprecate the legacy equipment exists

100. You examine your blue team cybersecurity toolkit and want to add a tool that produces proof of an exploit and supports JavaScript and Ajax-based applications. Which of these is *best* to use?

    A. SET

    B. Nmap

    C. Netsparker

    D. SQLi

101. You are a server administrator for a large enterprise using Windows, Linux, and macOS. You need to find a web service that enables HTTP and SMTP using XML-based protocols. Which technology is *best* for this way of exchanging information?

    A. HTTPS

    B. SSL

    C. SOAP

    D. SAMLv2

102. Which of the following *best* describes the code that consists of binary instructions that is directly understandable by the CPU?

    A. Byte code

    B. Machine code

    C. Source code

    D. JavaScript

103. Edwin is a senior security analyst for a large online news organization. He was briefed that his organization fell victim to an XSS attack that executed malicious web-scripting code in a trusted web page. How can Edwin prevent this from happening in the future?

    A. Make sure the web application can validate and sanitize input.

    B. Implement patch management immediately.

    C. Request an external penetration test.

    D. Edwin cannot prevent this from happening on a public-facing web server.

104. You logged into your bank account at `http://mycreditunion.com`. You open another tab and search for the best Italian restaurants. One of those sites is owned by a bad actor. This website has an image tag linking to:`<"http://mycreditunion.com/transfer.asp?to_acct123456&amount=500">`. What type of attack is this?

    A. CSRF

    B. XSS

    C. SQLi

    D. Directory transversal

105. You are examining SQL server logs and are seeing `userid: 101 or 1=1:--`. What is most likely happening on that SQL server?

   A. XMLi

   B. XSS

   C. SQLi

   D. Buffer overflow

106. Your mobile devices need configuring just like desktop and server systems. You were told to standardize all mobile devices, both iOS and tvOS. What do you deploy to these devices?

   A. Mobile device configuration profile

   B. Group Policy

   C. Root the devices and install a golden mobile image

   D. Containerization

107. Sandra is using native Lightweight Directory Access Protocol for her authentication solution. What is LDAP's biggest weakness?

   A. Hard to deploy.

   B. Passwords are passed in clear text.

   C. The session is easily replayed.

   D. Authorizations are not included in the header response.

108. Your organization is undergoing an external penetration test. You see the following data passed in a web page field: `password' OR 1=1;--`. What is this attack?

   A. CSRF

   B. XSS

   C. SQLi

   D. Buffer overflow

109. Allan is a network engineer. He enters the following commands on an Ethernet port of a router. The port is currently in its default configuration. What command must be entered after the following commands to bring up the interface?

```
Router>enable
Router# configure terminal
Router(config)#interface fastethernet 0/1
Router(config-if)#ip address 192.168.1.23 255.255.255.0
```

   A. `no shutdown`

   B. `up`

   C. `restart`

   D. `start`

110. What security mechanism does UEFI include that prevents the boot process from being hijacked by malware?

    A. Secure Boot

    B. Secure Bootup

    C. Secure Start

    D. Secure Run

111. Frederick is a security analyst reviewing corporate settings on multiple assets. He notices some settings were disabled and are allowing untrusted programs to be installed on mobile devices. What settings should be adjusted so that applications can be sandboxed and tested before deploying securely?

    A. Updates

    B. Digitally signed applications

    C. Containerization

    D. Remote wiping

112. You were asked to secure the Ethernet ports on the company's switches used to connect to host systems to prevent a VLAN hopping attack. Which of the following actions helps prevent this issue?

    A. Ensuring the Ethernet ports are statically defined as trunk ports

    B. Ensuring the Ethernet ports have DPT turned off

    C. Ensuring the Ethernet ports have DTP turned on

    D. Ensuring the Ethernet ports are configured as access ports

113. Jean's organization provides cloud computing for a highly classified project. She has implemented a virtual data center with multifactor authentication. Using the SIEM, she discovered a breach affecting confidential data. Sensitive information was found within the hypervisor. What has most probably occurred?

    A. Jean found a token and a RAM exploit that was used to move data.

    B. Jean found a local admin who could move data to their hard drive.

    C. A vulnerable server was unpatched, and the attacker was able to use VMEscape for access.

    D. A guest account used privilege escalation to move data from one virtual token to another.

114. The application you are developing has a vulnerability that can be mitigated by using SSL and TLS. Which of these attacks can be prevented by using cryptographic protocols?

    A. DDoS

    B. VLAN hopping

    C. On-path

    D. BGP hijacking

115. Your MDM for COPE devices neglected to restrict the use of NFC. What is the biggest worry for employees using NFC for transactions?

    A. No login/password

    B. Interception

    C. Breaches

    D. Legalities

116. You test an application by mapping out all areas where a user's input is used to reference objects. This input accesses a file, and you try to change the value, bypassing all authorization. What type of attack is this?

    A. CSRF

    B. DDoS

    C. Insecure direct object reference

    D. Click-jacking

117. A small insurance business implemented least privilege. Management is concerned that staff might accidentally aid in fraud with the customers. Which of the following addresses security concerns with this risk?

    A. Policy

    B. Job rotation

    C. Separation of duties

    D. Security awareness training

118. Bernie, a member of your board of directors, has asked your CEO about your company's proactive defense measures. In turn, the CEO asks you about proactive defense strategies. Which of these tools is an example of proactive defense measures?

    A. Running Nexpose/Nessus

    B. Installing botnets

    C. War chalking

    D. Rootkits

119. You build a team of cyber-investigators who actively seek out threats on your network. They purposefully seek out anomalies and attempt to find patterns in data to stay ahead of criminals. What is this type of team called?

    A. Black box

    B. Gray box

    C. Hunt team

    D. Data analytics

120. A competitor of your company was hacked, and the forensics show it was a social engineering phishing attack. What is the first thing you do to prevent this from happening at your company?

A. Educate all employees about social engineering risks and countermeasures.

B. Publish a new mission statement.

C. Implement IPSec on all critical systems.

D. Use encryption.

121. Alberto has been investigating deceptive technologies. He wants to configure a system that will gather information about intruders and the attack methods they are using. The system needs to have valuable information and be specifically designed to attract malicious activities. What type of tool would he build?

A. Botnet

B. Zombie master

C. Honeypot

D. Honeynet

122. Marilyn, your CISO, has asked what type of deception strategy the company is using. One of the tools that she has asked you to evaluate is an open source honeypot software called Deception Toolkit. What does honeypot software do?

A. Gathers information about intruders

B. Gathers information about external networks

C. Gathers information about botnets

D. Gathers information about network infections

123. Your CIO has asked you to identify control types and control functions for risk mitigation. What type of control type and function would a honeypot or honeyfile be?

A. Detective/technical

B. Preventative/physical

C. Corrective/administrative

D. Recovery/technical

124. Your organization experienced some network failures over the past year within the core part of its network, particularly with the static assignment of all IP addresses. These failures cost the company a lot of money in lost productivity. Upper management wants to stop the failures. The IT department explained to upper management that these failures can't be avoided but that the network can be reconfigured at a cost so that the impact of such failures is greatly reduced. Which network configuration is the IT department likely to propose?

A. Hub and spoke with all static IP addresses

B. Full mesh with static and dynamic IP addresses

C. Point-to-point with all dynamic IP addresses

D. Partial mesh with all static IP addresses

125. You are a blue teamer for a medium-sized business. You want to automate and simu-
late social engineering tests using a free Python-based tool. Which of these is the *best* tool
for the job?

    A. SET

    B. Nmap

    C. BurpSuite

    D. Metasploit

126. Eduardo's security department is maturing using processing pipelines and wants to represent
data in digestible data points. He will decide the next step beyond the pie chart in Excel will
be using a business intelligence tool. What is this process called?

    A. Visualization

    B. Hypervisor

    C. Data complexity

    D. Clarity

127. Your security compliance audit failed due to the lack of data streaming into a logging tool
and an inability to analyze this data. You were chosen to lead a team to implement a logging tool that will index and search logs proactively and mitigate this risk. What tool do you
implement to lead this team to becoming compliant?

    A. SIEM

    B. VM

    C. DNS

    D. LASE

128. Your company deployed various databases throughout its network. A solution is needed to
monitor the databases and to analyze the type of activity occurring on them. Which of the
following provides the *best* solution?

    A. DAM

    B. SIEM

    C. XSS

    D. WAF

129. Your CISO has asked you to evaluate an antivirus tool for all company-issued laptops. The
cost is $3,000 for all 90 laptops. From historical data you anticipate that 12 computers will
be affected, with a SLE of $1,500. What do you recommend to the CISO?

    A. Accept the risk.

    B. Mitigate the risk.

    C. Transfer the risk.

    D. Avoid the risk.

130. In the past, your global organization tasked individual locations and departments with creating their own separate disaster recovery plans with immutable infrastructure. The organization realizes those employees know best how their division works. Your new CISO tasked your team with creating a viable plan should your company experience a disaster. What is your mission?

A. Record as many separate plans as necessary.

B. Create one fully integrated business continuity plan.

C. Separate plans for each geographic location.

D. Keep separate plans for each logical department, regardless of the physical location.

131. You are a technical project manager on a VoIP/teleconference project. The customer has shared their requirements with your department. Availability must be at least five nines (99.999 percent), and all devices must support collaboration and be hardened for security. Which controls are the *best* to apply to this ecosystem?

A. All images must be standardized and double redundant.

B. Security policies of network access controls and high-speed processing.

C. RAID 0 and hot sites.

D. Enforced security policies, standard images/configurations, and backup on all storage devices.

132. You found a suspicious USB in the corporate parking lot and brought the USB back to your lab for detonation in a sandbox. It contains unreadable documents and audio files. You pick one that is abnormally large to analyze, looking for hidden information. What is this process referred to as?

A. Stego-analyzer

B. Stegoanalysis

C. Steganography

D. Steganalysis

133. Your organization needs to be able to use a third party's development tools to deploy specific cloud-based applications. Platform as a service (PaaS) is the choice that has been approved to launch these cloud services. Which of the following is *not* a true statement?

A. PaaS can use an API to develop and deploy specific cloud-based services.

B. Cloud storage is a term used to describe the use of a third-party vendor's virtual filesystem as a document or repository.

C. You can purchase the resources you need from a cloud service provider on a pay-as-you-go basis.

D. With PaaS, you must buy and manage software licenses.

134. Amos is creating allow lists and block lists of IP addresses while editing an ACL. What device is Amos most likely configuring?

A. A switch

B. A modem

C. A router

D. A hub

135. In software development, a timing problem can occur when time to check (ToC) is misaligned with time of use (ToU). This time gap can be exploited by an attacker when scheduled for execution after each operation by the victim. To prevent ToCToU (pronounced Toctoo), which of the following is most effective?

    A. Do not perform a check before use.

    B. Alter the file owned by the current user.

    C. Request the timing gap be closed.

    D. Limit multiple processes and operations.

136. You have deployed an operating system that uses atomic operations. Atomic operations are used in many modern operating systems at the kernel level and with parallel processing systems. Atomic operations in concurrent programming are program operations that run completely independently of any other processes. What is the biggest problem you can have with this type of operating system or programming?

    A. When two operations run in parallel and use the same data, you note a disparity between the results of the operation.

    B. Atomic operation can only exist in nonsequential processing environments.

    C. There is no guarantee of data integrity.

    D. You must have a great deal of RAM for this system to function properly.

137. You need to perform a repetitive task on a Linux machine. Which of the following is the *best* way to execute this type of task?

    A. Bash

    B. Python

    C. Cron job

    D. PowerShell

138. Your company has a fence around the perimeter of its data center. A light sensor is connected to the fence and trips an alarm whenever something impacts the fence or the sensor detects movement and automatically records it on video. The data center is located in an area with tumbleweeds that often impact the fence in the fall, causing alarm fatigue. In this scenario, what alert type is causing alarm fatigue?

    A. True positive

    B. True negative

    C. False positive

    D. False negative

139. Sean is walking into a secured office building in a governmental complex, escorting an approved visitor. He scans his RFID badge to gain access and guides his visitor to sign in. As the door is closing, someone behind him yells at Sean to hold the door for them. What is that person attempting to do?

    A. Tailgating

    B. Baiting

    C. Water holing

    D. Man in the middle

140. You are conducting a physical site security survey. This facility has an open area that leads into a confined space. You want to ensure that only one authenticated person at a time can enter the building at a specific point and that everyone who enters the facility is logged. What is the *best* way to authenticate, and what perimeter defense do you recommend?

   A. Use a badge for access through a turnstile

   B. Require signatures in a log book; then everyone can enter through a interlocking door controller.

   C. Require presentation of an ID at a closed gate.

   D. Use bollards and a physical locked door.

141. Your company is using a traditional signature-based IDS, and the system seems to have some problems. You and your fellow analysts are seeing more and more false positives. What might be the issue?

   A. Anomaly detection requires vast amounts of resources.

   B. FIM uses too much computing power.

   C. There is excessive FTP traffic.

   D. Signatures are poorly written.

142. You are the CIO of an organization with many governmental contracts. You were challenged by the board of directors to reduce staff and the need for staff to do repetitive, low-value, decision-making activities so that your staff can work strategically. What tool would you use for this?

   A. Machine learning

   B. Zero-day exploits

   C. Triaged threats

   D. Human resources

143. During the risk analysis phase of planning, what would *best* mitigate and manage the effects of an incident?

   A. Modifying the scenario the risk is based on

   B. Developing an agenda for recovery

   C. Choosing the members of the recovery team

   D. Implementing procedural controls

144. You work as a security analyst for a large banking organization that is about to disclose to the public that a substantial breach occurred. You are called into a meeting with the CISO and CEO to discuss how to ensure proper forensic action took place and that the incident response team responded appropriately. Which of these should you ensure happens after the incident?

   A. Avoid conflict of interest by hiring outside counsel.

   B. Create forensic images of all mission-critical servers.

   C. Perform a formal investigation yourself without law enforcement.

   D. Treat the incident as though a crime has been committed.

145. After an incident, it is important for you to create a lessons learned document. By conducting this critique, you evaluate the effectiveness of the response. With that after-incident mindset, what is the most important result you can derive from this document?

A. Areas for improvement

B. Magnitude of the problem

C. Proper assessment of an incident

D. Security assessment awareness

146. Your organization finished dealing with an incident that requires an after-action report (AAR). Your goal is to improve your organization's response to an event or a critical situation. Which of the following should *not* be included in the AAR?

A. Analyze the event to determine what your strengths are and areas of improvement for your future response plan.

B. Understand the entire event from multiple strategic, tactical, and operational viewpoints; compile a playbook for future training.

C. Improve the communication of your organization's critical response, disaster recovery, and business continuity plans.

D. Create network topology diagrams.

147. One of your end users contacted the security administrator because the mouse on his computer seems to be moving all by itself. If your company's focus is confidentiality, which of the following is the *best* action to take?

A. Delay the intruder.

B. Disconnect the intruder.

C. Record the intruder.

D. Monitor the intruder.

148. You are a security analyst working for a casino. You work with a security firm and have traced the origin of a ransomware attack to a connected fish tank in the casino lobby. The attack was stopped within seconds, and the threat was mitigated. What would have led to the quick discovery of the attack?

A. Signatures

B. Endpoint analysis

C. Machine learning algorithms

D. Immunity learning

149. What risks and mitigations are associated with BYOD?

A. Risk: Data exfiltrationMitigation: Remote wipe

B. Risk: Confidentiality leaksMitigation: Corporate policy

C. Risk: TheftMitigation: Minimal storage

D. Risk: GPS trackingMitigation: Minimal cost

150. Your company's CISO hired an external security consultant to perform a review of the organization's physical security. In the contract, the CISO noted a concern of unauthorized access to physical offices that result in a digital compromise. How should the consultant evaluate the potential risk?

    A. Automatically grant access to physical control systems and review logs.

    B. Conduct internal audits of access logs and social media feeds.

    C. Install CCTV on all entrances and exits to detect access.

    D. Gain access to offices using social engineering techniques and then attempt to compromise the network.

151. Your new role within a network operations center is to support the development of policies and to implement standard IT security practices of incident response. You will be writing the procedures for how your incident team will manually respond to events. This would be considered which type of response?

    A. Least privilege

    B. Automated

    C. Non-automated

    D. Forensic tasks

152. Your organization was breached, but you have been able to prove that sufficient due care and due diligence was taken. You have documented exactly when the workflow began and what the response tasks were. What is this document called?

    A. SOW

    B. NDA

    C. Runbook

    D. Playbook

153. You are working for the federal government as a vulnerability management supervisor. You are attempting to enable automated measurement and policy compliance to improve your security posture. What are you most likely to use?

    A. HTTPS

    B. SOAR

    C. STATE

    D. HIPAA

154. You are a project manager for an organization that just acquired another company. Your company uses mostly in-house tools, whereas the company you just acquired uses mostly outside vendors. Merging these two organizations needs to be quick, have an immediate return on investment (ROI), and retain the ability to customize systems. Each organization thinks their way is the best way. What do you do?

    A. Raise the issue with the CEO and board of directors to escalate the decision to outsource all services.

    B. Arrange a meeting between all department heads, project managers, and a representative from the board of directors to review requirements and calculate critical functions.

C. Perform a cost-benefit analysis of in-house versus outsourcing and the ROI in-house.

D. Calculate the time to deploy and support the new systems and compare the cost to out-sourcing costs. Present the document to upper management for their final decision.

155. Your company needs to decide on a data backup plan strategy. You established your RPO as 8 hours, and your RTO after any disaster, human-made or natural, as 48 hours. These RTOs were established by the business owner while developing the BIA. The RTO includes which of the following?

A. Recovery, testing, and communications

B. Decision time

C. Parallel processing

D. Only the time for trying to fix the problem without a recovery

156. Your bank outsourced the security department to an outside firm. The CISO just learned that this third-party outside firm subcontracted security operations to another organization. The board of directors is now pressuring the CISO to ensure that the bank is protected legally. What is the *best* course of action for the CISO to take?

A. Creating another NDA directly with the subcontractor

B. Confirming that the current outside firm has an SLA with the subcontractor

C. Performing a risk analysis on the subcontractor

D. Terminating the contract immediately and looking for another outside firm

157. Your new role with a law enforcement agency is to support the development of policies and to implement standard IT security practices. You will be writing the procedures for _____ such as collecting digital evidence, recording observations, and taking photographs.

A. least privilege

B. incident responses

C. master service agreements

D. forensic tasks

158. You had an incident and need to verify that chain of custody, due diligence, and identification processes were followed. You are told to verify the forensic bitstream. What will you do?

A. Employ encryption.

B. Instigate containment.

C. Compare hashes.

D. Begin documentation.

159. An attacker who compromised your network was caught and is being prosecuted. The logs from various pieces of equipment showing the attacker's actions are one of the key pieces of evidence. Upon examining the logs, you determined that the timestamps are inaccurate and off by years. What is likely to happen to the logs as related to the prosecution of the attacker?

    A. The defense attorney will likely be given an opportunity to correct the timestamps.

    B. The judge will likely enable a third party to correct the timestamps.

    C. The company will likely be given an opportunity to correct the timestamps, making them admissible in court.

    D. The logs will likely not be allowed in court because the timestamps are incorrect.

160. An employee uses a smartphone for both business and personal use. You think the phone is compromised, but you do not suspect the employee has malicious intent. What should you do?

    A. Confiscate the phone.

    B. Get a subpoena to access the phone.

    C. Ask the user to surrender the phone for testing.

    D. Get a warrant for the phone.

161. As a new director of security, you review your organization's security policy. The current policy states if a compromise is suspected or detected, you should immediately disconnect the system from the network, power it down, and physically secure the system. This mode worked well in the past. However, with malware authors reducing the footprint on a hard drive, storing as much as possible within RAM, which is cleared when the system is powered down, it is now widely recognized in forensics to do which of the following?

    A. Include volatile memory as part of the incident evidence collection, using tools that quickly analyze RAM.

    B. Power down because advanced persistent threats will still be evident on the hard drive.

    C. Pull the hard drive and RAM and then put them on dry ice indefinitely until they can be analyzed to store the digital evidence.

    D. Pull the plug and examine the network logs.

162. Your team is examining business continuity, incident detection, and response to determine its storage policy. One of the mitigating controls for this policy will be the hierarchy of evidence from most volatile to least volatile. For example, archival media is not volatile; the most volatile are registers, cache, and read-access memory. What is this called?

    A. Order of volatility

    B. IETF

    C. Guidelines of storage capacity

    D. RFC 3227

163. You are part of an IDR team building a team toolkit containing numerous tools from many sources—some open source and some prepacked with operating systems. Which of the following is a command-line tool that can be used to create a clone or image of any drive?

    A. nbtstat

    B. dd

    C. tshark

    D. netcat

164. Your agency was compromised but found no evidence of data exfiltration. What is the first thing that all employees should do?

    A. Proactively change their passwords.

    B. Clone all hard drives for backups.

    C. Contact a PR firm for customer relations.

    D. Hold a meeting of the board of directors.

165. After you are breached, one of the most difficult steps is to understand what actually occurred. Your technical team tells you which systems and data were violated, which vulnerabilities were used, and that the compromised systems are quarantined. What should your technical team do next?

    A. Ensure there are no backdoors or logic bombs left behind by attackers.

    B. Report directly to the board of directors.

    C. Place the CISO and CTO on administrative leave.

    D. Bring in a third party for a penetration test.

166. Your organization terminates an employee from the IT department. After the IT employee is escorted from the building, a complete forensic investigation on all systems that IT employee had access to shows a logic bomb installed on a server. Only three IT staff member had access to that server, and the remaining IT employees did not have admin access; therefore, they could not have installed the logic bomb. Which of the following factors supports the evidence you have collected?

    A. Authorized people accessing evidence

    B. Improper storage of evidence

    C. Mislabeled evidence

    D. Alteration of digital evidence

167. Your web application stores sensitive information, including credit card numbers and account records. Which of the following is an encryption mistake and can possibly lead to insecure storage in your website?

    A. Strong algorithm

    B. Initialization vectors

    C. Support for key changes

    D. Storage of certificates on USB

168. You have been appointed the new data custodian. What will your new role entail?

   A. Data protection

   B. Data classification

   C. Data backups

   D. Data entry

169. Your organization wants to start digging deeper into malware analysis and needs software to spot vulnerabilities that can be exploited. You do not have the budget for EnCase this year, so an open source tool is best. You also need to create your own plug-ins. Which of these tools meet that criteria?

   A. Ghidra

   B. Immunity Debugger

   C. AngryIP

   D. Hydra

170. You run a security verification process on a web server. You attempt to replace the decimal encoding of ../ with %2E%2E%2F. What type of attack are you attempting?

   A. Phishing

   B. Input validation

   C. Ransomware

   D. Double encoding

171. Your breached organization is in the middle of an investigation, gathering evidence, performing forensics, and giving a presentation to upper management of all the proof gathered. What is the organization's next action after all the technical incident forensics are completed?

   A. Notify the public.

   B. Notify the authorities.

   C. Notify your vendors.

   D. File for cyber-insurance coverage.

172. In forensics, what is the process that dictates how to control, protect, and secure evidence, should it ever need to be admitted to a court of law?

   A. Containment

   B. Cryptoanalysis

   C. Encryption

   D. Chain of custody

173. You are performing risk analysis on authentication systems in your enterprise. You are using a one-way encryption hashing algorithm. Which of the following is a hashing algorithm?

   A. AES

   B. Skipjack-128

   C. Blowfish

   D. SHA-512

174. As a new CISO, you are evaluating controls for integrity. Which set of controls should you choose?

   A. RAID 1, classification of data, and load balancing

   B. Digital signatures, encryption, and hashes

   C. Steganography, ACL, and vulnerability management

   D. Checksum, DOS attacks, and RAID 0

175. Your job as an information protection specialist is to prevent unauthorized individuals from examining or capturing intellectual property. What do you use to protect the confidentiality of this data?

   A. Cryptography

   B. Sanitization

   C. Legal documentation

   D. Zeroization

176. You investigate an incident of malware on a corporate computer, and you come across a steganography program on an employee's laptop. It turns out that this tool was downloaded for free onto the system and that the downloaded file is the source of the malware. What might explain this information?

   A. Company information may be extracted using the steganography tool by the employee who downloaded it as well as the developer of the program itself.

   B. Someone downloaded the steganography tool to protect data as a form of encryption.

   C. You should reverse-engineer the unauthorized software to determine how it works.

   D. You only need worry about the malware. You can always trust employees.

177. You purchase software from an online store. On the download page next to the link to download the software, there is a string of characters that looks like SHA256: e2ad113ea0d826d8c208bd0eabd3fb4b76c7d85618d4f38b5d54d4788a5ececa. What is the string of characters after SHA256 used for?

   A. Serial number of software

   B. Product ID of software

   C. Encryption key to decrypt the software

   D. Unique identifier of the software

178. You were hired to perform a white-hat penetration test and instructed to concentrate on a specific web server. You run the following command: nmap -sV -p80 192.168.1.6. This is the response: 80/tcp open http Apache httpd 1.3.30. What is this an example of?

   A. XSS

   B. Information leakage

   C. Request/response

   D. Error handling

179. You decided to ensure that your network is protected and will perform your own port scans using Nmap. To get accurate results, you must perform this port scan from a remote location using noncompany equipment and another Internet service provider (ISP). What must you do first?

   A. Get permission.

   B. Decide what range of IPs and ports to scan.

   C. Contact HR.

   D. Create a scan for 10 packet attempts to non-listening ports.

180. The second CIS control of the top 20 controls is knowing software inventory. A feature of Nmap is the ability to remotely detect operating systems. By default, Nmap will attempt to identify which of the following using the `nmap-os-db` file?

   A. Hostname and IP address

   B. OS vendor, generation, and device type

   C. FQDN and open ports

   D. OS patch level and DNS

181. You are using Nmap to complete a scan of your network. You want Nmap to perform all three steps of a TCP session. Which following command should be executed?

   A. `-sL`

   B. `-sn`

   C. `-sU`

   D. `-sT`

182. You are testing Group Policy and firewall settings on an end user's workstation. You want to see whether there are certain active TCP connections. What command do you use?

   A. `netstat`

   B. `netsh`

   C. `ping`

   D. `ipconfig`

183. Your incident detection toolkit has a command-line tool that captures packets over a network and displays them on the screen or saves them in a file. It is native in Linux and is installed on Windows when Wireshark is installed. What tool is this?

   A. TShark

   B. Zenmap

   C. Wireshark

   D. Netstat

184. Your pentester submitted a request to be allowed to use a port scanner tool internally on the network. Which port scanner do you recommend?

A. Nmap

B. Netcat

C. Tracert

D. Arp

185. You must use a computer networking utility to read and write network connections using TCP and UDP. Which one of the following commands is a network debugging tool enabling you to create nearly any kind of connection?

A. IPConfig

B. Netcat

C. Openbsd

D. Traceroute

186. Your toolkit needs an open source utility that works on the command line and gives descriptions of packet content. What tool do you pull out of your toolkit?

A. Tcpdump

B. dd

C. Netcat

D. Memdump

187. James is tasked with capturing network traffic and testing firewall rule sets for vulnerabilities and possible intrusions. He needs a granular tool that will support both hexadecimal and ASCII dumps. Which of these tools is *best* to use for this task?

A. Nmap

B. Wireshark

C. Traceroute

D. Packet Tracer

188. You are a security administrator. You are examining a packet capture file (PCAP) from Wireshark. You see traffic addressed to 119.0.23.5. What class address is this?

A. Class A

B. Class B

C. Class C

D. Classless

189. During a routine Wireshark capture on your network, you see a great deal of traffic over port 80. What protocol is typically running over port 80?

A. HTTPS

B. HTTP

C. HTML

D. NTTP

190. You need to capture network traffic and have downloaded Wireshark. What format does Wireshark use to save packet data?

A. PCAP

B. EXE

C. WSDATA

D. FERS

191. You are a forensic analyst for a financial company with a robust security program. You were told to analyze a tool that may contain a malicious payload and were given this code snippet to research:

```
Text2 += "Win32DiskImager_0_9_5_install.exe"; File.WriteAllBytes(text2,
Resources.Win32DiskImager) Process.Start);
```

What process do you use to find the location of the payload?

A. Reverse engineering

B. Fuzzing

C. Containerization

D. External auditing

192. Digital evidence is a part of many legal proceedings litigated by your organization. This evidence includes social media posts, photographs, videos, and text messages. With physical evidence alone, you were tasked with creating a chain of digital evidence. After law enforcement collects the digital evidence, what should happen next?

A. The original digital media should be forensically examined.

B. Law enforcement should make a public statement.

C. Forensic technicians should analyze the data before making a copy.

D. Your organization should immediately hash the original copy of the data.

193. Chain of custody begins with a crime scene. A digital forensic investigator carefully examines the scene and takes detailed notes for each single piece of evidence found, including the location, time, and date, before using any forensic carving tools. What may *not* be included in the chain of custody documentation?

A. Description

B. Condition

C. Unique attributes

D. Investigator CV

194. Your legal department requested files from a Linux machine due to a fraud investigation. Your team identifies, recovers, and preserves data from this machine using Foremost. You start transferring data to their office, enabling them to research relevance. They call in a forensic specialist to preserve the data for presentation in court. In what stage of e-discovery does this happen?

    A. Processing

    B. Inference

    C. Causation

    D. Collection

195. File carving is the process of reassembling computer files from fragments in the absence of filesystem metadata. Shawn is evaluating several different tools and needs one that will play an important role in forensic investigations because smart malicious actors will try to delete evidence of their unlawful acts. Which of these would work *best* for Shawn?

    A. Nessus

    B. Docker

    C. EnCase

    D. Autopsy

196. An analyst has been attempting to acquire a budget for a new security tool that will perform binary code analysis. Which of the following reasons should the analyst give to management to support the request for a binary code analysis tool?

    A. Provides threat and trend analysis reports

    B. Improves interconnection security agreements

    C. Creates a master service agreement

    D. Overcomes blind spots in assessing third-party software inventory and risk

197. You work with binary data, and you are unable to understand the format of a Linux file. What utility can you use to get file contents in much better readable format?

    A. Hexdump

    B. Grepper

    C. Clonezilla

    D. Office365

198. Susan, an analyst, is looking for a simple Linux tool for analyzing binary files for embedded files and executable code. She will use it mostly used to extract the content of firmware images. Which of these is her *best* option?

    A. Foremost

    B. Inception

    C. Binwalk

    D. QuickStego

199. Danio is a reverse engineer and just downloaded an open source tool shared by the NSA that is a reverse-engineering platform used to take "compiled," deployed software and "decompile" it. In other words, it transforms the 1s and 0s that computers understand back into a human-readable structure, logic, and a set of commands that reveal what the software you churn through it does. What software did Danio just download?

A. dd

B. Ghidra

C. Aircrack-ng

D. Netcat

200. Jaime is a software programmer, and he has written the implementation in a language that the compiler does not understand. What should he use to debug the software to find the source of his trouble?

A. SHA256sum

B. EnCase

C. Cobalt Strike

D. GNU Project Debugger (GDB)

201. An analyst is considering reverse-engineering malware to understand how it works and possibly repurposing it. Which of these tools would be *best* to use?

A. Hydra

B. ICS

C. hashcat

D. OllyDbg

202. Sirius's publishing company has experienced a breach and an analyst has found some ELF files on the Linux machines that are suspicious. What is the command similar to `objdump` but that goes into more detail?

A. `readelf`

B. `redgram`

C. `unwind`

D. `objcrack`

203. Martez has just typed the following line of code on his Unix system: `$ objdump -D -M intel file.bin | grep main.: -A10`. What will be the response?

A. Reassembly on the file «file.bin», with the assembly code shown in Intel syntax. redirect it to grep, which searches the main function and displays 10 lines of its code

B. Disassembly on the file «file.bin», with the assembly code shown in Intel syntax. redirect it to grep, which searches the main function and displays 10 lines of its code

    C. `Disassembly on the file «file.exe», with the assembly code`
    `shown in Intel syntax. redirect it to grep, which searches the`
    `main function and displays 10 lines of its code`

    D. `Disassembly on the file «file.bin», with the assembly code`
    `shown in Intel syntax. redirect it to grep, which searches the`
    `main function and displays 20 lines of its code`

204. You are a system administrator, and you are troubleshooting problems with programs for which the source is not readily available. What CLI tool can you use in Linux to help problem solve?

    A. `ptrace`

    B. `strace`

    C. `etrace`

    D. `otrace`

205. You are a systems analyst, and your work involves deep knowledge of executables and shared libraries in Linux. Which command can you use to access shared object dependencies?

    A. `cd`

    B. `mkdir`

    C. `ldd`

    D. `version`

206. After the latest acquisition, your security manager asked you to review the analysis done by an external firm. There was a live breach at the time of acquisition. What type of analysis is needed?

    A. Collection analysis

    B. Business analysis

    C. Forensic analysis

    D. Gap analysis

207. Ray has used the following command on his Linux machine: `$ file /etc/group`. The output is `/etc/group: ASCII text`. What is the purpose of the command?

    A. To see location of a file

    B. To make a file named group

    C. To display the filename along with the file type

    D. To display the filename along with the file extension

208. As a forensic analyst using analysis tools, you need to show that you did what any reasonable and prudent professional would do in certain circumstances for a legal defense. What is this minimum level of security called?

    A. Due diligence

    B. Due care

    C. Standards

    D. Policies

209. As a security analyst, Phil needs an open source CLI tool that can read, write, and edit embedded metadata in files. He was tasked to improve digital preservation workflows. Which analysis tool would be *best* for Phil to use?

    A. Nmap

    B. Wireshark

    C. Aircrack-ng

    D. ExifTool

210. Many organizations now use wireless networking and have their security compromised by rogue access points. Many attacks are perpetrated by insiders, and many penetration tests focus on public Internet-facing systems. Which of these tools would you use to evaluate the security of your organization's wireless network?

    A. Nmap

    B. Aircrack-ng

    C. Sn1per

    D. MiTM

211. What suite of tools can be used to capture a four-way handshake/wireless password?

    A. Aircrack-ng

    B. Ettercap

    C. Netstumbler

    D. Burp Suite

212. One of the important parts of malware analysis is random access memory (RAM) analysis. It helps to identify the malicious running processes, network activities, and open connections in the compromised system. What tool might you use to analyze crash dumps?

    A. Pentoo

    B. BackBox

    C. Buscador

    D. Volatility

213. You need a tool that allows you to examine filesystems of a suspect computer in a nonintrusive fashion. You need the tool to not rely on the operating system to process the filesystems because you want deleted and hidden content to be visible. Which of these would be the *best* tool to use?

    A. FindBugs

    B. Meterpreter

    C. TSK

    D. Nikto

214. You are conducting malware analysis in a sandboxed environment so it will not affect other systems. What kind of analysis is this?

    A. Dynamic

    B. Static

    C. Verification

    D. Validation

215. The containers you built are running, and software is currently undergoing a patch. These changes must be integrated into the application to reduce risk. What tool can you use to ensure that changes are *not* causing security issues on the containers in production?

    A. Container image scanner

    B. Container vulnerability scanner

    C. Container port scanner

    D. Container antivirus

216. You have taken your workstation into the hardware lab to get reimaged with the newest operating system using Clonezilla. While there, you notice some new machines on the workbench with the USB port filled with glue. What type of security approach is this?

    A. Redundant

    B. Reciprocal

    C. Vector oriented

    D. Protective oriented

217. You need to pull data into a tool from a suspected compromised system. Imaging has not been done, and you want to start media and network analysis as soon as possible. Which of these tools will allow you to create a forensic image of hard drives, preview files on network drives, and then export those files from a forensic image?

    A. MD5

    B. FTK

    C. SHA-1

    D. Duplicator

218. Kirsten is working in the forensics lab, and HR has brought her a hard drive for forensic analysis, specifically to recover files HR believes have been deleted. The very first thing Kirsten does is make a complete copy using which command on her Linux machine?

    A. cc

    B. mcopy

    C. dd

    D. sync

219. Paul has been tasked with creating a backup copy of a Linux system using the dd command. He has the source disk (sdb) and has chosen a destination disk (sdc). Which of these commands will clone the source drive to the destination drive?

A. `dd if=/dev/sdb of=/dev/sdc`

B. `fdisk -l /dev/sdb /dev/sdc`

C. `dd if=/dev/sdc of=/dev/sdb`

D. `dd of=/dev/sdc status=progress`

220. Sometimes your victim cannot afford to remove the system, or the only evidence of the incident may currently be in memory. Either way, a standard forensic duplication is impossible. What is your alternative?

A. String searches

B. Memory dumps

C. Live incident response

D. Encryption

221. You set up a meeting with your team to discuss an incident. Your incident response team tries to determine exactly what happened during the incident and brainstorm solutions to prevent recurring problems. Team members can work together to help an organization decide the best course of action to prevent future incidents. What type of process is this?

A. Premortem

B. Postmortem

C. Live collection

D. Running processes

222. Mike is debugging network problems on a Linux server; ping and traceroute are helpful, but he may need to have further network details on hand to help track down an issue and get it fixed. What tool might he use?

A. Netstat

B. Metasploit

C. LDAP

D. TSK

223. Shannan is troubleshooting a Linux server and needs to know what processes are currently running. What command does she run?

A. pwd

B. mv

C. ps

D. cat

224. You need to use a Linux command-line tool that reports various bits of system information. You need to report on memory, paging, processes, I/O, CPU, and disk scheduling. What is the command you run?

  A. chmod

  B. hostname

  C. ping

  D. vmstat

225. Timothy is a system admin, and his work involves complex knowledge of executables and shared libraries in Linux. There are several commands that he uses often; which one does he use to access shared object dependencies?

  A. tar

  B. zip

  C. ldd

  D. uname -a

226. You are working with Linux forensics and use the command ls to list files and find out some details about them. What command do you need to use to learn about all the other processes and devices that are being treated as though they were files?

  A. lsof

  B. man

  C. less

  D. var

227. You need to scan for open ports in the range 20–80. What command line would you run?

  A. $ nc -z -v 192.168.1.1 20-80

  B. $ nc -z -v 192.168.1.1 20 to 80

  C. $ nc -z -v 192.168.1.1 20=80

  D. $ nc +z +v 192.168.1.1 20-80

228. You are using netcat, and you type the following command:

```
nc -p 31337 -w 5 host.example.com 42
```

What is the purpose of this command?

  A. Opens a TCP connection to port 31337 using 5 as a source port with a timeout of 42 seconds

  B. Opens a TCP connection to port 5 using 31337 as a source port with a timeout of 42 seconds

  C. Opens a UDP connection to port 42 using 5 as a source port with a timeout of 31337 seconds

  D. Opens a TCP connection to port 42 using 31337 as a source port with a timeout of 5 seconds

229. What would the result be of using the command `tcpdump -i eth0`?

- **A.** Shows all network traffic hitting your interface
- **B.** Shows only HTTPS traffic hitting your interface
- **C.** Captures specific port traffic
- **D.** Shows only IPv6 traffic

230. Carl is using `tcpdump` to improve network troubleshooting and security testing. Which of these commands would write a standard capture file to a `test.pcap` file for future analysis?

- **A.** `$ sudo tcpdump -i eth0 host 10.10.1.1 |w|r test`
- **B.** `$ sudo tcpdump -i eth0 -s0 -l port 80 | grep test.hex`
- **C.** `$ sudo tcpdump -i eth0 -s0 -w test.pcap`
- **D.** `$ sudo tcpdump -A -s0 port 80`

231. You need to use a tool that is able to track and maintain Kubernetes and Docker connections and their states. What is the *best* tool to use for this?

- **A.** Conntrack
- **B.** Connpaths
- **C.** Wireshark
- **D.** Nmap

232. One of your users is unable to ping a system on the network. How can you use Wireshark to solve the problem?

- **A.** Check ICMP packets.
- **B.** Watch traffic on port 80.
- **C.** Have the user reboot the system.
- **D.** You cannot user Wireshark to troubleshoot.

233. You are a forensic investigator conducting an email investigation of different email messages your CEO has received, and you need to view the hash value of the data. Why is this important?

- **A.** Due diligence
- **B.** Due care
- **C.** Validating emails at sender's end
- **D.** Validating emails at recipient's end

234. You have downloaded a Linux OS ISO, burned a CD, and made note of the hash supplied by the vendor. You can check the integrity with which of the following commands?

- **A.** `$ sha256sum /dev/cdrom`
- **B.** `$ md sha256sum /dev/cdrom`
- **C.** `$ sha256sum /dev/c:`
- **D.** `$ cd download_directory sha256sum`

235. You are an analyst classifying samples into known and unknown malware. This is challenging due to the enormous number of code samples received, with limited amount of time and resources. Using fuzzy hashing, you are able to automate the process of grouping similar malware. Which program is *best* suited for this?

   A. SHA512

   B. MD6

   C. ssdeep

   D. FTP

236. Andre, the network operations manager, has asked you to run a command that will scan a target server, 192.168.2.14, using a TCP SYN scan. Which of the following commands would do that?

   A. $nmap -sn 192.168.2.14

   B. $nmap -sS 192.168.2.14

   C. $nmap -sU 192.168.2.14

   D. $nmap -sA 192.168.2.14

237. Cecil has found a live system with an IP address of 192.168.72.45. He does not have an inventory of the operating system of this machine. What nmap command will assist him?

   A. nmap -O

   B. nmap -OS

   C. nmap -p

   D. namp -oS

238. Felix is trying to tell at a hex level that a file has been deleted in FAT12. What tool could he use to tell if it is gone?

   A. ssdeep

   B. fsstat

   C. ldd

   D. Recuva

239. Henry has been instructed to make a copy of the Windows file that holds user passwords. What is the name of that file?

   A. BOB

   B. SAM

   C. users.exe

   D. ISO

240. You are looking for a tool that will assist in recovering and reconstructing Microsoft Event Viewer logs. Which of these would work *best*?

- **A.** EVTXtract
- **B.** MUI
- **C.** Ghidra
- **D.** Aircrack-ng

241. Jessica is conducting a digital forensics investigation and needs a fast file carver that is filesystem-independent and that will carve files from FATx and NTFS. Which of these would be her *best* option?

- **A.** OllyDbg
- **B.** Forceps
- **C.** Scalpel
- **D.** Nmap

242. You are using a file recovery tool called Foremost in Kali Linux. It can recover files based on their internal data structure, which is commonly referred to as file carving. Which of the following commands would allow you to search for all PDF files?

- **A.** `foremost -s 10 -t jpg -i image.dd`
- **B.** `foremost -t gif -i image.dd`
- **C.** `foremost -t pdf -i image.dd`
- **D.** `foremost image.dd`

243. You are trying to discover vulnerabilities via decomposition and disassembly of the binary and recognition of known vulnerability patterns. This can encompass some of the common weakness types such as buffer overflows, unhandled error conditions, cross-site scripting (XSS), and various injection attack vectors. What is this called?

- **A.** Code escrow
- **B.** Malware analysis
- **C.** Data mining
- **D.** Binary code review

244. You have an ASCII hex dump file and need a tool that will assist you in reading a temporary libpcap file. Which is the *best* tool to use?

- **A.** TSK
- **B.** Wireshark
- **C.** strace
- **D.** MD5

245. Mendon needs a cross-platform GUI tool that will assist his department's reverse-engineering efforts. Since his budget has been exhausted, he also needs a tool that is open source. Which of these would you recommend?

   A. OddJob

   B. EternalBlue

   C. DoublePulsar

   D. Ghidra

246. Nate has been assigned a project to analyze new hardware that was purchased overseas. He needs a tool that will allow him to analyze firmware binaries. He is suspicious that the firmware may be engineered to have malicious content. Which is the *best* tool for him to use?

   A. Binwalk

   B. Scalpel

   C. Foremost

   D. Strings

Chapter 3

Security Engineering and Cryptography

THE CASP+ EXAM TOPICS COVERED IN THIS CHAPTER INCLUDE:

✓ **Domain 3: Security Engineering and Cryptography**

- **3.1 Given a scenario, apply secure configurations to enterprise mobility.**
  - Managed configurations
  - Application control
  - Password
  - MFA requirements
  - Token-based access
  - Patch repository
  - Firmware Over-the-Air
  - Remote wipe
  - WiFi
  - WiFi Protected Access (WPA2/3)
  - Device certificates
  - Profiles
  - Bluetooth
  - Near-field communication (NFC)
  - Peripherals
  - Geofencing
  - VPN settings
  - Geotagging
  - Certificate management
  - Full device encryption

- Tethering
- Airplane mode
- Location services
- DNS over HTTPS (DoH)
- Custom DNS
- Deployment scenarios
- Bring your own device (BYOD)
- Corporate-owned
- Corporate owned, personally enabled (COPE)
- Choose your own device (CYOD)
- Security considerations
- Unauthorized remote activation/deactivation of devices or features
- Encrypted and unencrypted communication concerns
- Physical reconnaissance
- Personal data theft
- Health privacy
- Implications of wearable devices
- Digital forensics of collected data
- Unauthorized application stores
- Jailbreaking/rooting
- Side loading
- Containerization
- Original equipment manufacturer (OEM) and carrier differences
- Supply chain issues
- eFuse

- 3.2 Given a scenario, configure and implement endpoint security controls
  - Hardening techniques
  - Removing unneeded services

- Disabling unused accounts
- Images/templates
- Remove end-of-life devices
- Remove end-of-support devices
- Local drive encryption
- Enable no execute (NX)/execute never (XN) bit
- Disabling central processing unit (CPU) virtualization support
- Secure encrypted enclaves/memory encryption
- Shell restrictions
- Address space layout randomization (ASLR)
- Processes
- Patching
- Firmware
- Application
- Logging
- Monitoring
- Mandatory access control
- Security-Enhanced Linux (SELinux)/Security-EnhancedAndroid (SEAndroid)
- Kernel vs. middleware
- Trustworthy computing
- Trusted Platform Module (TPM)
- Secure Boot
- Unified Extensible Firmware Interface (UEFI)/basic input/output system (BIOS) protection
- Attestation services
- Hardware security module (HSM)
- Measured boot
- Self-encrypting drives (SEDs)

- Compensating controls
- Antivirus
- Application controls
- Host-based intrusion detection system (HIDS)/ Host-based intrusion prevention system (HIPS)
- Host-based firewall
- Endpoint detection and response (EDR)
- Redundant hardware
- Self-healing hardware
- User and entity behavior analytics (UEBA)

- 3.3 Explain security considerations impacting specific sectors and operational technologies
  - Embedded
  - Internet of Things (IoT)
  - System on a chip (SoC)
  - Application-specific integrated circuit (ASIC)
  - Field-programmable gate array (FPGA)
  - ICS/supervisory control and data acquisition (SCADA)
  - Programmable logic controller (PLC)
  - Historian
  - Ladder logic
  - Safety instrumented system
  - Heating, ventilation, and air conditioning (HVAC)
  - Protocols
  - Controller Area Network (CAN) bus
  - Modbus
  - Distributed Network Protocol 3 (DNP3)
  - Zigbee
  - Common Industrial Protocol (CIP)
  - Data distribution service

- Sectors
- Energy
- Manufacturing
- Healthcare
- Public utilities
- Public services
- Facility services
- 3.4 Explain how cloud technology adoption impacts organization security
  - Automation and orchestration
  - Encryption configuration
  - Logs
  - Availability
  - Collection
  - Monitoring
  - Configuration
  - Alerting
  - Monitoring configurations
  - Key ownership and location
  - Key life-cycle management
  - Backup and recovery methods
  - Cloud as business continuity and disaster recovery (BCDR)
  - Primary provider BCDR
  - Alternative provider BCDR
  - Infrastructure vs. serverless computing
  - Application virtualization
  - Software-defined networking
  - Misconfigurations
  - Collaboration tools
  - Storage configurations

- Bit splitting
- Data dispersion
- Cloud access security broker (CASB)
- 3.5 Given a business requirement, implement the appropriate PKI solution.
  - PKI hierarchy
  - Certificate authority (CA)
  - Subordinate/intermediate CA
  - Registration authority (RA)
  - Certificate types
  - Wildcard certificate
  - Extended validation
  - Multidomain
  - General purpose
  - Certificate usages/profiles/templates
  - Client authentication
  - Server authentication
  - Digital signatures
  - Code signing
  - Extensions
  - Common name (CN)
  - Storage area network (SAN)
  - Trusted providers
  - Trust model
  - Cross-certification
  - Configure profiles
  - Life-cycle management
  - Public and private keys
  - Digital signature
  - Certificate pinning

- Digital signature algorithm (DSA)
- Rivest, Shamir, and Adleman (RSA)
- Elliptic-curve digital signature algorithm (ECDSA)
- Protocols
- Secure Sockets Layer (SSL)/Transport Layer Security (TLS)
- Secure/Multipurpose Internet Mail Extensions (S/MIME)
- Internet Protocol Security (IPSec)
- Secure Shell (SSH)
- EAP
- Elliptic curve cryptography
- P256
- P384
- Forward secrecy
- Authenticated encryption with associated data
- Key stretching
- Password-based key derivation function 2 (PBKDF2)
- Bcrypt
- 3.7 Given a scenario, troubleshoot issues with cryptographic implementations.
  - Implementation and configuration issues
  - Validity dates
  - Wrong certificate type
  - Revoked certificates
  - Incorrect name
  - Chain issues
  - Invalid root or intermediate CAs
  - Self-signed
  - Weak signing algorithm
  - Weak cipher suite
  - Incorrect permissions

- Cipher mismatches
- Downgrade
- Keys
- Mismatched
- Improper key handling
- Embedded keys
- Rekeying
- Exposed private keys
- Crypto shredding
- Cryptographic obfuscation
- Key rotation
- Compromised keys

1. You decided to start a new consulting business. You began the risk analysis process and developed employee policies and researched and tested third-party security. What is the next riskiest problem for SOHO?

    A. Mobile devices

    B. Email

    C. Training

    D. Guidelines

2. Your company policy states that only authorized software is allowed on the corporate network, and BYOD needs to be configured by IT for the proper software and security controls to adhere to company policy. The marketing manager plugged in a USB received at a conference into their laptop and it auto-launches. What is the greatest risk?

    A. Employee transferring the customer database and IP

    B. Employee using nonapproved accounting applications

    C. Infecting the network with malware

    D. File corruption by the USB exiting out improperly

3. A new program that you are in charge of requires replacing legacy hardware and software. These applications will touch three major operational systems in the company. You establish security requirements and engage with the infrastructure and networking. What is your next step?

    A. Document all the requirements, both technical and nontechnical.

    B. Organize a tabletop exercise with all the technical personnel.

    C. Communicate the security requirements with all the stakeholders.

    D. Meet with database and application consultants for migration advice.

4. You want to ensure that there are no weak passwords on any mission-critical server, mobile, or networking device. You also want to ensure that none of the top 100 exposed passwords (i.e., 12345678) is on any device. What is the *best* tool to crack any weak password on your assets?

    A. Hashcat

    B. Netcat

    C. Wireshark

    D. Splunk

5. Your department is inundated with requests for PII. What type of controls should you put in place to protect this information?

    A. Use encryption, strong passwords, MFA, and backups.

    B. Keep old media with personal data indefinitely.

    C. Do not automate updates; it can break workflows.

    D. Use public Wi-Fi, not a corporate wireless network.

6. To facilitate ease of access for mobile device users, many apps use tokens. These tokens enable users to perform multiple actions without requiring users to reauthenticate their identity. Which of the following is a best practice in using this methodology?

   A. Generating new tokens with each access attempt.

   B. Keeping old tokens for a specific amount of time.

   C. Using token until the app or page is closed.

   D. Tokens should never expire.

7. Your security vulnerability management team has a specific timeline for patching all systems in your organization. Which of the following will automate this process?

   A. Patching the management system

   B. Using an automated patching system

   C. Updating the management system

   D. Automating the update system

8. Your organization deployed various mobile devices throughout the network. Unfortunately, many of these devices have few security mechanisms in place to protect them. What is one measure that can be taken to secure these mobile devices?

   A. Loading project management tools on them

   B. Using the MSM technology FOTA

   C. Installing a HIDS/HIPS on them

   D. Downloading the firmware update to your PC

9. An employee's company-issued cell phone was left in the back of a ride-sharing vehicle and has not been returned in a timely manner. Per the security policy, the employee contacted the IT department, and now you must perform a remote wipe on that asset. What type of server allows remote wiping of the device?

   A. MAM

   B. MDM

   C. RDP

   D. DNS

10. You are helping develop a security awareness policy that focuses on social engineering and email safety. You are working on a section that helps employees avoid malware downloads via phishing. What would *not* be beneficial in this policy?

   A. Not using public Wi-Fi on mobile devices

   B. Using antimalware and anti-phishing software

   C. Using digital certificates

   D. Not sharing personal information in email

11. A home user wants to secure their new wireless router. Which of the following should they *not* do?

    A. Change the default administrator name and use a strong password.

    B. Set SSID broadcast to nonbroadcast.

    C. Use WEP.

    D. Use MAC filtering.

12. You are in a large-scale enterprise organization, and your IT administrators do not have time to manually distribute certificates to mobile devices. What is the *best* protocol to use?

    A. MDM

    B. ICMP

    C. RDP

    D. SCEP

13. Your staff wants to use Bluetooth on their networked mobile devices, and you were asked to be the Bluetooth administrator. What type of network are you implementing?

    A. MAN

    B. LAN

    C. WLAN

    D. PAN

14. You work for a university and are monitoring your dedicated faculty wireless network. You have configured Wi-Fi profiles to deploy wireless network settings to users in your organization, but you still see many unauthorized mobile devices connected to the network. Malicious activity has been reported. Your IT security manager suggested adding contextual authentication. Which of the following falls in that category?

    A. GPS

    B. IDS

    C. MAC filtering

    D. Bluetooth

15. Some employees were issued NFC-capable corporate phones. As part of the security department, you are tasked with recommending how to use these devices securely. Which answer should be included in your recommendation?

    A. Keeping patches up-to-date

    B. Turning off pairing mode

    C. Turning off discovery mode

    D. Turning on NFC when not in use

16. You are employed in a high-risk geographically diverse production environment. Which of these options would be *best* reason to deploy link encryption to reduce risk?

    A. Link encryption provides better flow confidentiality and routing.

    B. Link encryption encrypts routing information and is often used with satellite communication.

    C. Link encryption is used for message confidentiality.

    D. Link encryption is implemented for better traffic integrity.

17. Your CISO wants to wirelessly share their phone or other mobile device screen with a larger screen in a conference room. They want to give presentations and directly share feedback from applications. Which of the following is their *best* option?

    A. Screen mirroring

    B. Videoconferencing

    C. IMS

    D. TPM

18. Instead of having salespeople travel back to the corporate office to upload customer information and to download new electronic marketing materials, upper management tasked the IT department with recommending a secure but simple-to-use solution. This solution should enable the salespeople to remain in the field but utilize Internet access to transfer the necessary information to and from the corporate office. All salespeople are familiar with using a web browser. What solution *best* suits this need?

    A. A VPN solution using SSL/TLS via a web browser

    B. A VPN solution using an application solution with IPSec

    C. A VPN solution using a web browser with WAF

    D. A VPN solution using an application solution with HIDS

19. Your organization includes employees who travel internationally and who occasionally post their business travel locations on their social media. In some social media platforms, physical location is shared or attached to a post or picture. What do employees need to be most aware of with these digital posts on the Internet?

    A. Credit card theft

    B. Phishing

    C. RFID cloners

    D. Geotagging

20. An audit for your mobile device policies found that your COPE devices are allowing unsigned applications. The default value on these assets is set to $true. After developing an app, the developer must sign it in or make it traceable and publish it to the Play Store. Is there a valid business need for installing unsigned applications on a company device?

    A. If a developer wants to test and troubleshoot an app.

    B. To validate the keystore: debug and release.

    C. To remove the app's digitally signed certificates.

    D. No, there is never a reason to use unsigned apps.

21. You were tasked with choosing the correct encryption for your mobile device management program. Which asymmetric encryption algorithm is *best* suited for mobile devices?

    A. AES

    B. ECC

    C. IDEA

    D. Serpent

22. You are traveling for work, and no Wi-Fi is available. You are in a public space and need to use your laptop to go online. If supported, you could tether through a mobile device to the Internet. What are the drawbacks of tethering?

    A. Your mobile connection will be slow, and the battery will draw down quickly on your mobile device.

    B. You must have an app to tether your phone to your laptop.

    C. Your phone calls will go straight to voicemail.

    D. Security will be an issue.

23. Meena has called the IT help desk and stated she has lost her corporate iPad. You attempt to use location services to physically locate the device, but she said she just returned from a trip and is afraid the device is in airplane mode. What would you recommend happen?

    A. Incident detection and response

    B. Remote lock and data wipe

    C. Replacement of a device and destruction of old one

    D. Termination of the employee

24. Your IT department is investigating the use of DNS over HTTPS (DoH). With DoH, all DNS resolutions occur over an encrypted channel, helping to further safeguard against which of these attacks?

    A. Insecure protocols

    B. Key mismanagement

    C. Man-in-the-middle attacks

    D. Bad sector on a hard drive

25. You have determined the ISP-supplied DNS servers are slow, or not properly configured for caching, and they have slowed down your connection. This is especially true when you load a page that draws content from many different domains, such as advertisers and affiliates. What is something that might be used to speed up your connection as well as increase security?

    A. TTL records

    B. Custom DNS server

    C. DHCP

    D. NS lookup

26. Your new CISO wants to implement a mobile device strategy. All staff have mobile devices, and you need something quickly implemented that is not very expensive. Which of the following strategies is the *best* one for your organization?

    A. BYOD

    B. CYOD

C. COPE

D. IDEA

27. Your global banking organization wants to use mobile devices in their main offices as well as remote branches. Employees handle sensitive financial documents, including bank statements, loan applications, and mortgage documents. Given that your organization is very risk averse, what type of mobile strategy would work *best* for them?

A. BYOD

B. CYOD

C. COPE

D. OSPF

28. In the next fiscal year, all your company's salespeople will get a company-issued cell phone. As you develop a security policy to address lost or stolen data, malware, and malicious applications, one major risk to address is a lost or stolen device. How do you approach this risk?

A. MDM

B. MAM

C. BYOD

D. TPM

29. Your organization is revisiting its mobile device strategies due to security's need to have vetted hardware on corporate networks. You want to give employees a choice, but you want to keep costs down. What is the *best* strategy to deploy?

A. BYOD

B. CYOD

C. COPE

D. TPM

30. You are a security analyst for a SOHO. Against your advice, upper management decided that BYOD for salespeople would be cost-effective, citing employee churn. You now have security challenges, including duplicate IP addresses and infected systems on the company's network. Which of the following should you implement to help with these issues?

A. NAC

B. HIDS

C. HIPS

D. Port security

31. You are asked to recommend a lightweight and mobile key management solution for your company's users. Which of the following provides this function?

A. EFS

B. TPM

C. microSD HSM

D. NTFS

32. Your marketing team wants to share files between local devices without using the network or a physical memory card at the next conference. Which of these terms is *best* suited for the preceding situation?

   A. Uploading

   B. Downloading

   C. Sideloading

   D. P2TP

33. Your mobile device wirelessly receives its over-the-air (OTA) update. The company determined it is not a security risk for your mobile device to receive new software or data this way. You do not want to lose access to your mobile device during business hours, so what type of OTA do you configure?

   A. Manual

   B. Instinctive

   C. Responsive

   D. Automatic

34. Mobile apps in your environment are causing concern because of the unintentional data leakage. "Riskware" applications pose the biggest problem for mobile users who give all permissions asked for without checking the need or security on their laptops, tablets, and wearable devices. These apps are usually the free fun apps and can be found in official app stores. What should you advise mobile device users about data leakage?

   A. Make sure that your network is fast.

   B. Instruct users to check for upgrades often.

   C. Only give apps permissions they must have, and delete any app that asks for more than is necessary.

   D. Give apps all the permissions they ask for.

35. Your terminated IT network administrator turned in their company iPhone. You found that they were able to remove the limitations put in place by the device's manufacturer. Third-party software is installed on the device. What did the IT network administrator do?

   A. Locking

   B. Rooting

   C. Jailbreaking

   D. Recompiling

36. Your system administrator attempted to gain access to low-level systems on their phone. They want to uninstall system applications and revoke permissions on installed apps. What is this type of access called?

   A. Malware

   B. Unlocking

   C. Rooting

   D. Jailbreaking

37. The corporate contract with your current mobile device provider is nearly over, and you are considering moving to a new provider. Many phones, particularly ones that are subsidized with a contract, come locked into a specific carrier. You also want to prevent any data theft or leakage from the devices. The phone is configured to operate only with that carrier. What action must you provide to move your mobile phone fleet to a new carrier?

A. Jailbreak

B. Root

C. Lock

D. Unlock

38. Data privacy is of utmost importance to your organization, and this includes PHI and PII. As a security architect, you are tasked with protecting instant messages. Which of the following is the *best* choice for protecting these messages?

A. SMS

B. Encryption

C. Surveillance

D. Transmission

39. Your organization creates a business case for purchasing company-owned, personally enabled (COPE) mobile devices. One issue with mobile device open source operating systems is increased disparity. Which *best* describes the problem with manufacturers creating their own version and updates?

A. Morphism

B. Instantiation

C. Fragmentation

D. Mutation

40. Your security manager has requested an addendum to your corporate security policy. This policy states that whenever a device is lost or stolen, the enterprise has the ability to protect its data on that device. Using applications to physically find the device once it has gone missing is not sufficient. What should this policy recommend?

A. Incident detection and response

B. Remote lock and data wipe

C. Replacement of a device and destruction of old one

D. Termination of the employee

41. You deployed containers to bundle and run applications in your production environment. You need a way to manage the containers and to ensure that there is no downtime. If one container goes down, another one needs to spin up. Which technology will allow you to *not* spin up machines manually in case of a failure?

A. Kubernetes

B. Instantiation

    C. Rollback

    D. Tiagra

42. You work for a large hospital complex as a security program manager. As your business partner, your supplier asked you to exchange documents using EDI. What does this mean to your hospital?

    A. Using purchase orders

    B. Postal mail, fax, and email

    C. Order management systems

    D. Using an electronic format

43. The system admins on your network have noticed that certain sub systems are failing, taking too long to respond, or consuming too much power. What IBM technology will allow you to dynamically reprogram a computer chip?

    A. Guardium

    B. eFUSE

    C. QRadar

    D. Veeam on IBM Cloud

44. For security reasons, during the system development life cycle you are looking at security at the hardware level as well as software. You need a CPU that will separate memory areas so that one is used for instructions and one is used for storage. What is this called?

    A. NX

    B. CN

    C. AR

    D. C++

45. An internal security audit of your organization shows consistent security configurations are needed. Your department implements a golden standard image to all servers and workstations. How can you detect unauthorized changes?

    A. Vulnerability assessments

    B. Compliance reports

    C. Audit logs continuously

    D. Scan computers against the baseline

46. Your CIO requests a meeting with you, the security manager, to discuss the SQL administrators' request for a service-oriented architecture (SOA) and an application programming interface (API). In SOA and APIs, services are provided over a network. What is your biggest concern?

    A. Users and services are centralized and available only during business hours.

    B. SOA manages all the legacy systems that are vulnerable.

    C. SOA is deployed using VMs and is exploited using VMEscape.

    D. Users and services are distributed over the Internet, which can be open to outside threats.

47. Your growing startup wants to take advantage of single sign-on (SSO). Which of the following is *not* an advantage?

A. Multiple user accounts and passwords can be eliminated.

B. Users can sign on once for access to resources.

C. SSO is convenient and leads to fewer tech support password resets.

D. The attacker needs only one password to compromise everything without two-factor authentication.

48. You work as a security analyst for a healthcare organization. A small legacy cluster of computers was acquired during an acquisition of a small hospital clinic. All virtual machines use the same NIC to connect to the network. Some of these machines have patient data, and others have financial data. One of these VMs is hosting an externally facing web application. What is the biggest problem you see with this scenario?

A. Confidentiality

B. Threats

C. Integrity

D. Utilization

49. You are a system administrator, and you are asked to draft a policy for several mission-critical legacy application servers that will be replaced in six months because of end of support from the server manufacturer. What policy do you create?

A. Data provisioning

B. Data remanence

C. Data retention

D. Data encryption

50. A governmental agency purchases new computers for its employees and wants to ensure that the computers' boot loader process is protected from rootkits loading during startup. What protection mechanism requires UEFI's Secure Boot process and TPM encryption to work together to ensure that an OS is allowed to load and to specify which parts of the process are allowed to execute?

A. Early Launch Antimalware

B. Integrity Measurement Architecture

C. Measured Launch

D. Attestation Services

51. You are exploring the best option for your organization to move from a physical data center to VMs hosted on bare-metal servers. Moving to a Type 1 hypervisor was discussed, but these hypervisors are difficult to deploy. Now, it has been decided to use hosted hypervisors on Windows 10 machines by enabling CPU virtualization. What is that type of environment called?

A. Type 1 hypervisor

B. Type 2 hypervisor

    C. iPaaS

    D. IaaS

52. What form of storage decays over time, must be refreshed constantly, and can be always encrypted, with data being decrypted only within the CPU?

    A. RAM

    B. Hard drive

    C. ROM

    D. BIOS

53. Robert has conferred with security and system admins as to what hardening should take place on end users' systems. Which of the following restrictions can limit use of commands, programs, and scripts?

    A. Port restrictions

    B. Web restrictions

    C. App restrictions

    D. Shell restrictions

54. In your role as a hospital's security architect, not only do you have to worry about confidentiality attacks like attackers stealing PHI, you also must worry about availability attacks like a DoS. One of the most popular attacks you want to thwart is a buffer overflow attack. Which of the following is a technique designed to protect against buffer overflow attacks?

    A. MAC

    B. OSPF

    C. ASLR

    D. RLSA

55. You are brought in as a consultant to improve the security of business processes. You improve security by applying the proper controls, including transport encryption, interface restrictions, and code review. What else can you do to improve business processes now that you've already done all the technical improvements?

    A. Modify the company's security policies and procedures.

    B. Meet with upper management to approve new company standards and a mission statement.

    C. Conduct another technical quantitative risk analysis on all current controls.

    D. Conduct a gap analysis and give a recommendation on nontechnical controls to be incorporated into company documentation.

56. Your security team is small and must work economically to reduce risk. You do not have a lot of time to spend on reducing your attack surface. Which of the following might help reduce the time you spend on patching internal applications?

    A. VPN

    B. PaaS

    C. IaaS

    D. Terminal server

57. As a new security administrator in a global organization, you discovered that no one at this company has addressed CVE 2017-5689, a critical firmware flaw in the Intel Management Engine that is more than a decade old and contains an undocumented kill switch. What do you implement immediately?

    A. Nothing. Most companies who bought the chip affected were notified directly from the company.

    B. Update the Intel ME firmware immediately and then block ports 16992–16995 on endpoints and firewalls.

    C. Request more input from upper management about prioritization.

    D. Ignore it because there is no real effect from this CVE.

58. You contracted with a company to develop a new web application for your retail outlets to process credit cards. Which of the following assessments gives you the *best* level of assurance for the web application they create?

    A. Penetration testing

    B. Vulnerability assessment

    C. Implementation

    D. Code review

59. You have event logging turn on so that you can build a chronological list of steps to provide documentary evidence of the sequence of activities that affect a specific operation or event. What is this called?

    A. Audit trail

    B. Vulnerability scanning

    C. Patch management

    D. Compliance and reporting

60. You feel comfortable with the security mechanisms your department has put in place for data at rest. You are more concerned about data in transit. Which of these do *not* concern you?

    A. Insecure protocols

    B. Key mismanagement

    C. Man-in-the-middle attacks

    D. Bad sector on a hard drive

61. What NSA project promoted the use of SELinux in Android devices?

    A. SEinAndroid

    B. SEAndroid

    C. SELinAndroid

    D. SAndroid

62. Your organization's container ecosystem handles extremely sensitive data. You want to scan and validate the configuration of each container as it is added to the container registry. Which of these is most important when securely locking down and monitoring the container registry?

    A. It can cost a lot of money to spin up containers that your team is not utilizing.

    B. It ensures that only containers meeting with the team's development processes and security policies are added to the environment.

    C. There is a limit to how many containers can operate in one single deployment.

    D. The hypervisor on the container image could have vulnerabilities that are now cloud-based and easier to take advantage of.

63. Your IT department discovered that some of your legacy computers and servers don't have a TPM chipset in them. What security feature is missing from these computers?

    A. Time synchronization of logs

    B. Program sandboxing

    C. Throttling of bandwidth protection

    D. Storage of cryptographic keys

64. You are a network engineer for an SMB. You are evaluating the placement of your new unified communications (UC) server. Your UC server does have some built-in capabilities for attack mitigation, but you do not want to solely rely on it. Where should you place this UC server?

    A. Sequestered behind a firewall

    B. Connected directly to the Internet

    C. Between two web servers, email and messaging

    D. Connected directly to your intranet

65. As a security engineer, you discovered that some of your computers are still using BIOS for hardware initialization. What security feature is missing from BIOS that is available using UEFI?

    A. Loads boot loader

    B. Setting system clock

    C. Secure Boot

    D. Initializes system hardware components

66. Your CIO has included the use of HSM in security baseline documentation. What is HSM used for?

    A. Managing keys for authentication

    B. Managing CRLs

    C. Managing data in transit

    D. Managing TPM

67. You are bidding on a military contract that requires the validation of hardware components for security reasons. What is the validation process from a third party called?

    A. Authorization

    B. Authentication

    C. Isolation

    D. Attestation

68. You are a SQL database administrator managing and implementing security initiatives from the kernel to middleware. Based on controlling the confidentiality of your customer's financial information, what controls *best* meet the need of your company?

    A. UPS and partial disk encryption

    B. IPS, generator, and strong authentication controls

    C. Vulnerability scanning and peer review of all changes

    D. CMDB and an analysis of all code modifications

69. A company outsourced payroll and is concerned about whether the right technical and legal agreements are in place. Data is viewed and stored by a third party, and an agreement needs to be set in place about that data. Which type of interoperability agreement can you use to make sure the data is encrypted while in transit and at rest?

    A. BPA

    B. MOU

    C. ISA

    D. NDA

70. Alice is responsible for PCI compliance for her organization. The policy requires she remove information from a database, but she cannot due to technical restrictions. She is pursuing a compensating control to mitigate the risk. What is her *best* option?

    A. Insurance

    B. Encryption

    C. Deletion

    D. Exceptions

71. You work as a security consultant for a petroleum chemical company. The company uses SCADA to monitor sensors and control valves throughout their facility. Which of the following options *best* secures the company's SCADA system?

    A. Installing HIDS on the devices that make up the SCADA system

    B. Implementing defense in depth in front of the SCADA system

    C. Ensuring devices within the SCADA system have implicit allow rules on the firewall

    D. Installing antivirus software on the devices that make up the SCADA system

72. Your CISO wants to install a security product capable of detecting and removing most malicious programs such as viruses, Trojans, ransomware, spyware, adware, and the like from high-value hosts within the organization. Which of the following is *best* suited to meet the criteria?

A. Antivirus

B. Antimalware

C. Anti-adware

D. Application controls

73. Your CISO asked you to implement a solution on the servers in your data center that can detect malicious activity and send alerts to IT staff once they are detected. Which solution accomplishes this task?

A. HIDS

B. NIDS

C. HIPS

D. NIPS

74. You finished a penetration test that identified a web server with a critical vulnerability. The web server's role is mission critical to your organization and has an uptime requirement of 99.9 percent. If you patch the vulnerability, it may break the application running on this server. How do you secure the web server until another solution is found?

A. Using a stateful inspection firewall

B. Installing antivirus protection

C. Using a circuit-level gateway

D. Via a HIDS/HIPS

75. Your incident detection team is responsible for finding intruders on the endpoints, on the network, and in your infrastructure. They try to trace intruder activity using endpoint protection tools, contain the threat, and then remove it. Learning how attackers gain access and move around your network is valuable. What is this called?

A. INS

B. IDR

C. CIA

D. DNS

76. While building out a new VoIP architecture, what also should be added to support redundancy?

A. Power

B. Budget

C. Legal

D. ISP

77. In large enterprise data systems, operation and maintenance work plays a crucial role in ensuring that service interruptions from hardware and software failures do not threaten the overall stability of platforms. Given the challenges of doing so in massive data environments, what type of automated solutions will simplify response efforts?

   A. EDR

   B. Self-encrypting devices

   C. SSO

   D. Self-healing hardware

78. One of your domain administrator's username and password combinations was compromised. An attacker with those credentials can engage your network in nefarious ways. What do you use to trigger a red flag alerting you of this type of behavior?

   A. IDR

   B. UEBA

   C. RBAC

   D. AM

79. What did the Mirai botnet used to launch a massive 2016 DDoS attack primarily consist of?

   A. IoT

   B. Servers

   C. Laptop computers

   D. Switches

80. The rise of the Internet of Things (IoT) has presented challenges for your organization's security team while trying to secure your corporate network. Attacks on IoT have been steadily trending upward as attackers enlist devices to launch attacks. What is the *best* method to combat this threat?

   A. Adding network intrusion devices

   B. Performing inventory management

   C. Adding more security tools

   D. Reducing the attack surface

81. You travel a great deal for work. What tool would you use to find a hidden infrared camera in your hotel room?

   A. Fuzzer

   B. Metal detector

   C. Tethering

   D. Smartphone

82. You are a security administrator for a network that uses a special microprocessor for environmental monitoring. What type of microchips would be used for this purpose?

    A. TPM

    B. ASIC

    C. CISC

    D. AAHA

83. Sandra is tasked with finding a hardware-based processor approach for intensive tasks, including face detection, performing calculations, and controlling programmable logic. What would Sandra use?

    A. FPGA

    B. SCADA

    C. PLC

    D. Closed circuit

84. Because of your facility's geolocation and its propensity for hurricanes, you are tasked with finding another data processing facility to provide you with a location in case of a natural disaster. You are negotiating a contract with an organization with HVAC, power, water, and communication but no hardware. What kind of facility are you building?

    A. PLC

    B. Warm site

    C. Safety Instrumented System

    D. Cold site

85. While you're presenting the business plan to migrate to a new SCADA system solution to upper management at your industrial plant, many questions arise regarding accuracy, security, and cost. One question asked at the meeting was how operators and stakeholders could review historical data. What do you tell them?

    A. Historian

    B. Ladder logic

    C. HMIs

    D. Modbus

86. Bob is the owner of a website that provides information to healthcare providers. He is concerned that the PHI data he is storing falls under the jurisdiction of HIPAA. How does he ensure that he removes the data correctly?

    A. By deleting the suspected PHI data on the drive

    B. By degaussing the drives that hold suspected PHI data

    C. By determining how long to keep the healthcare data securely encrypted and then using a drive-wipe utility

    D. By adding SSDs to the web server and storing used drives in a physically secured location

87. Your new line of software business is selling directly to public utilities to accept customer payments. Two major risks are your lack of experience with establishing and managing credit card processing and the additional compliance and encryption requirements. What is the *best* risk strategy?

  A. Transferring the initial risk by outsourcing

  B. Transferring the risk to another internal department

  C. Mitigating the risks by hiring additional IT staff

  D. Accepting the risks and log acceptance

88. Your energy organization has elected to opt into a public cloud solution for all of your business customers' testing environments. Which one of these is *not* a disadvantage?

  A. TCO can rise exponentially for large-scale use.

  B. It is not the best solution for security and availability for mission-critical data.

  C. Low visibility and control of the environment and infrastructure may lead to compliance issues.

  D. There are reduced complexity and requirements of IT experts because the vendor manages the physical environment.

89. You are a security engineer for a healthcare organization. You are evaluating controls for PHI as well as financial data. Based on this table, what is the *best* classification?

Data	Confidential	Integrity	Availability
PHI	High	Medium	Low
Financial	Medium	High	Low
PII	High	Medium	Low
Manufacturing	Low	Low	High

  A. High confidentiality, high integrity, low availability

  B. High confidentiality, medium integrity, low availability

  C. Medium confidentiality, high integrity, low availability

  D. Low confidentiality, low integrity, low availability

90. After the latest facility services acquisition, your security manager asked you to review the business continuity plan. Your organization is required to meet compliance and other regulatory requirements relating to confidentiality. Upper management is concerned that you may miss some of the requirements, which would make your newly blended organization fail an audit. What should you do to improve the existing business continuity plan?

  A. AAR

  B. BIA

  C. RPO and RTO

  D. Gap analysis assessment

91. An internal auditor has completed the annual audit of your public service company's financial records. The report has found several lapses in security procedures, including proper disposal and sanitization of financial transactions. What would be their recommendation?

    A. You should wait for an external audit.

    B. You should recommend a separation of duties.

    C. You should institute job rotation.

    D. You should implement mandatory training.

92. Elizabeth needs to create a low-power, low data rate and close proximity wireless ad hoc network for industrial equipment that requires short-range low-rate wireless data transfer. Which of the following would she use?

    A. Controller area network

    B. Distributed Network Protocol

    C. Zigbee

    D. Common Industrial Protocol

93. While developing your business continuity technical policies for your financial trading organization, your team is evaluating the need for real-time interaction for both publishers and subscribers in your application. Which of these *best* fit those needs?

    A. Controller service

    B. Domain Name System

    C. Dynamic Host Configuration Protocol

    D. Data Distribution Service

94. A software startup hired Pamela to provide expertise on data security. Clients are concerned about confidentiality. If confidentiality is stressed more than availability and integrity, which of the following scenarios should Pamela suggest is *best* suited for clients?

    A. Virtual servers in highly available environment. Clients will use redundant virtual storage and terminal services to access software.

    B. Virtual servers in highly available environment. Clients will use single virtual storage and terminal services to access software.

    C. Clients are assigned virtual hosts running on shared hardware. Physical storage is partitioned with block cipher encryption.

    D. Clients are assigned virtual hosts running shared hardware. Virtual storage is partitioned with streaming cipher encryption.

95. Your company decided to outsource certain computing jobs that need a large amount of processing power in a short duration of time. You suggest the solution of using a cloud

provider that enables the company to avoid a large purchase of computing equipment. Which of the following is your biggest concern with on-demand provisioning?

A. Excessive charges if deprovisioning fails

B. Exposure of intellectual property

C. Data remanence from previous customers in the cloud

D. Data remanence of your proprietary data that could be exposed

96. Pedro has responsibility for the cloud infrastructure in the large construction company he works for. He recorded data that includes security logs, object access, FIM, and other activities that his SIEM tool often uses to detect unwanted activity. Which of the following *best* describes this collection of data?

A. Due diligence

B. Syslog

C. IDR

D. Audit trail

97. You need to collect and review the logs in the finance department from application servers in the cloud to look for any malicious activity. What *best* describes your activity?

A. Identification

B. Authentication

C. Malware analysis

D. Accountability

98. A network engineer is concerned that the logs retrieved from various cloud-based applications as well as on-premise networked devices have inaccurate timestamps, making it difficult to correctly monitor and sequence the logs. What could the network engineer do to ensure the timestamps are current?

A. Configure NTP on all devices.

B. Manually set the date/time on all devices.

C. Reverse-engineer the correct date/time by using the current date/time and the original date/time of the device at boot.

D. Outsource the correction process to a third party.

99. Marcus is a remote employee needing to access data in cloud storage. You need to configure his Windows 10 client for a remote access VPN using IPSec/L2TP. Why is a VPN so important for remote employees?

A. VPN traffic is accessible.

B. VPN traffic is encrypted.

C. VPN gives you remote access.

D. VPN is an option if you are on your home network.

100. Dana has a three-layer line of defense working to protect remote access to his network and cloud applications, including a firewall, antivirus software, and VPN. What action should Dana's network security team take after standing up this defense?

   A. Log all security transactions.

   B. Monitor alerts from these assets.

   C. Check the firewall configuration monthly and antivirus weekly.

   D. Run tests for VPN connectivity once every 24 hours.

101. Jorge is reviewing the monthly itemized receipts from his cloud provider. He has noticed some VMs being spun up that were not authorized or that have been left running for extended time periods with no usage. In addition, configuration of some VMs has changed over time. What is this called?

   A. VM sprawl

   B. VM escape

   C. VM jacking

   D. VM migration

102. Serah has been added to the operations team to conduct the annual business impact analysis (BIA) evaluation with a focus on new cloud infrastructure. She has been charged with updating this document. This BIA will identify which of the following?

   A. The impact of vulnerabilities to the organization

   B. How best to reduce threats efficiently

   C. The exposure to loss within the organization

   D. How to bring about change based on the impact to operations

103. Your CIO approached you, the CISO, with the idea to configure IPSec VPNs for data authentication, integrity, and confidentiality for cloud assets. Which of the following reasons would help support the CIO's goals?

   A. IPSec only supports site-to-site VPN configurations.

   B. IPSec can only be deployed with IPv6.

   C. IPSec authenticates clients against a Windows server.

   D. IPSec uses secure key exchange and key management.

104. You need a hardware solution that will provide your employees with a secure way to store digital certificates and private keys. The solution must be mobile. Which of the following options *best* suits your need?

   A. PKI token

   B. PKI badge

   C. Token ring

   D. RAID

105. You examined your company's disaster recovery plans and are working on the proper response. If your mission-critical processes have an RTO of 36 hours, what would be the *best* recovery site to have?

A. Service

B. Warm

C. Hot

D. Cold

106. Carlos has primary responsibility for his hospital's business continuity and disaster recovery (BCDR) plan for the IT department. He wants to perform a test where the BCP is evaluated for effectiveness, but no actions take place. Due to his compliance requirements, it needs to be scheduled twice a year. Which of the following is the *best* type of test to perform?

A. Full interruption test

B. Parallel test

C. Structured walk-through

D. Simulation test

107. Frederick's company is migrating key systems from on-premises systems to a virtual data center in the cloud managed by a third party. Remote access must be available at all times. Access controls must be auditable. Which of these controls *best* suits these needs?

A. Access is captured in event logs.

B. Access is limited to single sign-on.

C. Access is configured using SSH.

D. Access is restricted using port security.

108. You completed the inventory of your existing virtual web applications and must sort them in order of priority. Your list is quite long, and if you do not prioritize, it will be difficult to know which application to focus on first. What would *not* be a category rating?

A. Normal

B. Baseline

C. Serious

D. Critical

109. Your organization is in the middle of a risk assessment for a new software-defined network (SDN) infrastructure upgrade. All planning is complete, and your plan must include which security controls are to be put in place during each stage of the upgrade. What risk response is most likely being considered while creating an SLA contract with a third party?

A. Accepting risk

B. Identifying risk

C. Transferring risk

D. Mitigating risk

110. Dale, a network engineer, is working on a misconfigured router at a remote office. He successfully connects a telephone line and modem to the router so that he can access the router if the single network circuit fails. What is this type of connection referred to as?

    A. Failover management

    B. Redundant management

    C. Out-of-band management

    D. Standby management

111. Your business cannot overlook the need for allowing remote access and collaboration tools to employees. You never know when an employee will need to connect to the corporate intranet from a remote location. The first thing to do is create a comprehensive network security policy. Which one of these will *not* fit into that policy?

    A. Definition of the classes of users and their level of access

    B. Identification of devices allowed to connect through a VPN

    C. The maximum idle time before automatic termination

    D. Allow list ports and protocols necessary to everyday tasks

112. You work for the power company that supplies electricity to three states. You rely heavily on the data you collect, and that is replicated in the cloud. Data is split into numerous arrays, and a mapper processes them to certain cloud storage options. What is this process called?

    A. Encryption

    B. Data dispersion

    C. Bit splitting

    D. Perimeter security

113. Jonathan is a cloud security sales consultant working for a cloud access security broker (CASB) company. His organization is advocating applying the highest level of protection across all your cloud assets. You suggest this is not what the priority should be. What would be a more strategic priority?

    A. Determining what to protect through data discovery and classification

    B. Running antimalware software on all cloud instances

    C. Using vulnerability scanning software on mission-critical servers

    D. Implementing threat mitigation strategies

114. You want to send an email securely to a colleague in such a way that the colleague is sure it came from you. What key would you use to sign the email so that the colleague is sure it came from you?

    A. Your public key

    B. Your private key

    C. Your colleague's public key

    D. Your colleague's private key

115. You manage a CA on your global corporate network. When a certificate authority revokes a certificate, what certificate information is placed on the revocation list?

   A. Certificate's private key

   B. Certificate's public key

   C. Certificate's serial number

   D. Certificate's hash

116. You work with an intermediate certificate authority to create digital certificates for your organization. What cryptographic key do you provide to the intermediate certificate authority?

   A. You don't provide keys to the certificate authority.

   B. You provide both the private and public keys.

   C. You provide the private key.

   D. You provide the public key.

117. You are a security engineer, and your legal department and human resources department have reached out to you because of employee fraud. They have asked you to prove the authenticity of an email an employee sent to the bank requesting an unauthorized wire transfer. What would you recommend for nonrepudiation?

   A. IPv4

   B. Physical signature

   C. Certificate

   D. Digital signature

118. Your company relies on certificates to verify entities it does business with. It is important that the validity of certificates is verified as quickly as possible. What method of checking certificate validity is *best* for this situation?

   A. CRL

   B. OCSP

   C. CLR

   D. OSCP

119. As a security architect, you decided to build a multiple virtual host with different security requirements, including a storage-attached network. Several virtual hosts will be used for storage, and others will be used as databases. You anticipate these VMs will change depending on data use and time it is sent. What should you do with these hosts?

   A. Encrypt all hosts with AES.

   B. Store each host on a separate physical asset.

   C. Move these virtual hosts to the cloud for elasticity.

   D. Verify that each server has a valid certificate.

120. You have done a quarterly audit and found a certificate signed by a CA that was compromised by an attacker used on a system. What should have happened to the compromised certificate?

- **A.** Added to the CRL
- **B.** Added to the OCSP
- **C.** Renewed with new expiration date
- **D.** Deactivated and added to the ACL

121. You are reviewing your annual budget and are looking for places to cut back. You want to find a way to get one certificate to cover all domains and subdomains for your organization. What type of certificate do you need?

- **A.** Registration authority
- **B.** Extended validation certificate
- **C.** Multidomain certificate
- **D.** Wildcard certificate

122. You receive an email with a document attachment from a known individual with a digital signature. The email client is unable to validate and cannot trust the signature. What should you *not* do?

- **A.** Contact the sender.
- **B.** Contact your security administrator.
- **C.** Open the attachment to see if the signature is valid.
- **D.** Determine why the signature is not valid before you open the attachment.

123. Your organization uses an authentication system that enables users to authenticate once and includes a service that grants tickets for specific services. Of the following options, which technology *best* matches this description?

- **A.** OSPF
- **B.** Kerberos
- **C.** LDAP
- **D.** Biometrics

124. Your colleague hashes a message, encrypts the associated hash with their private key, and sends it to you. What is this process called?

- **A.** Digital signature
- **B.** Nonrepudiation
- **C.** Digital transfer
- **D.** Digital privacy

125. You want to send a confidential message to a colleague in such a way that only the colleague can read it. You encrypt the message and then send it. What key is used to encrypt the message?

- **A.** Your public key
- **B.** Your private key

   C. Your colleague's public key

   D. Your colleague's private key

126. You want to send a confidential message to a colleague in such a way that only the colleague can read it. You encrypt the message and then send it. What key is used to decrypt the message?

   A. Your public key

   B. Your private key

   C. Your colleague's public key

   D. Your colleague's private key

127. How can you secure third-party libraries or applications and introduce only acceptable risk into your environment?

   A. Code review, simulation, and signing

   B. Round-table discussions

   C. Parallel trials

   D. Full deployment

128. Becca needs to secure a simple single website using an SSL certificate and traditional validation and vetting. Which of these would be *best* for her to use?

   A. General purpose

   B. Multidomain

   C. Extended validation

   D. Wildcard

129. Your colleague hashes a message, encrypts the message with your public key, encrypts the associated hash with their private key, and sends it to you. What will this process do?

   A. Provide confidentiality, integrity, and nonrepudiation

   B. Provide availability, confidentiality, and integrity

   C. Provide availability, integrity, and nonrepudiation

   D. Provide availability, confidentiality, and nonrepudiation

130. Daryl will be using a digital certificate to send encrypted messages on his network using public and private keys. What type of infrastructure is this called?

   A. P2P

   B. PKI

   C. PnP

   D. PPI

131. You want to verify the trustworthiness of a user's certificate signed by a certificate authority by using a trust anchor. What type of certification is this?

   A. Wildcard certification

   B. Perpetual certification

   C. Cross certification

   D. Root certification

132. Don has a list of all the CA profiles he would like to add to a trusted group. What component of the PKI process defines how the CA interacts with the CRL?

   A. Profile

   B. Enrollment

   C. Revocation

   D. Validation

133. Many devices need to check in with the certificate authority, and it is hard using OCSP in your organization because of the large-scale implementation. What process can you use to get that information directly from the device itself?

   A. Processing

   B. Stapling

   C. Pinning

   D. Revoking

134. You are creating a certificate signing request in order to receive an SSL/TLS certificate. Which of these are *not* the key pieces of information needed?

   A. FQDN

   B. Legal name of organization

   C. Two-letter code for country where organization is located

   D. Name of CEO and board of directors

135. Joaquin is tasked to investigate a web server directive that tells web browsers to handle the connection securely with a response header sent at the beginning of the connection because setting up redirects from http:// to https:// is not enough to secure his domain. What type of implementation should Joaquin suggest?

   A. HSTS

   B. OCSP

   C. cURL

   D. SSL certificate

136. The website you developed in JavaScript must be secured. What is the *best* way for you to encrypt the data being sent over the Internet while using your website?

   A. TLS/HTTPS

   B. SSL/FTP

    C. OTP

    D. MD5/SHA1

137. An Excel file on your Windows desktop is named Confidential. You want to hash this file using PowerShell and SHA1. What is the command that you run?

    A. `Get-FileHash '.\Confidential.ppt' -Algorithm SHA1`

    B. `Get-FileHash '.\Confidential.xls' -Algorithm SHA1`

    C. `Get-FileHash '.\Confidential.doc' -Algorithm SHA1`

    D. `Get-FileHash '.\Confidential.xls' -Algorithm MD5`

138. Kian is explaining cryptography to upper management, specifically hashing as one-way encryption. Which of these is *not* a hash algorithm?

    A. DES

    B. SHA-1

    C. MD5

    D. SHA-3

139. Russell and Otis are discussing a significant difference between an HMAC of input data and a hash of input data. What exactly is the difference between an HMAC and a hash of a span of input data?

    A. Keyed hash

    B. Hybrid

    C. SSL/TLS

    D. Cipher

140. A network engineer wants to configure a router so that remote connections to it via SSH are possible. Which of the following commands must be entered after the `line vty 0 4` command to ensure that only SSH connections are allowed?

    A. `transport secure`

    B. `transport ssh`

    C. `transport input secure`

    D. `transport input ssh`

141. Tristan's energy company opened a remote office and needs secure communications between the corporate office and the remote office. To save money, upper management wants to utilize the Internet access each location has to provide this secure link. Secure communication on the individual LANs is not required. Which solution provides the *best* option for this situation?

    A. VPN via SSL/TLS using a web browser.

    B. VPN via IPSec in transport mode.

    C. VPN via IPSec in tunnel mode.

    D. No additional configuration is needed because IPv4 includes IPSec.

142. Jerry is looking for something he can use to encrypt hard disk drives, email messages, and corporate payroll files. What do you suggest?

   A. ECC

   B. PGP

   C. LDAP

   D. EAP

143. While doing research on current best practices for encryption, you find the Internet Engineering Task Force (IETF) authored memorandums applicable to your new project. How does the IETF list these official documents?

   A. RFQ

   B. RFP

   C. RFC

   D. IAB

144. You intend to use asymmetric encryption to transmit various amounts of data from one endpoint to another over the Internet. You are concerned that if the private key used for this transmission is compromised, all encrypted data will be exposed. What technology could you use that generates temporary session keys based on your asymmetric keys?

   A. Perfect Forward Secrecy

   B. ECDH

   C. ECDSA

   D. RSA

145. A governmental agency is purchasing new Windows-based computers for some departments. The agency wants to ensure these computers have a security mechanism in place to detect whether files have been accidentally or maliciously altered. What mechanism provides this function?

   A. Secure Boot

   B. Attestation Services

   C. Integrity Measurement Architecture

   D. Early Launch Antimalware

146. You have been given a USB with hardware drivers from a co-worker. How can you ensure that the drivers have *not* been tampered with?

   A. MD5 hashes on the Internet

   B. SHA-1 hashes on the developer's website

   C. Scan with a vulnerability scanner

   D. Scan with asymmetric algorithms

147. What is it called when you have two different files that are hashed with the same symmetric encryption algorithm and it produces the same hash output?

    A. XOR

    B. Collision

    C. Array

    D. Variables

148. The military wants to encrypt data using symmetric encryption between its headquarters and a military unit. Which of the following devices could the military use to accomplish this task?

    A. Firewall

    B. Unified threat management system

    C. Proxy

    D. Inline network encryptors

149. Your company currently has a software-based cryptography and a security processing system that has slowed down over the years. You are tasked with recommending a new hardware solution to speed up the processes. What is the *best* option for completing this task?

    A. PCI

    B. Bcrypt

    C. RIPEMD

    D. HSM

150. Crawford's healthcare startup does not currently have any written security standards, so he is creating a security policy. Which of these statements should go into his security standards document?

    A. All personally identifiable health information (PHI) must be encrypted using AES to ensure customer privacy and confidentiality.

    B. First, you must select the data you want to encrypt, right-click the file, and select Encryption. Then, select a password.

    C. All data must be encrypted.

    D. HIPAA compliance requires customer privacy.

151. An employee has lost their private key. This key provides access to a database holding confidential health information. Without this key, the employee cannot perform their everyday tasks. As the security administrator, what do you do first?

    A. Revoke the key

    B. Reissue a key

    C. Recover the key

    D. Replace the key

152. Which method of encryption makes use of a single shared key?

   A. SHA

   B. ECC

   C. 3DES

   D. AES

153. The application you are building handles sensitive data, specifically PII. You want to encrypt the data and protect it from being stolen or altered. You are considering asymmetric cryptography in your application processes. What is this an example of?

   A. Secure by design

   B. Secure by default

   C. Secure by deployment

   D. Secure by download

154. Your company hired customer service representatives from a third-party vendor working out of a remote facility. What is the *best* way to prevent unauthorized access to your systems?

   A. Two-factor authentication (2FA)

   B. Site-to-site VPN

   C. Encrypted VDI

   D. IPSec to the required systems for the vendor

155. Hugh has an application that requires data to be encrypted on legacy equipment with minimum hardware resources. Which of the following ciphers *best* suits his needs?

   A. Twofish

   B. RC4

   C. AES

   D. Blowfish

156. Julia has a plaintext message that needs to be encrypted into equal-length ciphertext. After the data is encrypted, she will use a key and an IV to generate a secondary key. This second key will generate a keyed hash of the ciphertext. What type of encryption has Julia completed?

   A. AES

   B. RC4

   C. RIPEMD

   D. AEAD

157. You are a security architect and were asked to review the project for a new VPN. You were asked to review a solution that operates on the Network layer of the OSI model and uses authentication and encryption and cryptographic keys to protect data moving between hosts. What type of VPN remote access solution is this?

   A. L2TP

   B. XAUTH

    C. IKE

    D. IPSec

158. Your organization has a remote workforce and often works with multiple global offices, partners, and contractors. You are a security engineer and have been asked to collaborate on security goals. All communications must be encrypted and remain onsite. All users must use the same programs, and those programs must be patched regularly. Which solution do you recommend?

    A. Deploy an SSL reverse proxy and have end users use full-disk encryption with the TPM chip.

    B. Install an SSL VPN to your data center and have users connect with a virtual work-station image.

    C. Create a portal using web-based software. Your company hosts the database.

    D. Use a terminal server and use remote management tools to standardize workstations.

159. You are tasked with implementing security measures and with presenting to the board of directors what symmetric encryption, specifically the symmetric cipher called Salsa20, does. Your presentation will discuss which of the following?

    A. Accounting

    B. Authentication

    C. Nonrepudiation

    D. Integrity

160. You are a security architect and will be deploying encryption in your enterprise environment. Which encryption algorithm is the only one appropriate for streaming but has been found to be vulnerable?

    A. DES

    B. AES

    C. Blowfish

    D. RC4

161. Richard is a security analyst for a retail organization. He has upgraded from SSL to TLS on all his company's web applications. What type of encryption is TLS?

    A. Hybrid

    B. Hashing

    C. Steganography

    D. Asymmetric

162. You have built an extended ACL, which will allow you to be extremely specific as to what you allow into your environment. The extended ACL that you have written can process all *except* which of the following?

    A. ICMP

    B. TCP

    C. 3DES

    D. UDP

163. Elijah is configuring SNMP on a Windows server. He has found that this server is currently running SNMPv2c. Why would he want to upgrade to SNMPv3?

  A. Cryptographic security system

  B. Party-based security system

  C. Easier to set up

  D. Supports UDP

164. Percy is investigating a centralized key management for his organization. Which of these is *not* true in a centralized key management scheme?

  A. It supports a high level of control over the environment.

  B. It requires significant infrastructure.

  C. The CA creates both private and public keys.

  D. Users have full control over their keys.

165. Tammy is concerned with proving who is actually sending emails. What is the most obvious means of providing nonrepudiation in a cryptography system?

  A. Hashing

  B. Digital signatures

  C. Shared keys

  D. Public keys

166. Maddie is a systems analyst, and her computer systems participate in an asymmetric cryptography system using a digital signing algorithm (DSA). She has crafted a message to another user. Before transmission, she hashes the message and then encrypts the hash using her private key. She then attaches this encrypted hash to her message as a digital signature before sending it to the other users. What protection does the hashing activity provide?

  A. Nonrepudiation

  B. Integrity

  C. Availability

  D. Confidentiality

167. Chase has been instructed to implement a block cipher that supports variable bit length keys and variable bit block sizes. Which version of the Rivest cipher would work for Chase?

  A. RC5

  B. RC4

  C. RC2

  D. RSA

168. Alec has been told to provide rapid encryption for a large amount of data in transit over networks and data at rest stored in the data center. Speed is an advantage that symmetric encryption has over asymmetric. Which of these is an option for Alec?

   A. AES

   B. El-Gamal

   C. Diffie–Hellman

   D. SHA-1

169. Margaret is implementing AES in her computing environment. Which of the following statements is true of the operation modes of the AES algorithm?

   A. ECB is not used for databases.

   B. ECB is the slowest 3DES mode.

   C. CBC and CFB are best used for authentication.

   D. ECB repeatedly uses produced ciphertext to encrypt a message consisting of blocks.

170. Hayden works for a financial organization and needs to use message authentication code (MAC) to help prevent fraud in electronic fund transfers involved in online transactions. Which type of MAC should he evaluate implementing?

   A. EAP and P256

   B. HMAC and CBC

   C. SSH and IPSec

   D. SSL/TLS

171. Collin has accepted a new position in cybersecurity at a research company, and his first task is implementing a private key cryptographic system. What will be his biggest challenge?

   A. Protecting the CA

   B. Keeping the key secure

   C. Calculating return on investment

   D. Authenticating the end user

172. Claire is the IT manager and has informed her staff that the organization has just suffered a ciphertext-only attack. Which of the following statements is true regarding this type of attack?

   A. A cipher-only attack is the same as a birthday attack.

   B. A cipher-only attack is done during a man-in-the-middle attack.

   C. It is very difficult for an attacker to exfiltrate ciphertext.

   D. The ciphertext-only attack is focused on discovering the encryption key.

173. Abdul's organization is trying to decide whether to use RSA or ECC to encrypt cellular communications. What is the advantage of ECC over the RSA algorithm?

   A. ECC uses curves to improve reliability.

   B. ECC uses curves instead of keys.

   C. ECC requires fewer resources.

   D. ECC cannot be used for digital signatures.

174. Erin is using Diffie–Hellman encryption. Which of these is an example of the Diffie–Hellman encryption algorithm?

   A. Symmetric with authentication

   B. Asymmetric with authentication

   C. Symmetric with authorization

   D. Asymmetric with authorization

175. Lucio has decided to use message authentication code (MAC) to protect network messaging. What type of attack will this help prevent?

   A. Logic bomb

   B. SYN floods

   C. Denial of service

   D. Masquerading

176. Stanton is using RSA encryption. Which of the following is a characteristic of the RSA encryption algorithm?

   A. It is a symmetric algorithm.

   B. It uses prime numbers.

   C. It uses composite numbers.

   D. It uses identical keys for encryption and decryption.

177. Carmela is worried about key escrow for her organization. The purpose of key escrow is to enable a trusted third party to do which of the following?

   A. Back up encrypted data

   B. Decrypt backup data

   C. Verify identity using a digital certificate

   D. Access sensitive data if required

178. Stacy is a security analyst for her firm and is responsible for the security of all telecommunication and collaborating tools. Most recently, she has been investigating encryption in videoconferencing and decided to recommend keeping Zoom as their videoconferencing tool. What did encryption did Zoom upgrade to make Stacy feel more comfortable with the software?

   A. AES with ECB

   B. AES with GCM

    C. 3DES with GCM

    D. AES with DES

179. Orval is needing a simple counter-based block cipher for information security, including confidentiality and authenticity. Which of the following is the *best* option?

    A. CTR

    B. ECB

    C. CBC

    D. CFB

180. Ward is wanting to turn a block cipher into a synchronous streaming cipher where encryption and decryption is exactly the same. Which of these modes of operation is his only option?

    A. ECB

    B. AES

    C. SLA

    D. OFB

181. Santo wants to implement a cryptosystem based on algebraic structures, implementing all major capabilities of asymmetric algorithms, including encryption, digital signatures, and key exchange. Which of these would be *best* for Santo and his organization?

    A. AES

    B. ECC-256

    C. 3DES

    D. MD5

182. David is investigating ECC cryptography and analyzing which size curve to use. Which of these is recommended by the National Security Agency?

    A. P-192

    B. P-256

    C. P-384

    D. P-128

183. Bess needs to use encryption that provides better protection due to the fact that it creates a unique session key for each transaction. Which of these is her *best* option?

    A. FS

    B. Skipjack

    C. P-256

    D. Bcrypt

184. Alberto has to enable TLS v1.2 in order to keep compatibility with the Internet's main browsers. He needs to understand what cipher suites will be an option if he chooses AEAD. Which of these will be an option?

    A. ChaCha20

    B. SHA-3

    C. P-384

    D. AES

185. Raphael would like to make it more difficult for an attacker to brute-force possibly weak passwords being used in his environment. What technique could he use?

    A. Key-deduplication

    B. Key-monetization

    C. Key-stretching

    D. Key-derivation

186. Valentino is looking to use a simple function to make encryption keys more resistant to dictionary attacks. What function *best* meets his need?

    A. IPSec

    B. PBKDF2

    C. S/MIME

    D. EAP

187. Billy wants to secure the passwords in his database in case of a data leak. What type of hash should he use if he wants an integrated salt function?

    A. MD5

    B. SHA-256

    C. SHA-512

    D. Bcrypt

188. Your small company wants to utilize asymmetric encryption to send secure emails but doesn't want the expense of using a certificate authority. Which of the following options is a good alternative?

    A. PKI

    B. CA/RA

    C. GPG

    D. Kerberos

189. As security engineer, you are asked to recommend a file encryption technology that your end users can use to secure individual files. All the end users have Windows 10 systems. Which of the following is the *best* option available?

    A. FAT32

    B. EFS

    C. BitLocker

    D. FAT64

190. You have Ubuntu servers within your organization. You are looking for an economical software package that can be installed on these systems and provide file and communication encryption. Of the following options, which can provide this functionality?

    A. GNU Privacy Guard

    B. BitLocker

    C. EXT4

    D. EFS

191. You work for a company that has the Microsoft Windows OS deployed on its computers. Various versions of Windows are being used within your organization. You want to take advantage of EFS to secure individual files on these systems. Which filesystem supports EFS?

    A. FAT16

    B. EXT4

    C. FAT32

    D. NTFS

192. Your CISO is notified by a three-letter agency that your network is compromised. The first thing your security department needs to understand is what the attackers stole. After security knows what was stolen, what is the *best* follow-up question to ask?

    A. Can the attackers use our data?

    B. How did they get in?

    C. How do we keep it from happening again?

    D. How did they know we had been hacked?

193. Brantley is attempting to view a shopping website but is seeing that the website is untrusted. What could the issue be?

    A. Validity dates

    B. Processing power

    C. FIM

    D. Randomization

194. You need to prevent attackers from being able to access data from a group of transactions, even if they are able to break the encryption for a single communication sent over the web by devices creating a unique session key for each transaction. What is this called?

    A. Perfect Forward Secrecy

    B. Pretty Good Privacy

    C. GNU Privacy Guard

    D. IETF standards

195. While doing risk analysis, you realize that you set up a collaboration tool using the URL `mycompanyname.appname.com`. What should you do to protect this collaboration tool from an attacker randomly finding this login portal?

   A. Choose a tool that enables your IT team flexibility to control security settings and to determine a URL structure that is customizable.

   B. Make sure that the entire team using the tools understands encryption.

   C. Require strict usernames and passwords.

   D. Check for compliance if you are a healthcare organization.

196. Quinton is a website developer who has just been made aware that customers visiting the corporate site is seeing this message: `NET::ERR_CERT_AUTHORITY_INVALID`. What could the problem be?

   A. The website is without an SSL/TLS certificate or is mismatched with the domain name.

   B. There is an internal server error.

   C. The service is temporarily overloaded.

   D. Authorization is required.

197. Nathan is experiencing an error in his Chrome browser that means there is an issue with an SSL certificate being withdrawn. Which error would he see?

   A. `NET::ERR_FIX_CERT`

   B. `NET::ERR_CERT_RESET`

   C. `NET::ERR_CERT_REVOKED`

   D. `NET::ERR_WEAK_KEY`

198. Carol is a security engineer and has noticed unauthorized takeover of several computer's resources to mine cryptocurrency. The malware that has been injected caused performance issues and has increased electricity usage. What is this called?

   A. Social engineering

   B. Bitcoin hijacking

   C. Malware analysis

   D. Cryptojacking

199. You are a security analyst assigned a ticket put in by a website designer, stating, "Our website has an invalid or missing intermediate certificate. This may not break the padlock on all browsers but will on others. Please contact our SSL vendor." What should you do first?

   A. Check that the certificate is installed correctly.

   B. Contact the SSL vendor.

   C. Reassign the ticket back to the website designer.

   D. Test all browsers.

200. Gale is working on the corporate local intranet project. He has to decide what certificate to use, and he has no budget. What type of certificate is most feasible for Gale's project?

A. Hybrid

B. Self-signed

C. Multidomain

D. Wildcard

201. You have privacy concerns regarding the WLAN. You decide to disable SSID, enable MAC filtering, and enable a security method adhering to IEEE 802.11i standards. Which of the following do you enable?

A. WPA

B. PEAP

C. WPA2

D. WEP

202. Colin is an amazing developer you have on staff. He is a great problem-solver and works very well with others. However, this developer continues to perform risky behavior on the network with his administrator account even after a security awareness session. What should you do next?

A. Begin a separation of duties.

B. Terminate him and perform an exit interview.

C. Employ mandatory vacation.

D. Decrease permissions.

203. Eddie is a developer and gets a report of Apache error logs with multiple errors: `err_ssl_version_or_cipher_mismatch`. What is the most probable issue?

A. Problem with authentication

B. Problem with SSL certificate

C. Problem with SSH certificate

D. Problem with DNS

204. Les is investigating what he believes to be ARP poisoning or a rollback attack. He first must see the mappings between IP addresses and MAC addresses on a specific segment of the network. What command-line tool does he use?

A. ARP

B. Netstat

C. Wget

D. TraceRT

205. Harley is getting the error in Chrome and other browsers: ERR_SSL_VERSION_OR_
CIPHER_MISMATCH. What does this error mean?

    A. The browser is not compatible with the website.

    B. The browser requires a credit card on file.

    C. The browser needs updating.

    D. The browser has deemed the website unsafe.

206. Dwayne wants to make sure the encryption keys are protected. What is a common mistake organizations make with encryption key management that is easy to fix?

    A. Innovation

    B. Number of keys

    C. Location of keys

    D. Return on investment

207. Bobby has discovered the previous web developer simply hard-coded encryption keys in the source code. A copy of the offending source code is all that is needed for someone to get the keys. What can Bobby do to mitigate this issue?

    A. Use a keystore.

    B. Use a certificate.

    C. Change the key.

    D. Remove the offending encryption.

208. Evan has been placed in charge of key management and deciding how long the crypto period is for each key. A crypto period is the time span in which a key is authorized for use. What happens after that key expires?

    A. The key is deleted.

    B. The key is rekeyed.

    C. The key is revoked.

    D. The key is recut.

209. Charles has become suspicious that his private key has been compromised and an unauthorized person gained access to the identity the certificate was supposed to protect. What should he immediately do?

    A. Contact human resources.

    B. Email IT and wait for a response.

    C. Submit revocation request to the CA.

    D. Put in a ticket for a new key.

210. Carla is learning about compliance requirements now that her organization is doing business in the United Kingdom. A customer in the UK has requested her data be deleted, and per GDPR, Carla has to completely erase this customer. She could just delete the customer in the database, but she must address the backups of that data. What will help solve this issue?

    A. Crypto-shredding

    B. Cryptojacking

    C. Destroying all backups

    D. Using a hot site to make new backups of the altered database

211. Gerald is writing code specifically to make it hard to understand and thus make it more difficult to attack or to copy. What technique is he using?

    A. Encoding

    B. Obfuscation

    C. Encrypted

    D. Hashing

212. Demetrius is writing a new security policy regarding encryption. One of the new line items is rotating root keys regularly and during special events like a system admin getting terminated. What does regular rotation of root keys provide?

    A. Quantum-safe protection

    B. Protects the user from obfuscation

    C. A new key just in case the old one is compromised

    D. Protects the encryption algorithm

213. John is looking for a system to mitigate threats to keep his company's encryption keys safe. Any key management system should have a hardware security module (HSM) to create and protect keys as well as which of the following?

    A. Strict policy-based controls to prevent the misuse/reuse of keys

    B. Full life cycle management of keys

    C. Automatic key rotation

    D. All of the above

Chapter 4

Governance, Risk, and Compliance

THE CASP+ EXAM TOPICS COVERED IN THIS CHAPTER INCLUDE:

✓ **Domain 4: Governance, Risk, and Compliance**

- 4.1 Given a set of requirements, apply the appropriate risk strategies

  - Risk assessment

    - Likelihood

    - Impact

    - Qualitative vs. quantitative

    - Exposure factor

    - Asset value

    - Total cost of ownership (TCO)

    - Return on investment (ROI)

    - Mean time to recovery (MTTR)

    - Mean time between failure (MTBF)

    - Annualized loss expectancy (ALE)

    - Annualized rate of occurrence (ARO)

    - Single loss expectancy (SLE)

    - Gap analysis

  - Risk handling techniques

    - Transfer

    - Accept

    - Avoid

    - Mitigate

- Risk types
  - Inherent
  - Residual
  - Exceptions
- Risk management life cycle
  - Identify
  - Assess
  - Control
  - People
  - Process
  - Technology
  - Protect
  - Detect
  - Respond
  - Restore
  - Review
  - Frameworks
- Risk tracking
  - Risk register
  - Key performance indicators
  - Scalability
  - Reliability
  - Availability
  - Key risk indicators
- Risk appetite vs. risk tolerance
  - Tradeoff analysis
  - Usability vs. security requirements
- Policies and security practices
  - Separation of duties
  - Job rotation

- Mandatory vacation
- Least privilege
- Employment and termination procedures
- Training and awareness for users
- Auditing requirements and frequency
- 4.2 Explain the importance of managing and mitigating vendor risk
  - Shared responsibility model (roles/responsibilities)
    - Cloud service provider (CSP)
    - Geographic location
    - Infrastructure
    - Compute
    - Storage
    - Networking
    - Services
    - Client
    - Encryption
    - Operating systems
    - Applications
    - Data
  - Vendor lock-in and vendor lockout
  - Vendor viability
    - Financial risk
    - Merger or acquisition risk
  - Meeting client requirements
    - Legal
    - Change management
    - Staff turnover
    - Device and technical configurations

- Support availability
- Geographical considerations
- Supply chain visibility
- Incident reporting requirements
- Source code escrows
- Ongoing vendor assessment tools
- Third-party dependencies
  - Code
  - Hardware
  - Modules
- Technical considerations
  - Technical testing
  - Network segmentation
  - Transmission control
  - Shared credentials
- 4.3 Explain compliance frameworks and legal considerations and their organizational impact.
  - Security concerns of integrating diverse industries
  - Data considerations
    - Data sovereignty
    - Data ownership
    - Data classifications
    - Data retention
    - Data types
    - Health
    - Financial
    - Intellectual property
    - Personally identifiable information (PII)
    - Data removal, destruction, and sanitization

- Geographic considerations
  - Location of data
  - Location of data subject
  - Location of cloud provider
- Third-party attestation of compliance
- Regulations, accreditations, and standards
  - Payment Card Industry Data Security Standard (PCI DSS)
  - General Data Protection Regulation (GDPR)
  - International Organization for Standardization (ISO)
  - Capability Maturity Model Integration (CMMI)
  - National Institute of Standards and Technology (NIST)
  - Children's Online Privacy Protection Act (COPPA)
  - Common Criteria
  - Cloud Security Alliance (CSA) Security Trust Assurance and Risk (STAR)
- Legal considerations
  - Due diligence
  - Due care
  - Export controls
  - Legal holds
  - E-discovery
- Contract and agreement types
  - Service-level agreement (SLA)
  - Master service agreement (MSA)
  - Non-disclosure agreement (NDA)
  - Memorandum of understanding (MOU)
  - Interconnection security agreement (ISA)
  - Operational-level agreement
  - Privacy-level agreement

- 4.4 Explain the importance of business continuity and disaster recovery concepts.
  - Business impact analysis
    - Recovery point objective
    - Recovery time objective
    - Recovery service level
    - Mission essential functions
  - Privacy impact assessment
  - Disaster recovery plan (DRP)/business continuity plan (BCP)
    - Cold site
    - Warm site
    - Hot site
    - Mobile site
  - Incident response plan
    - Roles/responsibilities
    - After-action reports
  - Testing plans
    - Checklist
    - Walk-through
    - Tabletop exercises
    - Full interruption test
    - Parallel test/simulation test

1. A corporation expanded their business by acquiring several similar businesses. What should the security team first undertake?

    A. Development of an ISA and a risk analysis

    B. Installation of firewalls between the businesses

    C. Removal of unneeded assets and Internet access

    D. Scan of the new networks for vulnerabilities

2. Your organization was the victim of brute-force attacks where the attacker discovered usernames and continually tried to log in to the corporate network using various passwords until the account was compromised. Which option could reduce the likelihood of a brute-force attack being successful?

    A. Allow only one attempt for privileged users.

    B. Configure Group Policy in Active Directory to lock out an account for 10 minutes after 5 unsuccessful login attempts.

    C. Create federated identities with SSO.

    D. Enforce stricter password requirements.

3. You have a web server in your network that is the target of a distributed denial-of-service attack. Multiple systems are flooding the bandwidth of that system. Which information security goal is impacted by this type of an attack?

    A. Availability

    B. Baselines

    C. Integrity

    D. Emergency response

4. When you looked at the business impact analysis given to your office for approval, you notice it is less narrative and more mathematical calculations. What will make this BIA more balanced?

    A. More qualitative analysis

    B. More quantitative analysis

    C. More gap analysis

    D. More risk analysis

5. You oversee hardware distribution for your global enterprise. You conduct a data analysis to figure out failure rates of a certain brand and model of laptop. You need to calculate the average number of times that specific model is likely to break in a year. Which of the following *best* describes your calculation?

    A. Annualized rate of occurrence

    B. Exposure factor

    C. Single loss expectancy

    D. Annualized loss expectancy

6. Your senior management wants to measure how risky an activity will be. This metric is used to provide a signal of increasing risk exposure. You need to identify which of the following?

   A. Key risk indicators (KRIs)

   B. Key performance indicators

   C. Total cost of ownership

   D. Risk assessment

7. Bob is conducting a risk assessment and wants to assign an asset value to the servers in the data center. His organization wants to ensure there is a budget to rebuild in case of a natural disaster. What method should Bob use to evaluate the assets?

   A. Depreciated cost

   B. Purchase cost

   C. Replacement cost

   D. Conditional cost

8. With traditional network architecture, one best practice is to limit network access points. This limitation allowed for a concentration of network security resources and a protected attack surface. With the introduction of 802.11x into enterprise network architecture, what was introduced into the network?

   A. Increased capability and increased risk and higher TCO

   B. Decreased capability and increased risk and higher TCO

   C. Increased capability and decreased risk and lower TCO

   D. Decreased capability and decreased risk and lower TCO

9. You need a strategy for managing your organization's overall governance, risk management, and compliance regulations. What is the structured approach to aligning IT with business objectives?

   A. GRC

   B. ITIL

   C. PMI

   D. CRMA

10. One of the requirements for a new device you're adding to the network is an availability of 99.9 percent. According to the vendor, the newly acquired device has been rated with an MTBF of 20,000 hours and an MTTR of 3 hours. What is the most accurate statement?

    A. The device will meet availability because it will be at 99.985 percent.

    B. The device will not meet availability because it will be at 99.89 percent.

    C. The device will not meet availability because it will be at 99.85 percent.

    D. The device will meet availability because it will be at 99.958 percent.

11. You need to calculate the annual loss expectancy (ALE) for an important server on your network. Which of these is the proper formula?

    A. ARO × EF × AV

    B. ARO × AV

    C. EF × SLE

    D. EF × SLE × AV

12. Your organization is attempting to make the best use of all the resources allocated to a security project. If your organization is not making the best use of currently held resources, the project may not perform as planned. What type of analysis needs to be done?

    A. BDR

    B. BIA

    C. Gap

    D. Risk

13. Your organization experiences a security incident that costs $20,000 in downtime each time it occurs. It has happened twice this fiscal year. The device causing the issue is scheduled to be upgraded next year. The cost of implementing a fix is more than $250,000 and also requires maintenance contracts. What is the *most* cost-effective way to deal with this risk?

    A. Mitigate the risk

    B. Avoid the risk

    C. Accept the risk

    D. Transfer the risk

14. You have joined an ERM team and completed a risk assessment for your organization. After evaluating all cyber-risk, you have found an area that needs to be mitigated by risk transfer mechanisms. Which of these would be an example of risk transfer?

    A. Patching

    B. Pentesting

    C. Insurance

    D. Simulations

15. Your company has set up a new e-commerce website. It is agreed that risks exist, but the benefit of the added cash flow outweighs the risk. What is this called?

    A. Risk acceptance

    B. Risk reduction

    C. Risk transference

    D. Risk rejection

16. An audit identified a lack of security controls regarding employee termination. The current company policy states that the terminated employee's account is disabled within one hour of termination. The audit found that more than 10 percent of terminated employees still have active accounts. What is the *best* course of action?

    A. Review the termination requirements.

    B. Implement a monthly review of terminated employees.

    C. Update the policy to accommodate the delay.

    D. Review the termination policy with managers.

17. Qualitative risk assessment is explained by which of the following?

    A. Can be completed by someone with a limited understanding of risk assessment and is easy to implement

    B. Must be completed by someone with expert understanding and uses detailed analysis for calculation

    C. Is completed by subject-matter experts and is difficult to implement

    D. Brings together SME with detailed metrics to handle a difficult implementation

18. Your CISO mandates the security department implement the Center for Internet Security Top 20 controls, starting with the first control, Inventory and Control of Hardware Assets. This control states that an organization must actively manage all hardware devices on a network. The main function of this control is to prevent which of the following?

    A. Authorized access

    B. Indefinite access

    C. Unauthorized access

    D. Continuous access

19. Because of time constraints and budget, your organization has opted to hire a third-party organization to begin working on an important new project. From a security point of view, what *best* balances the needs of the organization and managing the inherent risk of a third-party vendor?

    A. Outsourcing is a valid option and not much of a concern for security because any damage is the responsibility of the third party.

    B. If the company has an acceptable security record, then it makes perfect sense to outsource.

    C. You should never outsource. It leads to legal and compliance issues.

    D. The third party should have the proper NDA, SLA, and OLA in place and should be obligated to perform adequate security activities.

20. Your software company is acquiring a competitor start-up. All the people working with that company will become your employees. They will retain all access to their former network and resources for two weeks to ease the transition. For productivity, the decision was made to join the two networks. Which of the following threats is the highest risk for your company?

    A. IP filters

    B. Loss of code

    C. Malware

    D. Comingling the networks

21. Your company began the process of evaluating different technologies for a technical security-focused project. You narrowed down the selection to three organizations from which you received formal requests for information (RFIs). What is the next request that you will make of those three vendors if you want to discover the total value required for purchase with items and deliverables?

   A. RFQ

   B. RFP

   C. RFC

   D. RFI

22. Edgar has been tasked with reviewing existing technology security policies. Which of these should *not* be covered in his security policy?

   A. Details and procedures

   B. Exceptions to policy

   C. Password policy

   D. Access control of client data

23. If you wanted to require that employees follow certain steps to avoid malware, you would create a procedure. If you wanted to require employees to use specific software to avoid malware, which of the following would you create?

   A. Policy

   B. Standard

   C. Baseline

   D. Scope

24. What is the customary practice of responsible protection of an asset that affects an organization or community?

   A. Due diligence

   B. Risk mitigation

   C. Insurance

   D. Due care

25. The security awareness training informed employees that within their operating systems an auditing feature was enabled. What form of control is used when end users are informed that their actions are monitored on the network?

   A. Directive

   B. Corrective

   C. Detective

   D. Preventive

26. As a risk manager, accurate inventories are critical for many reasons. You receive an alert of multiple failed logins on a root account on a server. How do you decide the criticality of responding to the alert?

    A. Use the inventory to find what service this server provides and what data is stored on it.

    B. Use the inventory to find the physical location and unplug the machine from the network.

    C. Use the inventory to find the environment the asset services and send an email to operations.

    D. Log into the machine and watch tasks that are running while deploying antivirus software.

27. As a security engineer, you are comfortable with the security aspect of information technology. However, real security requires being able to communicate with stakeholders. You read security reports, and any findings that are related to risk are given to department heads for review. This collaboration technique is which of the following?

    A. Independent review

    B. Structured review

    C. Strategic alignment

    D. Security controls

28. An external audit is a formal process involving an accredited third party. It can be expensive and time intensive. What is a key to component having an external audit?

    A. An independent authority against a recognized standard

    B. An internal agent and a security framework

    C. A global internal assessment with gap analysis

    D. A validated outcome and scheduled future audits

29. Given recent high-profile cyberattacks, your CISO asks for your input on cybersecurity control frameworks to better define what the internal auditors should use for information security management systems (ISMS) guidance. Which internal auditing framework do you recommend?

    A. SEC

    B. CISM

    C. ISO/IEC 27001

    D. CIS

30. Your department started to plan for next year. You need to clarify what your key performance indicators are for the current year. Which of the following is *not* found in a KPI?

    A. Measurement

    B. Target

    C. Risk register

    D. Data source

31. Your organization opted into a private cloud solution for all your large highly regulated technical customers. Which one of these is a disadvantage?

 A. Dedicated environment

 B. Compliance to regulations

 C. Scalable and high SLA performance

 D. Expensive solution and difficult to scale

32. Your company purchased new computers and wants consistent reliability and performance out of them. You recommend that an operating system and software application configuration be installed on these systems prior to the addition programs. What is this process called?

 A. Base configuration

 B. Production operating environment

 C. Standard operating environment

 D. Standard configuration

33. You were hired for a role in healthcare as a system architect. You need to factor in CIA requirements for a new SAN. Which of the following CIA requirements is *best* for multipathing?

 A. Confidentiality

 B. Threat

 C. Integrity

 D. Availability

34. Your organization decided to outsource systems that are not mission critical. You have been tasked to calculate the risk of outsourcing these systems because a recent key risk indicator review shows that core business functions are dependent on these outsourced systems. What is the *best* tool to use?

 A. Business impact analysis

 B. Annual loss expectancy

 C. Total cost of ownership

 D. Gap analysis

35. You live and work in an area plagued by hurricanes. What *best* describes the effort you made to determine the consequence of a disruption due to this natural disaster?

 A. Business impact analysis

 B. Risk assessment

 C. Table top exercises

 D. Mitigating control analysis

36. As CIO, you took the proper steps to implement a standard of due care by fostering an environment of due diligence. You created an ecosystem that enforces more than the minimum level of required security. What are these efforts called?

    A. Best practices

    B. Due care

    C. Baseline

    D. Modeling

37. You have an accountant who refuses to take their required time off. You must institute a policy that will force people in critical financial areas of the organization to take time off. Which of the following standard security practice do you institute?

    A. Separation of duties

    B. Mandatory vacation

    C. Forensic tasks

    D. Termination procedures

38. Your organization has a new policy to implement security based on least privilege and separation of duties. A key component is deciding on data access. They decided it is *best* made by which of the following roles?

    A. Data steward

    B. Data owner

    C. User/manager

    D. Senior management

39. A security administrator is reviewing an audit and finds that two users in human resources also have access to finance data. One of these users is a recruiter, and the other is an intern. What security measure is being violated?

    A. Job rotation

    B. Disclosure

    C. Mandatory vacation

    D. Least privilege

40. You work in the training department of a software company and have only one full-time trainer. What can you do to prevent a single point of failure if that trainer should become ill and unable to teach?

    A. Job rotation

    B. Dual control

    C. NDA

    D. Mandatory vacation

41. Disciplinary actions for noncompliance should be included in security policy. These actions should be strong enough to deter violating policy, including suspension, termination, or legal prosecution. Who has to endorse the security policy?

  A. Senior management

  B. Human resources

  C. All employees

  D. Contractors

42. Over the last month, you reviewed security reports that state there was a significant increase in the number of inappropriate activities on the network by employees. What is the first step in improving the security level in your organization?

  A. Awareness sessions

  B. Stronger auditing

  C. Reduce employee permissions

  D. Termination

43. Your HR recruiter is having difficulties finding qualified applicants for an open IT security manager role. Your department discussed moving deployment solutions to a third party that will operate and maintain the processes. Which of the following deployment solutions is this most likely to be?

  A. Cloud

  B. Hosted

  C. On-premise

  D. Automated

44. You are leading a project for your organization moving to a thin client with the server architecture hosted in the cloud. You are meeting with upper management, and they have asked for your advice of using thin clients. Which of the following is a security advantage?

  A. Thin clients are economical and require less security. There is no storage, and the server is protected in the cloud.

  B. Thin clients are encrypted with AES, both at rest and in transit.

  C. Attackers will have less opportunity to extract data from thin clients.

  D. Thin clients do not require external security auditing.

45. You need an agreement that lets your business implement a comprehensive risk allocation strategy and provides indemnification, the method that holds one party harmless against existing or future losses. What contract should you negotiate?

  A. Master service agreement

  B. Business impact agreement

  C. Interconnection security agreement

  D. Memorandum of understanding

46. Your company has a subscription to use a third party's infrastructure, programming tools, and languages to develop and build out a new cloud-based ESB application. Which acronym properly defines this type of service?

A. PaaS

B. IaaS

C. SaaS

D. MaaS

47. Your newly formed IT team is investigating cloud computing models. You want to use a cloud computing model that is dedicated to your organization. The data center and all resources are located at the vendor's site but are isolated through a secure network and not shared with any other customer. Which of the following is the *best* choice for this situation?

A. Public

B. Private

C. Agnostic

D. Hybrid

48. Your company is considering a new vendor to add a new host to a computer cluster. The cluster will be connected to a single storage solution. What are you most likely trying to accomplish?

A. Availability

B. Provisioning

C. Integrity

D. Confidentiality

49. Human resources is advertising on several websites for a new position in IT. This applicant for this role needs to be familiar with specific networking and security products. Since the advertisement, you have seen targeted external scans looking for open default ports on the networking and security products you use. What has most likely occurred?

A. Auditors have done their due diligence on your organization.

B. Attackers have used job boards to find information about your company.

C. Regulators are responding to requirements.

D. Self-assessment using tabletop exercises is being performed.

50. You believe attackers set up fake access points in high-traffic public locations near your hospital campus. These access points have common names like Hospital Guest. What is this type of attack called?

A. Network hacking

B. Network spoofing

C. Phishing

D. Whaling

51. A web developer builds a web form for customers to fill out and respond to the company via a web page. What is the first thing that a developer should do to prevent this page from becoming a security risk?

  A. SQLi

  B. Input validation

  C. Cross-site request forgery

  D. Fuzzing

52. As security engineer, you were asked to recommend a disk encryption technology that your end users can use to secure an entire disk or partition. All the end users have Microsoft Windows 10 systems. Which of the following is the *best* option available?

  A. EFS

  B. FAT32

  C. NTFS

  D. BitLocker

53. Your MDM allows for the use of mobile payments using virtual smartphone wallets. Paying with your smartphone replaces swiping a card. Your end users are skeptical, but your security analysts support it. What is the security analyst's argument for using this technology?

  A. Mobile wallets use encryption to mask payment card numbers.

  B. Mobile wallets use encryption to mask the phone's number.

  C. Mobile payment methods are not more secure than cards or cash.

  D. Loss of a smartphone is like losing a credit card.

54. You are a healthcare provider accessing a cloud-based server where your collaboration tool resides. What is the most important question you need to ask the vendor/host of this cloud-based server?

  A. Is this server HIPAA and HITECH compliant?

  B. Is this server SCADA compliant?

  C. What is your SLA if the server goes down?

  D. What is my TCO of this software?

55. You want to access your company's network equipment on the corporate LAN remotely. A colleague suggests using the program PuTTY. After downloading and running PuTTY, you find that it offers various means of remote connectivity. Which of the following options is the most secure option?

  A. Telnet

  B. SSH

  C. FTP

  D. HTTP

56. Your CIO, Kenneth, is reviewing a contract with a new startup software vendor. He has asked the software vendor for a clause to be added for software escrow as well as to not automatically renew. He also asks you to investigate other ways to avoid vendor lock-in. Why is software escrow necessary?

    A. Vendor bankruptcy

    B. Off-site backup

    C. Payment over time

    D. Performance measurements

57. A data user reached out to the data custodian to request permission to give access to sensitive information to a third-party marketing agency. The third-party vendor has been vetted by security to make sure they are trusted and viable. Who should be contacted next before access is granted?

    A. Data owner

    B. CEO

    C. Board of directors

    D. Marketing VP

58. Your organization is now under legal investigation after a merger. Your data is placed in a legal hold, which means it cannot be destroyed. You are pursuing a vendor for enterprise data archiving because failure to preserve this data can lead to fines. What type of metadata would these documents *not* contain?

    A. File properties

    B. Time-date stamps

    C. Author/recipient

    D. Ink

59. While implementing best practices, the security fix quoted from a vendor for a specific asset costs more than the asset is worth to the organization. What must be maintained?

    A. SSH

    B. Due care

    C. CVE

    D. Fiscal responsibility

60. Your organization's security policy specifies a length of time to keep data, after which the data must be destroyed to help mitigate the risk of that data being compromised. This type of policy helps reduce legal liability if the data becomes unrecoverable. What type of policy is this?

    A. Data protection

    B. Data remanence

    C. Data retention

    D. Data destruction

61. Your FIM initial deployment went well but is now experiencing some issues. FIM's purpose is to detect change, and it is necessary to tune the solution carefully to minimize issues with false positives and volume. The issues revolve around performance and noise. What must you integrate with FIM to ensure the solution is holding up to your organizational needs?

- **A.** Project management
- **B.** Program management
- **C.** Change management
- **D.** Staff management

62. A security consultant on your team was written up for a multitude of offenses. The latest transgression left you no choice but to terminate this employee. Which of the following is *most* important to do when informing the employee of their separation from the company?

- **A.** Allowing them to complete their project
- **B.** Giving them two weeks' severance
- **C.** Allowing them to collect their personal belongings
- **D.** Disabling network access and changing the passwords to devices to which they had access

63. You are on hold with tech support, and they have guided you to the command screen. Your computer has a command prompt, and you need to see all the current TCP/IP network configuration values for this specific asset. What command do they have you enter?

- **A.** ipconfig
- **B.** arp
- **C.** rarp
- **D.** dns

64. Your global organization has tech support offices that "follow the sun." This means tech support is open 24 hours a day, 7 days a week, and some of those support offices are located in other countries. Depending on the time of day, it may be necessary for tech support personnel to access systems remotely over the Internet, managing your own server without using a centralized service. What is the *best* choice in this list to accomplish the support personnel needs?

- **A.** MRA
- **B.** VNC
- **C.** RDP
- **D.** TeamViewer

65. You work for a global manufacturer of computer parts. You have been tasked with a goal of keeping something from happening. What type of control would you want to put in place?

- **A.** Detective
- **B.** Preventive
- **C.** Corrective
- **D.** Recovery

66. Forming a response team and assigning responsibilities is a critical step in emergency response planning. If your team is not familiar with their assigned role, important actions could be missed when a security incident occurs. Overall, a cyber-emergency response team should analyze incident data, discuss observations, manage communications, remediate, and close the incident with what response?

    A. Understanding lessons learned

    B. Negotiating a contract

    C. Building an SOC

    D. Performing risk analysis

67. As a security analyst for a hospital, you rely on some assets running high-end customized legacy software. What precaution should you implement to protect yourself if this developer goes out of business?

    A. Access control

    B. Service level agreement

    C. Code escrow

    D. Outsourcing

68. You are a service provider responsible for ensuring that an audit for PCI DSS occurs and that the correct documentation is completed by the relevant parties. This is part of the assessment you provide. What is this process is called?

    A. Service provider request

    B. Attestation of compliance

    C. Payment requests

    D. Security standards council

69. You are developing an information security program to protect critical business processes, data, and assets. What are the three components to implementing information security programs?

    A. People, processes, policies

    B. Assets, authentication, authorization

    C. Backups, broadband, BCPs

    D. Servers, SaaS, supply chains

70. You are a developer for a research organization and are tasked with testing a new team member's code. You must gather as much diagnostic information as possible to troubleshoot any problems. Which of the following options is your *best* option?

    A. Memory dump

    B. Pivoting

    C. DNS records

    D. Internal audit

71. An organization installed various Ethernet ports in its facility. Anyone can walk up to a port and plug their computer into the network unabated, gaining network access. Even with network segmentation, a security audit found this situation to be a security risk. What technology should be implemented to ensure only authorized computer equipment can connect to the network using these Ethernet ports?

- **A.** Network access control
- **B.** Proxy
- **C.** Next-generation firewall
- **D.** Security information and event management system

72. You are shopping on a popular website for computer parts. As you move from page to page, cookies are being used to maintain session state during transmission of data. This means the cookie is used to store needed information, such as the selections made on previous pages. Not all websites protect cookies when they are transmitted over HTTP because HTTP is stateless. If an attacker gets ahold of your cookie, what can they *not* do with it?

- **A.** Modify the cookie content.
- **B.** Rewrite session data.
- **C.** Inject malicious content.
- **D.** Eat it.

73. You completed a vulnerability scan on your network without using any type of SMB or SSH service credentials. It gives you an idea of what your network looks like to the outside world. The next step is to use shared IT service account credentials. What type of vulnerability scan is this called?

- **A.** Authenticated
- **B.** Unauthenticated
- **C.** Secured
- **D.** Accessible

74. Employees in your organization must use a Windows 10 desktop with a multicore CPU, a minimum of 8 GB of memory, and a solid-state drive. Which of these describes these technical aspects?

- **A.** A policy
- **B.** A procedure
- **C.** A standard
- **D.** A responsibility

75. One of your salespeople has been asked to travel overseas on business and wants to make sure the corporate Windows laptop will be secure if it were stolen or lost. What do you tell the salesperson?

- **A.** Make sure they change their password before they leave.
- **B.** The laptop has a TPM chip and BitLocker enabled.
- **C.** Always use VPN.
- **D.** Install WS-Security and enable RDP.

76. You are a developer for a security software company. Your CISO tasks you with conducting a "white-box" test. The advantages include optimization and thoroughness, given the fact that the developer has full knowledge of the code and libraries used. Which of the following should be considered a disadvantage to a white-box test?

    A. Complexity and duration

    B. Simplicity and impartiality

    C. Redundancy and simplicity

    D. Accuracy and superficiality

77. Your global software organization is required to conduct a BIA for any new company acquisition. Your organization has acquired a new software startup. Your organization as well as the startup outsources the LMS and CMS for education to noncompatible third parties. What are you most concerned about?

    A. Data sovereignty

    B. Encryption

    C. Data migration

    D. Disaster recovery

78. You must identify a person who will have the administrative control and be accountable for a specific set of information and data set. It could be the most senior person in a department. What is their role?

    A. Data custodian

    B. Data user

    C. Data owner

    D. Data administrator

79. You work for a university, and the registrar is the data owner for student data. This department is responsible for managing access, classification, and regulatory requirements. Who does the data owner work with to enforce the technical control?

    A. Other data owners

    B. Data user

    C. Data custodian

    D. Data classifier

80. Your organization finds it difficult to distinguish what data can be shared with a customer and what should remain internal. They assigned you the task of data classification. What is the primary purpose of this task?

    A. Justifying expenses

    B. Assigning value to data

    C. Defining necessary security protections

    D. Controlling user access

81. You researched and conferred with your legal department as to what your data retention policy should be. Which of the following place restrictions on data retention?

    A. GLBA

    B. HIPAA

    C. SOX

    D. All of the above

82. In a healthcare organization, what data role is responsible for assigning access, producing reports, and logging access, as well as implementing physical safeguards to protect the confidentiality, availability, and integrity of a dataset?

    A. Data owner

    B. Data custodian

    C. Data user

    D. Data protector

83. As a data user, you are required to follow policies and procedures by the business unit, including ensuring the security of any sensitive data. You visited a website holding sensitive financial information about your organization. What should you do first?

    A. Hack the site to remove the information.

    B. Visit WhoIs and find out who owns the site and contact them directly.

    C. Report the suspected security/policy violation to the appropriate authority.

    D. Try to find out how the information was shared.

84. You have a well-configured firewall and IDS. Which of the following can *best* steal intellectual property or trade secrets because there is no system auditing?

    A. Hacktivist

    B. Auditors

    C. Malware

    D. Employees

85. Your company holds large amounts of company data in electronic databases as well as personally identifiable information (PII) of customers and employees. What do you do to ensure that implemented controls provide the right amount of protection?

    A. Best practices

    B. Forensics

    C. Due diligence

    D. Auditing

86. Your research determines what type of data your organization should preserve and the length of time the data should be stored. Which of the following is *not* another part of a good data retention policy?

    A. Format

    B. Certification

    C. Access control

    D. Destruction

87. You are hired by an insurance company as their new data custodian. Which of the following *best* describes your new responsibilities?

    A. Writing and proofing administrative documentation

    B. Ensuring accessibility and appropriate access using policy and data ownership guidelines

    C. Conducting an audit of the data's strategic, tactical, and operation (STO) controls

    D. Improving the data consistency and increasing data integration

88. As a marketing analyst for a large retail enterprise organization, you want to deploy a technology that will responsibly personalize the in-person shopping experience. What technology do you explore using with your retail app?

    A. Home delivery

    B. Personal shoppers

    C. Geotagging

    D. Customer feedback

89. Your organization is in an area susceptible to wildfires. Within the last 30 days, your employees were evacuated twice from the primary location. During the second evacuation, damage occurred to several floors of the building, including the data center. When should the team return to start recovery?

    A. In 72 hours.

    B. You should not return to the primary location.

    C. Immediately after the disaster.

    D. Only after it is deemed safe to return to the primary location.

90. You would like to periodically update records in multiple remote locations to ensure the appropriate levels of fault tolerance and redundancy. What is this known as?

    A. Shadowing

    B. Mirroring

    C. Archiving

    D. Fail safe

91. Your objectives and key results (OKRs) being measured for this quarter include realizing the benefits of a multitenancy cloud architecture. Which one of these results is *not* applicable to a multitenancy cloud service?

   A. Financial

   B. Usage

   C. Location

   D. Onboarding

92. Your company hired a third-party company to fulfill compliance requirements to test for weaknesses in your company's security before an audit. The contractor attempted to hack wireless networks and enter secure areas without authorization and used phishing to gain access to credentials. What *best* describes this process?

   A. Vulnerability scans

   B. Active reconnaissance

   C. Penetration test

   D. Passive reconnaissance

93. Your healthcare organization decided to begin outsourcing some IT systems. Which of the following statements is true?

   A. All outsourcing frees your organization from any rules or requirements.

   B. All compliance and regulatory requirements are passed on to the provider.

   C. The IT systems are no longer configured, maintained, or evaluated by your organization.

   D. The outsourcing organization is free from any rules or regulations.

94. Your organization must comply with PCI DSS and regulations that mandate annual and ongoing penetration testing after any system changes at both the network and application layers. What is the primary purpose of penetration testing?

   A. Creates security awareness

   B. Evaluates IDS

   C. Tests the security perimeter

   D. Accesses the internal guidelines

95. Your U.S.-based company manufactures children's clothing and is contemplating expanding their business into the European Union. You are concerned about regulation and compliance. What should your organization examine first?

   A. Payment Card Industry

   B. General Data Protection Regulation

   C. Children's Online Privacy Protection

   D. Family Educational Rights and Privacy Act

96. You are hired by a burgeoning retail startup that needs to evolve their IT operations into a more mature model. Which of the following frameworks is *best* to use while doing the first internal audit of the organization?

    A. ITIL

    B. CISA

    C. COBIT

    D. ISO 27001

97. You look to implement best practices and have identified other departments or people who have experience with their implementation. Where else might you look for guidance on cybersecurity best practices?

    A. NIST

    B. ADA

    C. FBI

    D. GLBA

98. As part of your Capability Maturity Model Integration (CMMI), capturing lessons learned is an ongoing effort you have implemented in your technical project management. You will use this data in the future for process improvements. Not learning from project failures can lead to which of the following?

    A. Repeating the failure

    B. Missing opportunities

    C. Implementing good processes

    D. Preparing for current projects

99. You are using a process where the product or system being evaluated is called the "target of evaluation" and rated on evaluation levels of E0 through E6. What is this process called?

    A. COPPA

    B. CSA STAR

    C. ITSEC

    D. Common Criteria

100. Your organization was breached, but you have been able to prove that sufficient due care was taken. What burden is eliminated?

    A. Liability

    B. Investigation

    C. Financial loss

    D. Negligence

101. Your organization opened new offices on a different continent. This expansion requires internal security as well as compliance, especially when it comes to export controls. Existing policy also states that all employee activity could be monitored. What would be the reason that policy could change?

    A. Teams in other countries fall under different legal or regulatory requirements.

    B. The time it takes to export data to the data warehouse.

    C. Cybersecurity shortage of qualified analysts.

    D. Social networking initiatives.

102. Your company decides to shift the eDiscovery processes from external third parties to in-house. Which of the following is *not* a stage of eDiscovery?

    A. Identification

    B. Interpretation

    C. Collection

    D. Processing

103. While running IaaS environments, you retain the responsibility for the security of all operating systems, applications, and network traffic. Which of these would *not* be technically advantageous to deploy to protect this cloud environment?

    A. Advanced antimalware applied to the OS

    B. Application whitelisting and machine learning–based protection

    C. Memory exploit prevention for single-purpose workloads

    D. Negotiation of an SLA spelling out the details of the data the provider will share in case of an incident

104. An analyst has been attempting to acquire a budget for a new security tool. Which of the following should the analyst give to management to support the request?

    A. Threat reports and a trend analysis

    B. Interconnection security agreement (ISA)

    C. Master service agreement (MSA)

    D. Request for information (RFI)

105. You chose a vendor for your collaboration tool and will sign an agreement that requires that a vendor not disclose confidential information learned during the scope of the proof of concept, deployment, and usage of the tool. Which document needs to be signed by both your organization and the vendor?

    A. SLA

    B. MOU

    C. NDA

    D. RFP

106. You work for a software company and are building an SLA template. The SLA is what the IT organization as a whole is promising to the customer. Which of the following documents *best* can be used to support the SLA?

A. PLA

B. OLA

C. NDA

D. DBA

107. You are tasked with conducting a risk analysis based on how it affects business processes. What activity are you actually performing?

A. Gap analysis

B. Disaster recovery

C. Intrusion detection system

D. Business impact analysis

108. Your organization's primary network backup server went down at midnight. Your RPO is nine hours. What time will you exceed the business process recovery tolerably, given the volume of data that has been lost in that time frame?

A. 6 a.m.

B. 9 a.m.

C. Noon

D. 3 p.m.

109. Your company just experienced an emergency and needs to initiate a business continuity plan (BCP). Who is responsible for initiating the BCP?

A. Senior management

B. Security personnel

C. Recovery team

D. Database admins

110. You completed a structured walk-through of your disaster recovery plan. Senior management would like you to use the absolute best way to verify that the DRP is sufficient and has no deficiencies. What test do you choose next?

A. Round-table exercises

B. Dry-run exercises

C. Full interrupt test

D. External audit

111. You want to create an IT disaster recovery solution for your organization, and your budget is small. The MTD for your company is five days. Any downtime more than five days will harm the company. Which of the following is your *best* option?

    A. Hot site

    B. Warm site

    C. Cold site

    D. Mobile site

112. You work in the computer lab provisioning hardware to be deployed throughout your enterprise. Your company policy states that end users are responsible for backing up their files. After an operating system upgrade, some people lost mission-critical files and are coming to your lab to salvage lost files. What is this process called?

    A. Data salvaging

    B. Data retrieving

    C. Data recovery

    D. Data destruction

113. You were tasked with building a team that will handle computer security incidents. This team will use the incident response plan. What has this team been called historically?

    A. NIST

    B. CERT

    C. ADA

    D. Red Cross

114. You have been handling an incident and have finally arrived at the final step of the incident response process. What is the final step?

    A. Recovery

    B. Announcement

    C. Public relations

    D. Lessons learned

115. As a CISO, you built a team of security developers, managers, educators, architects, and administrators. Some of the people in these roles are finding they are duplicating efforts and not using their time well. What can you do to initiate solid administrative control over the situation?

    A. AUP

    B. TCO

    C. Mandatory vacation

    D. Job descriptions

116. Your company has a new CIO, who has a favorite vulnerability management tool and a relationship with that software company. You are migrating to the new software. What document would require the most changes?

   A.   Policies

   B.   Guidelines

   C.   Baselines

   D.   Procedures

117. Your internal auditor completed the quarterly PCI DSS audit of the financial systems and found that accounts payable has not followed proper procedures during a tabletop exercise. What is your recommendation?

   A.   Review procedures and retrain employees.

   B.   Wait until the external auditor completes their annual review.

   C.   Delete all unnecessary financial transactions.

   D.   Do a complete parallel test of account payables systems.

118. Your team was tasked with a penetration test of a large automotive corporation. The proper documentation was signed by both organizations. Because this is a black-box penetration test, where should your team start?

   A.   Vulnerability scanning

   B.   Social engineering

   C.   Reconnaissance

   D.   Malware distribution

119. You need a way to enable tech support from your organization to have complete remote access to your systems. It has become difficult to have end users walk through a complicated set of steps, so it is best to let a well-trained technician do it for them. Which of the following are the major risks with desktop sharing and remote access?

   A.   Authentication and access control

   B.   Authorization and verification

   C.   Validation and isolation

   D.   Regulation and application

120. You want to test the fault tolerance of your hardware systems. Which of the following is a way of preventing a disruption arising from a single point of hardware failure during a test?

   A.   A database with customer information backed up in a data warehouse

   B.   Duplicate alternative power sources

   C.   Using an identical server with all operations running in parallel

   D.   A duplicate database

121. You want to gather your team together to evaluate potential corrective and recovery controls for your company. You want to encourage them to contribute and evaluate, taking an active role in the discussion. The three-tiered approach consists of brainstorming ideas for solutions, evaluating the best possible solutions, and which of the following?

A. Deciding

B. Committing

C. Administering

D. Recovering

122. Your team is conducting a risk evaluation to assign an asset value to the collaboration servers in your data center based on an after-action report of the last incident. The primary concern is how and what to replace in the case of a disaster. Which one of the following is the *best* choice?

A. Purchase cost

B. Depreciated cost

C. Retail cost

D. Replacement cost

123. Your organization is analyzing the risk of using more and more diverse technology. Your task is to look at collaboration tools because such a tool houses your most important information, customer data, and innovative ideas in one single space. With data security in mind, what do you suggest doing to protect against privileged users compromising sensitive data?

A. Deploying flexible levels of access across the platform

B. Creating alerts when specific data file types have been uploaded

C. Putting individual projects in their own dedicated spaces with restricted access

D. Creating a strict password policy

124. You are working on a business continuity and incident response plan for your health organization. What is the control type of this function?

A. Detective

B. Preventive

C. Corrective

D. Reconciliation

Chapter

5

Practice Test 1

1. You have an asset that is valued at $1,000. The EF for this asset is 10 percent. The ARO is 2. What is the ALE?

    A. The ALE is $200.

    B. The ALE is $100.

    C. The ALE is $400.

    D. ALE cannot be calculated with the numbers provided.

2. You are a consultant for a cybersecurity firm and have been tasked with quantifying risks associated with information technology when validating the abilities of new security controls and countermeasures. What is the *best* way to identify the risks?

    A. Vulnerability management

    B. Pentesting

    C. Threat and risk assessment

    D. Data reclassification

3. Which of the following security programs is designed to provide employees with the knowledge they need to fulfill their job requirements and protect the organization?

    A. Awareness

    B. Training

    C. Indoctrination

    D. Development

4. Alice discovered a meterpreter shell running a keylogger on the CFO's laptop. What security tenet is the keylogger mostly likely to break?

    A. Availability

    B. Threats

    C. Integrity

    D. Confidentiality

5. You are a security administrator for a network that uses Fibre Channel over Ethernet (FCoE). The network administrator would like to access raw data from the storage array and restore it to yet another host. Which of the following might be an issue to availability?

    A. The new host might not be compatible with FCoE.

    B. The data may not be in a usable format.

    C. The process could cause bottlenecks.

    D. Deduplication will occur.

6. As a network administrator, you are asked to connect a server to a storage-attached network. If availability and access control are the most important, which of the following fulfills the requirements?

    A. Installing a NIC in the server, enabling deduplication

    B. Installing a NIC in the server, disabling deduplication

    C. Installing an HBA in the server, creating a LUN on the SAN

    D. Installing a clustered HBA in the server, creating two LUNS on a NAS

7. Which of the following confidentiality security models ensures that a subject with clearance level of Secret can write only to objects classified as Secret or Top Secret?

   A. Biba

   B. Clark–Wilson

   C. Brewer–Nash

   D. Bell–LaPadula

8. Your organization needs a security model for integrity where the subject cannot send messages to object of higher integrity. Which of the following is unique to the Biba model and will accommodate that need?

   A. Simple

   B. Star

   C. Invocation

   D. Strong

9. You need to assign permissions so that users can access only the resources they need to complete specific tasks. Which security tenet did you use to meet the need?

   A. Separation of duties

   B. Need to know

   C. Job rotation

   D. Least privilege

10. You are tasked with hiring a third party to perform a security assessment of your manufacturing plant. What type of testing gives the most neutral review of your security profile?

    A. White box

    B. Gray box

    C. Black hat

    D. Blue hat

11. Alice needs some help developing security policy documentation. She turns to you for help in developing a document that contains instructions or information on how to remain in compliance with regulations. What document do you need to develop?

    A. Procedures

    B. Standards

    C. Policy

    D. Guidelines

12. Prioritization is an important part of your job as a security analyst. You are trying to calculate the ALE for all assets and risks. What purpose will this serve?

    A. To estimate insurance

    B. To arrive at a budget and head count

    C. To prioritize countermeasures

    D. To inform design

13. One of the software developers made a change in code that unintentionally diminishes security. Which of the following change control processes will be most effective in this situation?

    A. Rollback

    B. Logging

    C. Compiling

    D. Patching

14. Your external auditor submitted the final report to the board of directors and upper management. Who is responsible for implementing the recommendations in this report?

    A. End users

    B. Internal auditors

    C. Security administrators

    D. Senior management

15. A security vulnerability was discovered while a system went through the accreditation process. What action should come next?

    A. Start the accreditation process over again once the issue is fixed.

    B. Restart the accreditation process from when the issue was discovered.

    C. Reimage the system and start the accreditation from the beginning.

    D. Reimage the system and start from the current point.

16. Your department was tasked with implementing Bluetooth connectivity controls to mitigate risk. Which of these *best* describes the network you will create?

    A. PAN

    B. LAN

    C. WAN

    D. WLAN

17. You are planning the site security for a new building. The network administrators would like the server room door to be secured with RFID. The security team would like to use a cipher lock. Loss of the data on these servers is high risk. What should your plan start with?

    A. A meeting to discuss security options

    B. Smartcards

    C. TFA, both cipher lock and RFID

    D. A keyed lock only

18. You are a systems analyst conducting a vulnerability assessment. Which of the following is *not* a requirement for you to know?

    A. Access controls

    B. Understanding of the systems to be evaluated

    C. Potential threats

    D. Passwords

19. You are made aware of a threat that involves a hacking group holding large amounts of information about your company. What *best* describes the threat you face from this hacking group?

    A. DoS

    B. TCO

    C. Latency

    D. Data mining

20. You are evaluating the risk for your data center. You assigned threat, vulnerability, and impact a score from 1 to 10. The data center scores are as follows: Threat: 4, Vulnerability: 2, Impact: 6. What is the risk?

    A. 12

    B. 16

    C. 48

    D. 35

21. Your customer-facing website experiences some failures. The security engineer analyzed the situation and believes it is the web application firewall. Syslog shows that the WAF was down twice, for a total of 3 hours in the past 72 hours. Which of the following is your mean time to repair (MTTR)?

    A. 2.5 hours

    B. 1.5 hours

    C. 34.5 hours

    D. 3 hours

22. Intrusions are usually detected in one of three basic ways. Which detection method can reassemble packets and look at higher-layer activity?

    A. Signature recognition

    B. Heuristic detection

    C. Anomaly detection

    D. Protocol decoding

23. What is the lookup table used to store MAC addresses on a switch called?

    A. Content addressable memory

    B. Random access memory

    C. Read-only memory

    D. Nonvolatile memory

24. If loaded into a router, which set of commands allows a network engineer to log into it if they know the correct password?

A. Router>enable

Router# configure terminal

Router(config)#line vty 0 4

Router(config-line)#password secret

B. Router>enable

Router# configure terminal

Router(config)#line vty 0 4

Router(config-line)#password secret

Router(config-line)#login

C. Router>enable

Router# configure terminal

Router(config)#line vty 0 4

Router(config-line)#password

Router(config-line-password)# secret

Router(config-line)#log in

D. Router>enable

Router# configure terminal

Router(config)#line vty 0 4

Router(config-line)#password secret

Router(config-line)#log in

25. Several payload variables can be configured in a mobile device configuration profile—you can configure each mobile device and user to which you are giving the profile. If you wanted to include a unique identifier in the profile, which of these would you choose to populate?

A. $DEVICENAME

B. $SITENAME

C. $USERNAME

D. $UDID

26. You build a web application for your new retail organization. Your developer failed to check the length of input before processing his code. What is this code susceptible to?

    A. Session management

    B. XSS

    C. Privilege escalation

    D. Buffer overflow

27. Which of the following application security threats is mitigated by the use of garbage collection?

    A. Object reuse

    B. XSS

    C. Ransomware

    D. Sandboxing

28. In a social engineering campaign, you were provided with the birthday of your victims. You invent a scenario to engage the victim using this information. What is this type of social engineering called?

    A. Pretexting

    B. Phishing

    C. Baiting

    D. Diversion

29. Your CFO received an email from a vendor requesting payment for services rendered. The CFO reached out to your team because the vendor's name is spelled with an extra vowel. What type of social engineering technique was being used?

    A. Spear phishing

    B. Water holing

    C. Pretext

    D. Bait and switch

30. Your office manager received a voicemail from a vendor wanting to confirm a delivery time and address. The delivery time is correct, but the address is not. What possibly happened?

    A. Baiting

    B. Water holing

    C. Phishing

    D. Diversion

31. As a security analyst, you conducted a security assessment that was divided into internal and external exploitation. The external activities have a time limit set by the statement of work. Which of the following methods would you attempt after the time limitation expired?

    A. Social engineering

    B. OSINT

    C. Vulnerability scan

    D. Pivoting

32. Your compliance auditor requires an inventory of all wireless devices. What is the *best* search engine to use?

    A. Shodan

    B. WiGLE

    C. Wireshark

    D. BurpSuite

33. A member of your development team was fired for harassment. The company is concerned with the security of the project and proprietary code this developer had access to. What is the *best* way to ensure the integrity of this project?

    A. Peer review

    B. Red-box test

    C. Gray-box test

    D. Black-box test

34. As a security architect, you are responsible for making all systems come together and work properly and securely. Your tester is logged into the system as a user, testing the internal mechanisms of the application. This enables an exhaustive test very similar to what an attacker might accomplish. What type of test is this?

    A. A gray box

    B. A black box

    C. A red box

    D. A clear box

35. You need a security assessment that imitates real-world attacks. What type of team should you hire to conduct this test outside of the organization that has limited or no knowledge of your company?

    A. Red team

    B. Blue team

    C. Yellow team

    D. White team

36. You are a member of the blue team for your company. This team is tasked with engaging with a red team of mock attackers. What team referees this engagement?

    A. White team

    B. Stakeholders

    C. CISO

    D. Yellow team

37. Your new CISO wants to upgrade from open source to an enterprise vulnerability management tool. Which tool satisfies your organization's need for comprehensive vulnerability management?

A. Nexpose

B. Optimi

C. Splunk

D. Security Analytics

38. Your FIM deployment solution leverages the ability to install on target systems for the most powerful analysis. The difficulty is that it needs regular updating. What term describes this use of FIM?

A. Agentless

B. Agent-based

C. Cloned

D. SaaS

39. Your organization is concerned with the security of using RFID. Several issues exist with using RFID, but which of the following is *not* an issue?

A. Sniffing

B. Tracking

C. Counterfeiting

D. Destruction

40. An employee brings you a computer to retrieve data from, but you're unable to boot it up by turning on the power button. You ask the employee if they have their files backed up, and the answer is no. What should you do to recover all the data possible?

A. Pull out the hard drive, place it in new machine, and attempt to boot up from the hard drive.

B. Use the data recovery wizard in the operating system and move files to the cloud.

C. Remove the power, battery, and then the hard drive. Connect to a new PC, boot, and access the hard drive, if possible.

D. If the machine will not boot up in its natural state, no recovery is possible.

41. You are part of a small startup nonprofit that has grown to a development stage where a security policy is necessary. Which of these do you *not* include in your security policy?

A. Purpose

B. Scope

C. Compliance

D. Procedures

42. You consider yourself to be a white-hat hacker with expertise in social engineering. Are you a good candidate for a red team black-box engagement?

A. No, the skill set is exactly the same.

B. Yes, the skill set is not the same.

C. No, the skill set needed is completely opposite.

D. Yes, the skill set is similar.

43. You conduct a physical penetration test for a jewelry store chain. The organization wants to prevent drivers from using a vehicle to smash through the front of the store and grab valuable merchandise. What type of defense do you suggest?

A. Security guards

B. Iron gate

C. Motion detector

D. Bollards

44. You test forms on a school's websites by using some odd information in a given field. Where a ZIP code is supposed be five numerical characters, you used the numerical characters 1234, in addition to the ZIP code. What type of testing did you conduct?

A. PDCA

B. Boundary

C. White hat

D. Form testing

45. You assisted your networking organization in upgrading the speed and capabilities of your wireless local area network (WLAN). Currently, everyone utilizes equipment based on 802.11g using central access points. Which of the following would enhance the speed?

A. 802.11a

B. 802.11b

C. 802.11n

D. WiMAX

46. You decide to use a Type 2 hypervisor to deploy commercial software to test for suitability, vulnerabilities, and functionality. Your CISO questions your decision to use a Type 2 hypervisor instead of a VMM. Which of these is *not* a valid explanation?

A. A virtual machine monitor (VMM) is another name for a hypervisor. A hypervisor is software that is able to virtualize the physical components of computer hardware.

B. A Type 1 hypervisor is installed on a bare-metal server, meaning that the hypervisor is its own OS. Type 2 hypervisors use a host OS that is compatible with commercial software.

C. A virtual machine (VM) is an instance of a device running on a hypervisor. It is a computing virtual environment that relies on a hypervisor to communicate with the physical hardware it is installed on.

D. A virtual machine is a term used to describe Internet-enabled streaming services or web applications that give end users the ability to activate software locally.

47. A new business was acquired by your organization. Your CISO tells you that you will oversee the project merging the two organizations. As the security manager, what do you do first?

A. Develop an interconnection policy and perform a risk analysis.

B. Deploy a golden image operating system to all end users' computers.

    C. Develop criteria and rate each firewall configuration.

    D. Implement an NIDS on all desktops and conduct security awareness training for all new employees.

48. You are an IT manager, and the software list your employees must use has grown to the point that it is mandated that you implement federated identity SSO. It needs to be an extensible markup language used to exchange provisioning requests for account creation. Which of the following is *best* for this task?

    A. SAML

    B. cURL

    C. SOAP

    D. SPML

49. New zero-day attacks are released on a regular timeline against many different technology stacks. Which of the following would be *best* for you, as a security manager, to implement to manage the risk from these attacks?

    A. List all inventory, applications, and updated network diagrams.

    B. Establish some type of emergency response hierarchy.

    C. Back up all router, firewall, server, and end-user configurations.

    D. Hold mandatory monthly risk assessment meetings.

50. You are hired by a large enterprise as a systems security consultant to evaluate and make recommendations for increasing the network security posture. It is your first meeting with the stakeholders. What is your first question?

    A. What are your business needs and the corporate assets that need to be protected?

    B. What hardware and software do you currently have, and what would work best for securing your network?

    C. What is your budget?

    D. When is your next audit, and who will be on my team to carry out this security plan?

51. In an enterprise environment, which common security services would include firewalls and enterprise-grade border routers?

    A. Access control

    B. Cryptography and encryption

    C. Boundary control

    D. Authentication and automation

52. You are exploring the best option for your organization to move from a physical data center to virtual machines hosted on bare-metal servers. Which of the following is the *best* option for that move?

    A. Type 1 hypervisor

    B. Type 2 hypervisor

    C. iPaaS

    D. IaaS

53. Your company hires a third party to provide cloud-based processing that will have several different types of virtual hosts configured for different purposes, like multiple Linux Apache web server farms for different divisions. Which of the following *best* describes this service?

   A. SaaS

   B. PaaS

   C. IaaS

   D. AaaS

54. A guest OS escapes from within VM encapsulation to interact directly with the hypervisor. If the VM becomes compromised, this can give an attacker access to all the VMs as well as the host machine. What is this scenario called?

   A. DoS

   B. VM escape

   C. VM jacking

   D. VM isolation

55. One of the concerns you have for your hypervisor environment is the flooding of network traffic to leverage a host's own resources. The availability of botnets to rent on the dark web makes it easy for attackers to carry out a campaign against specific virtual servers or applications with the goal of bringing services down. What is this type of an attack called?

   A. VM DoS

   B. VM scraping

   C. VM isolation

   D. VM migration

56. You decided to create your own company that will be a service provider integrating security services into a corporate entity with a subscription model. This will be cost effective for companies when they investigate the total cost of ownership (TCO) of cybersecurity. What business model have you just created?

   A. DaaS

   B. PaaS

   C. SECaaS

   D. IaaS

57. Your organization wants to automate the process of assigning corporate resources to employees. For example, when an HR rep enters data into the HR system for a new employee, the organization wants the HR system to reach out to various other systems like the email system to configure resources for the new employee automatically. What automated identity management solution could perform this task?

   A. SPML

   B. SOAP

   C. Active Directory

   D. SSO

58. Your organization has partnerships with various other companies that require employees of each company to access information from the others. Of course, each company has an authentication process for their employees. What identity management system would allow employees of each company to log in to their respective company and also access the needed information at the others?

   A. SSO

   B. SSL

   C. Federal Identity Management

   D. Kerberos

59. You are managing a new project to bring the OAuth framework into the organization. Which one of these statements is incorrect?

   A. OAuth gives a third-party application access to resources.

   B. OAuth is an open standard authorization framework.

   C. OAuth is designed around four roles: owner, client, resource server, and authorization server.

   D. OAuth shares password information with third-party applications.

60. You suspect that an employee is stealing company information, but you're not sure how they are removing the information from the premises. During an investigation, you find a folder with numerous pictures in it. Later, you also discover that many of these pictures were emailed to an external email account. What may you deduce from this information and want to investigate further?

   A. Someone loves photography and sharing photos via email.

   B. Information could be hidden in the photos.

   C. The recipient of the photos could be in the marketing department.

   D. You could reach out to human resources to bring this person in for a discussion and review the NDA they signed.

61. Your end users are using mobile devices to access confidential information on the corporate network. You need to ensure the information is kept secure as it is transmitted to these mobile devices. Encryption is a requirement. Of the following options, which one *best* describes a major concern with implementing encryption on mobile devices?

   A. Mobile devices have more processing power than other computing devices.

   B. Mobile devices typically have less processing power than other computing devices.

   C. Increased complexities.

   D. Obfuscation.

62. You must decide what to do to formulate an efficient and effective security policy that includes the network. What type of an assessment should you do?

   A. Risk assessment

   B. Penetration test

   C. Compliance audit

   D. Black-box testing

63. You have decided that an IPSec VPN is not a good fit for your organization. Employees need access only to specific applications, not the entire network. What VPN option would work *best* in this situation?

   A. SSH

   B. SSL

   C. IKE

   D. RDP

64. Your SMB organization is exploring a tool that combines VoIP, video, chat, and email together in one messaging system. What type of tool is this called?

   A. Cloud computing

   B. Unified communications

   C. Global transformation

   D. Competitive collaboration

65. What is the *best* security practice for keeping your collaborative software updated with patches and bug fixes as well as knowing how those updates will impact the system?

   A. Patch management

   B. Vulnerability management

   C. Encryption

   D. Security policy and procedures

66. The art of having people divulge sensitive information about the organization or about themselves by masquerading as a valid identity in your collaboration platform is known as which of the following?

   A. Dumpster diving

   B. Phishing

   C. Social engineering

   D. Active reconnaissance

67. You are choosing a collaboration tool to be used across the finance department. For evaluation, which of the following questions is *not* as important as the others?

   A. How established is the solution?

   B. What support is required to roll out the solution?

   C. Can we change the brand logo and color scheme?

   D. What training and best practices can you offer to avoid issues in the future?

68. You have completed the SDLC's accreditation process for a system your organization is going to deploy globally. Management has approved the system. What phase in SDLC comes next?

   A. Documentation

   B. Acceptance

   C. Accreditation

   D. Implementation

69. Your organization has a policy that passwords must be at least 12 characters long; include a combination of upper and lowercase letters, numbers, and special characters; and be changed every 30 days. Which of the following solutions will enforce this policy organizationwide?

    A. Active Directory GPO

    B. LDAP

    C. RADIUS

    D. DIAMETER

70. To enter your facility, a guest must sign in and present a picture ID. A security guard will check both for accuracy, and if both match, the guest is allowed to entry into the building as long as they are escorted by a sponsor. What has the security guard performed?

    A. Identity proofing

    B. Identity authentication

    C. Identity accounting

    D. Identity confidentiality

71. Phishing is a successful way to initiate a security breach. One of the collaboration-based attacks your company suffered last quarter was phishing using malicious URLs via an instant messaging tool. Which of the following is why this attack is so successful?

    A. Your guard was down, you were worried about deadlines, and you trusted those people.

    B. You logged into the collaborative tools with credentials.

    C. Phishing is only used for emails.

    D. Malicious files or URLs are not blocked automatically in IMs.

72. You are evaluating remote desktop software that enable help-desk personnel to remotely access a user's computer for troubleshooting purposes. For ease of use, you want the product to be browser based. While evaluating a product, you notice a padlock next to the URL in the browser. What does the padlock indicate?

    A. You are connected using HTTP.

    B. You are connected using SSH.

    C. You are connected using TLS.

    D. You are connected using TPM.

73. You are a network engineer and need to access network equipment on the corporate LAN remotely. The solution to provide this function must include a secure login per user that is easily managed. Tracking login activity is also important. Which of the following is the *best* solution?

    A. Common passwords should be set on each network device.

    B. A common username and password should be set on each network device.

    C. Unique usernames and passwords should be set on each network device.

    D. Use a RADIUS solution and have each network device configured to use it.

74. You are evaluating a remote desktop solution that is browser based. While performing the evaluation, you discover that the latest version of SSL is used to encrypt data. Which statement is true about this connection?

    A. The connection is using SSL, and it is secure.

    B. The latest version of SSL is version 1.96.

    C. SSL is obsolete. TLS should be used instead.

    D. TLS is obsolete. SSL is the best solution.

75. You found that an attacker compromised a web conferencing server utilizing a known vulnerability of the software. Which option should be performed to prevent this intrusion?

    A. Install a firewall in front of the server.

    B. Keep the web conferencing software patches up-to-date.

    C. Install AV on the web conferencing server.

    D. Ensure HTTPS is always used.

76. You have a user, Charles, who wants to conduct videoconferences from his computer. He finds a free program that does what he wants and downloads it. The program was published for only a few months. Unfortunately, the free program includes malware and infects his system and others. What technology could have prevented this situation from occurring?

    A. Redlisting

    B. Blacklisting

    C. Graylisting

    D. Whitelisting

77. Your CISO is concerned that employees are posting confidential information on social media. Which of the following options *best* addresses this issue?

    A. Block social media sites from corporate resources.

    B. Train employees on the importance of not divulging company information on social media.

    C. Forbid employees from having social media accounts.

    D. Create a corporate policy outlining the requirement not to divulge corporate information on social media sites and the consequences of doing so.

78. Your best practices are outlined in the compliance requirements of Payment Card Industry Data Security Standard (PCI DSS). This standard specifies the digital framework for what type of organization?

    A. Any organization, regardless of size or number of transactions that stores any cardholder data

    B. The financial industry, excluding trading companies

    C. Only publicly traded mortgage companies and banks

    D. Retail organizations that have more than 30,000 transactions a month

79. As a security analyst for a large retail organization, you research best practices for PCI compliance levels. How do you know to what level your organization must build the security framework?

    A. Transaction volume for 6 months

    B. Transaction volume for 12 months

    C. Financial total for 6 months

    D. Financial total for 12 months

80. New security technology is necessary because data thieves found another way of stealing your company's information. The inadequacy of usernames and passwords is well known. Which of these is a new and more secure form of authentication to research?

    A. Hardware authentication

    B. Rule-based access control

    C. Vulnerability management

    D. Incident detection

81. You examine activity in a data center on the corporate network. There is nonuser behavior that is malicious and suspicious. What type of model would you use to determine your reaction?

    A. COBIT

    B. Advanced threats

    C. Machine learning

    D. GDPR

82. Your organization migrated to the cloud to host your traditional on-premises IT. Which on-premises security technique should you *not* research and adopt in the cloud?

    A. Virtual firewalls

    B. Virtual IDS and IPS

    C. Virtual security hardware

    D. Virtual physical security

83. You and your organization are performing an annual threat-modeling exercise. You look for potential threats coming from physical or digital vulnerabilities. Using the most popular Microsoft IT threat-modeling methodology, you try to find threats that align to your product. What is this methodology called?

    A. STRIDE

    B. PASTA

    C. TRIKE

    D. VAST

84. You have mission-critical software running on a server in your data center with a known security flaw. The software vendor does not have a patch in place to fix the problem, and there is potential attacker exploitation. What is this called?

    A. No-day vulnerability

    B. Zero-day vulnerability

    C. Patch vulnerability

    D. Java vulnerability

85. Your security manager petitioned management to disallow social media account access on company-issued property. Upper management feels that giving up social media is not a reasonable option. You were tasked with taking steps to protect your company against common social media threats. Which one of these is a big risk to your company?

    A. Unattended social media accounts

    B. Strict privacy settings

    C. Social media policy

    D. Audits

86. You believe you successfully locked down your company's social media accounts. While doing more research, you find another malicious attack vector regarding social media. Which of these could enable an attacker to gain access to your social media account through app vulnerabilities?

    A. Imposter accounts

    B. Third-party apps

    C. Privacy settings

    D. Authentication

87. You have a team of people working on social media messaging and customer service. While you may focus on threats coming from outside the organization, research has shown that employees are more likely to cause cybersecurity incidents. What is your first line of defense?

    A. Limit the number of people who can post on your company's social media accounts.

    B. Share the individual login information for social network accounts with only marketing personnel.

    C. When someone leaves the organization, disable their social media access.

    D. Create brand guidelines that explain how to talk about your company on social media.

88. Your business is using social media and created a social media policy. These guidelines outline how your employees will use social media responsibly and protect you from security threats and legal trouble. Which of the following would *not* be included in your social media policy?

    A. Guidelines on brand and copyright

    B. Rules regarding confidentiality and personal social media use and who to notify if a concern arises

    C. Guidelines on password creation and rotation

    D. Latest threats on social media

89. You were tasked with performing a quarterly audit on your social media accounts. Social media security threats are constantly changing. Attackers are coming up with new strategies, so a regular audit should keep you ahead of an attacker. Which of the following is *most* important and should be included in your regular audit?

    A. Privacy settings, access, and publishing privileges

    B. All network attack vectors and access management

    C. Social network trending of competitors

    D. All mentions of your company on the Internet

90. Your manufacturing company uses sensor data to detect production processes that malfunctioned. You are concerned that an attacker could undermine the quality of your big data analysis by fabricating data. What would this vulnerability revolve around?

    A. Fake data

    B. Fraud detection

    C. Alarming trends

    D. Wrong quality

Chapter

6

Practice Test 2

1. You are tasked with creating a security plan for your point-of-sale systems. What is the *best* methodology when you begin architecting?

    A. Outside-in

    B. Assets-out

    C. No write-up

    D. No write-down

2. Which of the following *best* describes how a frame is forwarded through a switch?

    A. The destination MAC address of an incoming frame and the CAM table are used to find the destination port out of which the frame is to be forwarded.

    B. All frames entering a switch are forwarded out of all ports except the port it originated from.

    C. All frames entering a switch are forwarded out of all ports, including the port it originated from.

    D. The destination IP address of an incoming frame and the CAM table are used to find the destination port where the frame is to be forwarded out.

3. What address type does a switch use to forward frames?

    A. IP address

    B. Frame address

    C. TCP/IP address

    D. MAC address

4. Which is an example of a routable protocol and a routing protocol?

    A. Frames and OSPF

    B. Frames and RIP

    C. IP and OSPF

    D. Segments and RIP

5. The firewall administrator implemented the following rules. Which statement is true concerning these rules?

Rule #	Rule	Protocol	Source	Destination	Port
1	Permit	IP	10.1.2.25	10.1.0.224	80
2	Permit	TCP	10.2.45.123	10.1.0.235	23
3	Deny	TCP	Any	10.1.0.130	22
4	Deny	TCP	10.2.45.123	10.1.0.235	23
5	Deny	IP	Any	Any	Any

A. TCP traffic from source IP 10.2.45.123 will be allowed to destination IP 10.1.0.235 port 23 because rule 2 will be performed.

B. TCP traffic from source IP 10.2.45.123 will not be allowed to destination IP 10.1.0.235 port 23 because rule 4 will be performed.

C. TCP traffic from source IP 10.2.45.123 will be allowed to destination IP 10.1.0.235 port 23 because rule 5 will be performed.

D. TCP traffic from source IP 10.2.45.123 will not be allowed to destination IP 10.1.0.235 port 23 because of the implicit deny at the end of the firewall list.

6. You set the following command on a switch port, and a host sends frames to it. Assuming defaults for all other settings, which of the following statements is correct?

```
Switch(config-if)#switchport port-security mac-address 00:0E:08:34:7C:9B
```

A. When a frame enters the port with a source MAC address other than 00:0E:08:34:7C:9B, the port will be placed in restricted mode.

B. Nothing. The command format is incorrect.

C. Enables only frames without source MAC address 00:0E:08:34:7C:9B into the port.

D. Enables only frames with source MAC address 00:0E:08:34:7C:9B into the port.

7. Understanding normal traffic patterns for your organization can help identify which of the following?

A. Malware

B. DDoS attack

C. Ransomware

D. Spoofing attack

8. Your CISO wants to put in place a technique that helps mitigate a DDoS attack, should one be launched against the company. The CISO tasks you with identifying a technique that would drop malicious DDoS traffic destined for an IP address, or a range of IP addresses, under attack. What technique performs this task?

A. Remotely triggered black hole

B. Transport security

C. Trunking security

D. Port security

9. Your IT group decided to do limited filtering of known malicious traffic entering the border router from the Internet. Which traffic with the following source IP addresses should *not* be filtered inbound from the Internet?

A. 127.0.0.0/8

B. RFC 1918 addresses

C. 172.32.0.0/16

D. 0.0.0.0/8

10. As a security analyst, you analyzed suspicious traffic flowing from a host on your network. After further examination, it appears that the data consists of website addresses, items downloaded, emails sent and received, and other data. You suspect malicious software is on the host. You want to install a product on the host to discover and remove the expected software. Which of the following products will likely discover the program performing this malicious activity?

   A. Anti-adware

   B. Antivirus

   C. Antispyware

   D. Antimalware

11. Your organization has a problem with users downloading programs from untrusted Internet sites. Some of these programs included malware that has infected the systems. Your CISO wants to stop users from doing this. What technique permits only approved programs to be downloaded to an end user's system?

   A. Blacklisting

   B. Pinklisting

   C. Whitelisting

   D. Graylisting

12. To curtail end-user visits to known malicious websites, the security team decided to block users from accessing them. Which of the following solutions performs this task?

   A. Pinklisting

   B. Graylisting

   C. Whitelisting

   D. Blacklisting

13. If a packet received by a router is examined by an ACL and no statement in the ACL matches the packet, what happens to the packet?

   A. The packet is dropped.

   B. The packet is forwarded.

   C. The packet is sent to another queue for further examination.

   D. The packet is returned to the sender.

14. A network engineer wants to prevent people outside of the corporate network from pinging systems within the network but to allow all other traffic. The router's Ethernet 0 interface is connected to the Internet. Which ACL prevents this type of traffic?

   A.

```
!
interface ethernet0
ip access-group 101 in
!
```

```
access-list 101 deny icmp any any
access-list 101 permit ip any any
```

B.

```
!
interface ethernet0
ip access-group 1 in
!
access-list 1 deny icmp any any
access-list 1 permit ip any any
```

C.

```
!
interface ethernet0
ip access-group 101 in
!
access-list 101 permit ip any any
access-list 101 deny icmp any any
```

D.

```
!
interface ethernet0
ip access-group 1 in
!
access-list 1 permit ip any any
access-list 1 deny icmp any any
```

15. As a security professional, you were asked to provide tips on how to best protect Bluetooth-enabled devices. Of the following answers, which is *not* a recommended way to protect your device?

    A. Turn Bluetooth off when not needed

    B. Ensure Bluetooth is in hidden mode

    C. Turn Bluetooth pairing off unless needed

    D. Ensure Wi-Fi is off when not needed

16. You are explaining the differences between various IEEE standards to a colleague. The colleague asks which IEEE standard concerns Wi-Fi. Which IEEE standard is the umbrella standard for Wi-Fi networks?

    A. 802.11

    B. 802.2

    C. 802.3

    D. 802.5

17. As a mobile application management administrator, you want to set specific policy elements to be applied to your company's mobile devices. You do not want to change the underlying application. Which of the following should you implement?

    A. Sandboxing

    B. App wrapping

    C. Risk analysis

    D. USB OTG

18. You want to use a USB drive with your phone to read data from the USB device without a PC. What type of cable do you need?

    A. USB to USB

    B. Paraflex Matrix

    C. MicroUSB to C

    D. USB OTG

19. You want to evaluate the most secure authentication method on a mobile device, primarily your phone. Authentication includes many options and could possibly use multiple methods for secure access. Which of the following is *not* something you know?

    A. Password

    B. Pattern lock

    C. Fingerprint

    D. PIN

20. Your new program using biometrics for authentication is going well. Biometrics are hard to fake and increase convenience. Which of these is *not* an advantage of using biometrics for authentication?

    A. Servers require less database memory.

    B. Ease of use.

    C. Stable and enduring with little variation.

    D. Technical accuracy; partial capture of data.

21. As a security analyst, you received a phone call from your CFO. The CFO received the same email three times this week asking for approval of a bank transfer. You investigate the email and find it is not legitimate. What type of attack is this?

    A. Phishing

    B. Introspection

    C. Ransomware

    D. Buffer overflow

22. You want to find a way for your shop's new mobile app to notify people when there is a sale without the user opening the application. What do you need to create?

    A. Push notification

    B. Text message

    C. Email

    D. SMS

23. You are investigating a method to send information over radio waves that is fast and secure while sending data, primarily taking payments. What is the *best* option in this list?

    A. Bluetooth

    B. Infrared

    C. RFID

    D. NFC

24. Your risk audit for mobile devices shows the best way to deal with data lost in a breach is coverage from financial losses. Which of the following is the *best* choice to accomplish this?

    A. Cyber liability insurance

    B. Risk acceptance

    C. Risk avoidance

    D. Encryption

25. You attempt to fix a problem with a workstation and discover that the end user installed unauthorized software. The workstation now conflicts with security policy. You uninstall the software and make sure the system is compliant. What do you do next?

    A. Report the user to human resources.

    B. If the user is a direct report, document the problem and confiscate all the installation media.

    C. Have the end user request the software be placed on the approved list.

    D. Give the end user a list of all approved software.

26. Your role in developing secure software requires that you follow a methodology for defense in depth called SD3. What type of strategy is this?

    A. Secure by design, default, and deployment.

    B. Secure review code three times.

    C. An outside SD3 audit as recommended by NIST.

    D. No methodology is called SD3.

27. A subset of programmers in your organization tested the beta of your application. During the testing phase, you asked that they install the software by selecting optional components during the setup procedure. For any changes they want to make in the future, they will need to rerun the installation process. What is this called?

    A. Secure by design

    B. Secure by default

    C. Secure by deployment

    D. Secure by download

28. In the event of application failure or error, a system should be set in place so that your end users have a general error indicator but that the events are logged for future reference. What is this called in production?

    A. Secure by design

    B. Secure by default

    C. Secure in deployment

    D. Secure in download

29. You are a penetration tester, searching for unlinked content on a web server. What type of an attack is this?

    A. CSRF

    B. Forced browsing

    C. SQLi

    D. Click-jacking

30. You implement a CAPTCHA system on your corporate web server to prevent spam. Which of the following other attacks are most likely to be prevented?

    A. XSRF

    B. XSS

    C. Two-factor authentication

    D. XMLi

31. Your company's HR department alerted IT that an end user is complaining of a suspicious web page on the intranet. The user said they clicked a button to download software updates, and instead, it opened their personal bank account homepage. What type of attack was most likely perpetrated against your organization?

    A. CSRF

    B. Phishing

    C. Social engineering

    D. Click-jacking

32. Your penetration test of several SQL databases returned the following:
ERROR: unterminated quoted string at or near " .'.' ". What should you call this in your report?

    A. Improper error handling

    B. Proper error handling

    C. Vulnerability

    D. XSS

33. You conduct a privacy audit for your organization and are concerned about possible violations. Which of the following is most concerning?

A. FTP

B. VPN

C. Rogue access points

D. Cookies

34. The performance on the server running SQL is degrading and occasionally fails. You ran diagnostics, and despite having adequate RAM, your OS is not correctly managing the resources. What is most likely happening?

A. Memory leak

B. Dysfunctional dependency

C. SQLi

D. Virus

35. Which of these helps prevent accidental data loss by making sure a class defines the data it needs?

A. Modules

B. Classes

C. Segmentation

D. Encapsulation

36. Your database administrator (DBA) reached out to you because the relational database that the security department uses has modified data, so secret projects are being referred to by an identification number instead of a name. What is the security control implemented?

A. Encryption

B. Randomization

C. Pseudonymization

D. Tokenization

37. Your web application is going through a user experience (UX) review. The application grew to the point that issues have developed because of the complexity of the text fields, radio buttons, and other input fields impacted by the state of other text fields and radio buttons. What type of issue are you experiencing?

A. State management

B. Redundant libraries

C. Request frameworks

D. Centralized data store

38. You have JavaScript installed as the foundation of most of your web applications because it is fast and interactive. You attempt to harden systems found with JavaScript vulnerabilities. Which of the following are the most commonly exploited JavaScript attacks?

    A. Click-jacking

    B. DNS and ARP

    C. XSS and CSRF

    D. SQLi and XMLi

39. Your company undergoes a three-year cycle of tech refreshes on mobile devices and a five-year cycle on servers and workstations. You look at the newest version operating systems and try to decide which operating system is the safest with the most functionality for your mission-critical assets. What do you do first?

    A. Build a threat model.

    B. Conduct developer interviews.

    C. Write a report.

    D. Triage results.

40. One of your teammates is struggling with understanding why a program is not responding the way she expects when it runs. What would you suggest she try next to troubleshoot?

    A. Kernel dumping

    B. Check internal data flow

    C. Runtime debugging

    D. Automation

41. As a network security analyst, you notice web traffic increasing from your organization to a specific shopping site. What social engineering attack can take advantage of this type of traffic?

    A. Tailgating

    B. Baiting

    C. Phishing

    D. Watering hole

42. As part of your security audit, your CISO suggested leaving an infected USB in the break-room with "wedding pics" written on it. By the time you drop the USB next to the refrigerator in the breakroom and make it back to your desk, someone has found the USB and plugged it in, and the malicious file left on the USB has been installed. What is this type of social engineering technique called?

    A. Mantrap

    B. Quid pro quo

    C. Watering hole

    D. Baiting

43. IT support called you and told you to disable your antivirus software because they have a patch that needs to run on your machine to keep you safe. What social engineering technique did this attacker use?

  A. Tailgating

  B. Honeytrap

  C. Quid pro quo

  D. Rogue access point

44. You work for a security organization that performs penetration tests for large corporations. A corporation asks for a black-box test. You begin the process of passive reconnaissance. What should you access first?

  A. DNS

  B. Nmap

  C. Netcat

  D. Social media

45. Your company is concerned about Internet-facing servers. They hired a security organization to conduct a black-box test of www.yourcompany.edu to make sure it is secure. Which of the following commands helps the tester determine which servers are externally facing before they take any additional actions?

  A. Whois

  B. WhatIs

  C. SMTP

  D. IPConfig

46. You are a network security administrator on a network of more than 50,000 nodes. In the past week, your end users have complained that specific pages on the Internet are not loading. You test the pages from your tablet with cellular service and access them just fine. What do you expect to find in the router logs after you have verified firewall rules?

  A. Route poisoning

  B. Device fingerprinting

  C. Gray-box testing

  D. PKI

47. You are a security analyst and were tasked by your company with finding all external Internet-connected devices, webcams, routers, servers, and IoT devices on your corporate network. What is the *best* search engine to use to accomplish this task in the least amount of time?

  A. Yahoo

  B. Shodan

  C. Google

  D. Bing

48. A company must comply with a new HIPAA regulation that requires the company to determine whether an external attacker is able to gain access to systems from outside the network perimeter. What should the company do to meet this new regulation?

   A. Code review

   B. Black-box penetration test

   C. Inventory of hardware and software

   D. Vulnerability scan

49. Your new CTO is concerned that the IT staff is not able to secure and remediate new vulnerabilities found in the latest financial software adopted by the company. The CTO is focused on reliability and performance of the cloud software. Which of the following is the *best* way to meet the CTO's testing requirements?

   A. A small firm does a black-box test.

   B. A large firm does a white-box test.

   C. An internal team does a black-box test.

   D. An internal team does a white-box test.

50. You were informed of an upcoming external PCI DSS audit and need to find a way to remediate thousands of vulnerabilities on production servers that will cause you to fail the audit. You want to prioritize which vulnerability is the most dangerous in your environment, not just the rating by CVSS. What type of test is *best* to conduct prioritizing vulnerability remediation?

   A. Black box

   B. Gray box

   C. White box

   D. Clear box

51. One of your internal security tests finds it is not detecting the newest security threats. Management wants you to investigate what type of IDS is the best tool to implement. Which of the following is your suggestion?

   A. Protocol based

   B. Hash based

   C. Pattern matching

   D. Anomaly detection

52. You remove hard drives from old servers, workstations, and copy machines. Your security policy requires that no sensitive data remains on those drives. It is not in the budget to replace the drives, so you must be able to use them again. What type of tool do you use to accomplish this task?

   A. DeFraggler

   B. KillDisk

   C. Nmap

   D. OS .iso

53. One of your reports is on a server that you usually access by `ftp.myserver.com`. You are unable to download it from that address, but you can access the file server by the IP address 192.168.1.2. What tool do you check first?

    A. ARP cache

    B. DHCP server

    C. FTP server

    D. DNS server

54. Your company acquired a new company. As the lead security administrator, you want to start a vulnerability scan against a new network that joined your domain. You want to scan this new network from the outside looking in. What type of scan is this called?

    A. Authenticated

    B. Unauthenticated

    C. Secured

    D. Accessible

55. You are working on the maturity of your vulnerability management processes. You established network vulnerability testing but are concerned about the internal applications and web forms that are on the intranet. What type of tool should you use to scan for Common Weakness Enumerations (CWEs)?

    A. Application scanner

    B. Fuzzer

    C. Attack scanners

    D. CIS scanners

56. Your company contracts a security engineering consultant to perform a black-box penetration test of the client-facing web portal. Which of the following is the most appropriate?

    A. Increase protocol analyzation against the site to see if ports are being replayed from the browser.

    B. Scan the site with a port scanner to identify vulnerable services that are running on the web application server.

    C. Create network enumeration tools to see where the server is residing.

    D. Scan the site with an HTTP interceptor to identify areas for code injection.

57. Your web application designers handed the program over to your department for a Q&A review. Which of these tools is *best* to find any flaws like SQLi or CSS in the web application requiring approval?

    A. Nessus

    B. LogRhythm

    C. Acunetix WVS

    D. Autopsy

58. Your pentester is looking for an infrastructure to add their own custom tools to. You prefer free software for this purpose. What is the top choice?

    A. Meterpreter

    B. Exploitation

    C. Metasploit

    D. BurpSuite

59. Most modern attacks surprisingly begin with nontechnical techniques. You want to use an open source tool to mine for information about your organization used to conduct a targeted phishing campaign. Which of these tools helps you create a real-world link between people, websites, and your company?

    A. NIST

    B. Wireshark

    C. Maltego

    D. Nmap

60. You downloaded a driver to the C: drive for a component you must install on a Linux machine. The file is called `printer_driver.dll`. One of the first things to do is verify that the file was not corrupted during download. What is the command you used in CLI to ensure this file has *not* been tampered with using the 128-bit MD5 algorithm?

    A. `md5_C:printer_driver.dll`

    B. `md5 "C:\printer_driver.dll"`

    C. `md5 printer_driver`

    D. `cd/ "printerdriver.dll" md5 -n`

61. You view a command prompt and need to find if there is connectivity between you and another machine on the network. What command do you run?

    A. `arp`

    B. `vnstat`

    C. `ipconfig`

    D. `ping`

62. You have a command prompt at a terminal window and need to find the path an IP packet is taking through the network. What command do you issue?

    A. `fms`

    B. `ipconfig`

    C. `traceroute`

    D. `ping`

63. Your business has PCI requirements that includes standards and regulations. Those standards and regulations state that data must be monitored and managed to ensure its integrity. What software will you institute?

A. SOX

B. FIM

C. IaaS

D. Cloud

64. Your organization is undergoing a physical penetration test. Which of these tools is most likely in the tester's toolkit?

A. Buttset

B. Toner probe

C. Amp set

D. Lock picks

65. Your facility was broken into, but the cameras did not have sufficient light to capture anything of substance. Your manager tasks you with exchanging the cameras with ones that are a better choice for night recording. What type of camera do you choose?

A. IDR

B. IR

C. CDR

D. Dome

66. Your division must maintain expensive equipment that ranges in price from several hundred dollars to several thousand dollars. You have multiple facilities monitoring these tools. You must be able to track them to decrease replacement costs and increase employee productivity. What do you choose?

A. RFID tags

B. QR codes

C. Bar codes

D. ISBNs

67. RFID gained popularity in your organization because of low maintenance cost. You consider expanding the use of RFID, but your security analyst warns that the backend database is vulnerable. What could be the biggest worry of your analyst?

A. Virus attack

B. IR

C. Lockpicking

D. Credentials

68. Your CFO accidentally deleted an important folder from their computer. They brought their system to you to attempt data recovery. You know the files are still on the drive, but there is no reference to them in the directory structure. What should you do first?

   A. Do not save any documents or files.

   B. Turn off the computer.

   C. Restart the computer.

   D. Install a new program to rescue the files.

69. Your department is examining the CIA triad and how it applies to storage. You want to maintain confidentiality, integrity, and availability for all authorized users. At the same time, you are asked to focus on strong enough systems so that attackers expend more work (i.e., work factor) than the data is worth. What does this hinge on?

   A. Cost and value of data

   B. Cost and value of privacy

   C. Cost and value of encryption

   D. Cost and value of potential breach

70. Your CISO tasks you with creating an addendum to the security policies and procedures as it relates to security at rest. Which of these is *not* a concern to address in your high-level security policy and more granular procedures?

   A. Data and cyberattack growth

   B. Cost of breaches and increased data value

   C. Regulation and business continuity

   D. Network topology and subnets

71. Your main SCSI storage is embedded with an array controller, and redundancy is managed by hardware-level RAID. What is this type of storage called?

   A. SAN

   B. NAS

   C. DAS

   D. RAS

72. You work for an organization that subscribes to 99.99 percent network uptime. You must find a way to decrease downtime in case of an internal DAS hardware failure, which has happened twice in the past six months. What solution do you deploy?

   A. USB

   B. SSD

   C. SAN

   D. DASv2

73. Your security team needs to stay up-to-date and worked hard to develop a training program. They were taught to identify and report the early warning stages of an attack campaign. Which of these is *not* an indicator of a compromise?

    A. Slow Internet and unexplained system reboots

    B. Multiple failed logins and locked-out accounts

    C. Anomalies in network traffic, especially after hours

    D. Patch management

74. Your organization was just informed by a three-letter agency that your organization's POS systems were compromised. You avoided panicking and focused on gathering your incident team and assigning roles. Which role is *not* as important in a data breach incident response team immediately after a breach?

    A. Legal

    B. Public relations

    C. Technical

    D. Sales

75. Your hunt team wants to prove compliance at a glance. You want them to have a strong security posture, but you need some help mapping regulations. What should they map regulations to in order to show compliance?

    A. Security metrics

    B. Security standards

    C. Security threats

    D. Threat intelligence

76. Your security policy was rules based until now, requiring specific conditions matching either good or bad events. While important, you need these rules to be more agile based on patterns. Which of the following *best* describes that type of correlation?

    A. Threat intelligence

    B. Heuristics

    C. Complexity

    D. Categorical

77. You receive a phone call from one of your employees because their machine has BSOD. What happens when a Windows machine blue-screens?

    A. Collects all operating system data

    B. Machine just needs a reboot

    C. Creates a `tcpdump`

    D. Creates a crash dump

78. The impact of an incident or breach can be measured in several different levels. Which of the following is *not* included in the various levels?

    A. Critical

    B. High

    C. Low

    D. Junior

79. Your incident response team attempts to estimate the cost of a breach. This estimate is based on if the data records were customer and employee or employee only. Another factor is the scope of the breach, such as how many people were affected. Now that you know who and how much, what else do you need to know?

    A. When

    B. Where

    C. What

    D. How long

80. A hard disk fails in a mission-critical server, and there is no redundancy. Many options exist when it comes to recovering data from a hard disk failure. Sometimes the corrective action has the potential to result in rendering the data unrecoverable. What is the first rule of recovering data?

    A. Install a recovery tool.

    B. Open the drive to examine the platters.

    C. Minimize access to the drive.

    D. Attempt to boot the drive in another machine.

81. The after-action report (AAR) received from the incident response team contains lessons learned. It states that security policies were not sufficient when it comes to dealing with the current level of vulnerabilities found in the enterprise environment and the timeline allotted for patching. Attackers had a large window of time to take advantage of unpatched software. What should the security department do based on the AAR and lessons learned?

    A. Investigate the current patch management system and look for ways to improve or automate.

    B. There is no way to improve an already existing patch management program.

    C. Hire more IT analysts.

    D. Hire a third-party agency to conduct a review of the AAR and make suggestions of software to eliminate all vulnerabilities.

82. Your organization currently uses FTP to transfer files, and you are tasked with upgrading a file transfer solution that answers the need for both integrity as well as confidentiality. Which of the following is true about the current state of business?

    A. Port 20 used for transfer and port 21 used for control

    B. Port 20 used for control and port 21 used for transfer

    C. Port 20 used by the client and port 21 used by the server

    D. Port 20 used for integrity and port 21 used for confidentiality

83. You are the new CISO for a software organization revising security best practices. Which of these statements regarding best practices is the most accurate?

    A. They should be endorsed by end users.

    B. They should be extremely specific.

    C. They should by extremely general.

    D. They should be as short as possible.

84. A virtual machine hosted on an ESX server in your data center contains confidential data that is no longer needed by your company. You recommend shutting down the virtual machine and deleting the VM disk (VMDK) from the host. What is the security risk?

    A. Data retention

    B. Data encryption

    C. Data protection

    D. Data remanence

85. Your organization has grown and needs to hire someone for information management. This role is responsible for security marking and labeling. Which of the following *best* describes the role's responsibility?

    A. Security marking/labeling is the process of using internal data structure from within information systems to determine criticality.

    B. Security labeling is more important than security marking and is required for all information, including marketing information released to the general public.

    C. Security marking and security labeling are the same.

    D. Security marking and labeling will reflect compliance, requirements, applicable laws, directives, policies, and standards.

86. As a security architect of a medical complex, you are concerned that attackers can steal data from highly secure systems. You are trying to prepare for a system attack that exfiltrates data through existing channels in small increments. What are you trying to prevent?

    A. Encryption

    B. Backdoors

    C. Covert channels

    D. Viruses

87. A third-party software vendor disclosed that a backdoor was left in a product by mistake. What is this called?

    A. A security patch

    B. A rootkit

C. A virus

D. A maintenance hook

88. You are building a decentralized privilege management solution for your financial organization with user accounts that are defined on each system rather than a centralized server. Which of these *best* describes this?

A. A workgroup

B. RADIUS/DIAMETER

C. Client/server

D. Terminal services

89. The National Institute of Standards and Technology (NIST) recommends the physical destruction of data storage media at what stage of media life?

A. Initial

B. Backups

C. Final

D. Retention

90. You work for a luxury car manufacturer. Your CEO wants to use machine learning and artificial intelligence to build models of customer-buying patterns and to use those models to make future predictions for a competitive lead. Machine learning engines learn for themselves and constantly evolve. Optimization is hard and nearly impossible to trace how decisions are made. You risk ending up with a car that no one wants. What is this called?

A. Transparency

B. Computational power

C. Massive datasets

D. Model drift

Appendix

Answers to Review Questions

Chapter 1: Security Architecture

1. **A.** An incident is an event that could lead to loss of, or disruption to, an organization's operation, services, or functions. Incident management is a term describing the activities of an organization to identify, correct, and analyze to prevent a future occurrence. Forensics are performed to find artifacts in an environment. Mandatory vacations and job rotation are administrative controls.

2. **A.** RAID 1 is for redundancy; the data's level of sensitivity is classified based on importance, which is correlated to security measures and who has access, and load balancers determine which server in a pool is available and route requests to that server. The other answers all pertain to either confidentiality or integrity, not availability.

3. **C.** An intrusion detection system (IDS) is used to detect against intrusion from the outside untrusted network into an internal trusted network. It can be deployed to watch behind the firewall for traffic that was successful in circumventing the firewall, as well as for activity originating from inside the trusted network. A RAS (remote access service) is a combination of hardware and software to enable remote access tools connecting a client to a host computer. A private branch exchange (PBX) is a private telephone network used in a company. DDT is a modern synthetic insecticide originally used to combat malaria.

4. **A.** You want to protect your endpoints from malware, viruses, and spyware. A host-based firewall will prevent malicious traffic, where the IDS will only report there is an intrusion. All two-factor authentication (TFA) is multifactor authentication (MFA), but not all MFA is TFA. Multifactor authentication grants a user access after presenting several separate pieces of evidence that belong to different categories (including something you are, something you know, and something you have). TFA is two pieces of evidence.

5. **B.** A network-based intrusion detection system (NIDS) monitors traffic traversing the network and can alert based on observing attacks and intrusions. The alerts can come in various forms, including email and text messages. HIDSs (host-based intrusion detection systems) and HIPS/NIPS are intrusion prevention systems.

6. **A.** A host-based intrusion prevention system (HIPS) is an intrusion prevention system used to detect intrusions on a host system like a server and stop those intrusions from compromising a system. A HIPS can also alert personnel of the intrusion detected. NIPSs are network-based, and HIDSs/NIDSs are detection only and can be configured to alert but not actually stop anything.

7. **B.** Wireless intrusion detection system (WIDS) solutions can locate and identify Wi-Fi devices as well as Bluetooth, Bluetooth Lower Energy, and devices emitting cellular signals. This means a WIDS can discover a cell phone even when the Wi-Fi and Bluetooth are not active. Network-based IDSs and IPSs are looking for malicious network-based activities. A firewall is used to filter content flowing through the unit.

8. **A.** Data loss prevention (DLP) systems, also called data loss protection systems, are designed to examine data as it moves off the host system looking for unauthorized transfers. Examples

of unauthorized transfers are moving data to a cloud provider, via USB, and sending via email. Network-based IDSs and IPSs are looking for malicious network-based activities. A firewall is used to filter content flowing through the unit.

9. A. Some more advanced FIM solutions are a part of a host-based intrusion detection system (HIDS). As a general rule, they can detect threats in other areas, not just files. An NIDS is network intrusion detection, and change management is an administrative control. ADVFIM is made up.

10. D. Encrypted packets are not processed by most intrusion detection devices. Other potential issues with NIDSs are high-speed network data overload, tuning difficulties, and signature development lag time.

11. D. A security information and event management (SIEM) system is used to collect logs from various devices on a network and to analyze those logs, looking for security issues. Because a SIEM can review logs from various devices, it gets a holistic view of actions going on over the network, as opposed to a single appliance analyzing only traffic flowing through it. A syslog server is a place to collect and monitor network devices. NIPSs and WIPSs are network and wireless intrusion protection systems that examine traffic flows to detect and prevent vulnerability exploits.

12. D. A web application firewall (WAF) is used to inspect OSI Layer 7 data for malicious activity. HTTP/HTTPS/SOAP are all web application protocols that operate at OSI Layer 7. Screened host firewalls and packet filter firewalls don't inspect OSI Layer 7 data. A DMZ is a type of screened subnet that permits external users' access to a part of a private network.

13. A. The 802.1x standard from IEEE provides for port-based network access control (NAC). It provides a means of authenticating devices that attempt to connect to the network. Based on authentication, the Ethernet port can be placed in the appropriate VLAN for that device. If a device does not authenticate, the port could be placed into a quarantined VLAN or configured for Internet access only.

14. B. Not only can network access control (NAC) authenticate network devices, but it can also ensure the enforcement of corporate policies governing these devices. If a system is not in compliance with the corporate policy, the device can be quarantined until such time when the policy failures are remediated. An HIDS is for host detection. An agent is a software program that acts on behalf of a user or other program in a relationship. NIPS is for network protection.

15. C. The software installed on devices that will connect to the network using NAC is called an agent. A program is a set of instructions that allow for a certain kind of digital operation. A process is a set of activities and outcomes that produces a software product. A thread of execution is the smallest sequence of programmed instructions, typically part of the operating system.

16. D. Data at rest is stored on a device. A VPN contains data moving, which means data in transit. VPNs provide secure communications over an insecure network like the Internet. A variety of encryption protocols can be used to protect data as it moves across a VPN. A SAN is storage-attached network. NAS is network-attached storage, and an SSD is a solid-state hard drive.

17. B. A virtual private network (VPN) enables employees to access sensitive data and systems on mobile devices while away from the secure corporate network. A VPN's traditional role is to enable employees to authenticate from anywhere in the world and seamlessly access the company's network. Wi-Fi is wireless networking technology that allows equipment to connect to the Internet. The Remote Desktop Protocol (RDP) is a Microsoft technology that gives end users a graphical user interface to connect to another computer. A network interface card (NIC) is hardware that connects a computer to a network.

18. D. In a full tunnel, all network traffic is forced to go through the VPN. Depending on how it's configured, you may only have access to the internal network while the VPN is active. Split VPN tunnels only partially encrypt traffic. DNS tunneling turns the Domain Name System (DNS) into a weapon. It can hide data within DNS queries that are sent to an attacker-controlled server. An ARP cache is a collection of Address Resolution Protocol (ARP) entries that are made when an IP address is resolved to a MAC address.

19. A. DNSSEC strengthens authentication using digital signatures based on public/private key cryptography. With DNSSEC, you have data origin authentication as well as data integrity. Transport Layer Security (TLS) is a cryptographic protocol designed to bring security to communication on a computer network. Secure Sockets Layer (SSL), like TLS, is a protocol used for encryption in web browsing, email, and VoIP, but it has been replaced by TLS. Keeping the entities separate was not an option.

20. B. Authentication traffic is the most commonly captured and reused network traffic used in a replay attack. If an attacker is able to replay the stream of authentication packets correctly, they gain access to the same systems as the original user. A packet header is the portion of an IP packet that comes before the body, and it contains addressing. FTP is File Transfer Protocol, and Domain Name System (DNS) is a naming system for computers, services, and other resources connected to the Internet or private network. It associates domain names like www.wiley.com with an IP address.

21. A. A packet filter firewall inspects packets traversing the network and allows you to control the traffic based on source and destination IP, source and destination port, and the protocol utilized for communication. A proxy server is a server application or appliance that acts as an intermediary for requests from client machines looking for resources. A hardware security module (HSM) is a physical computing device that stores, manages, and safeguards digital keys and performs other cryptographic processes. A DMZ (demilitarized zone) is a physical or logical network segment that contains and exposes external-facing services to the Internet.

22. B. A unified threat management (UTM) system is a single device that provides multiple security functions, including antivirus protection, antispyware, a firewall, and an IDP. A concern with using a UTM is that it could become a single point of failure. A next-generation firewall (NGFW) combines a traditional firewall with other network device filtering functions such as deep packet inspection or IPS. A quantum proxy is a signature scheme that makes a proxy signer generate a signature on behalf of the original signer. There is no security model for quantum proxy, and it is susceptible to forgery attacks. There is no such thing as a next-generation IDP.

23. A. An Address Resolution Protocol (ARP) scan is performed to learn MAC addresses. You run an ARP request to query the MAC address of a device with a known IP address. When the ARP reply is received, you populate the ARP table, which maps the IP to a MAC. A NAT gateway enables cloud resources without public IP addresses access to the Internet without exposure to incoming connections. IPConfig is a Windows DOS utility that is used from the command line that program displays all current TCP/IP network configuration, including the currently assigned IP, subnet mask, and default gateway addresses. IFConfig is IPConfig on a Unix operating system.

24. A. A proxy firewall is also known as an application-level gateway firewall. It is used primarily to hide the source of a network connection by terminating the connection and initiating a new connection. This allows you to hide the true source of the traffic. An Internet gateway is a node on a network that is a stopping point for data on its way to or from other networks. A Layer 3 switch combines the functionality of a switch and a router. It acts as a switch to connect devices on the same subnet and has IP routing built in to immolate a router. A bastion host is a specially built host to withstand attacks generally hosting just one application such as a proxy server to reduce the threat landscape.

25. C. A reverse proxy performs the function mentioned in the question. Because traffic intended for the servers goes through the reverse proxy, it can provide filtering of malicious traffic destined for the servers. A proxy sits in front of clients, receiving their request and forwarding them on to the destination. Replies associated with these requests are also forwarded through the proxy to the clients. A basic firewall filters traffic based on packet header information. A network-based intrusion detection system (NIDS) examines traffic, looking for malicious content.

26. B. Spam filters inspect and filter malicious emails before they reach the end user. A basic firewall does not examine emails for malicious content. A web application firewall (WAF) examines web traffic for malicious activity. A forward proxy is an Internet-facing proxy that retrieves data from a wide range of sources. The requested server will send a response to a forward proxy server, and then the proxy server will forward the response to the client that requested it on the internal side of the network.

27. A. A DoS attack is a single-source computer system initiating the attack. A distributed DoS (DDoS) attack is much more orchestrated, enlisting the help of hundreds (if not thousands) of other source computers to completely overload the system. Spamming is the use of messaging systems to send an unsolicited message in large numbers. IP spoofing is the creation of IP packets with a false source IP address to impersonate another computer system. Containerization is an alternative or companion to virtualization involving encapsulating software code and all dependencies so it can run consistently on any infrastructure.

28. B. Denial-of-service (DoS) and distributed denial-of-service (DDoS) are attacks that do not give unauthorized access but rather block legitimate users from access. Typically, attackers generate large volumes of packets or requests, overwhelming a target system. Most DDoS attacks can be mitigated by reducing the attack surface. Minimizing the surface area that can be attacked limits the attacker's options. Another mitigation is knowing what normal and abnormal traffic is on your network and deploying firewalls for sophisticated application attacks.

29. D. Secure Shell (SSH) encrypts the data being sent to and from the router, ensuring that if an attacker captures the traffic, the attacker cannot read it. The other protocols send traffic in clear text that can be read, if captured.

30. B. Software-as-a-service (SaaS) providers use an Internet-enabled streaming service or web application to give end users access to software that would have to be installed locally or on a server. Gmail and Hotmail are examples of SaaS providers. IaaS is infrastructure as a service, and PaaS is platform as a service. BaaS doesn't actually exist.

31. A. A sandbox is an environment that is used for opening files or running programs without interfering with production environments. It is used to test software as safe or unsafe. A cloud sandbox adds another layer of security than an on-premises sandbox as it is completely separate from your corporate network. A service level agreement (SLA) defines the level of service you should expect from a vendor. A hypervisor is a virtual machine, which you can use in a sandbox but you would not want it attached to your corporate network.

32. A. There are two web service formats: SOAP and REST. Simple Object Access Protocol (SOAP) is used for interchanging data in a distributed environment. Representational State Transfer (REST) is an architectural style for hypermedia (think hyperlinked) systems. Of the two, SOAP has extensions for specific security concerns, whereas REST focuses on how to deliver and consume. HTTPS stands for Hypertext Transfer Protocol Secure and is widely used for secure communication over a computer network. Extensible Markup Language (XML) defines a set of rules used for encoding documents for both humans and machines.

33. C. Asynchronous JavaScript and XML (Ajax) is a pattern where web pages use web services using JavaScript and XML. It is used to create fast dynamic web pages, enabling parts of a web page to update, rather than reloading the entire page. Simple Object Access Protocol (SOAP) is used for interchanging data in a distributed environment. Representational State Transfer (REST) is an architectural style for hypermedia (think hyperlinked) systems. Of the two, SOAP has extensions for specific security concerns, whereas REST focuses on how to deliver and consume. Cross-site scripting (XSS) is a type of injection attack where scripts are injected into websites.

34. B. A switched port analyzer (SPAN) port is a dedicated port on a switch that takes a mirrored copy of a network from within the switch to be sent to a destination. That destination is typically a monitoring device. The proper way to bring a switch port out of the error-disabled state is to go to the interface and issue the `shutdown` and then the `no shutdown` commands.

35. D. A passive vulnerability scanner can intercept network traffic and analyze its content for malicious activity while not interfering with the host computer. A system scanner and application scanner are both active vulnerability scanners that do interact with a host computer and, because they do so, could cause a host computer to crash.

36. D. Not only do you have the business issue of lost data by attacks or by accident, you also must consider whether the vendor can verify that your data was securely deleted on demand and that remnants of the data are not still in the cloud for others to see. The public cloud is more cost effective and utilizes elasticity to scale machines. Both public and private can deploy assets on demand, so the biggest security concern would be public data remnants.

37. A. If you place an IDS sensor somewhere in your network for intrusion detection, your end goal is important. If you want to see what threats are being aimed at your organization from the Internet, you place the IDS outside the firewall. If you want to see potentially malicious internal traffic that you have inside the perimeter of your network, you place the monitor between the firewall and the internal LAN. Considering what traffic is most important, find the relevant point in the network that traffic *must* pass through to get there.

38. D. A network TAP is an external network device that creates a copy of the traffic for use by various monitoring devices. It allows traffic mirroring and is an intricate part of an organization's network stack. The network TAP device is introduced at a point in the path of the network that is felt should be observed so that it can copy data packets and send them to a monitoring device. Deploying the correct ACL rule will immediately prevent data coming or going anywhere on port 445. The other options could work, but they would take more time than you have to stop the spread immediately.

39. D. A SIEM monitors servers on your network, ideally providing a real-time analysis of security incidents and events. SIEM (pronounced "SIM") can be performed with hardware or software by examining and correlating logs the servers produce. A SIEM can be used to monitor alerts from an IDS and to perform trend analysis. If an anomaly is detected, rules are then written to inform security administrators.

40. A. File integrity monitoring (FIM) is a security technique used to secure IT infrastructure and business data. If an attacker or malicious insider generates changes to application files, operating system files, and log files, FIM can detect these changes, indicating a breach. The PCI Standard is mandated by the card brands but administered by the Payment Card Industry Security Standards Council. The Domain Name System (DNS) is a hierarchical and decentralized naming system for computers, services, or other resources connected to the Internet or a private network. Transmission Control Protocol (TCP) is one of the main protocols of the Internet Protocol suite. It originated in the initial network implementation where it complemented the Internet Protocol, and the entire suite is commonly referred to as TCP/IP.

41. A. SNMP version 3 (SNMPv3) adds encryption and authentication, which can be used together or separately.

42. A. NetFlow is a feature that was introduced on Cisco routers around 1996 that provides the ability to collect IP network traffic as it enters or exits an interface. Cisco IOS NetFlow efficiently provides a key set of services for IP applications, including network traffic accounting, usage-based network billing, network planning, security, denial-of-service (DoS) monitoring capabilities, and network monitoring. NetFlow provides valuable information about network users and applications, peak usage times, and traffic routing.

43. A. By using encryption and tokenization, you can be assured that even if data is stolen, it cannot be sold. It can also help move data securely around a large enterprise, and analytics can be performed on the data, which reduces risk and is required by certain compliance such as PCI, PII, and PHI.

44. C. A heuristic antivirus application examines the code and searches for specific commands or instructions that would not normally be found in an application. A behavioral detection antivirus program watches the operating system, looking for anything suspicious or out of the normal range of behavior.

45. C. A virus is malicious code capable of destroying data and corrupting systems. It generally needs help moving from one system to another. Antivirus products are designed to recognize and remove viruses from a system. Antimalware products are able to detect various types of malware, including viruses. Anti-adware products detect and remove programs designed to display advertisements on an infected user's screen.

46. A. With the invasion of IoT, employees and customers find these devices valuable, but they can introduce risk. Updating the corporate security policy for IoT and conducting a security awareness campaign are effective mitigation tools. After you perform the proper technical risk analysis, compensating controls, segmentation, and stringent network access controls can be put into place.

47. C. A flat network topology in a single large broadcast domain means any device sending an ARP broadcast will receive a reply. This provides potential access to every system. Network segmentation using virtual local area networks (VLANs) creates a collection of isolated networks where each network is a separate broadcast domain. If configured correctly, VLAN segmentation hinders unauthorized access to systems, giving you time to find a solution to using old, vulnerable protocols.

48. D. Network microsegmentation enables you to increase network security by creating defense in depth. In today's threat environment, you should assume that you are always under attack and will eventually experience a breach. Network microsegmentation makes it much more difficult for an attacker to perpetrate an attack over your entire network, as they could with a flat network infrastructure.

49. B. A demilitarized zone (DMZ) is a type of screened subnet. It is considered the public-facing part of a network because the public can reach it (i.e., customers). A local or wide area network describes the entire topology. Egress in networking is traffic leaving a device or network boundary.

50. C. A host-based intrusion prevention system (HIPS) is an intrusion detection system used to detect and stop intrusions on a host and stop the activity. Jump servers, sometimes called jump boxes, are typically placed between a secure zone and a DMZ to provide management of devices on the DMZ once a management session has been established. The jump server acts as a single audit point for traffic. A prospective administrator must log into the jump server in order to gain access to the DMZ assets.

51. B. In a split DNS infrastructure, you create two zones for one domain. One of these domains is to be used by the internal network, and the external network is used by users on the Internet. This is done to hide internal information from outsiders.

52. D. Most assets on a network produce logs to different degrees and in different formats. Log analysis is extremely important for compliance. A security information and event management (SIEM) tool collects data from various assets, servers, domain controllers, hosts, and more. The SIEM tool will normalize that data, which is analyzed to discover and detect threats. A fuzzer is an automated software tester that will provide invalid and random data and then monitor the software for crashes or memory leaks. An HTTP interceptor will interrupt incoming or outgoing HTTP requests and possibly modify or change the values in the request. A port scanner is a tool that allows you to find open ports on a network and see versions of programs running on those ports.

53. A. A directional Wi-Fi antenna is not going to boost any signal—it directs the energy from the transmitter. You can adjust a directional antenna's signal gain and angle to provide the specific range you need. You do not want unauthorized personnel in the parking lot able to use your corporate guest Wi-Fi.

54. A. In these options, Remote Desktop Protocol (RDP) is the only protocol. It is a protocol that can be used to access a Windows system remotely via a network connection and can provide the user with a graphical interface of the desktop. Virtual Network Computing (VNC) uses the Remote Frame Buffer (RFB) protocol to enable a desktop to be viewed and controlled over a network connection. Virtual Desktop Infrastructure (VDI) is a remote desktop-hosting environment where a desktop image is hosted on a virtual machine and accessed remotely over a network. Data loss prevention is the process of detecting and preventing data exfiltration from the data owner's system.

55. B. Virtual Network Computing (VNC) uses the Remote Frame Buffer (RFB) protocol to enable a host desktop to be viewed and controlled over a network connection. Because it is a program that runs within the operating system, it is not possible to use VNC to access the BIOS of the host as it boots up, nor is it available if the OS experiences a critical failure and crashes, showing the blue screen of death.

56. C. By subdividing the network, you create an additional routing layer for messages. This additional layer can increase security or allow assigning each subnet available to individual network administrators. Ease of troubleshooting and bandwidth utilization are other benefits as well as customizing rules between subnetworks. Availability zones are isolated locations within a data center region where the public cloud operates.

57. B. When network access control or NAC is used but an agent is not installed on the devices, we refer to it as an agentless configuration. When using agentless NAC, the policy enforcement component is integrated into an authentication system like Windows Active Directory. The enforcement of policies is performed when the device logs on or off the network.

58. B. Standard versions of Linux use a discretionary access control (DAC) system that enables the creator of files to control the permissions of those files. Security-Enhanced Linux (SELinux) is a security architecture of Linux that uses mandatory access control (MAC), where a security policy dictates the permissions associated with a file.

59. B. When the cost of controls is more than the benefits gained by implementing a response, then the best course of action is risk acceptance for a certain period, and then the risk is reevaluated.

60. C. Implementing controls for confidentiality ensures that data remains private. Steganography can hide messages in pictures, music, or videos. Access control lists (ACLs) are tables that tell who has permission to see an object or directory, and vulnerability management refers to finding weaknesses in software to deal with any associated confidentiality risks.

61. B. A dedicated system functioning at a single level of a specific classification and all the users of that system have the same clearance and the same need to know as a dedicated system. High mode is a single level of classification, but not everyone has the same level of need to know. Multilevel consists of multiple levels of classification and various clearance levels where not everyone has a need to know. Peer-to-peer computing or networking is a distributed application architecture that partitions tasks or workloads between peers who are equally privileged.

62. C. Zero trust is a security concept centered on the belief that organizations should not automatically trust anything inside or outside its perimeters and instead must verify anything and everything trying to connect to its systems before granting access.

63. D. The database is in a secure air-gapped network with limited access. It is probably compliant and inaccessible to most attackers. A key-value pair (KVP) is a set of two linked data items: a key, which is a unique identifier for some item of data, and the value, which is either the data that is identified or a pointer to the location of that data. Key-value pairs are frequently used in lookup tables, hash tables, and configuration files. The best answer is inappropriate administrator access.

64. D. When using the cloud, it is difficult to know where your data is stored. The company you are using may be incorporated in the United States with server farms in Brazil. Many companies outsource to reduce costs. The other three are of more importance when considering cloud computing.

65. A. The most important security controls of any device that will be mobile are the ability to wipe that device should it become lost or stolen, as well as the ability to control access to that same device. Encryption provides a layer of physical and digital security. The track record of the vendor in correcting security flaws plays an important part in the risk assessment.

66. C. The act of encrypting nonvolatile memory will make the biggest impact and increase the work factor of anyone who attempts to break into the phone. A PIN would not be a strong enough deterrent, not when this phone has apps that connect to the corporate intranet. A complex password is better than a PIN.

67. D. The interconnection security agreement (ISA) is a contract between a telecommunication organization for the purpose of connecting networks and exchanging traffic. It is found detailed in NIST SP 800-47. This document regulates the security-relevant aspects of two entities operating under distinct authorities. An MOU (memorandum of understanding) is an agreement between two or more parties but is not legally binding. Disclosure of assets is intended to ensure there is no conflict of interest and acts as a deterrent against collusion and is usually required of public officials. An OLA (operation level agreement) describes the responsibilities of each support group to other support groups.

68. C. Infrared Data Association is an infrared communication organization supporting protocols for wireless infrared technology using infrared signals. Because infrared signals work line of sight, they are considered very secure, given that sniffing traffic is difficult.

69. B. It is highly recommended to reach out to all administrators found on the domains on Whois for any migration of mail and web services. Netstat is a command-line network utility that will show network connections. SSH is used for encryption. TCPDump is a packet analyzer.

70. B. Network-attached storage (NAS) offers file-sharing services over file-based protocols. The number of peered devices is not limited by physical limitations like port space. The performance of a NAS is based on congestion and the speed of the network. A SAN typically is a dedicated network of storage devices not accessible through the local area network (LAN). Although a SAN provides only block-level access, filesystems built on top of SANs do provide file-level access and are known as shared-disk filesystems. A DAG (directed acyclic graph) is a direct graph with no cycles. A DAS (distributed antenna system) is a network of antenna nodes connected to a common source and provides wireless service to a limited geographic area.

71. D. On-premises deployment solutions are the only way that an organization has complete control over the network, hardware, and software. A solution that is entirely created and deployed onsite could cost more up front than a hosted or cloud-based solution, but the local organization would have access to the system and all the data.

72. D. Legal should always have a seat at the table when it comes to discussing how to control sensitive information. The legal team should be aware of all new laws and acts that affect your business when it comes to safeguarding this resource.

73. A. All Internet usage begins with DNS. DNS was designed in the 1980s before security was a priority. The Internet Engineering Task Force (IETF) created a solution with DNS Security Extensions (DNSSEC). DNSSEC uses digital signatures and public key cryptography on the DNS data itself, signed by the owner of the data.

74. A. A public cloud is the cloud computing model where IT services are delivered across the Internet. The defining features of public cloud solutions are elasticity and scalability for IT services at a low cost. A public cloud offers many solution choices for all types of computing requirements.

75. A. Multifactor authentication can include two or three different factors, whereas two-factor authentication is always limited to two factors. Requiring users to authenticate with three factors is more secure, but users will expect an MFA solution to be easy to use. Remember, your end users will try to bypass your security controls if you do not make it easy to use.

76. A. By default, LDAP communication between client and server is not encrypted. This means it would be possible to capture traffic and view the information between client and server, which can be dangerous when transmitting usernames and passwords. LDAPS adds SSL encryption.

77. D. Software-defined networking (SDN) divides the function of a network device like a router or switch into planes. The control plane consists of the programmable (i.e., controlled) function of the network device. This function is separated from the network device and placed on a controller. The data plane consists of the core function of the networking device. In the case of a router, the data plane is concerned with the forwarding of data. The data plane remains on the router. The control plane communicates with the data plane to perform the overall function of the router.

78. C. A hybrid SDN (software-defined network) is a network where both traditional networking and SDN protocols operate. Sending the logs to a syslog server allows log retention in the event the device fails, reboots, or is compromised by an attacker and the attacker is able to turn logging off.

79. A. A vast amount of open source intelligence (OSINT) can help organizations stay safer. Overlay networking (aka SDN overlay) is a method of using software to create layers of network abstraction that can be used to run multiple separate, discrete virtualized network layers on top of the physical network, often providing new applications or security benefits.

Using indicators of compromise (IOCs) to aid information security processes on your specific network design helps detect data breaches and malware/ransomware infection. With this information, you can sweep your network to identify matches, sandbox anything suspicious, and contact the authorities.

80. B. Network Mapper (Nmap) is the most popular network discovery and port scanner. It is free and open source and is used by many system administrators and network engineers for auditing local and remote networks. Port scanning sends a request to connect to a target computer on each port sequentially and records which ports respond. The separation of control and forwarding planes in software-defined networking (SDN) networks is a key issue of the SDN technology. It offers the complete functionality of the Nmap utility to a network administrator, who controls the SDN network through the out-of-band control plane.

81. A. A private cloud or public cloud or a combination of both depends on a variety of factors, use cases, security needs, compliance, and limitations. Organizations as they grow and evolve will use all three types of cloud solutions.

82. A. Most attackers are going after vertical privilege escalation where a lower privilege user or application accesses functions reserved for a higher privileged one. Smart attackers also use horizontal privilege escalation where you have a normal user who accesses certain functions from another normal user. A wealth of information can be stolen with horizontal privilege escalation, which is rarely monitored.

83. D. Think strategy! You need to test for resilience and reliability of the rebuilt site before you restore any mission-critical function. The financial department and communication would be restored only after you know the foundation is good.

84. B. If you have only a single primary firewall, you have a single point of failure (SPoF), which could be catastrophic to an HA network. If all traffic must pass through a single point and it fails, no communication can happen. Clustered servers, high-speed redundant links, and switched networks all support HA by providing performance and reliability.

85. B. Heterogeneous computing refers to systems that use more than one kind of processor or core. These types of systems gain performance and/or efficiency by adding different coprocessors, usually incorporating specialized processing capabilities to handle specific tasks. A system of this type has also been referred to as a "diverse" chipset.

86. D. You may not have heard of Collaborative Automated Course of Action Operations (CACAO), but you are probably familiar with a playbook. Research from the Ponemon Institute in summer 2020 states that the volume and severity of cyberattacks continues to rise and to create resilience, and that the adoption of a companywide cybersecurity incident response playbook will help guide a business through its response to an attack.

87. D. Cyberthreat intelligence is extremely beneficial to every organization. However, of those listed, it is least beneficial to your marketing plan. Properly applied, it can provide insight into cyberthreats, enabling for faster response as well as resource allocation and distribution.

88. A. Not all vendors offer secure data center environments with multiple power sources and remote backups. Some cut costs and pass that risk on to you, the customer. This risk can knock you out of compliance if there is equipment failure for any reason.

89. A. Most companies use 125 kHz cards for access doors secured with electric locks. These cards have no encryption or authentication and will broadcast company information when any reader is nearby, making it easy for anyone with the right equipment to replicate these cards.

90. D. The biggest security risk is that multiple VMs using the same transport could possibly lead to exposure of sensitive data of the database as well as the mortgage application information of their customers.

91. B. Most enterprises use three types of provisioning. Self-provisioning is where a cloud customer fills out an online request for services with the provider. This tends to be the most expensive arrangement. Another type is provisioning in advance by signing a contract allocating a certain number of resources per unit of time with the customer receiving a discounted rate. The last type is dynamic provisioning. In this model, the customer dynamically receives the requested level of resources on an as-needed basis. When the customer needs more resources, the provider delivers them, and when the customer needs fewer resources, the provider takes some away. This model is also known as autoscaling.

92. B. Applying, cataloging, scheduling, and implementing change are all part of the Change Control process. Changes should be made in the most organized manner possible. Vulnerability management tools will scan an organization looking for hardware, operating systems, and software, looking for vulnerabilities. A security information and event management tool will digest and analyze logs, giving alerts. Automation is performing a task with as little human interaction as possible with a script, a program, or batch processing.

93. A. SOAR stands for security orchestration, automation, and response. It consists of technologies that enable an enterprise to collect data that is monitored by a security team. SOAR tools help an organization define incident analysis and response procedures in a digital workflow.

94. A. Containers' speed, agility, and portability make them a great tool for streamlining software development, which can also be called bootstrapping. Bootstrapping can refer to the development of successively more complex, faster programming environments.

95. D. With containerization, benefits include reduced IT management resources, quicker application deployment, less code to move, easier-to-deploy security updates, and the greatly reduced snapshots' size.

96. B. VMs are a great choice when you are running applications that need all the operating system's resources and functionality when you run multiple programs on servers or when you have several operating systems to manage. Containers are better when you need to maximize the number of applications running on a minimal number of assets. All the other answers are reversed.

97. C. A standard hardening practice is to turn off any unused services. If a feature is not used, do not enable it. If you use the UC server for voice, video, and instant messaging but not email, then turn off the email functionality. There will be less protocol traffic, and the server will do less work.

98. A. A proxy can be thought of as a go-between, where all traffic flows from a host through the proxy and out to the rest of the network or the Internet. Because the traffic flows through the proxy, the proxy can inspect the data for malicious activities. It can also help conserve bandwidth by caching data that has been requested and serving it to other users when needed.

99. D. A CDN (content delivery network) is a geographically distributed network of proxy servers and their data centers. The goal is to provide high availability and performance by distributing the service spatially relative to end users. If a DDoS attack is launched against a server in a CDN, the server may not be able to withstand the attack if the server resources are not adequate to withstand it. However, if a DDoS is launched against a server with load-balancing technology implemented in it, the attack can be distributed across multiple servers, lessening the impact of the attack on any one server by distributing the attack over multiple servers.

100. A. Configuration baselining is the process of configuring a base configuration for a system that includes basic capabilities and, in this case, a basic level of security. From this baseline (also known as a *gold image*), additional features can be added.

101. A. Are Alexa's speech capabilities and recordings HIPAA or PCI compliant? If Google, Siri, or Alexa are listening to confidential business or patient discussions, the results could be horrible for the hospital.

102. C. Option C is not a best practice. Options A, B, and D are what cloud providers *should* be doing.

103. D. Containers are *not* sandboxes. If an attacker gains access to a container, there is a risk of container escape. If they get access to the host, they get access to all other containers on the host, which is why security controls must be deployed on the containers as well.

104. A. Versioning is a way to control software so that everyone knows the latest and greatest version. Major revisions of software require the first number to change (i.e., 1.0 to 2.0). Minor revisions would increase like 1.7 to 1.8.

105. C. The threat in this scenario is the hacker/hacktivist or nation-state hacker who wants to use this third-party vendor as a gateway into your organization. Vetting a third-party organization is mission critical if that vendor is going to be working with any type of sensitive data or project.

106. B. Typically, app wrapping is performed through the use of a software development kit (SDK) that enables a developer to administer management policies. This includes controlling who can download a mobile app and whether data accessed by that app can be copied and pasted.

107. B. Setting API access and a secret key pair is the most commonly used option. Key pairs provide access to the API and give each individual a secret token. If the access and secret key pairs do not match, you will not have access. Large enterprise organizations and applications use this methodology for the validation of users.

108. A. A web application security plan should outline your organization's goals as well as contain a checklist based on infrastructure, individuals in the organization who are involved in maintaining web application security, and cost. Middleware includes web servers, application servers, and similar tools that support application development and delivery and should be included.

109. D. White-box testing validates inner program logic and security functionality. Software assurance (SwA) is defined by the National Institute of Standards and Technology as "the level of confidence that software is free from vulnerabilities, either intentionally designed into the software or accidentally inserted at any time during its lifecycle, and that the software functions in the intended manner."

110. C. A sandbox enables developers to download, install, and manipulate software in a quarantined location to test before putting it into production. Sandboxes are incredibly important to patch management and upgrading software.

111. B. When development merges with operations, it is called DevOps. The collaboration between developers and operations requires an agile model, which follows a flow of information between coders and users. More recently, DevOps has turned into DevSecOps, where security is integrated into the flow of information.

112. A. Browsers and websites use HTTP to communicate, and a web session is a serious of requests and responses created by an individual user. HTTP is stateless, which means each response and each request is independent of each other. A web administrator uses session management to track visits to a website and movement inside the site when the user logged in.

113. A. Many Android phones come with a locked bootloader. A locked bootloader won't boot anything but the approved version of a specific Android ROM. Unlocking the bootloader enables you to install a custom ROM, which is an alternate version of the Android operating systems. As far as a third-party library, attackers have shifted their focus from servers and operating systems directly to applications. This is the easiest route to accessing sensitive enterprise data, and attackers are doing everything they can to do to exploit third-party software components, even if the software has been validated. That still won't change the fact you still have to unlock the bootloader before uploading the new ROM.

114. A. Code signing is the process of digitally signing executables and scripts to confirm the software author and guarantee that the code has not been altered or corrupted since it was signed. The process employs the use of a cryptographic hash to validate authenticity and integrity. Hashing is a mathematical function used to compute a unique identifier for a particular input. You can compute the hash for the software code and post it on the server along with the software. When an end user downloads the software code, they can run the software through the same hash function. If the output of the hash function matches what is posted on the servers, then the software has not been altered.

115. A. You test for different things at different stages of the web application development cycle. With static application security testing (SAST), the tester has access to the framework and design and will test from the inside out. SAST does not need the application to be deployed. Because the scan can be executed early in the SDLC, it can find problems sooner.

116. C. You test for different things at different stages of the web application development cycle. With dynamic application security testing (DAST), the tester has no knowledge of the technology or framework. DAST tests from the outside in, which represents what an attacker would do. DAST does not check source code. It analyzes by executing the application itself. Unfortunately, DAST must be done at the end of the SDLC when you actually have an application to test, and therefore, the vulnerabilities will be more expensive to fix.

117. C. Interactive Application Security Testing (IAST) combines the best of a SAST and a DAST. IAST security tools provide the advantages of a static view because they can see the source code, and also the advantages of a web scanner viewing the execution flow of the application during runtime. Static application security testing (SAST) tools can scan binaries in software to find errors, vulnerabilities, and flaws in web, movie, and desktop applications. SAST is often called *white-box testing*. Dynamic application (DAST) tools are used for black-box testing, employing injection techniques like SQLi and CSS. Interactive application (IAST) is a combination of both SAST and DAST testing, applying analysis to all code, runtime controls, and data flow. Vendor application security testing (VAST) is a third-party risk assessment.

118. D. A hybrid cloud is the cloud computing model where IT services are integrated public and private solutions. Organizations can use a mix of both for security, performance, scalability, cost, and efficiency.

119. D. Downtime is not an option for many organizations. The best thing you can do is to be prepared for attacks. An RPO is how much data can be lost in a measured time frame, and an RTO is how long it takes to restore data from an incident. The people closest to those processes, such as business unit managers and directors, are best aligned to knowing what those metrics would be.

120. C. Asset management is the mostly likely use case for configuration management software (CMS). CMS is used to ensure that configurations are deployed on new systems and are maintained in their secure state. It can also be used for compliance, standardization, change control, and license management.

121. C. A configuration management database (CMDB) is a repository that acts as a data warehouse, storing information about your IT environment and the components that are used to deliver IT services. The data stored in a CMDB includes lists of assets and the connection between them. CMDBs and the configuration management processes that surround them are the core of modern IT operations, enabling the company to IT components in one place. A recovery point objective (RPO) indicates the amount of data loss or system unavailability measured in units of time that a business can endure. The RPO can help you decide how often systems should be backed up.

122. A. CRM (customer relationship management) is the process of managing interactions with existing as well as past and potential customers. It is one of many different approaches that allow a company to analyze interactions with its past, current, and potential customers. The first phase of any future attack will be active and passive reconnaissance. Using social media capriciously will open your organization to knowledge that can be used against you. Even job descriptions can be used to find out what technology your organization is using to craft social engineering attacks—HR advertises a need for a CCNP and an attacker knows you are probably using Cisco devices in your network.

123. D. You will want to build a centralized organizationwide access control system, bringing together multiple organizations for standardization, identity management, and authentication with the ability to repeat this with the next iteration of mergers and acquisitions.

124. D. Kerberos, directory services, and SAML 2.0 are all examples of single sign-on solutions. You provide your logon credentials and do not have to provide them again while in a specific environment. A workgroup is not a form of single sign-on. You have to authenticate each time to access a system.

125. C. DNS suffers from lack of authentication of servers and, therefore, an authenticity of records. During DNS hijacking, for example, the client's configuration is changed so that DNS traffic is redirected to a rogue server that sends the client wherever the attacker wants them to go.

126. B. The biggest security risk to adopting service-oriented architecture (SOA) is a lack of understanding, and because understanding is lacking, you have lack of governance. It can also increase solution costs. You need all the applications to work together to save money and to not be in isolation from each other. SOA should be deployed where everyone—customers, suppliers, and employees—is enabled as a partner in the system.

127. D. An enterprise service bus (ESB) is a communication system for software inside service-oriented architecture (SOA). It is a special type of client-server model focused on agility and flexibility. ESBs are built into the SOA "middleware" to overcome integration problems between incompatible systems. One of the systems may be a slow receiver; another may need messages in binary format.

128. D. The need for usability and productivity sometimes get prioritized over security. Problems with many organizations are the silos of people, the processes, and a lack of communication. This is an instance where risk management and strategies must communicate with those users and decision-makers and influence their behaviors. Not many outside of IT will know what the SDLC is, and it's our job to teach them.

129. A. When the exam uses the acronym SDLC, reread the question to clarify if it is the software development life cycle or the system development life cycle. They have different stages but will use the same acronym. The SDLC this question refers to is focused on software. There are six stages beginning with (1) requirement analysis, (2) planning, (3) design, (4) development, (5) testing, and finally (6) deployment.

130. A. The SDLC has several steps, beginning with requirements. This is where the idea develops, and it includes documenting objectives and answering questions. This stage of the SDLC means getting input from all stakeholders, including customers, salespeople, industry experts, and programmers. Learn the strengths and weaknesses of the current system, with improvement as the goal.

131. A. The SDLC has been evolving ever since there has been software development. Deployment has been known as "fielding" in the past, which is delivering the working system to the customer. If the system was designed to run on the customer's equipment, then you would need to install the software and test it. Some other nuances you might see as you study include testing, which is sometimes called system validation or quality assurance. Design can be called architecture definition. Planning is sometimes called inception. Licensing is not a phase in the SDLC, and you are not responsible for this process.

132. A. Security-related patches and upgrades should be applied as quickly as possible after testing on a system in a sandbox or not in production. Waiting until after you have a problem is not advantageous, and neither is having other organizations test the patch first. No two networks are identically built.

133. A. When you implement garbage collection, a process cleans up and controls what is left in memory. Garbage collection can ensure that credentials are erased from memory when they are no longer needed. Data validation is the process of making certain data has undergone data cleansing to ensure quality—that is, that data is both correct and useful. The SDLC can be either software or system development life cycle. OOP (object-oriented programming) is based on the concept of "objects," which can contain data and code: data in the form of fields, and code, in the form of procedures.

134. D. An HTTP interceptor is used to inspect requests before they are handed to a server and responses before they are handed over to the application. HTTP interceptors are used for error handling and authentication for requests and responses. Fuzzing or fuzz testing is an automated software testing technique that involves providing invalid, or random, data as inputs to a computer program and is monitored for exceptions such as crashes or memory leaks. A vulnerability scanner is a computer program designed to assess computers, networks, or applications for known weaknesses. Fingerprinting is the process of finding information about an asset to test security.

135. D. Regression testing happens after software is changed to make sure the program works as intended. Whenever developers change or modify their software, even a small tweak can have unexpected consequences. Regression testing is testing existing software applications to make sure that a change or addition has not broken any existing functionality. White-box testing is a software testing technique where internal structure, design, and coding of software are tested to verify flow of input-output and to improve design, usability, and security. Black-hat hackers are criminals who break into computer networks with malicious intent. They may also release malware that destroys files; holds computers hostage; or steals passwords, credit card numbers, and other personal information. A code review is a process where someone other than the author of a piece of code examines that code.

136. A. When doing unit testing, you test individual modules, or programs, to see whether the module is accepting input properly and whether it provides the right output to the next part of the program.

137. A. Fuzzing is a technique used in software testing that uses invalid data or random input called fuzz. It is done to discover implementation bugs in the software. The definition of compliance means following a rule or order. Access control is the selective restriction of access to a resource whereas access management describes the process. The act of accessing may mean consuming, entering, or using. Permission to access a resource is called authorization. Integration testing is defined as a type of testing where software modules are integrated logically and tested as a group. A typical software project consists of multiple software modules, coded by different programmers. The purpose of this level of testing is to expose defects in the interaction between these software modules when they are integrated.

138. A. Encryption for data at rest is a key protection against a data breach. Data at rest is stored and usually protected by a firewall or antivirus software. Defense in depth is important to data at rest and begins with encryption.

139. A. The primary purpose of change control is to prevent unmanaged change. All changes need to be managed and approved. Unmanaged change can introduce severe reduction in security.

140. C. Agile software development has been in use since 2001 when the waterfall methodology was too strict and rigid. Agile emphasizes teamwork and feedback, which changes the direction of the software. There are two major types of the agile methods: Scrum and Kanban. Scrum defines roles and events, whereas Kanban is simple with a lot of flexibility.

141. D. A spiral software development process is beneficial because of risk management; development is fast, and there is always room for feedback. It is not advisable if it is a small project because it is known to be expensive. There is more documentation with the spiral model because it has intermediate phases that require it. To be effective, the model has to be followed precisely.

142. B. The waterfall method of software development begins with long planning phases and design with a very rigid path through a set of phases. Waterfall is a common methodology for large projects. It tends to be among the less iterative and flexible approaches, as progress flows in largely one direction like an actual waterfall. The phases are conception, initiation, analysis, design, construction, testing, deployment, and maintenance.

143. A. Once a system is in production, the postinstallation phase in which the system is used in production is called operations and maintenance support. The system is monitored for weaknesses and vulnerabilities that did not appear during development. The system's data backup and restore procedures are also tested. If changes need to be made, it enters the phase of revision and system replacement.

144. D. Continuous integration (CI) and continuous delivery (CD) is a set of operating principles and collection of practices that enable application development teams to deliver code changes more frequently and reliably. The implementation is also known as the CI/CD pipeline. It is an agile methodology best practice, as it enables software development teams to focus on meeting business requirements, code quality, and security because deployment steps are automated. Many teams find that this is an economical and streamlined way to work because errors are identified and handled quickly. It lets a team bring software to production faster than other approaches.

145. A. A best practice can be described as a procedure that is accepted or prescribed as being most correct. The results it produces are better than other means because it has become a standard way of doing things. In 1995, one of the first vulnerability assessment tools, known as Security Admin Tool for Analyzing Networks (SATAN), was shared with the community and at first was widely disparaged. Today, the Center for Internet Security (CIS) recommends constantly scanning for vulnerabilities as the number 3 of the top 20 controls.

146. A. Shodan is a phenomenal website that crawls the Internet looking for publicly accessible IoT devices. The Open Web Application Security Project (OWASP) is an online community that produces articles, methodologies, documentation, tools, and technologies in the field of web application security. VirusTotal is a website where you can upload files and have them checked for viruses from various antivirus vendors. Maltego is a program, not a website, that performs data mining, perfect for reconnaissance.

147. A. Many tools can be used to fingerprint assets. These tools gather information for you to test known vulnerabilities and exploitation. Netcat, Nmap, Telnet, or crawling cookies are all tools or techniques used to gather information about an application to further your security testing. Authentication confirms that a user is who they say they are. Authorization gives those users permission to access a resource. Code review is the act of consciously and systematically checking others' code for mistakes and has been shown to accelerate and streamline the process of software development.

148. A. Data loss prevention (DLP) is a technology term that can mean either a methodology or a tool that monitors the system, the user, and data events on an endpoint, looking for and blocking suspicious activity. You can use DLP solutions to classify and prioritize data security. You can also use these solutions to ensure access policies meet regulatory compliance, including HIPAA, GDPR, and PCI-DSS. DLP solutions can also go beyond simple detection, providing alerts, enforcing encryption, and isolating data. NIDS and NIPS are for network intrusion detection and prevention. HIPS could have been the answer if DLP was not an option. HIPS tools can take a variety of actions, including sending an alarm to the computer user, logging the malicious activity for future investigation, resetting the connection, dropping malicious packets, and blocking subsequent traffic from a suspect IP address. Most host intrusion prevention systems use known attack patterns, called signatures, to identify malicious activity. Signature-based detection is effective, but it can only protect the host device against known attacks. It cannot protect against zero-day attacks or other signatures that are not in the software provider's database.

149. D. Of the options provided, option D is the most appropriate. Managing USB usage via a Group Policy can be used strategically, preventing some users from having USB access while enabling others' access.

150. C. One of the easiest, nontechnical ways to reducing the attack surface for dumpster diving is to control what leaves the facility by way of disposal and what form that takes. Larger enterprise organizations will hire third-party organizations for their shredding, whereas some organizations will create a policy based on what type of document has been manufactured. Either way, this information must be included in your policies and procedures, communicated to staff, and periodically audited. However, one of the best and most technical ways to prevent dumpster diving is to not allow the printing of documentation based on data classification.

151. B. A virtual desktop infrastructure (VDI) hosts desktop images on a server within a virtual machine and is accessed over the network via a desktop client. A virtual private network (VPN) is a way of establishing a secure link between two devices. Virtual Network Computing (VNC) is a graphical desktop-sharing system. Remote Desktop Protocol (RDP) is a Microsoft proprietary protocol used to provide a graphical desktop-sharing system.

152. B. When RDP is configured to allow access from anywhere on the Internet, it becomes highly susceptible to attacks. Attackers all over the world are constantly scanning the Internet, looking for devices configured for RDP. Once found, they will use tools to try to crack or break into your system. Because RDP is so widely used, it is a common target for man-in-the-middle cyberattacks. Best-practice protocol to prevent exposure to RDP security issues starts with creating a policy to handle endpoints and making sure the port is not accessible to the Internet. A proactive approach can help you focus on preventing initial access by minimizing RDP security risks, including limiting RDP users, using a VPN, using a remote desktop gateway, and following a very strong security policy that includes very strong passwords as well as appropriate logging.

153. D. Organizations have evolved, and people are doing more work remotely and while traveling. The need for constant access and connection is real in a fast-moving organization. Security policies must evolve to enable usability, risk evaluations must be done, and all mobile device must be encrypted. One such risk evaluation must be clipboard privacy on mobile devices. The collection of all clipboard data is not a practice that the average user reasonably expects. The data we copy and paste on our phones using the clipboard features can reveal sensitive information about us: our passwords, credit card numbers, notes, conversations, website URLs, as well as any corporate data. The average end user believes that the data is secure and shared with the apps only when we post the data into them, and sometimes that is not the case.

154. A. The process of data classification is extremely important to making processes repeatable. Once you have a document classified as Secret or Classified, you know exactly how to treat it according to the CIA triad. Each organization is unique, so you must develop the right security controls based on risk analysis and decide which security controls to implement. The purpose of data classification is to ensure that we know exactly what data we have, where it is located, and how sensitive the data is. Yet, despite how crucial it is to have this knowledge, it is an area of data security that is often overlooked.

155. A. Most experts agree that a rise in misconfiguration because of a lack of experience and education will lead to more breaches of cloud environments. Data protection is one of the primary concerns when adopting cloud services. According to McAfee Threats Report 2021, the average enterprise uses 1,427 cloud services, and employees often introduce new services on their own. Analyzing cloud usage data for 30 million users, McAfee found that 18.1% of documents uploaded to file-sharing services contain sensitive information, such as personally identifiable information (PII), protected health information (PHI), payment card data, or intellectual property, thus creating compliance concerns. Employing the right DLP solution in the cloud focusing on accuracy, real-time monitoring, analysis of data in motion, incident remediation, and data loss policy authoring is essential for successful cloud adoption.

156. B. Steganographic watermarking is a way of using steganography to watermark data. In this case, the watermark is hidden in the document so that it does not distort the document contents but still provides a means of proving where it originated. Sometimes you may see this as digital or invisible watermarking. Plain watermarking can be an embedded text or logo over a digital image indicating ownership. Blowfish provides a good encryption as a symmetric block cipher. No effective cryptanalysis of it has been found to date, and it has been used as a replacement for DES or IDEA. Digital signatures work by proving that a digital message or document was not modified—intentionally or unintentionally—from the time it was signed. Digital signatures do this by generating a unique hash of the message or document and encrypting it using the sender's private key. Public key infrastructure (PKI) governs the issuance of digital certificates to protect sensitive data; provide unique digital identities for users, devices, and applications; and secure end-to-end communications.

157. B. Sometimes controversial, digital rights management (DRM) is important to publishers of any electronic media since it is used to control the trading, protection, monitoring, and tracking of digital media. DRM helps publishers limit the illegal propagation of copyrighted works. DRM can enable online video and audio services to enforce that the content they provide is used in accordance with their requirements. This technology may restrict some of the things you can do in the browser.

158. D. Deep packet inspection is the process of inspecting the payload of a packet for malicious content. Other packet inspection techniques only check the header information for signs of malicious activity. The main techniques used for deep packet inspection include either pattern or signature matching. The data evaluated by the deep packet inspection provides a more robust mechanism for enforcing network packet filtering, as DPI can be used to identify and block a range of complex threats hiding in network data streams, including malware or data exfiltration, more accurately.

159. A. When traffic increases in the double digits over a short amount of time, you are usually under attack. Wireshark is the leading network traffic analyzer and captures packets to analyze. The UDP port being attacked is port 123, which is the Network Time Protocol. End devices should be talking to an internal NTP server or reaching out to a configured NTP server. You know this is a client-side attack because it is taking place on your machine. Server-side means the action is taking place on the server side.

160. A. The classification of data almost always is used for confidentiality. Once you classify data, you will know to the extent you need to provide access, encryption, etc., on that specific piece of data.

161. A. Data provenance is a big data security concern. Unauthorized changes in metadata lead to the wrong dataset, which makes it nearly impossible to find the correct information. Untraceable data sources can be a huge impediment to finding security breaches as well as any fake data that has been injected into real data.

162. A. Prevention obfuscation makes it difficult for a computer to decompile code to reverse engineer or copy the code. An example includes renaming metadata to gibberish. Data obfuscation is aimed at obscuring data and data structures. Control flow obfuscation uses false conditional statements to confuse decompilers while keeping code intact.

163. C. Security is increased, and risk is reduced when using tokens. The mapping from the original data to the token should be irreversible in the absence of the system that created it.

164. D. In simple terms, a logical unit number (LUN) is a slice or portion of a configured set of disks that is presentable to a host and mounted as a volume within the OS. The disks in an array are usually configured into smaller sets (RAID groups) to provide protection against failure. Logical unit numbering is an authorization process that makes a LUN available to a select number of hosts.

165. D. Data obfuscation consists of changing sensitive data or identifying a person (PII). A successful obfuscation is when the data maintains referential integrity as well as its original characteristics, which guarantees that the development, testing, and installation of the applications are successful. Other named for data obfuscation are data masking, data scrubbing, de-identification, depersonalization, and data scrambling.

166. D. The CIA triad principle is a security model that stands for confidentiality, integrity, and availability. All three should be guaranteed in any type of secure environment. Confidentiality is the ability to hide information. Integrity ensures that the information is accurate. Availability ensures that the information is readily accessible, and authenticity is needed for proof of origin. The definition of anonymous is of unknown name or origin. An author who does not put their name on their books is an example of someone who is anonymous. Cryptography and encryption are used to ensure data remains secure during transit, remains unchanged, and can be used to prove who sent it. Availability is the only one not affected by encryption.

167. C. The responsibility of secure development is on the developer and on the organization to enforce encryption standards. It isn't just that encryption is used, but that *good* encryption is used.

168. D. Data provisioning and processing and encrypting data in transit and at rest is the best description of the data life cycle end to end. The data life cycle begins with data creation, then storage, usage, archival, and eventually destruction. Having a clearly defined and documented data life cycle management process is key to ensuring data governance can be carried out effectively within your organization.

169. A. Establishing a process for offsite backups is most important. If you do not have access to the company's data that has been created, the rest of these options, while important, mean nothing.

170. B. The act of input validation is the proper testing of any input supplied by a user or application. It prevents invalid data from entering the database or information system. Unchecked user input can be a type of vulnerability in computer software that may be used for security exploits.

171. D. Web-based meeting software for collaboration has become increasingly important to organizations. You cannot disallow completely; otherwise, you lose competitiveness. Our job is to perform quantitative and qualitative software analysis and to choose the best, least expensive, and securest software and configure it properly.

172. C. Flashcards and USBs pose a security threat because they can store data. The storage size of the drive does not matter. Whether it is a 512 MB or a 1 TB SD card, they can host malware that runs when plugged in. They are small, cheap, and easy to use, and they can be connected to a system with little possibility of detection. They can also be infected with malware so that when they are inserted, the malware spreads, creating problems for an organization.

173. D. The best thing to do is add more disk space and employ some type of RAID configuration for speed and redundancy. With certain compliance, you need to know how long to keep the data, and if the cost is high, you must consider what type of backup medium is best for your organization. You should not use a cloud-based backup solution unless you feel that the solution provider can completely secure your data. Sensitive financial records must have the proper security controls in place.

174. B. A breach of physical security can be instigated by a trusted insider or an untested outsider. Intruders, vandals, and thieves remove sensitive information, destroy data, or physically damage or remove hardware.

175. B. The identification phase identifies data custodians, as well as potential data, information, documents, or records that could be relevant. To ensure that there is a complete identification of all resources, use data mapping to reduce complexity.

176. A. In a computer cluster, all the participating computers work together on a particular task. By utilizing a shared client server and storage, the goal you are working toward is increased customer data availability. Depending on how it is configured, it could also lead to increased performance, but that was not an answer choice.

177. A. The best answer is data quality procedures, verification and validation, adherence to agreed-upon data management, and an ongoing data audit to monitor the use and integrity of existing data.

178. A. Redundancy = availability. There are several different types of RAID. The most popular ones are RAID 0 (striping) for speed, RAID 1 (mirroring) for redundancy, and RAID 5 (parity) for error correction. You can combine RAID 0 and 1, or RAID 1 and 0, in different ways to accomplish speed and redundancy.

179. A. The Security Account Manager (SAM) is a database file in Windows located on your system at C:\Windows\System32\config\. They are also stored in the registry at HKEY_LOCAL_MACHINE\SAM.

180. A. Account lockout is not password management. Account lockout is access management.

181. A. The best way to ensure that email is kept secure is to verify that all logins to the system are encrypted and that the cloud provider has signed both a nondisclosure agreement (NDA) and a service level agreement (SLA) with your organization.

182. D. The majority of IoT devices are not developed with security in mind. Many of these devices send data over the network in clear text, use hard-coded passwords that are easily found, and have firmware that is not updated to address known vulnerabilities.

183. A. Two-factor authentication (2FA), sometimes called *multifactor authentication*, is an authentication methodology where a user is granted access only after presenting two or more pieces of evidence, such as something they are, know, or have. One of the best ways to use two-factor authentication is with an application or separate device. Using 2FA with a password manager adds complexity to your defense in depth and is a great way to stop the attacker.

184. D. Separation of duties is an access control mechanism that creates a system of checks and balances on employees with privileged access. Separation of duties requires more than one user to participate in a critical task. One person writes the check, and another person signs the check.

185. D. Attackers seek domain or administrator privileges. Some tools like Metasploit harvest credentials, verify they are still active, and escalate a user account into an administrator account, bypassing all user account controls (UACs). One of the easiest ways to mitigate this is to change passwords often and to enforce strong password policies, including complexity and uniqueness, as well as multifactor authentication.

186. C. The application performs authentication, so you would be checking for the appropriate vulnerability for this process. Privilege escalation is the only vulnerability that has anything to do with authentication.

187. D. The dictionary brute-force attack technique uses hundreds of likely possibilities, including real words. It cycles through them, attempting to find a legitimate password and to defeat a cipher or authentication mechanism. The other choices in this list are actually password industry best practices, including character length. The more characters, the more difficult to crack, but eight is usually the absolute minimum. Use a combination of ASCII characters, which will narrow your chances of a password being compromised. The password should not be listed in a popular password dictionary, and you should use a password manager if you have too many passwords to remember. Popular opinion is that passwords should be changed every 30, 60, or 90 days. However, recent research from the National Institute of Standards and Technology (NIST) discourages frequent password changes and says it is counterproductive to good security practices. For the exam, change your password. For future research, go to https://www.nist.gov/cybersecurity.

188. C. If two-factor authentication (2FA) is not an option, then creating a virtual private network between your organization and the SaaS provider is the best option.

189. A. The best answer here is to use strict password guidelines. Require users to change their passwords and use a device-based recovery tool rather than common password challenges like mother's maiden name. Audit password usage and require password history monitoring, complexity, length, and special characters. Every attacker worth their salt has an account at Ancestry.com.

190. B. Of all these, a password is typically the easiest to compromise. A password is a string of characters associated with a username. Users will create passwords that are easy to remember. Some of the most commonly used passwords are still 123456, password, and qwerty. Sometimes it can be as easy as checking under a keyboard for a written-down password. A more complicated scenario would be an operating system storing passwords with reversible encryption. Storing encrypted passwords in a way that is reversible means that the encrypted passwords can be decrypted. A knowledgeable attacker who is able to break this encryption can then log on to network resources by using the compromised account.

191. B. Federated identity management (FIM) is an arrangement that can be made among multiple enterprises that lets subscribers use the same identification data to obtain access to the networks of all enterprises in the group. The use of such a system is sometimes called identity federation. A trust is a relationship established between domains that enables users in one domain to be authenticated by a domain controller in the other domain. Trust is typically between AD domains, typically within the same company. The actual federation authentication is still a function of AD, so if there are AD trusts between the various domains, federation will give access to all of them.

Testing tip: Be careful of acronyms. FIM can also mean file integrity monitoring, which involves examining files to see if and when they change, how they change, who changed them, and what can be done to restore those files if those modifications are unauthorized.

192. B. The transitive trust is a two-way relationship automatically created between parent and child domains in a Microsoft Active Directory forest. When a new domain is created, it shares resources with its parent domain by default, enabling an authenticated user to access resources in both the child and the parent.

193. D. OpenID is a means of propagating identity information to different web services. For OpenID to work, the web services must have an existing trust relationship either among the web services or via a common third party.

194. C. Security Assertion Markup Language (SAML) is the best one to use for a web-based SSO environment. SAML is XML-based, which is an open standard used for authentication and authorization. Shibboleth is an open source software product that implements SAML. It consists of three functional parts: the identity provider (IdP), the service provider (SP), and the browser. The client is usually a web browser, although SAML can support enhanced clients and proxies.

195. A. Decentralized access control requires more administrative overhead. Centralized access control administration does not require as much, because all the accounts are centrally located.

196. D. The role-based access control is an approach to restricting system access to authorized users that supports the separation of duties and facilitates the administration of security for administrators and users.

197. A. Multifactor authentication is a method where a user is granted access only after giving more than one pieces of evidence to authenticate. It could be something the user knows, is, or has.

198. A. The data owner is responsible for determining who has authorized access to information about certain assets in their area of control. A data owner could take this on a case-by-case basis, or they could define a set of rules called rule-based access control. Access is granted on the security principle of separation of duties, least privilege, and need to know.

199. C. Attribute-based access control (ABAC) is an authorization model that evaluates attributes (or characteristics), rather than roles, to determine access. The purpose of ABAC is to protect objects such as data, network devices, and IT resources from unauthorized users and actions—those who do not have approved characteristics as defined by security policies. Runtime self-protection controls are internal to the application. These controls should be used to manage vulnerabilities in extremely specific lines of code. Simple mistakes result in vulnerabilities.

200. C. A mandatory access control (MAC) policy is a means of assigning access rights based on regulations by a central authority. This class of policies includes examples from both industry and government. The philosophy underlying these policies is that information belongs to an organization rather than individual, and the organization should control the security policy. Role-based access control (RBAC) is a form of access control, which is suitable to separate responsibilities in a system where multiple roles are fulfilled. Discretionary access control (DAC) is the way to go to let people manage the content they own. With attribute-based access control (ABAC), an organization's access policies enforce access decisions based on the attributes of the subject, resource, action, and environment involved in an access event.

201. A. Remote Authentication Dial-In User Service (RADIUS) can provide authentication, authorization, and accounting (AAA) functions to users, in this case, VPN users. RADIUS has evolved far beyond just the dial-up networking use cases it was originally created for. Today it is still used in the same way, carrying the authentication traffic from the network device to the authentication server. Layer 2 Tunneling Protocol (L2TP) is an extension of the Point-to-Point Tunneling Protocol (PPTP) used by an Internet service provider (ISP) to enable the operation of a virtual private network. Lightweight Directory Access Protocol (LDAP) is a lightweight client-server protocol for accessing directory services, specifically X.500-based directory services. Active Directory (AD) is a database. It is a set of services that connect users with the network resources they need. This database contains critical information about your environment, including what users and computers there are as well as the permissions those users have.

202. D. Terminal Access Controller Access Control System Plus (TACACS+) is a Cisco proprietary protocol used for authentication, authorization, and accounting (AAA). It provides device administration for routers, network access servers, and other networked computing devices through one or more centralized servers. RADIUS is a widely deployed protocol for AAA control, and Diameter is the successor. The protocols resemble each other. The packet formatting is similar, and they provide support for the same kind of AAA functions. On the Transport layer, RADIUS uses connectionless UDP, while Diameter utilizes either SCTP or TCP. RADIUS and Diameter do not encrypt usernames. Challenge-Handshake Authentication Protocol (CHAP) is an identity verification protocol. CHAP is based on a shared secret, but in order to authenticate, the authenticator sends a "challenge" message to the access-requesting party, which responds with a value calculated using a "one-way hash" function that takes as inputs the challenge and the shared secret. Once the hash is checked by the authenticator and it matches, authentication succeeds.

203. A. Kerberos is a network authentication protocol. It was designed to provide strong authentication for client-server applications by using secret-key cryptography. A major drawback of Kerberos is that it can be a single point of failure. It requires availability of a central server, and if the server is down, no new users can log in.

204. D. OAuth does not share passwords with a third-party application. With OAuth, the role of owner is to ask the application to perform a function, and the application then tells the server the owner wants to delegate access with a token and secret key. The owner authorizes the token, and the application asks the resource server to exchange the token for an access token and a secret key. MAC can stand for many things, like mandatory access control or media access control or an Apple computer. Extensible Authentication Protocol (EAP) is an authentication framework, not a specific authentication mechanism, frequently used in wireless networks and point-to-point connections. Security Assertion Markup Language (SAML) is an open standard for exchanging authentication and authorization data between an identity provider and a service provider. Basically, OAuth is for authorization of resources, and SAML covers identity management.

205. D. Accountability is the best reason to develop a logging process. When establishing a logging process, you should be aware of storage capabilities and create a log-reviewing policy that trains reviewers how to analyze those logs periodically. Authentication is proving who you are, and authorization is giving you access to resources based on who proving who you are. Two-step verification, also called 2FA (two-factor authentication), is where you add an extra layer of security to your account just in case your password is stolen.

206. D. The best solution is to have identification and authentication carried out with a message to the customer's mobile number, which generates a one-time password to be entered into the corporate web portal to reset passwords. SMS-based one-time passwords (OTPs) are the most common form of out-of-band authentication (OOBA). In-band authentication factors are generally regarded as inferior to out-of-band authentication factors, which are proofs of identity that do not arrive on or depend on the very same system that is requesting authentication.

207. A. Kerberos is a single sign-on solution from Microsoft used to authenticate users once and then allow them to permit the resources they are authenticated to access. Typically, SSL is used to secure credit card transactions, data transfer, and logins, and more recently is becoming the norm when securing browsing of social media sites. HOTP and TOTP are the two main standards for one-time passwords. HMAC-based One-Time Password (HOTP) is the original event-based one-time password algorithm, and it relies on two pieces of information: the secret key and the counter. The counter is stored in the token and on the server. A time-based OTP uses 30–60-second increments in which the OTP is valid only for that duration.

208. B. A Trusted Platform Module (TPM) is a chipset that can be included on a computer's motherboard to store encryption keys. It is also known as "hardware root of trust."

209. B. Open Authorization (OAuth) is an authorization standard that enables a user to authorize the access of the user's data without the users sending authentication credentials. The word *attestation* is almost always used to describe that an individual has confirmed or witnessed the truthfulness to some claim or assertion. In cybersecurity, this could take the form of a digital signature on a legal document or statement. Attestation is about the assignment of responsibility for actions with the goal of holding the person accountable for those actions. JSON Web Token (JWT) is an open standard (RFC 7519) that defines a compact and self-contained way for securely transmitting information between parties as a JSON object. Again, JWT is a standard, meaning that all JWTs are tokens but not all tokens are JWTs. Cookies are text files with small pieces of data—like a username and password—that are used to identify your computer when on a network. HTTP cookies are used to identify specific users and are used to improve your web browsing experience.

210. B. The main difference between Type 1 and Type 2 hypervisors is that Type 1 runs on bare metal and Type 2 runs in an operating system.

211. D. The process of scraping data is also called data extraction. It is the process of importing data from a local file or a website—extracting the data that is usually not human readable but that can be parsed to extract output intended to be human readable.

212. D. When using containers, host them in a container-focused OS and reduce the initial attack surface by disabling unnecessary services. Add monitoring tools for additional visibility, and then develop a strong set of security controls to preserve the integrity of the systems.

213. C. Virtual desktop infrastructure (VDI) is the hosting of desktop environments on a central server. This has been called providing desktop as a service (DaaS). Thin clients are protected from unauthorized software, and data is saved in another location than the server. It uses centralized processing for better management and monitoring.

214. C. Emulation is important in fighting obsolescence and keeping data available. Emulation lets you model older hardware and software and re-create them using current technology. With emulation, you can use a current platform to access an older application, operating system, or data while the older software still thinks it is running in its original environment. Type 1 hypervisor is a hypervisor installed on a bare-metal server, meaning that the hypervisor is its own operating system. Type 1 hypervisors usually perform better due to the direct access to physical hardware. Type 2 hypervisors run inside an operating system of a physical machine. Platform as a service (PaaS) is a kind of cloud computer service that enables a customer to develop and manage applications without a need to build and maintain the usual infrastructure.

215. D. The only answer that is a benefit to virtualization is faster provisioning and disaster recovery. Risks to virtual environments include patching, maintenance, and oversight, but the biggest is probably sprawl. It is easy to create VMs, push them out, duplicate machines, and forget about them. Once you bring them up, they could be up for weeks or months and get behind in patching, which creates a vulnerability.

216. D. While seemingly harmless, with every photo shared, a vast amount of information is attached to each one, including location with an accuracy of within 15 feet. While you are sharing posts on social media, you are also at risk from the criminal element because that photo you took can divulge where you physically are.

217. B. The Common Vulnerabilities and Exposures (CVE) list includes a number for identification, a description, and a public reference for all known cybersecurity vulnerabilities. The CVE system provides a reference method for officially known information security vulnerabilities and exposures and would be best for this goal-setting activity.

218. A. The management of your application requires end-to-end monitoring, so a connection from your location to the cloud environment is the best way to have great control over and visibility into attacks that threaten your environment.

219. D. A community cloud is defined by National Institute of Standards and Technology (NIST) as a collaborative effort in which infrastructure is shared between several organizations from a specific community with shared concerns. It can be managed and controlled by a group of organizations with shared interests so that costs are spread over several users. The public cloud model is the most widely used cloud service. This cloud type is a popular option for web applications, file sharing, and nonsensitive data storage. A public cloud model is available to anyone, but a private cloud belongs to a specific organization. That organization controls the system and manages it in a centralized fashion. A hybrid cloud environment is a combination of public, private, or community.

220. D. While single tenancy is more secure due to isolation and you control access and backups and cost with scaling, it requires more maintenance because single-tenant environments need more updates and upgrades that are managed by the customer.

221. D. A virtual private cloud (VPC) customer has exclusive access to a segment of a public cloud. This deployment is a compromise between a private and a public model in terms of price and features. Access can also be restricted by the user's physical location by employing firewalls and IP address whitelisting. Using the cloud is a trade—you gain speed, performance, and cost, but you still lose control over the security processes.

222. B. Electronic vaulting will enable you to transmit bulk data to an offsite data backup storage facility. You can choose to back up weekly, hourly, and daily. If a server fails, you can restore data quickly, but because the information is sent over the Internet, it should be encrypted. File storage organizes and represents data as a hierarchy of files in folders; block storage chunks data into arbitrarily organized, evenly sized volumes; and object storage manages data and links it to associated metadata.

223. C. A growing number of organizations are choosing to store some or all of their data in the cloud. Some people argue that cloud storage is more secure than on-premises storage, but it adds complexity to storage environments and requires old dogs to learn new tricks. Often with movement to the cloud, IT personnel needs to learn how to implement cloud securely.

224. A. A digital signature provides a means of verifying that an email originated from a particular user and that the email has not been altered. The term *nonrepudiation* describes the result of the user signing the email, but not the technology used.

225. A. Simple Object Access Protocol (SOAP) uses XML so that it can be neutral among web services. It can run on Windows, macOS, and Linux, and it allows clients to use web services and get responses independent of platform or language.

226. C. Key escrow is a means of securing cryptographic keys so that a lost key can be recovered. By breaking the key up into parts, no single escrow agent has the complete key, lending to the security of the entire key.

227. A. On Microsoft servers, the most secure authentication is Extensible Authentication Protocol-Transport Layer Security (EAP-TLS), which can utilize smart cards. It requires public key infrastructure (PKI). Public-key infrastructure (PKI) manages trust in electronic transactions.

228. A. Transport Layer Security (TLS) is an encryption protocol intended to keep data secure when being transferred over a network. It encrypts data to ensure that eavesdroppers or other students are unable to see what you transmit, which is useful when using passwords or credit cards.

229. A. Leveraging machine learning and innovating artificial intelligence will help find and respond to threats. Unfortunately, like with every tool, attackers are using this technology as well. In the future, we will see new machine learning malware and AI spear fishing that increases the length and breadth of cyberattacks.

230. A. An asymmetric encryption algorithm has easier key exchange and management but needs a bigger key than a symmetric algorithm to have the same work factor. Quantum computing is the use of quantum phenomena such as superposition and entanglement to perform computation. Computers that perform quantum computations are known as quantum computers. Hashing is the transformation of a string of characters into a usually shorter fixed-length value or key that represents the original string. Hashing is used to index and retrieve items in a database because it is faster to find the item using the shorter hashed key than to find it using the original value. The Scytale cipher is a type of transposition cipher used since the 7th century BCE. The first recorded use of the scytale cipher was by the Spartans and the ancient Greeks, who used it to transport battle information between generals.

231. D. A PIN is something you create and memorize. The other options are a part of your physical attributes.

232. C. A blockchain, as the name implies, is a chain of digital blocks that contain records of transactions. Each block is connected to all the blocks before and after it. Participants have their own private keys, and it would take massive amounts of computing power to access every instance of a blockchain and alter them all at the same time. Homomorphic encryption allows you to perform calculations on encrypted data without decrypting it first. Secure multiparty computation (SMPC) is a cryptographic protocol that spreads a computation across multiple participants where no other party can see the other user's data. Secure multiparty computation protocols can help data scientists and analysts to contribute compliantly, securely, and privately on distributed data. A blockchain system relies on distributed consensus protocol for ensuring all nodes in the network agree on a single chain of transaction history, given the influence of malfunctioning or malicious attackers.

233. A. Private information retrieval (PIR) is a protocol that allows someone to retrieve an element of a database without the database owner knowing which element was selected. Strong private information retrieval (SPIR) is private information retrieval with the additional requirement that someone learns only the elements they are querying for and nothing else, which answers the need for privacy of a database owner. Secure function evaluation (SFE) and private function evaluation (PFE) are special protocols used in cryptography based on secretly or privately sharing of all the inputs to search for potentially malicious computations that benefit an attacker, primarily used in digital currency, blockchain, and multiparty computations. A National Institute of Standards and Technology report defined big data as "extensive datasets, primarily in the characteristics of volume, velocity, and/or variability that require a scalable architecture for efficient storage, manipulation, and analysis." Some have defined big data as an amount of data that exceeds a petabyte—one million gigabytes.

234. D. An AR cloud-related challenge is structural because it becomes integrated into processes and applications in your enterprise. Once committed to a cloud service, companies become dependent on that service provider, often with no easy way to change to another provider that might be cheaper or faster or deliver a better product. IT departments need to build up the skill set to work in the cloud safely and reliably. The business proposition of AR is causing it to be adopted before the risks have been vetted or having tech developed by companies without significant IT experience, leading to technologies that are vulnerable. Wearable devices can host malware, enabling cameras, collecting data, corrupting work instructions, or disrupting operation. It is fairly easy to steal network credentials off wearable devices using Android and exposing networks. The only one that does not make sense here is micro/nano technology. Micro and nano technologies include a wide range of advanced techniques used to fabricate and study artificial systems, with dimensions ranging from several micrometers (one micrometer is one millionth of a meter) to a few nanometers (one nanometer is one billionth of a meter; a human hair is about 60,000 nanometers wide).

235. B. The one thing all 3D printers share, whether proprietary or open source, is that they are computer-controlled. Those computers run software, which may be prone to development errors that result in security vulnerabilities. The rest of these options are important, but hardening existing systems first should be the priority.

236. C. The use of passwordless authentication methods like biometric and facial recognition has become a norm on mobile devices, but that's not the only place it's used. Both Windows and Linux support passwordless authentication. In a 2018 update to the Active Directory LDAP service, Microsoft added native support for passwordless authentication through FIDO2 keys. This means that with the proper server-level configurations, AD users can walk up to any domain-connected workstation and insert their key to log in to their accounts without making changes at the machine level. Linux also has native support for software keys, which can replace passwords. When passwordless authentication is implemented on a Linux server, users can remotely log into their SSH consoles by presenting their software key instead of typing in their password.

237. C. Machine learning uses algorithms to parse data, learn from that data, and make informed decisions based on what it has learned. Deep learning structures algorithms in layers to create an "artificial neural network" that can learn and make intelligent decisions on its own. Deep learning has enabled many practical applications of machine learning and, by extension, the overall field of AI. Deep learning breaks down tasks in ways that makes all kinds of machine assists seem possible—like driverless cars, better preventive healthcare, and even better movie recommendations on Netflix.

238. A. Chatbots are evolving, and advancements in natural language processing (NLP) have increased their usefulness to the point that live agents no longer need to be the first point of communication for some customers. Some features of chatbots include being able to help users navigate support articles and knowledge bases, order products or services, and manage accounts. NLP describes the interaction between human language and computers. It is a technology that many people use daily, and it has been around for years, from spell-check to Siri, Alexa, or Google Assistant. Biometrics are body measurements related to human characteristics such as fingerprints or retina scans. Virtual reality is a simulated experience that is created by computer technology, placing the user in that reality. Deep fakes refer to a manipulated image or video produced by artificial intelligence that makes someone appear to do or say something they did not.

Chapter 2: Security Operations

1. B. You do not want security analysts chasing irrelevant alerts down rabbit holes. Modern cyberattacks take place over a long time period, progressing through multiple stages of the kill chain. Organizations must detect attack campaigns, not isolated alerts, and you cannot do that with periodic logging—you must have consistent logging.

2. D. Commodity malware can be purchased online and is used by a wide variety of threat actors. The scope of a breach or incident is measured in how widespread or how far the range of the incident reached. The scope of this type of breach, which is limited to just one machine, is considered minimal.

3. A. Any organization that experiences a breach has the opportunity to learn from the incident. Communicating strategic intelligence to the organization as a whole will ensure that the risks the organization experiences are met with expertise and that company assets, including people, are safe.

4. D. If you examine the kill chain for cybersecurity, then you know that attackers will use phishing campaigns to target insiders. Once compromised, an attacker will use privilege escalation to move laterally and attempt to gain enhanced permissions across the network, specifically targeting domain administrators and other privileged accounts to cause the most damage or to find intellectual proprietary information.

5. A. Strategic cyber-intelligence informs decision-makers on long-term issues and overall intent. Operational cyber-intelligence guides support and response operations and usually comes as a forensic report. Tactical intelligence assesses real-time events and supports day-to-day operations.

6. B. Organizations have petabytes of data, and it is impossible for a human team to do any sort of threat hunting manually. A security incident and event management (SIEM) tool organizes that data and can use external threat intelligence for pattern matching or to find data anomalies.

7. B. Threat emulation picks up malware at the exploit phase before hackers can apply evasion techniques. Files are quickly quarantined and inspected, running virtually to discover malicious behavior before it enters your network. Threat emulation can convert newly identified unknown attacks into known signatures, making it possible to block these threats before they have a chance to become widespread.

8. C. CASB is mainly focused on security. Companies need visibility and access control on cloud assets, in addition to a method for data loss prevention as well as protection from malware and insider threats. Insiders can maliciously or unwittingly steal, erase, or expose sensitive data for a variety of reasons.

9. D. The vital new healthcare system being exploited might ruin the company. The healthcare industry is a prime target of cyberattacks and faces hostile cybersecurity issues that have financial and reputational impacts for hospitals, pharmaceutical company, and other healthcare institutions.

10. B. Most social networks are monitored for malicious activity and false information. A post that is instantly reposted by the thousands is a clear indicator that there is malicious activity on that social media network. The original posting account is usually banned and is called the martyr bot. The original account of the hacktivist is sacrificed to spread the attack.

11. B. A script kiddie is a person who uses existing software, computer scripts, or code to hack into computers, lacking the expertise to write their own. A port scan with malicious intent by any attacker, beginner or advanced, must not go undetected. An experienced attacker would conduct the port scan in strobe or stealth mode, limiting the ports to small targets and slowing down the scan over a longer time period to reduce the chance the IT administrator will get an alert.

12. D. Social engineering is malicious activity where data is disclosed by accident. It is typically performed by an attacker outside of the organization. The goal is to get the victim to disclose confidential or sensitive information. Espionage, fraud, and embezzlement are all malicious, and the attacker is internal but commits these crimes on purpose.

13. A. The *best* definition of a risk in IT is a vulnerability in your ecosystem and the high probability of compromise with a known active threat actor. Threat actors fall into categories such as the cyber-criminal who is motivated by money; nation-state actors who are state-funded and have access to many resources; and insiders who can be malicious, looking for financial gain or revenge.

14. C. The risks associated with a supply chain attack have never been higher. Due to recent supply chain attacks, there is growing public awareness of these threats and increased oversight from regulators. Meanwhile, attackers have more resources and tools at their disposal than ever before. A supply chain attack, also known as a third-party attack, happens when someone infiltrates your enterprise through an outside partner, vendor, or provider who has access to your software, systems, updates, patches, and/or data.

15. A. All organizations have vulnerabilities. There's a saying that the only completely secure asset is the one encased in concrete and buried 6 feet under. If you have no budget and minimal vulnerabilities that are protected under compensating controls, then accepting risk is the only option. If the vulnerability has a critical score of 0 and you know there are compensating controls preventing the exploit of that vulnerability, most vulnerability management tools can create an exception to exclude that vulnerability from future reports.

16. C. Configuring a BIOS password ensures that an attacker with physical access to the computer could not reconfigure the boot sequence to boot to a removable drive.

17. A. XSS is an attack that can be mitigated by using input validation and sanitization. Like an XSRF attack, an XSS attack attempts to steal information from a user. If a web application is not able to properly sanitize input from a user, the attacker can use form input to inject malicious code.

18. C. Using open source intelligence sources and threat databases, you can generate your own IDS rules, leveraging the knowledge of third-party sources. By using your own threat landscape as a model, your IDS rules are tailored for your specific use case.

19. B. Passive reconnaissance is gaining information about a company without actively engaging any systems or people by using tools like social media or OSINT. Active reconnaissance is gaining information by actively engaging with people or technologies, such as making a phone call or doing a port scan. Open source intelligence (OSINT) is a multimethod methodology for collecting, analyzing, and making decisions about data that is publicly available. HUMINT is human intelligence, and according to the Central Intelligence Agency (CIA), it is collected through clandestine acquisition of pictures, documents, and other materials from people.

20. B. The deep web refers to a part of the Internet that has to be accessed by navigating to a specific database that is not indexed publicly by a search engine. The dark web is a part of the Internet that is more private, generally needing a specific browser that favors anonymity. Proprietary means owned by a specific business or organization. The Clearnet portion of the Internet is any information that can be found by a search engine such as Google or Bing.

21. C. A hunt team is not a new concept in cybersecurity but is usually afforded only by large enterprise organizations. Hunt teams play an important part in efficiently detecting, identifying, and understanding advanced persistent threats (APT) to correlate this data and to find the bad actors. By using intelligence feeds, they can look for specific actions or malware that will assist in finding perpetrators.

22. C. The MITRE ATT&CK framework is a matrix of tactics and techniques used by threat hunters, red teamers, and defenders to better classify attacks and assess an organization's risk. The aim of the framework is to improve post-compromise detection of adversaries in enterprises by illustrating the actions an attacker may have taken. Organizations can use the framework to identify holes in defenses and prioritize them based on risk. NIST is the National Institute of Standards and Technology; 800-53 is specific to software development life cycles. ISO is the International Organization for Standardization, and 27001 is a list of 14 controls for information security. PCI DSS is a standard for the payment card industry, not a framework.

23. A. An industrial control system (ICS) is a control system that is used for monitoring industrial processes. It can be composed of just a few controllers or a complex network of interactive control systems made up by thousands of connections. Remote sensors will check machinery and then send it to the industrial control system. If it sees that the machinery is overheating, the ICS will tell the machinery to shut down. The ICS gives operators an easy way to manage, monitor, and control industrial processes. ATT&CK for Industrial Control Systems is a knowledge base useful for describing the actions an adversary may take while operating within an ICS network. The knowledge base can be used to better characterize and describe post-compromise adversary behavior. ATT&CK for ICS will describe the actions of an attacker who seeks to cause significant risk to the health and safety of human lives or serious damage to the environment.

24. D. The Diamond Model of Intrusion Analysis (DMIA) applies underlying relationships between the attacker and victim as well as infrastructure and capability. The DMIA applies a scientific approach and produces improvements in analytic effectiveness, efficiency, and accuracy. Ultimately, the model provides opportunities to integrate intelligence in real time for network defense, classifying events with confidence and forecasting what the adversary could do. Gap analysis is a method of assessing the differences in performance between a business's information systems or software applications to determine whether business requirements are being met and, if not, what steps should be taken to ensure they are met successfully. Disaster recovery (DR) is an area of security planning that aims to protect an organization from the effects of significant negative events. Having a DR strategy in place enables an organization to maintain or quickly resume mission-critical functions following a disruption. Intrusion detection systems (IDSs) are software or devices that monitor a network for malicious activity, intentional or unintentional. Any malicious activity is reported to the security information and event management (SIEM) tool.

25. C. The cyber kill chain is a security model that describes how an external attacker is taking steps to penetrate a network and steal its data, breaking down the steps of the attack to help organizations prepare. There are several core stages in the cyber kill chain. They range from reconnaissance (often the first stage in a malware attack) to lateral movement (moving laterally throughout the network to get access to more data) to data exfiltration (getting the data out). All of your common attack vectors—whether phishing or brute force or the latest strain of malware—trigger activity on the cyber kill chain.

26. B. Wireshark is a well-known packet capture tool that can help a pentester examine traffic on a network. It can help find vulnerabilities as well as firewall rule sets. It analyzes live packets and saves them in a PCAP file.

27. A. In a security information and event management (SIEM) tool, you get near real-time alerts and analysis of what is happening on network hardware, servers, and applications. It does this by capturing logs from all those devices, aggregating the data, correlating it, looking for commonalities, and linking events together that are out of the normal range. QRadar, ArcSight, and Splunk are leading SIEM vendors. A VM is a virtual machine. DNS is the Domain Name System, which is the phone book of the Internet. LASE is a word used in conjunction with physical processes in a laser.

28. A. The first step after an intrusion is to document. Creating backups of logs will ensure that investigators have information about the problem. If you are unable to discover the attacker's identity, it might show other important details. After you secure the audit trail, the other answers are options.

29. D. Creating an audit trail is vital. Security policy often specifies which data should be collected, how it should be stored, and how long it will be kept. An audit trail is often used to find unauthorized activity on a network. Due diligence is the reasonable steps taken by a person in order to satisfy a legal requirement, especially in buying or selling something. Syslog is a protocol used to send system log or event messages to a syslog server. It is primarily used to collect various device logs in a central location for monitoring and review. IDSs (intrusion detection systems) use two methods while acquiring and analyzing information. IDSs can use signature-based detection, which takes data activity and compares it to a signature or pattern in the signature database. The other detection method is anomaly-based or behavior-based detection, which detects any anomaly and gives alerts when detecting new types of attacks.

30. A. If the administrator received approval, perhaps the technical catastrophe could have been avoided with a more senior administrator's wisdom. Gaining approval is the first step in managing a needed change. Once approved, testing can be performed. Implementation, deployment, and documentation should follow after testing.

31. D. An Apache log is a record of the events that have occurred on the web server. There are two types: access and error. Access logs contain information about requests coming into the web server whereas error logs contain information about errors the web server encountered when processing requests such as files are missing. An error log will usually have `[error]` in the log as well as what the error was, such as `file does not exist`. In this case, the `500` found in the log line is the error.

32. D. The NetFlow protocol is used by analysts as a network traffic analyzer to determine its point of origin, destination, volume, and paths on the network. Before NetFlow, network engineers and administrators used Simple Network Management Protocol (SNMP) for network traffic analysis and monitoring. SNMP was effective for network monitoring; it did not provide insight into bandwidth usage. NetFlow is now part of the Internet Engineering Task Force (IETF) standard, and the protocol is widely implemented by network equipment vendors.

33. A. If sensitive data is encrypted properly, there is the possibility of no repercussions. Organizations that are the target of attackers usually face serious costs due to notification of quantitative and qualitative losses. Organizations with PII face even higher liabilities.

34. D. File integrity monitoring (FIM) exists because change is constant in your IT department. FIM monitors and detects changes in files that could indicate there has been a breach. FIM is a critical security control involving the examination of files to see when, how, and who changes a file and if those modifications are authorized. FIM is also useful to detect suspicious modifications and detect malware. It is required for certain compliance regulations like PCI DSS.

35. C. Synchronizing time across a network requires Network Time Protocol (NTP). An NTP client will send out a UDP packet to sync time from a configured NTP server, and the NTP client adjusts its time. For certain authentication methodologies like Kerberos, NTP is a must for the process to work properly.

36. A. Backups provide protection for availability. It will protect your company from data loss as well as data corruption. When there is another copy of a file, if the primary copy is damaged, it can be replaced. Organizations should have a data loss prevention policy that defines how the organization will share and protect data. A DLP will specify how data is used in decision-making without exposing it to people who have no "need to know."

37. A. An after-action report (AAR) is a review process that ensures learning and improved performance. It analyzes what happened, why it happened, and how it can be avoided in the future.

38. B. Because Windows Active Directory is available within your corporate environment, using Group Policy to install the antivirus product on all systems is the most efficient method for installation.

39. C. In measuring the severity of an incident, the five measurable factors are scope, impact, cost, downtime, and legal ramifications. Disclosure should be in the disclosure policy, which ensures that the required information is shared with the public, investors, customers, employees, and other stakeholders at the proper time after an event, incident, or breach.

40. A. Netstat, or "network statistics," gathers information about the system, traffic statistics, number of open connections, and number of closing or pending connections. Watching these metrics enables you to determine whether a compromise has occurred or whether it's a performance issue on a server.

41. A. When changing or adding firewall rules, all rules should be tested with matching traffic. It is possible that the rule is not configured properly or that there is a contradicting rule higher up the firewall rule list that could negate the new rule. Only by testing all the rules on the firewall can the validity of the rules be verified.

42. B. Option B denies inbound traffic to the router from a computer with an IP address of 192.168.1.25. Option A permits all inbound traffic. Options C and D deny all inbound traffic. Note that option C is an empty ACL applied to an interface that denies all traffic.

43. B. Installing an IPS and creating the right rules will monitor traffic moving to and from the Internet to stop attacks. Monitoring internal traffic is critical to your defense because attackers can get a foothold in a container environment and expand their reach.

44. A. The command `bash /r` is not a valid Bash command. All of other commands listed place Bash in restricted mode.

45. B. Data security means keeping it private and out of the wrong hands. Data protection is about ensuring that data remains available after there is a failure. A data loss protection (DLP) policy will help protect that data. It should have detailed rules to prevent data from being deleted or stolen. The policy should focus on the protection of valuable, sensitive, or regulated data such as medical or financial records. A good DLP will involve both the technology as well as the policy, such as blocking the use of USB and detailing how to share confidential intellectual proprietary information via email.

46. A. A vulnerability is a weakness in system design, procedure, or code. It can be exploited for a threat to destroy, damage, or compromise an asset. A threat is the circumstance or likelihood of a vulnerability being exploited. The likelihood of the threat is the probability of occurrence or the odds that the event will actually occur. Using a vulnerability scanner like Nexpose or Nessus will help you find vulnerabilities to fix them. Using threat intelligence will help you identify your threat landscape.

47. C. Networks can be built with a multitude of hardware and software. When you are attempting to join two disparate networks, many problems can occur with connectivity, latency, and vulnerabilities due to the two separate entities becoming one. Before making any technical changes, both networks should be examined and documented, and a risk analysis should be performed, beginning with a credentialed vulnerability scan. A credentialed scan allows the vulnerability scanning tool to log in and get more information, such as version of operating system, patch level, and software installed, as well as misconfigurations such as default passwords left on a system. An uncredentialed scan cannot do that. It makes an educated guess on operating system, viewing that machine from the outside by guessing how it responds to TCP/UDP packets.

48. A. Many vulnerability scanners offer an agent-based scan rather than a server-based scan. A small piece of software is installed on the laptops being taken home and can send information directly back to the vulnerability software. Since it is installed on the hard drive using administrative credentials, it acts as a credentialed scan. A server-based scan is optimal for assets that remain stationary.

49. C. The most important aspect of vulnerability management processes is to understand assessing what risks exist to your organization and who/what threatens to use your vulnerabilities against you. Risk = Threat × Vulnerability. All publicly disclosed vulnerabilities are listed by their Common Vulnerability and Exposures (CVE) number. That list is maintained by MITRE, a nonprofit organization funded by the U.S. government. Vulnerabilities will be ranked by things like exploitability or attack vector and given a score called the Common

Vulnerability Scoring System (CVSS), which is maintained in the National Vulnerability Database (NVD) by the National Institute of Standards and Technology (NIST). Scores will range from 0 being not vulnerable and 10 being horrifically vulnerable.

50. B. There are two approaches to network vulnerability scanning: active and passive. Active scanning tools are used where constant vigilance is required. They have a specific area of focus that the product is programmed to monitor. The passive approach allows security personnel to monitor which operating systems are in use; what is being sent to, from, and within the system; which services are available; and where parts of the system may be vulnerable to security threats. The active approach offers much information about system and application vulnerabilities. Both approaches can be used in the same environment. Credentials and non-credentialed scans refer to the use of usernames/passwords to log into a system during the scan process.

51. B. The Security Content Automation Protocol (SCAP) is used for standardizing automated vulnerability management, measurement, and policy compliance. The Extensive Configuration Checklist Description Format (XCDDF) is a specification language for checklists and benchmarks. The Open Vulnerability and Assessment Language (OVAL) is a standardizing language for reporting machine state. The Common Platform Enumeration (CPE) Dictionary is a structured naming scheme for systems and software. The dictionary is provided in XML format and is available to the general public.

52. D. The Security Content Automation Protocol (SCAP) is an open standard used to find security flaws and configuration issues related to security and compliance. SCAP specifications standardize naming conventions and formats used by vulnerability management and policy compliance. The SCAP checklist standardizes computer security configurations, and the SP 800-53 controls framework. HTTP (Hypertext Transfer Protocol) is an application layer protocol designed for communication between browsers and web servers. Asset Reporting Format (ARF) is a data model that facilitates the reporting, correlating, and fusing of asset information. The last release of ARF by NIST was in 2011. CCE used to be an effort by MITRE to assign unique entries called Common Configuration Enumeration to configure guidance statements and controls. As of November 28, 2014, according to the MITRE website: "Activity on the CCE effort has been suspended, and the CCE Web site has been moved to 'Archive' status."

53. A. The best strategy for patch management is to test all updates in a safe environment before deploying them to production.

54. D. A patch management system can automate the process of installing patches on systems. Automating this process makes it more likely that all systems will be patched and none will be mistakenly missed. A security assessment identifies the current security posture of an organization. Vulnerability management is the continual process of identifying, evaluating, treating, and reporting on security vulnerabilities. A vulnerability scanner scans a network, looking for and reporting on known vulnerabilities.

55. D. Hardening a system so that it provides only the required functionality is the best way to mitigate any zero-day issues an organization may have. A zero-day vulnerability has no fix. Hardening the system involves removing any services or applications that are not required.

56. A. Information sharing and analysis centers (ISACs) help critical infrastructure owners and operators protect their facilities, personnel, and customers from cyber and physical security threats and other hazards. ISACs collect, analyze, and disseminate actionable threat information to their members and provide members with tools to mitigate risks and enhance resiliency. By appropriating an organization's specific hashtag, bots can distribute spam or malicious links that will appear in an organization's circle. Trend-jack is similar in that attackers will pick the tops trends of the day to disseminate the attack, making a "social media watering hole" and plant the payload where the potential users are gathering.

57. D. A dynamic application security test (DAST) is used by developers to analyze an application while in runtime to identify any security vulnerabilities or weaknesses. DAST examines an application while it's working and attempts to hack it as an attacker would. Static application security testing (SAST) should be performed early and often against all files containing source code to find flaws and weaknesses such as SQL injection. Reverse engineering is taking apart an object to see how it works in order to duplicate or make it better. Side-channel analysis allows an attacker to infer information by observing nonfunctional characteristics of a program, such as execution time or memory consumed.

58. A. When purchasing hardware, you do not have control of the hardware's design and process. Therefore, you must purchase hardware from vetted and responsible vendors. Researchers in December 2018 discovered a UEFI rootkit called Lojack used globally by APT groups. Lojack took advantage of firmware vendors and enabled the remote flashing of firmware.

59. B. Dumb fuzzers can provide completely random input to software with no intelligence to test for bugs. Sometimes, a program will perform certain processes only if there is specific input like a protocol definition or a rule for a file format. That allows for valid input, which is a smart fuzzer.

60. A. Network analysis is most likely going to begin with a review of web server logs using a SIEM tool like Splunk, QRadar, or AlienVault. Network analysis can be done on live traffic or on logs that were recorded in a logging file. An analyst who suspects that a web server has been attacked should acquire and then analyze the logs to determine if, when, and how an attacker might have gained access. Hardware analysis is the examination of the electrical or electro-mechanical devices, which often contain firmware or embedded software. Software composition analysis (SCA) is a segment of the application security testing (AST) that deals with managing open source component use. SCA tools perform automated scans of an application's code base, including containers and registries, to identify all open source components and any security vulnerabilities.

61. B. Pivoting is a methodology that pentesters (and attackers) use to compromise deeper into a network. After the initial compromise, the attacker can use that system on a network to attack other systems to avoid network detection, firewall rules, or IDS. In Metasploit, you have the ability to create proxy pivots and VPN pivots to expand the attack.

62. D. There are several cyberattack models, including the Mandiant Attack Model and Lockheed Martin's Cyber Kill Chain. Most steps are remarkably similar in nature. Reconnaissance attempts to identify vulnerabilities in the target network. Persistence is an attacker creating a backdoor or alternative access methods should their first intrusion be detected. Weaponization is creating remote access like a virus or a worm. Post-exploitation refers to any action taken after a session is open from a successful exploit or brute-force attack.

63. D. Security Content Automation Protocol (SCAP, pronounced "ess-cap") is currently at version 1.3. SCAP is a number of open standards widely used to enumerate software and configuration issues as they pertain to security. These specifications help standardize formats used by policy compliance.

64. A. An organization can easily control their vulnerability management life cycle to scan specific assets during specific times. A tabletop exercise is a dry run through policies and procedures that anticipates the readiness of an organization to respond to an incident or event. Sandboxing is a process used to execute suspicious code without risking harm to a device or network, which can add another layer of protection against possible malware. Social engineering is a deceptive act used to manipulate a user into sharing information that can be used for nefarious purposes.

65. C. On a Windows server, `nbtstat` displays NetBIOS over TCP/IP (NetBT) statistics. NetBIOS displays tables for both the local and remote computers. It refreshes names registered with the Windows Internet Name Service (WINS).

66. B. Domain Name System (DNS) uses port 53 for both TCP and UDP. TCP is used for DNS zone transfers, and UDP is for DNS queries. Dynamic Host Configuration Protocol (DHCP) is a network management protocol used to automate the process of configuring devices on IP networks, allowing them to use network services such as DNS, NTP, and any communication protocol based on UDP or TCP. A DHCP server dynamically assigns an IP address and other network configuration parameters to each device on a network so they can communicate with other IP networks. DHCP can run on ports 67–68. Internet Message Access Protocol (IMAP) is an Internet standard protocol used by email clients to retrieve email messages from a mail server over a TCP/IP connection, usually over port 143. Hypertext Transfer Protocol Secure (HTTPS) is an extension of the Hypertext Transfer Protocol. It is used for secure communication over a computer network and is widely used on the Internet over port 443.

67. B. An HTTP or HTTPS interceptor like BurpSuite by PortSwigger is one of the best tools out there to do web application assessments. You can read and manipulate web traffic. Additionally, you can scan a target machine; interrupt the flow of traffic; and manipulate, modify, and forward information.

68. C. John the Ripper is a fast password cracker. It is free and open source.

69. D. A white-box white-hat penetration test means the good guys know everything about the network, hardware, and software as well as policies and procedures the company has. This would be included within the Scope of Work. Rules of Engagement (RoE) is a document that deals with the manner in which the penetration test is to be conducted. Some of the directives that should be clearly spelled out in RoE before you start the penetration test are client contact information, sensitive data handling, and status reporting. Since it is a white-box white-hat test, a list of assets could be included as well. What would *not* be included is the malware the penetration testers would use during the engagement.

70. B. User training and policy enforcement are critical to preventing social engineering attacks. Technical countermeasures can prevent automated attacks. Social engineering is attacking human nature.

71. A. Active reconnaissance requires interaction. As the "attacker," you may start to appear in logs because you interact with systems. Active reconnaissance is invasive. Passive reconnaissance involves making use of the vast amount of information available on the web, collecting as much information as possible on a target. Passive reconnaissance is noninvasive. There can be passive and active reconnaissance done on a facility to test how buildings are accessed and if the facility is secure. Physical penetration testing must be documented in the scope of work.

72. B. The best-known vulnerability management tools on the market today are Nessus by Tenable, Nexpose by Rapid7, and Qualys Vulnerability Management. A vulnerability scanner compares details about the target attack surface to a database of vulnerabilities, which are known securities issues with services, ports, operating systems, and protocols. For a complete list of assets, make sure you are using a credentialed scan with the proper permissions and access. It should also be documented how often to rescan for assets that are added to the network.

73. A. The five steps in risk assessment are as follows: (1) Identify hazards or anything that can do harm to the health and safety of assets, including people, (2) Decide what the vulnerabilities are and who/what could be harmed, (3) Assess the threat landscape and take action after you have recorded the impact of that exposure to the organization, (4) Make a record of the findings, and (5) Review the risk assessment.

74. C. In computing environments, race conditions in software or on a network can occur if two tasks are performed at the same time or if two users attempt to access a specific channel at the same instant. Attackers take advantage of the confusion of race condition vulnerabilities by gaining access to the data or unauthorized access to a network.

75. B. An overflow occurs when a program writes more data to a field than is expected. An attacker can take advantage of this situation by injecting their own malicious code or variables. Because these commands don't check size, they make a program susceptible to overflow attacks.

76. A. Buffer overflows occur when software code has too much input and the programmer failed to include any data input validation checks. Extra data in a buffer overflow is pushed into the execution stack and is processed, enabling the attacker to perform any system operation. SQL injection (SQLi) is a type of an injection attack that makes it possible to execute malicious SQL statements. These statements control a database server behind a web application. Attackers can use SQLi vulnerabilities to bypass application security measures. Integer overflow occurs when an arithmetic operation attempts to create a numeric value that is outside of the range that can be represented with a given number of bits—either larger than the maximum or lower than the minimum representable value. (Think of an odometer on your car rolling over from 999999 back to 000000.) Insecure direct object references (IDORs) are a cybersecurity issue that occurs when a web application developer uses an identifier for direct access to an internal implementation object but there is no additional access control and/or authorization checks. An IDOR vulnerability would happen if the URL of a transaction could be changed through client-side user input to show unauthorized data of another transaction.

77. A. Single sign-on (SSO) is an authentication solution that allows a user to log in once and have access to multiple computer systems. With single sign-on, a user only has to enter their login credentials (username, password, etc.) one time on a single page to access all of their applications. SSO is often used when user applications are assigned and managed by an internal IT team. Remote workers who use multiple applications also benefit from using SSO.

78. B. A fuzzer, fuzzing utility, or fuzz testing is a type of testing where techniques are used to discover coding errors and loopholes in software, networks, or operating systems by inserting invalid random data called *fuzz*. The software, network, or operating system is monitored for crashes or exceptions.

79. D. Your organization can avoid all these security vulnerability examples by conducting regular secure configuration assessments. Security misconfiguration vulnerabilities occur when a web application component is susceptible to attack due to a misconfiguration or insecure configuration option. Misconfiguration vulnerabilities make your application susceptible to attacks that target any part of the application stack.

80. A. In forensics, when you are recovering only specific files based on headers, footers, or data structure, it is called *data carving*. Foremost was created by the USAF and can be downloaded at SourceForge.

81. A. Public relations must disclose the hack. If you disclose the breach, you control the message. You can present the information correctly and reinforce your business reputation by demonstrating that you are handling the breach in a responsible way. For example, if a limited number of customers are affected, notify them in a proper and timely manner.

82. A. There are two ways to enroll in SCEP: an SCEP server CA automatically issues the certificate, or an SCEP is requested and set to PENDING, and the CA admin then manually approves or denies the certificate.

83. C. The primary concern with Bluetooth for business considerations is that Bluetooth uses a weak encryption cipher, E0. E0 uses a 128-bit key, but cryptanalysis has shown that the E0 cipher is only as strong as a 38-bit key.

84. A. A stream cipher encrypts data bit by bit. It doesn't require as many hardware resources as other types of ciphers like block ciphers.

85. D. The cipher lock on the server room door is a physical security control as opposed to technical controls.

86. C. A peer review is sometimes called a code review. You inspect and analyze all the code to make sure that it works as it's supposed to and that all security and business needs are met, but it can take a long time to perform. The time and effort can result in delays that may outweigh the benefits.

87. C. All an attacker needs is just one vulnerability to gain access to your network. At a minimum, even with quarterly compliance requirements, if you are patching weekly, then you must scan for vulnerabilities weekly. The only way to know if the patch or compensating controls you set in place have worked is to follow the vulnerability life cycle and scan after patching.

88. D. Financial loss would be the threat combined with a vulnerability, which is better described as an impact or result to the organization.

89. C. Containerization is a standardized unit for development and deployment. It is a stand-alone lightweight instance of software that includes code, system tools, third-party libraries, and settings. The two most popular containerization tools are Docker and Kubernetes.

90. A. A distributed denial-of-service (DDOS) is an attack performed through a multitude of systems on a single target. A website, or in this case, VoIP, receives a massive amount of incoming data in the form of messages, requests, or calls. All of this incoming data forces the site, or service, to shut down and deny the service to customers and users dependent on the service.

91. B. An application that uses a large amount of data, especially when done with an HTML editor, is at a high risk of injection attacks if proper prevention measures are not enforced.

92. C. This is hardware. You can put an operating system on most any hardware out there. When old equipment has maintenance issues, it is sometimes difficult to find the parts and perform regular updates to those assets.

93. D. Any type of transition to new software or hardware should be projectized so that processes roll out smoothly. Plans for decommissioning the existing OS, implementing testing, and verifying compliance with applicable regulations is the best life cycle. In addition, with any type of change or upgrade, be sure to have a rollback or regression process just in case the project fails.

94. A. The vulnerability time is the time from when the vulnerability is discovered and the vulnerability is patched. The vulnerability window is when an IT asset is most vulnerable. This window has become increasing important because it is currently much larger than in the past. The cycle of creating malware based on inherent vulnerabilities keeps getting shorter and shorter.

95. D. Patching, hardening, and firewalls are all mitigation techniques used to prevent server-side attacks. Identity management is about access control.

96. A. An application programming interface (API) is a tool that can allow two applications to talk to each other. One of the key advantages of APIs is that they provide a great deal of flexibility. Data is not tied to resources or methods, so Representational State Transfer (REST) can handle multiple types of calls, return different data formats, and even change structurally with the correct implementation of hypermedia. REST is an architectural style for providing standards between computer systems on the web, making it easier for systems to communicate with each other. REST-compliant systems, often called RESTful systems, are characterized by how they are stateless and separate the concerns of client and server.

97. B. Trojans present themselves as one thing, when in reality they are something else. According to new research published by Kaspersky Lab, the malware known as Razy is a Trojan that uses some of the more unusual techniques on record when infecting systems. The Razy Trojan is targeting legitimate browser extensions and is spoofing search results in the quest to raid cryptocurrency wallets and steal virtual coins from victims.

98. A. Microsoft ActiveX controls are dangerous and should be installed only when needed, removed when no longer necessary, and downloaded only from a trusted source. Active X controls are small programs sometimes also called add-ons, and they are insecure by design and deprecated, effective August 31, 2020. Flash was an Adobe product used for viewing multimedia content and streaming audio. Adobe stopped supporting Flash and concluded end of life (EOL) as of December 31, 2020, and it strongly recommends immediately uninstalling Flash Player to protect systems.

99. A. HTML 5 is a revision of the Hypertext Markup Language (HTML), the standard programming language for describing the contents and appearance of web pages. HTML5 was developed to solve compatibility problems that affect the current standard, HTML4. One of the biggest differences between HTML5 and previous versions of the standard is that older versions of HTML require proprietary plug-ins and APIs. This is why a web page that was built and tested in one browser may not load correctly in another browser. HTML5 provides one common interface to make loading elements easier, so there is no need to install a Flash plug-in in HTML5 because the element will run by itself. HTML5 is a solution that defines the behaviors of web page content and encourages more interoperable implementations.

100. C. Netsparker is a popular web application scanner that supports JavaScript and Ajax-based apps. It can find flaws like SQLi and local file inclusion and even suggests remediation actions. With Netsparker, you do not have to verify the vulnerability. If Netsparker cannot verify the flaw, it alerts you. JavaScript is a client-side scripting language, which means the source code is processed by the client's web browser rather than on the web server. This means functions can run after a web page has loaded without communicating with the server. Ajax (short for Asynchronous JavaScript and XML) is a technique for creating better, faster, and more interactive web applications with the help of XML, HTML, CSS, and JavaScript.

101. C. Simple Object Access Protocol (SOAP) is exactly that—simple. It is used as a messaging protocol for exchanging information via web services with disparate protocols and operating systems. This enables developers to authenticate, authorize, and communicate using Extensible Markup Language (XML).

102. B. Machine code is a set of instructions that is directly machine-understandable and is processed by the central processing unit (CPU). Machine code is in binary (0s and 1s) format, which is completely different from the byte code and source code. It is regarded as the lowest-level representation of the source code. Machine code is obtained after compilation or interpretation. It is also called machine language. Byte code is an intermediate code between the source code and machine code. It is a low-level code that is the result of the compilation of a source code, which is written in a high-level language.

103. A. XSS is an attack that can be mitigated by using input validation and sanitization. Like an XSRF attack, an XSS attack attempts to steal information from a user. If a web application is not able to properly sanitize input from a user, the attacker can use form input to inject malicious code.

104. A. When the browser loads that page, the victim's browser makes the request using the legitimate cookie from the initial login. Cross-site request forgery, also known as one-click attack or session riding and abbreviated as CSRF or XSRF, is a type of malicious exploit of a website where unauthorized commands are submitted from a user that the web application trusts. Cross-site scripting attacks (also known as XSS attacks) target scripts embedded in a page that are executed on the client side (in the user's web browser) rather than on the server side. SQL injection is a web security vulnerability that allows an attacker to interfere with the queries that an application makes to its database. It generally allows an attacker to view data that they are not normally able to retrieve. The directory traversal attack (also known as a path traversal attack) gives an attacker access to files, directories, and commands that are stored outside the root directory. This attack uses the "no./" special-character sequence to alter the resource location requested in the URL. If an attacker is able to perform directory traversal on the site, in some cases they might be able to read or write to arbitrary files on the server, allowing them to modify application data or behavior and ultimately take full control of the server.

105. C. This log is SQL injection. The SQL is valid and will return all rows from the UserID table because OR 1=1 is a true statement. Without additional SQL, it is hard to know the table is UserID because the SQL is likely checking the userid column looking for a row where the userid is 101; generally, select * from `<table>` where userid=`<Input from web page>`. So the injection here is their userid, `101 or 1=1;--'`, which will then test true. The semicolon and double hyphen is important; if there was also a check on the password to log in, the semicolon completes the SQL, ignoring the rest. Developers should validate all end-user input to prevent injection attacks.

106. A. Mobile device configuration profiles are XML files, defining all settings and restrictions that should belong on your mobile devices. The Extensible Markup Language (XML) is a simple text-based format for representing structured information: documents, data, configuration, books, transactions, invoices, and much more. It was derived from an older standard format called SGML (ISO 8879), in order to be more suitable for web use. XML is one of the most widely used formats for sharing structured information today: between programs, between people, between computers and people, both locally and across networks.

107. B. Sending LDAP passwords in clear text has never been a good idea because it makes it easy for attackers with the ability to sniff network traffic to steal credentials. In large organizations, it is extremely time-consuming to identify and fix all the applications that still use this insecure method of LDAP. Microsoft recommends that sysadmins turn on in-depth diagnostic logging on their domain controllers to identify offending applications. It is very noisy and will probably cause a flood of events into the Directory Service event log.

108. C. Input fields in web applications can be vulnerable to SQL injection. An attacker can use SQL commands in the input field in a way to change the statement executed on the server. Running the command shown executes the following SQL query: SELECT id FROM users WHERE username='username' AND password=' password' OR 1=1;. Because OR 1=1 will always test true, the attacker will gain access to the account with the passed username in the field.

109. A. By default, Ethernet ports on a router are shut down. To bring the port up, the no shutdown command must be entered after the last command listed in the question.

110. A. Secure Boot is a security mechanism included in a Unified Extensible Firmware Interface (UEFI) that ensures an OS boot loader is certified before loading it. Certification is verified using signed certificates.

111. C. Containerization establishes a separate and encrypted space on employees' mobile devices where business data is kept apart from everything else on the device. This can enable an administrator to manage what is in the container and restrict access to the corporate network.

112. D. VLAN hopping is an attack where the attacker changes the VLAN tag of a frame so that the attacker's frame is able to access a different VLAN. To launch this attack, an attacker must establish a trunk link between the target switch port and the attacker's system. If the switch port is configured either as a static trunk port or has Dynamic Trunking Protocol (DTP) enabled on the port, a trunk link can be established. To prevent this, ensure that the Ethernet ports are configured as access ports only. DPT is a misspelling of DTP.

113. C. Virtual Machine Escape is an exploit in which the attackers can run code on a VM that enables an OS to interface directly with the hypervisor. This type of exploit of a vulnerability can be a huge risk. The attacker could then have access to the host operating system and all other VMs running on that host.

114. C. The security offered by SSL and TLS can help prevent on-path attacks, formerly known as man-in-the-middle (MiTM) attacks. These protocols are used to encrypt segments of TCP/IP traffic. An on-path attack happens when an attacker gains access to traffic sent between two devices. If the data is unencrypted, the attacker can view all the traffic. SSL and TLS are used by HTTPS over port 443. A distributed denial-of-service (DDoS) attack is when attackers attempt to make it impossible for a service to be delivered. In a DoS attack, it's one system that is sending the malicious data or requests; a DDoS attack comes from multiple systems. These attacks work by drowning a system with requests for data, like sending a web server so many requests to serve a page that it crashes under the demand. The result is available Internet bandwidth, CPU, and RAM capacity becomes overwhelmed. VLAN hopping (virtual local area network hopping) is a method of attacking a network by sending packets to a port that is not normally accessible from a given end system. Border Gateway Protocol (BGP) hijacking is an illicit process of taking control of a group of IP prefixes assigned to a potential victim. Either intentionally or accidentally, it is achieved by changing paths used for forwarding network traffic, exploiting the weaknesses of BGP.

115. A. Mobile device management (MDM) for company-owned, personally enabled (COPE) devices using near-field communication (NFC) was built for convenience, not security. All you have to do is bump, tap, or swipe against an NFC reader and the connection is valid. No login or password is necessary. NFC is concerned only with distance. Turn off NFC by default when not in use. Interception of data is a worry but not the biggest one.

116. C. Insecure direct object references enable an attacker to bypass authorization and directly access a resource that they should not have access to, such as database records, files, or other application pages.

117. D. Security awareness training is vital to any customer-facing organization because 80–85 percent of most compromises today begin with some form of social engineering. Unfortunately, it's usually the first thing cut from the IT budget.

118. A. Using a vulnerability scanner like Nexpose or Nessus is a good example of an organization proactively in finding vulnerabilities in systems on their network. If vulnerabilities are found, they can be patched or the services disabled, hardening the system to make it resistant to future attacks.

119. C. A hunt team is not a new concept in cybersecurity but is usually afforded only by large enterprise organizations. Hunt teams play an important part in efficiently detecting, identifying, and understanding advanced persistent threats to correlate this data and to find the bad actors.

120. A. Training and policy enforcement are key examples of how to prevent social engineering attacks. Many end users are not aware of the risks involved. Training raises awareness and should provide clear instructions for dealing with and reporting suspicious activity, including where end users should forward any suspected email.

121. C. A honeypot will attract malicious users. Administrators then are able to use that information to protect legitimate assets. The location of the honeypot, as well as the services running on it and data it contains, will determine what kind of attacks it will be vulnerable to. A honeynet is an entire network, not just a single system, set up to attract attackers. A botnet is a collection of compromised computers called zombies and is controlled by a zombie master.

122. A. A honeypot is a tool used to gather information about intruders and their methodologies. This valuable threat intelligence analyzes the tools used in an attack and then uses the information to protect legitimate assets.

123. A. A honeypot or honeyfile would be a detective control function and a technical control type. Control functions include preventive, detective, and corrective functions. Control types are physical, technical, and administrative.

124. B. A full mesh network configuration provides for maximum redundancy in a network with all the network devices, in this case, in the core connected to each other. If one device fails, network traffic can always find another path to its destination. Most users don't need static IP addresses. Static IP addresses normally matter more when external devices or websites need to remember your IP address. One example is VPN or other remote access solutions that trust (whitelists) certain IPs for security purposes. A static IP address is not required if you are hosting a server, although it can simplify the setup process. Most devices use dynamic IP addresses, which are assigned by the network when they connect and change over time.

125. A. The Social-Engineer Toolkit (SET) by David Kennedy's TrustedSec is a framework for simulating attacks such as credential harvesting, phishing, and PowerShell attacks. You may have seen the SMS spoofing attack on the TV show *Mr. Robot*. It is Python based and will automate these attacks, create malicious web pages, and more.

126. A. Data visualization quickly transfers information from machine analytics to the human brain efficiently and meaningfully. With visualization tools like Domo or Google Analytics, you see the clarity of the message that the data holds.

127. A. In a security information and event management (SIEM) tool, you get near real-time alerts and analysis of what is happening on network hardware, servers, and applications. It does this by capturing logs from all those devices, aggregating the data, correlating it, looking for commonalities, and linking events together that are out of the normal range. QRadar, ArcSight, and Splunk are leading SIEM vendors.

128. A. Database activity monitors (DAMs) monitor databases and analyze the type of activity occurring on them. A DAM is like a SIEM, except that the DAM is concerned specifically with databases, whereas a SIEM is concerned with various networked devices.

129. B. ARO × SLE = ALE or 12 × $1,500 = $18,000. If the computers are not protected, the company can lose $18,000 a year. You recommend mitigating the risk by purchasing the antivirus tool. Antivirus software is a type of program designed and developed to protect computers from malware like viruses, worms, spyware, botnets, rootkits, and keyloggers.

130. B. A BCP and DRP are never complete. They are updated and improved over time. Management oversees one single fully integrated plan, which needs approval and testing, and may consist of multiple subplans. Immutable infrastructure is an approach to managing services and software deployments on IT resources wherein components are replaced rather than changed. A device, component, application, or service is effectively redeployed each time any change or disaster occurs.

131. D. The question said nothing about speed. Speed is good. Actually, speed is great, but still, the question targets availability. For availability focus, create and enforce security policies appropriately, create a standard image and configuration for hardening, and have a backup.

132. D. The process of looking for hidden information in steganography data is called steganalysis.

133. D. PaaS enables you to avoid the expense and complexity of having to buy and manage software licenses, application infrastructure, development tools, and other resources. You manage the applications and services that you have developed, and the cloud provider does everything else.

134. C. A router is most closely associated with access control lists (ACLs). An ACL is the basic firewall control used to either allow or disallow traffic into a network.

135. A. Software can check the state of a resource, but the state can change between the time of check (ToC) and the time of use (ToU). This change can cause the software to crash or be a security risk if an attacker can influence the state of the resource between check and use. The most basic fix is to not to perform a check. It limits the false sense of security given by the ToC.

136. A. The biggest problem comes when two operations running in parallel (concurrent operations) use the same data and there is a difference between the results. Locking is a method that allows locking in variable data and forces sequential operation of atomic processes that will use the same data.

137. C. `cron` is a Linux command for scheduling a task (command). Cron jobs allow you to automate certain commands or scripts on your server to complete repetitive tasks automatically. This can be a very resourceful tool, because a cron job can be set to run by 15-minute or hourly increments, a day of the week or month, or any combination of these. For example, you could set a cron job to delete temporary files every week so that your disk space is not being used up by unnecessary files. Bash is the default user shell on most Linux installations. The main purpose of a shell is to allow users to interact effectively with the system through the command line. Shells have mechanisms to send the output of one program as input into another and facilities to interact with the filesystem, such as a user traversing the filesystem or directing the output of a program to a file. Python is a popular general-purpose programming language that can be used for a wide variety of applications. It includes high-level data structures, dynamic typing, dynamic binding, and many more features that make it useful for complex application development. PowerShell is a powerful tool for automating tasks and simplifying configuration, and it can be used to automate almost any task in the Windows ecosystem, including Active Directory and Exchange.

138. C. A false positive alert is an alert that is generated but that is not associated with a true attack. Having tumbleweeds hitting your fence, triggering alerts, is an example of a false positive alert. A true positive is an alert triggered from an attack. A true negative is no alert triggered because no attack occurred. A false negative is an attack happening with no alert triggered.

139. A. Tailgating is used by social engineers to gain access to a building or some secure area. A tailgater waits for an authorized user to open a door and time it so they can pass right behind. They will attempt to catch their victim unaware or sidetracked with other tasks.

140. A. A turnstile ensures that only one authenticated person enters at a time. It is a means of physical access control and prevents tailgating, which is when an unauthorized individual attempts to follow an authorized person into a secured area. Badges will authenticate each user who uses the turnstile. If managed correctly, physical security can tell you who is in the building during an emergency.

141. D. The most common disadvantage to using a signature-based IDS is false positives, which can happen when the IDS identifies legitimate traffic as an attack. IDS signatures are updated by the IDS vendor in response to vulnerabilities in the wild. If you have a poorly written signature, it can produce both false positives and false negatives. False negatives occur when the signature fails to correctly identify malicious activity.

142. A. Many organizations today are using AI and machine learning to triage threats so that workers can focus on critical attacks. Machines can handle the repetitive work so that you can free up time to deal with strategic issues such as modernizing infrastructure.

143. D. Risk analysis involves looking at how objectives might change due to the impact of an event or incident. Once a risk is identified, it is analyzed both qualitatively and quantitatively so that the proper steps can be taken to mitigate them. These steps are documented in procedure controls and should be implemented as soon as an incident occurs.

144. D. In digital or cyber-forensics, no matter what action has been taken and what the implied burden of proof is, you must treat the incident as if a crime had been committed. If the process is broken, the risk of challenging or diminishing the value of the evidence could make it inadmissible and reduce its value to the company. The IRT should have well-documented policies and procedures in place and have chain-of-custody rules. According to the National Institute of Standards and Technology (NIST), there are four steps: 1) Preparation, 2) Detection and Analysis, 3) Containment and Eradication and Recovery, and lastly, 4) Post-Incident Activity, better known as lessons learned.

145. A. After an incident, managers can evaluate the effectiveness of their response and then identify areas that need improvement, specifically, assessment, detection, notification, and evaluation. The lessons learned document details how your emergency response process can be improved.

146. D. In an after-action report (AAR), it is time for reflection and to record what was done well and the areas that need improvement. Capturing and regularly updating the lessons learned can keep the incident response on track. In the long run, it can also help continually improve how organizations execute incident response.

147. B. Disconnecting the intruder is the best response if confidentiality is of utmost importance. Allowing any more time to the intruder might enable them to pivot deeper into the network. Delaying, auditing, or monitoring the intruder is the correct response if you are going to prosecute the intruder. This is the type of scenario that has already been discussed so that you know exactly what the response should be in an incident/event.

148. C. This actually happened. A casino in North America detected a ransomware attack that used the network-attached fish tank as a point of entry. The attack was spotted due to machine learning algorithms that detected the intrusion, and no damage was done.

149. A. The biggest issue with any type of BYOD is the loss of data (data exfiltration), and the biggest fix is to remotely wipe the device should it become lost or stolen.

150. D. According to Gartner, social engineering is the single greatest security risk faced in cybersecurity. Social engineering is the art of manipulating, influencing, or deceiving to gain information or control of a system, process, or finances.

151. C. When a situation arises, such as a service interruption or some other significant incident, the security operations center (SOC) receives word via their monitoring system. Once it has identified an issue, you must initiate an incident response, which will in turn notify the appropriate parties, providing the necessary information so they can begin working to resolve the problem. Critical issues must be addressed quickly, as any downtime can have a tremendous negative impact on the organization, from lower revenue to lost customers. This puts a lot of pressure on NOC managers to handle any and all incidents with the utmost attention given to quality and turnaround time. The problem comes into play when businesses are still relying on antiquated systems to manage their incident response processes. The result is a huge margin for human error and unnecessary delay.

152. C. Due care is acting responsibly. Due diligence is verifying those actions are sufficient. An organization that shows due care means they took every reasonable precaution to protect their assets and environment. A statement of work (SOW) is a document used in project management. It is the narrative description of a project's work requirement. It defines project-specific activities, deliverables, and timelines for a vendor providing services to the client. A nondisclosure agreement (NDA), also known as a confidentiality agreement, confidential disclosure agreement, or secrecy agreement, is a legal contract or part of a contract. Runbooks are often confused with playbooks, and some IT professionals use the terms synonymously. While runbooks define individual processes, playbooks deal with overarching responses to larger issues or events and may incorporate multiple runbooks and personnel within them—think of a runbook as a chapter within a playbook.

153. B. Security orchestration and automation response (SOAR) helps teams improve their security posture and create efficiency—without sacrificing control of important security and IT processes. SOAR technology helps coordinate, execute, and automate tasks between various people and tools, allowing companies to respond quickly to cybersecurity attacks and improve their overall security posture. SOAR tools use security "playbooks" to automate and coordinate workflows that may include any number of disparate security tools as well as human tasks.

154. D. Because time is important, as a project manager you need to estimate how long the merge will take and then look at ROI—how much to sustain and how much to change. Involve the stakeholders and present them with a communication plan clarifying who is involved in the decision-making process.

155. A. The recovery time objective (RTO) is the duration of time that can pass before a disruption begins to affect the flow of normal business operations. It can include the time for trying to fix the problem even if it does not work; the actual recovery itself; testing the fix; and communicating with others.

156. B. The best option for the CISO is to investigate whether the outside firm has a service level agreement (SLA) with the subcontractor, which will protect the organization legally. If the contract does not exist, the CISO must insist that one be created, or they should exit the contract as soon as possible.

157. D. The role of a digital forensic analyst or a digital forensics examiner is to protect computer systems, recover files, document and analyze data, and to provide reports and feedback or testify in court. This role also assists in the creation of documentation for best practices.

158. C. The golden rule of forensics is never touch, change, or alter anything until it is documented, identified, measured, and photographed. An image is a complete image of all the contents of a storage device. A bitstream copy of an image copies all areas of a storage device. When documenting for an incident, you need to list the software/hardware used, its source and destination name, the start/end timestamp, and hashed values.

159. D. If the logs are evidence, then as evidence they cannot be altered. If the timestamps are from years before the crime occurred, they may not be allowed in court.

160. C. Asking a user to surrender evidence is an option if the user is unaware of the breach. If the phone owner is involved directly with the activity, then confiscation is the better option. With data breaches, the chain of custody is important, and you do not want the user destroying evidence, either by accident or on purpose.

161. A. Understand what can be contained in volatile memory before you power down a machine that you believe is compromised. Use a tool that is able to quickly analyze RAM and add that data to digital evidence.

162. A. The Internet Engineering Task Force (IETF) released guidelines for evidence collection known as RFC 3227. This document explains the order of volatility, which is least volatile to most—archives, physical, logging, disk, temporary files, routing and ARP tables, registers, and cache.

163. B. Using dd enables you to clone a drive and flash a USB, hard disk, or any file without data loss. It is the most widely used free tool for collecting evidence. You can also use it to back up your system.

164. A. Have every individual change their password immediately. If you were using the same password on multiple sites, change those as well. A single breached password can take down other accounts if you are reusing passwords. Just don't reuse passwords.

165. A. Once you determine which machines were compromised, make sure that nothing was left behind that will do more damage or allow the attackers access again. Collect all evidence and logs that are appropriate; then ensure that other assets are protected against the method the attackers used to get into your organization.

166. A. In criminal cases, a defendant can petition the court to exclude evidence that the prosecution obtained if someone breaks the chain of custody for any reason.

167. D. Insecure storage of keys, certificates, and passwords is a common mistake. Encryption is fairly easy to implement, but developers may overestimate the level of protection gained and not perform due diligence over other parts of the web application.

168. C. Backing up data is the role of a data custodian. The data custodian is usually responsible for data backups, network and endpoint security, systems maintenance, as well as disaster recovery. The data owner makes high-level security decisions, and the data custodian carries them out.

169. A. The U.S. NSA recently outsourced Ghidra, a reverse engineering tool used to forensically analyze malware.

170. D. A double encoding attack is used to bypass a web application's directory traversal security check. HTTP accepts both decimal and hexadecimal values. The new doubled value bypasses input validation and sanitization.

171. B. A well-organized attack by skilled individuals is extremely difficult to solve with a technical investigation, but your data will be extremely helpful for detectives (i.e., authorities). They may have parts of a puzzle that you do not have access to or have established a modus operandi of hacking groups in your specific industry.

172. D. Chain of custody must be followed, should evidence need to be admitted in a court of law. Chain of custody indicates the collection, control, transfer, protection, and analysis of the evidence. It is important to maintain the chain of custody to preserve integrity and to prevent contamination.

173. D. SHA-512 is one of the strongest encryption algorithms used today. Authored by the NSA, it has up to 256 bits with 80 rounds. The other two secure hashes used today are RIPEMD-320 and Whirlpool.

174. B. Digital signatures are a standard element of most cryptographic standards and are used to verify that a message was sent by a known sender and not altered in transmission. Encryption converts information or data into code to prevent unauthorized access. Hashes are one-way algorithms that take a variable value and create a fixed output value, which can prove that something is the same as something else without actually revealing the original value.

175. A. Data protection is the process of preventing the capture of sensitive data by those unauthorized to see or use it. Most often, encryption or cryptographic techniques are used to protect confidentiality.

176. A. The presence of unapproved software could be suspicious. Finding steganography tools on a system is a sign that information may be extracted inappropriately. Further investigation should be performed to determine whether information was stolen.

177. D. The characters make up a hash value of the software using SHA 256. A hash is a mathematical function that, with an input of characters, provides a unique output string of characters. In this case, it is used to ensure that the software has not been altered during download.

178. B. Developers and administrators forget or ignore how much information is shared in a server banner or a hostname. If your server is running Apache and you return the server header in your response, the attacker can use that information to find vulnerabilities in your web server version.

179. A. You must ensure that you have approval from appropriate stakeholders before taking on this task. If you do not, you could find yourself violating terms of service and, even worse, the law.

180. B. You can use Nmap detect to detect OS vendor, generation, and device type. Nmap probes the target with TCP and UDP packets and examines OS specifics like initial sequence numbers (ISNs), IP identifier, timestamps, explicit congestion notifications (ECNs), and window sizes. Every operating system has distinctive responses to these probes, which results in an OS fingerprint.

181. D. When taking the CASP+, you should be comfortable using a tool like Network Mapper (Nmap). Of the options listed, -sL and -sn are both used for host discovery. -sU and -sT are used for UDP and TCP, respectively. TCP uses a three-way handshake to establish a reliable connection.

182. A. netstat will display active TCP connections. With certain options, it can also display listening ports, statistics, and the IP routing table.

183. A. Using TShark helps an IT analyst capture bytes on a computer network and enables the analysis of a captured file. The more accurate the capture, the easier and faster the analysis will be.

184. A. Network Mapper (Nmap) is a port-scanning tool. It is a free and open source tool that enables network discovery and security auditing. It uses IP packets to determine which hosts are available, what services are running, the operating system, and more.

185. B. Netcat is a utility that features port scanning and listening and can transfer files. It can even be used strategically as a backdoor.

186. A. Tcpdump is a packet analyzer utility that monitors and logs TCP/IP traffic between a computer and the network.

187. B. Wireshark is a well-known packet capture tool that can help a pentester examine traffic on a network. It can help find vulnerabilities as well as firewall rule sets. It analyzes live packets and saves them in a PCAP file. Wireshark can read in an ASCII hex dump and write the data described into a temporary libpcap capture file. It can read hex dumps with multiple packets in them and build a capture file of multiple packets.

188. A. Classful routing classifies IPv4 addresses that start with 0.0.0.0 to 127.255.255.255 as a Class A address. The first 8 bits, or the first octet, denote the network portion, and the last 3 octets belong to the host portion. There are several reserved spaces within the Class A network space to include 127.x.x.x, which is reserved for loopback addressing.

189. B. Hypertext Transfer Protocol (HTTP) runs typically over port 80.

190. A. PCAP files are data files created by Wireshark. The NIC is in promiscuous mode on a system using Wireshark default settings. In a PCAP file, you will see the time, source/destination IP, protocol, and length of the data traversing your network.

191. A. When dealing with malware, reversing binaries is important. Oftentimes, you will not have the source, so reverse engineering is how you find the location of the payload. This may also be called *binary reverse engineering*. On a side note, a code snippet is a slightly modified version of a popular bitcoin-stealing malware found on a software download site.

192. C. Just like with physical evidence, digital evidence must have a chain of custody should you ever need to present this information in court. A technician may install a password or write blocker to reduce the risk of altering the copy of the data, and some forensic specialists will hash the drives with tools like sha256sum or ssdeep to secure evidence.

193. D. In this situation, until the evidence is presented in court, it is not necessary for the investigator to provide their credentials in the chain of custody documentation.

194. D. In the collection phase, data is sent to legal for examination. The length and breadth of this data collection are determined by the identification phase. Foremost is a forensic data recovery program for Linux used to recover files using their headers, footers, and data structures through a process known as file carving. Although written for law enforcement use, it is freely available and can be used as a general data recovery tool.

195. C. EnCase is the shared technology within a suite of digital investigations products by Guidance Software. The software comes in several products designed for forensic, cybersecurity, security analytics, and e-discovery use. EnCase is traditionally used in forensics to recover evidence from seized hard drives. Some other important data recovery tools are Foremost, Scalpel, and FTK.

196. D. A new approach for application security testing and software security is binary code analysis. As cybersecurity threats have shifted from the network perimeter to the application layer in recent years, application security assurance has become a priority for the enterprise. To ensure that the software is secure, organizations must test it before purchase or deployment and remediate any flaws that may expose the enterprise to threats.

197. A. Hexdump is a very useful Linux utility for developers and application debuggers. It has the ability to dump file contents into many formats like hexadecimal, octal, ASCII, and decimal. The hexdump command takes a file, or any standard input, as an input parameter and converts it to the format of your choice.

198. C. Binwalk is a Kali-Linux built-in Python tool that is used to analyze, reverse-engineer, and extract firmware images. A lot of people who play CTFs use this tool to analyze the files they find.

199. B. Ghidra (pronounced "GEE-druh" with a hard *g*) is a reverse-engineering framework, developed by the U.S. National Security Agency (NSA). Security engineers often perform reverse-engineering activities to understand the behavior of malware or to develop exploits against applications. Ghidra runs on OpenJDK 11 and supports analysis of machine-level binaries across a range of architectures, including servers and embedded systems.

200. D. The GNU Project Debugger (GDB) is a powerful tool for finding bugs in programs. It helps you uncover the reason for an error or crash by tracking what is going on inside the program during execution. SHA256sum is a tool that will check SHA256 checksums. EnCase is for forensically carving out data, and Cobalt Strike is a threat emulation software.

201. D. OllyDbg is a 32-bit disassembler/debugger for Windows binary files. It has an easy-to-use and fairly intuitive GUI, making it a relatively quick study. Although OllyDbg is free, it is *not* open source since we do not have access to the source code. It comes preinstalled in KaliLinux. Hydra is a password cracker, and hashcat is a password recovery utility. ICS stands for many, many things, and none would answer this question.

202. A. ELF is the abbreviation for Executable and Linkable Format and defines the structure for binaries, libraries, and core files. The formal specification allows the operating system to interpret its underlying machine instructions correctly. ELF files are typically the output of a compiler or linker and are a binary format. With the right tools, such files can be analyzed and better understood. readelf displays information about one or more ELF format object files. This program performs a similar function to objdump but goes into more detail.

203. B. objdump displays information about one or more object files. The options control what particular information to display. This information is mostly useful to programmers who are working on the compilation tools, as opposed to programmers who just want their program to compile and work.

204. B. A system call is the programmatic way a program requests a service from the kernel, and strace is a powerful tool that allows you to trace the thin layer between user processes and the Linux kernel. Strace is a diagnostic, debugging, and instructional user space utility for Linux. It is used to monitor and tamper with interactions between processes and the Linux kernel, which include system calls, signal deliveries, and changes of process state.

Ptrace is a kernel feature that allows observation and control over execution of another process. Etrace is an Internet-based firearms tracing agency. Otrace is a Python-based object-oriented debugger.

205. C. The `ldd` command prints the shared libraries required by each program or shared library specified on the command line.

206. C. Forensic analysis is a term for in-depth analysis. It is an investigation to objectively identify and document the attackers, reasons, course, and consequences of a security incident or violation of state laws or rules of the organization. The main purpose of a forensic analysis is to analyze, recover, document, and preserve evidence in an investigation. Gap analysis is a tool used to find the space between current performance and desired performance. It evaluates where you started and the actual performance and then identifies the necessary improvements.

207. C. The `file` command classifies files based on a series of tests and determines the file type based on the first successful test. In its simplest form when used without any option, the `file` command will display the filename along with the file type.

208. B. Due care is using reasonable care to protect the interests of your enterprise. Due diligence is the actual practice of specific activities that maintain due care. If proper due care is not taken, you open the organization up to legal liability.

209. D. ExifTool is an open source software program used for manipulating, updating, reading, and writing metadata of media files. ExifTool, developed by Phil Harvey, is platform independent and is available as a Perl library as well as a command-line application. ExifTool is extremely flexible and is compatible with a large collection of file types.

210. B. AirCrack-ng is the best-known tool available for cracking WEP and WPA-PSK in Windows. Knowing how to use Aircrack-ng to break WEP with mathematical analysis or WPA-PSK with brute force is important for the blue team as well as the red team. Nmap is for network mapping, sn1per is used for vulnerability scanning, and MiTM is a man-in-the-middle attack, not a tool.

211. A. The weakness in WPA/WPA2 wireless passwords is that the encrypted password is shared in what is known as a four-way handshake. When a client authenticates to an access point, the client and the access point go through a four-step process to authenticate the user to the access point. We can then capture the password with Aircrack-ng and attempt to crack it. Ettercap is one of the best tools for network and host analysis. Netstumbler is a great tool used to detect wireless networks. Burp Suite is used to test application security.

212. D. The Volatility Foundation is an independent 501(c) (3) nonprofit organization. The foundation's mission is to promote the use of Volatility and memory analysis within the forensics community, to defend the project's intellectual property (trademarks, licenses, etc.) and longevity, and to help advance innovative memory analysis research. Volatility is an open source memory forensics framework for incident response and malware analysis. Volatility also provides a unique platform that enables research to be immediately transitioned into the hands of digital investigators. Pentoo is a security-focused tool on Gentoo. BackBox is an Ubuntu system designed for penetration tests, and Buscador is a Linux virtual machine configured for online investigators.

213. C. The Sleuth Kit (TSK) is a collection of command-line tools and a C library that allows you to analyze disk images and recover files from them. It is used behind the scenes in Autopsy, the GUI version of TSK, and many other open source and commercial forensics tools. FindBugs is a free static analyzing tool for Java. Meterpreter is an advanced, dynamically extensible payload that uses in-memory DLL injection stagers and is extended over the network at runtime. Nikto is black-box web server and web application vulnerability scanner.

214. A. Malware can behave differently depending on what it is programmed to do, which makes it all the more important to understand its functionalities. There are basically two methods to do so: static analysis and dynamic analysis. Dynamic analysis is a detailed process of malware detection and analysis carried out in a controlled environment, and the whole process is monitored to observe the behavior of the malware. Static analysis is a process of determining the origin of malicious files to understand their behavior without actually executing the malware.

215. A. You can ensure that your containers are free from malware and vulnerabilities and are not exposing secrets by running a container image scanner. This scanner looks at the environment and searches for custom indicators of compromise (IoCs), enabling you to mitigate any risk before additional development takes place or before deploying to a live ecosystem.

216. C. Vector-oriented security is an approach in layering defense mechanisms to protect valuable information and data. Vector-oriented security focuses on common attack vectors like permanently disabling USB ports so they cannot be used.

217. C. Forensic Toolkit (FTK) is a computer forensics software application made by Access-Data. The toolkit includes a standalone disk imaging program called FTK Imager. FTK Imager is a free tool that saves an image of a hard disk in one file or in segments that may be reconstructed later. It calculates MD5 or SHA-1 hash values of the original and the copy, confirming the integrity of the data before closing the files. A duplicator is hardware that allows you to swap drives in and out as needed and can be used to copy information or erase it.

218. C. Disk cloning is the process of creating an image of an entire disk. This can be useful for copying disks, backups, recovery, and more. The dd command is easy-to-use tool for making such clones.

219. A. There are several reasons you may need to clone your hard disk or partition. With a cloned hard disk, you do not need to reinstall and configure the applications again. dd is a simple and powerful command for a Linux-based operating system, used to create a perfect copy of drives, partitions, and filesystems. With the dd command, you can back up the boot sector of a hard disk and also obtain a fixed amount of random data. Be careful before using the dd command—a small mistake can destroy your whole hard disk. Option A is the proper command for cloning the correct source to the correct destination. Option B is the command for checking the size of both hard drives. Option C is backward—it would clone the destination to the source. Option D gives you a display of the total data transferred.

220. C. Live data is collected in nearly every incident response investigation. The main purpose of the collection is to preserve volatile evidence that will further the investigation. You should also collect any additional information that can be collected quickly, such as log files and file listings. This is done so that you have answers to investigative questions without performing a lengthier drive duplication. The first responder will look for rogue connections or mysterious running processes, and it is sometimes possible to capture an image of the running memory.

221. B. Incident "postmortem" refers to a process that enables an incident response team to learn from past downtime, outages, and other incidents. During postmortem, the team determines what happened during an incident, identifies what was done right and what can be corrected, learns from its mistakes, and proceeds accordingly.

222. A. Netstat, short for "network statistics," is a Linux tool (as well as other operating systems such as Windows and macOS) that can display incoming and outgoing network connections. It can be used to get information on network statistics, protocol statistics, and routing tables. You can use netstat to find network problems and measure the amount of network traffic, so it can be a really useful tool to help you gather the information you need to solve any outage, slowdown, or bottleneck issues on your network.

223. C. The Linux command line provides a great deal of flexibility. Whether you are managing a server or launching a terminal window on a desktop system, the command line brings with it an extensive toolkit to update files, tweak system performance, and manage processes. The ps command is short for "processes status" and displays the currently running processes. The command pwd is used to show which directory you are in. It gives you the absolute path, which means the path that starts from the root. Use the mv command to move files through the command line. You can also use the mv command to rename a file. Use the cat command to display the contents of a file. cat is also used to easily view programs.

224. D. The command vmstat (virtual memory statistics) is a computer system monitoring tool that collects and displays summary information about operating system memory, processes, interrupts, paging, and block I/O. You can use vmstat to specify a sampling interval, which permits you to observe system activity in near-real time. You use chmod to make a file executable and to change the permissions granted to it in Linux. You can use the hostname command to view or set a computer's hostname or domain name. ping will check your connection to a server.

225. C. The man page explains ldd as printing the shared objects (shared libraries) required by each program or shared object specified on the command line. The command tar is used to work with tarballs (or files compressed in a tarball archive) in the Linux command line. You can use the command zip to compress files into a zip archive, and use unzip to extract files from a zip archive. Use uname to display information about the system your Linux distro is running. Using the command uname -a prints most of the information about the system. It prints the kernel release date, version, processor type, and more.

226. A. The lsof command lists the open files in the system as well as anything that is being handled as though it were a file. Many of the processes or devices that lsof can report on belong to root or were launched by root, so you will need to use the sudo command with lsof.

227. A. Netcat is cross-platform, and it is available for Linux, macOS, Windows, and BSD. You can use `netcat` to debug and monitor network connections, scan for open ports, transfer data, as a proxy, and more. The `netcat` package is preinstalled on macOS and popular Linux distributions like Ubuntu, Debian, and CentOS. The `-z` option will tell `netcat` to only scan for open ports, without sending any data to them, and the `-v` option is used to provide more verbose information.

228. D. It is sometimes useful to talk to servers "by hand" rather than through a user interface. This approach can aid in troubleshooting, when it might be necessary to verify what data a server is sending in response to commands issued by the client. This command opens a TCP connection to port 42 of `host.example.com`, using port 31337 as the source port, with a timeout of 5 seconds.

229. A. This command will show you what's going on by displaying the network traffic hitting your interface. You could use `-i any` to see all traffic on all interfaces.

230. C. You can build queries to find just about anything you need. The key is to first figure out precisely what you are looking for and then to build the syntax to isolate that specific type of traffic.

231. A. Connection tracking is the basis of many network services and applications. Conntrack is essentially a table that maintains information about all incoming and outgoing connections (also known as sessions) to the host. Maintaining a reasonable number of conntrack sessions is important. There may be times during peak usage when servers can briefly exceed this number.

232. A. Ping uses ICMP. Wireshark can be used to check if ICMP packets are being sent out from the system. If they are sent out, Wireshark can also check if the packets are being received.

233. D. The Internet is full of attackers who want to change, edit, or delete data being transmitted. There is no guarantee that the receiver will get the exact message without any alteration. Hashing is a method to ensure integrity and make sure that the correct data is received at the other end. The application of message digest includes verifying that correct data is received. The originator creates a hash value using a digitally signed private key and sends it across. The recipients check it at their end by decrypting the message using the public key. Then, the recipient creates a digest on their system and compares with the original value.

234. A. After running `$ sha256sum /dev/cdrom`, you would compare the calculated hash against the one the vendor has for the ISO file. `sha256sum` is designed to verify data integrity using SHA-256 (the SHA-2 family with a digest length of 256 bits). SHA-256 hashes used properly can confirm both file integrity and authenticity. SHA-256 serves a similar purpose to a prior algorithm recommended by Ubuntu, MD5, but it's less vulnerable to attack. Comparing hashes makes it possible to detect changes in files that would cause errors.

235. C. ssdeep is a program for computing context triggered piecewise hashes (CTPH). Also called fuzzy hashes, CTPH can match inputs that have sequences of identical bytes in the same order, although bytes in between these sequences may be different in both content and length. ssdeep attempts to automate the process of grouping similar malware. Fuzzy hash functions hold a certain tolerance for changes and can tell how different two files are by comparing the similarity of their outputs.

236. B. Option B is the TCP SYN scan. -sS is one of the most popular nmap scans because it is fast and difficult to be seen by the target machine. It never completes the three-way handshake. The -sn option will only ping the system. -sU will scan for UDP ports, and -sA is a TCP ACK scan and can be used to determine if a firewall is stateful or not.

237. A. One of nmap's coolest features is remote operating system detection by using the -O option. It sends TCP and UDP packets to the system and looks at how that system responds. It will check a database with more than 2,600 known operating systems and will share the results.

238. B. Felix could run fsstat against the FAT partition to gather details. He could run fls to get information about the image files. This will return information about deleted files and the metadata information. Ssdeep is for hashing, ldd is for library dependencies of an executable, and Recuva is a tool for file recovery.

239. B. A SAM (Security Accounts Manager) file is a file specifically used in Windows computers to store user passwords. It is used to authenticate both remote and local Windows users and can be used to gain access to a user's computer.

240. A. EVTXtract is actually a Python script, which you can easily run on any platforms such as Windows, Linux, and macOS. Just invoke the script, provide the path to a binary image, and wait until EVTXtract writes its results to the standard out stream. EVTXtract recovers and reconstructs the fragments of EVTX log files from raw binary data, memory image, and unallocated space.

241. C. The Scalpel file carving tool is based on pattern recognition that describes a particular file or data fragment types. The patterns can be based on either binary strings or regular expressions. You can find the number of default patterns in the configuration file included in the distribution scalpel.conf. Overall, it is an exceptionally good data carving tool for a large amount of data.

242. C. Option B would return all GIF files. Option A would search for JPEGs after skipping the first 10 blocks, and option D would run the default case.

243. D. Binary code review is particularly suited for malicious code detection and low-level issues like backdoors and rootkits. This is a result of its inherently ultra-low-level analysis of the machine-level instruction sets. Binary analysis or binary code review is a form of static analysis that deals only with the binary executable of an application without visibility into the source code. It usually consists of a multistep approach that attempts to model data types, flows, and control paths through various means without the need to reverse-engineer.

244. B. Wireshark can read in an ASCII hex dump and write the data described into a temporary libpcap capture file. It can read hexdumps with multiple packets in them and build a capture file of multiple packets. It is also capable of generating dummy Ethernet, IP and UDP, TCP, or SCTP headers, in order to build fully processable packet dumps from hexdumps of application-level data only.

245. D. Released at the RSA conference in 2019 by the National Security Agency, Ghidra is an open source GUI tool for most platforms that features a reverse compiler, as well as help menus that assist in editing assembly and recompiling binaries. OddJob, EternalBlue, and DoublePulsar are all hacking tools that have been stolen and leaked from the NSA by the Shadow Brokers in 2017.

246. A. Binwalk is a tool for analyzing and identifying the contents of binary blobs. Its features include detecting and extracting known file types, analyzing binary entropy, and detecting differences between binaries. Binaries can be examined and analyzed for known file types contained within them. Device firmware can be obtained by downloading software updates from the device manufacturer or by pulling them off the device itself. Once an image is obtained, it can be analyzed to determine how it is put together and what it contains. Scalpel, Foremost, and Strings are data carving tools.

Chapter 3: Security Engineering and Cryptography

1.   A. Mobile devices represent the weakest security link. Every mobile device represents a potential vector of compromise by attackers. Even with passcodes, facial recognition, thumb-print scanners, and remote wipe capabilities, BYOD remains a vulnerability for many organizations.

2.   C. A great many people view USBs as passive storage when, in fact, it is one of the best vehicles for transferring malware. Many penetration testers use a USB type of attack, knowing that end users do not understand the repercussions.

3.   C. After you have established security requirements when replacing core legacy equipment, those requirements need to be escalated and communicated to all the stakeholders in the project.

4.   A. Hashcat is a fast password cracking (or recovery) tool. You can do straight and brute-forcing cracking, as well as reverse masking and dictionary attacks. Hashcat takes a password, hashes it, and then compares the resulting hash to the one it is trying to crack. If the hashes match, we know the password. If you are curious, visit https://www.scrapmaker.com/data/wordlists/dictionaries/rockyou.txt, where you will find a list of 14 million passwords that Hashcat can start the hashing process with. Double-check that your passwords are not in this list.

5.   A. There are many ways to protect personally identifiable information (PII). You can use encryption, strong passwords, MFA, and backups. You will also want to have policy in place that dictates how long to keep personal information, how often to update systems, and to always use a secure wireless network when working with PII.

6.   A. New tokens must be generated with each access attempt. Improper session handling occurs when apps accidentally share session tokens with malicious attackers, enabling them to impersonate legitimate users.

7. A. A patch management system provides an automated process of retrieving, testing, and installing patches on systems. Patching software tends to be an annoyance for end users, and sometimes recommended patches go ignored. System admins may find it difficult to ensure all systems are adequately patched. Software patches and updates are of paramount importance—they can prevent your software and systems from being vulnerable to bugs, malware, and major issues. A software patch consists of updates changing the code of existing programs to fix potential security vulnerabilities or other issues. Patches are designed and then tested and can be applied either by an admin or by an automatic tool.

8. B. Maintaining the latest firmware on a mobile device eliminates known vulnerabilities on the device. Firmware Over-the-Air (FOTA) is a mobile software management (MSM) technology in which the operating firmware of a mobile device is wirelessly upgraded and updated by its manufacturer. FOTA-capable phones download upgrades directly from the service provider. The process usually takes 3 to 10 minutes, depending on connection speed and file size.

9. B. When a device is enrolled to a mobile device management (MDM) server, that server is enabled to set device-level policies and push security commands to that asset like a remote wipe or lock. It can query the device to see what is installed on that device or install needed/updated applications.

10. A. Public Wi-Fi can be dangerous if not used correctly, but it would not be as important in this policymaking situation. Public Wi-Fi rules and guidelines would belong in your Internet usage policy. Having this policy in place helps to protect both the business and the employee. The employee will be aware that browsing certain sites, connecting corporate assets to public Internet providers, or downloading files is prohibited and that the policy must be adhered to or there could be serious repercussions. This should lead to fewer security risks for the business as a result of employee negligence.

11. C. Wireless Equivalent Protection (WEP) is obsolete and should not be used. WPA2/3 or newer should be used. Attackers love unsecured home Wi-Fi networks. Securing your Wi-Fi network can also shield you from unwelcome connections that may be using your network for illegal activities. It is extremely important to protect your Wi-Fi network with strong encryption. Every router has a different menu, but you should be able to find encryption under the Wireless or Security menu. If you still have an older router, you want to select one that starts with WPA2. If your router is not WPA3 compatible, then WPA2-PSK AES is your best option right now.

12. D. The Simple Certificate Enrollment Protocol (SCEP) is a standard protocol used for certificates. It is mostly used for certificate-based authentication where access to Wi-Fi, VPN, and email is deployed using certificates. Advantages are no intervention by users and secure encrypted network communication.

13. D. Bluetooth is best described as a personal area network (PAN). A PAN is used to create a network to connect and share data with devices that are close together. A network of a PC, a phone, a printer, and wireless headphones would be a PAN. A MAN is a metropolitan area network, a LAN is a local area network, and a WLAN is a wireless LAN.

14. A. A common contextual authentication method is using a geographic location or the time of day. If a professor typically accesses their account during their planning period while in a certain location like their office or classroom, any login attempt that falls outside those parameters will fail.

15. A. Keeping your near field communication–capable device up-do-date and off when not in use are two recommendations that should be mentioned. Like most things in cyber: if you do not need it, turn it off to shrink your attack surface.

16. A. Link encryption is a way to secure your data by encrypting the information at the Data Link layer as it is transmitted between two points.

17. A. Screen mirroring requires two devices: a sending one and a receiving one. The sending one uses a screen-mirroring protocol like Apple AirPlay on an iPhone, Google Cast on Chromebook, or Miracast on Windows devices.

18. A. A VPN using SSL/TLS via a web browser is likely the best solution. It provides secure communication with the corporate office as well as ease of use because it uses a web browser interface.

19. D. Some social networking sites are very precise when featuring locations associated with a post. This can be dangerous should the information fall into the wrong hands, putting the poster in danger.

20. A. Android requires that all apps be digitally signed with a certificate before they can be installed by end users. This certificate proves authorship and that the app came from you and not a suspicious entity.

21. B. The Elliptic Curve Cryptography (ECC) algorithm is ideal for mobile devices because it requires less computational power to calculate yet is considered very secure. AES encryption is commonly used in wireless security, processor security, file encryption, and SSL/TLS. IDEA was used in Pretty Good Privacy (PGP) v2.0, and Serpent encryption was a runner-up to AES and has not been patented.

22. A. The benefits of tethering include getting Internet access to upload and download files and check your account balances securely through your PAN. The downsides are that there is a possible cost with your carrier, the mobile connection will be slow, and the battery on your phone or tablet can die quickly.

23. B. One of the most important ways for an organization to limit mobile device risk and threats is to enforce a strict remote lock and data wipe policy. It is another layer of protection for the organization's mobile devices. Even in airplane mode, the remote lock and wipe will take effect when the device is powered on and brought out of airplane mode. This is why it is the answer, even though in airplane mode the device will not receive the instructions immediately.

24. C. When you navigate to a website, your browser first needs to determine which server is responsible for delivering the website you asked for, a process called DNS resolution. With DoH, all DNS resolutions occur over an encrypted channel, strengthening security and privacy by preventing eavesdropping and manipulation of DNS data.

25. B. Customizing your DNS servers to optimize for efficiency can speed up web surfing. DNS servers can filter out malicious websites at the DNS level, so the pages never reach an employee's browser. They may also filter out other work-inappropriate sites.

26. A. There is no one-size-fits-all solution, and each mobile device strategy has its own pros and cons. With bring your own device (BYOD), no wireless carrier needs to be engaged, and fast deployment is available and has a lower cost because the employee owns the device. Choose your own device (CYOD) is business supplied, but employees get to choose the devices they want. Corporate-owned, personally enabled (COPE) architectures provide the flexibility of allowing both enterprises and employees to install applications onto organization-owned mobile devices. IDEA is an encryption algorithm.

27. C. When you are in a situation where security and data protection of the utmost importance, company-owned, personally enabled (COPE) is the best mobile device strategy to use. COPE has strict specific procurement standards and the highest hardware costs of the three options.

28. A. Mobile device management (MDM) is responsible for managing the hardware and cellular connection of the device. Mobile application management (MAM) is more granularly controlling the apps, storage, and restrictions on the device itself.

29. B. A mobile strategy that works well for some organizations is choose your own device (CYOD), and there are a few models from which to choose (for example, an organization may ask if you want a Mac laptop or a PC tablet when starting a job).

30. A. Network access control (NAC) is a solution to support visibility and access management on a network using policy enforcement on devices and users. Organizations have to deal with mobile devices and the risks that they bring to an organization. It is important to increase visibility into those assets and strengthen the security of your network infrastructure.

31. C. A microSD HSM provides hardware security module functionality on a microSD card. The microSD HSM is lightweight and mobile. Encrypted File System (EFS) is a system used on computer devices for encryption purposes, not key management. A Trusted Platform Module (TPM) is a chip that is installed on a computer's motherboard for key management purposes. NTFS is a Microsoft filesystem.

32. C. Sideloading is a term that applies to transferring a file from one local device to the other using a USB, a lightning cable, or Bluetooth. The process involves establishing a connection between two devices and moving files to the right location.

33. A. With manual OTA updates, an end user is notified when there is an available update and can decide to accept or refuse the download. This allows the end user to decide an appropriate time to install the update. An automatic OTA is done from the back end, and the update is pushed to the device.

34. C. Only give apps permissions they must have and delete any app that asks for more than is necessary. For example, there is no need for your flashlight app to record your voice and have access to all your pictures and videos.

35. C. Some people have the perception that jailbreaking is used only to do nefarious things or piracy. Jailbreaking enables you to do things like change the default browser and mail client. It also enables you to use software that the manufacturer does not approve of. Not only should your company have an inventory of mobile devices, but a security policy and a scanning process should be required as well. Some companies have an annual "eyes on inventory," where mobile devices are scanned physically by IT once a year.

36. C. Rooting is the process of gaining root access on a mobile device. This is usually done on an Android, whereas jailbreaking is usually performed on iPhones. Rooting gets around security architecture and can cause damage if users make a mistake. Manufacturers generally do not want end users having root access.

37. D. If you try to insert a SIM card from a competing carrier into a phone that was locked to another carrier, a message will appear saying the phone is locked. Although some carriers will unlock a phone when the contract is up; others may refuse to unlock them.

38. B. A service provider could be compromised, causing important or sensitive information to be leaked. For this type of scenario, using end-to-end encryption reduces the exposure of attack.

39. C. When an original equipment manufacturer (OEM) creates a new phone, the manufacturer can take the open source operating system and customize it for their specific device. There are many, many manufacturers, so the operating system becomes more fractured over time.

40. B. One of the most important ways for an organization to limit mobile device risk and threats is to enforce a strict remote lock and data wipe policy. It is another layer of protection.

41. A. Kubernetes provides a framework to run resilient distributed systems. It takes care of scaling systems, failovers, and load balancing, and it can even be configured to kill containers that fail a health check.

42. D. Electronic Data Interchange (EDI) is the computer-to-computer exchange of business documentation in a standard electronic format. EDI can cut down on cost, increase processing speed, and reduce errors if implemented correctly. The exchange of EDI documents is usually between business partners.

43. B. These are all IBM products. eFUSE is a technology invented by IBM that allows for the dynamic real-time reprogramming of computer chips. Speaking abstractly, computer logic is generally *etched* or *hard-coded* onto a chip and cannot be changed after the chip has finished being manufactured. By utilizing a set of eFUSEs, a chip manufacturer can allow for the circuits on a chip to change while it is in operation. The primary application of this technology is to provide in-chip performance tuning. IBM Guardium is protection specifically for databases and compliance. QRadar is a security incident and event management (SIEM) tool. Veeam on IBM Cloud combines backup, restore, and replication to manage virtual environments.

44. A. NX is an abbreviation for *no execute*, which is a bit used in a CPU that keeps storage and instructions separate. Some companies use proprietary acronyms so that they can market security features. For example, Intel calls it XD, which means *execute disable*. AMD calls it EVP, for *enhanced virus protection*.

45. D. Many different products allow for configuration baseline scans. Each configuration item is evaluated on a schedule or could be evaluated with agents.

46. D. SOA is the architecture that enables the service to work, whereas the API is the service. Some concerns are that applications will run more slowly and need more processing power, leading to higher costs. Scalability can become an issue, and there are no industry security standards, which can lead to exposure to outside threats. One of the most important hardening techniques is to remove unneeded services and disable unused accounts from these systems.

47. D. To prevent losing everything with just one password being exposed, enterprise-level single sign-on requires two-factor authentication, such as texting a mobile phone or using a one-time password, biometrics, or proximity card, making systems much harder to compromise. Remember hardening techniques like disabling unused accounts and removing unneeded services running.

48. A. Visibility into the data through the traffic on these virtual machines can impact confidentiality as well as compliance issues—that is, PCI for financial data and HIPAA for patient data. You should have a plan in place to replace these legacy machines at end of life.

49. C. A data retention policy is documentation that your organization has created to stipulate when data no longer serves its purpose and should be deleted, or if the data retention period has been met. Implementing a data retention policy begins by knowing what kinds of data your organization holds and then classifying that data. This policy is critical to ensuring all local and federal regulations and retention schedules are being met. This includes retaining data and records for the specified period of time, as well as deleting or destroying records once the retention policy is up and specifying how to migrate that data to new systems.

50. C. Measured Launch is a boot loader protection mechanism and relies on UEFI's Secure Boot and TPM encryption to ensure that an OS is allowed to load and specify which parts are allowed to execute. It is sometimes referred to as a *measured boot*.

51. B. Type 2 hypervisors are applications installed on host OSs like Microsoft Windows or Linux. They are also called hosted hypervisors, because there is a host OS that translates between the OS, the VM, and the server hardware. Type 2 hypervisors are easier to deploy, but Type 1 hypervisors usually have better and faster performance. As a best practice, virtualization should be explicitly disabled unless required. Although it is true you should not enable VT unless you really use it, there is no more risk whether the feature is on or not.

52. A. Dynamic RAM is a form of storage on a motherboard that must be constantly refreshed because the stored information changes over time. A hard drive, ROM, and a BIOS are not as volatile as RAM and do not need refreshing over time. RAM can be encrypted, with data being decrypted only within the CPU; however, RAM is where everything goes when it's actively being used, which means it can't be encrypted *and* useful at the same time. There are solutions for this issue, but they sacrifice convenience and functionality. You might want to run servers in an environment that's not trusted or safe physically, and you want some way to protect against a side-channel attack against RAM, like a cold boot attack. The general solution is that you only handle encryption keys and sensitive operations in the CPU. Everything else in RAM is encrypted at all times. It is resource intensive, but there are organizations doing this at scale.

53. D. A shell provides you with an interface to a Unix system. It gathers input and executes programs based on that input. When a program finishes executing, it displays that program's output. Shell is an environment in which we can run commands, programs, and shell scripts. There are different flavors of a shell, just as there are different flavors of operating systems. Each flavor of shell has its own set of recognized commands and functions. To secure end users' machines, one best practice is to limit who has access to the shell features.

54. C. In a buffer overflow attack, an attacker knows where the code for a certain function accepts input. The attacker feeds more information into that spot and can include a malicious payload. Major operating systems today support address space layout randomization (ASLR). ASLR randomizes the location of different portions of the code. Basically, ASLR turns this attack into buffer overflow "whack-a-mole" where the attacker has to properly guess the location of the address space.

55. D. Gap analysis involves comparing the actual performance with desired or potential performance. If the organization does not properly use the resources available, it might be performing below its potential.

56. D. Terminal servers enable businesses to centrally manage host applications, permitting access to company resources from anywhere and any device. Applications are installed once and regularly updated.

57. B. As soon as an organization learns of a firmware vulnerability, the company should evaluate if they are vulnerable and if a fix exists. Then they must patch, as soon as the patch is available from the vendor. If a patch is unavailable, compensating controls should be put into place if the assets affected are mission-critical. As more attackers learn about vulnerable firmware, the risk of exploit rises exponentially. This vulnerability exfiltrates data over ports 16992–16995 by default.

58. D. A code review, also called a *peer review*, is a way that one or many people systematically check a program by reviewing its source code for mistakes.

59. A. The body of data that is gathered by event logging is called an audit trail. Audit trails allow a security professional to build a timeline of events and actions that happened on a system to prove an individual or entity is responsible for malicious activity.

60. D. Data in transit is more vulnerable than data at rest. Data in transit has a greater risk that it will end up compromised. The keys to securing data in transit are to use mandatory access control and authentication and to be able to track suspicious behavior and threats.

61. B. SEAndroid, later renamed SEforAndroid, was an NSA project that promoted the use of SELinux in Android devices.

62. B. When you securely lock down and monitor the container registry, you ensure there are no rogue container environments operating insecurely that touch your systems or their sensitive data. Locking down and monitoring the container registry also ensures that only containers meeting the team's development processes and security policies are being added.

63. D. A Trusted Platform Module (TPM) is used to store cryptographic keys. The TPM can be embedded on a motherboard or added via a PCI card.

64. A. Using a device for its intended purpose will keep your network most secure. A UC server should be protected by a firewall, which is designed to block all unknown traffic into a network and allow traffic only from trusted resources. A properly configured firewall is designed to sort through traffic, whereas a UC server is not.

65. C. Secure Boot is a security feature available in Unified Extensible Firmware Interface (UEFI). It only allows OS boot loaders certified by the software vendor.

66. A. A hardware security module (HSM) is a physical device that is used to manage keys for strong authentication. It is usually an external device that plugs into a network server or a plug-in card and is a secure, tamper-resistant cryptographic processor designed specifically to protect the life cycle of cryptographic keys and to execute encryption and decryption routines. An HSM provides a high level of security in terms of confidentiality, integrity, and availability of cryptographic keys and any sensitive data processed.

67. D. Attestation is the process of validating something is true. In this case, you hire a third-party organization to verify that the hardware components are secure.

68. B. Of all these answers, having a generator for backup power, intrusion prevention, and strong authentication would best meet the need of protecting your customer's information.

69. C. An interconnection security agreement (ISA) specifically identifies the technical requirements for secure connections (NIDS or NIPS) and ensures that the data is encrypted properly—for example, the use of self-encrypting drives (SEDs). A BPA is a business partnership agreement, and an MOU is a memorandum of understanding between two parties that need to work together. An NDA is a nondisclosure agreement or confidentiality agreement that is signed by two parties and outlines confidential material, knowledge, or information that the parties need to share with each other.

70. B. If Alice encrypts her database, she is using an algorithm to transform readable data into unreadable data. Without knowing the key or algorithm used, you cannot reverse-engineer the data. The purpose of this is to protect data from theft, malicious intent, or misuse.

71. B. Unfortunately, most SCADA systems have little, if any, securing mechanisms in place. Therefore, two ways to secure these systems is, first, to ensure that the systems have up-to-date firmware loaded. Second, implement defense in depth whereby multiple security devices are placed in front of the SCADA systems so that they can filter out malicious content. Most SCADA systems don't support the installation of software on the systems like HIDS and anti-virus products.

72. B. Anti-malware products can detect various types of malware, including viruses, Trojans, ransomware, spyware, adware, and similar malicious programs/code. Antivirus products are designed to recognize and remove viruses. Antispyware products detect and remove programs designed to covertly collect information on the infected system. Anti-adware products detect and remove programs designed to display advertisements on an infected user's screen. Application controls are a form of security that is designed to improve the quality of the data that is input into a database. An example of an application control is the validity check, which reviews the data entered in a data entry screen to ensure that it meets a set of predetermined range criteria.

73. **A.** A host-based intrusion detection system (HIDS) is an intrusion detection system used to detect intrusions on a system and to alert on those intrusions. The alerts can come in various forms, including email and text messages. A host-based intrusion prevention system (HIPS) monitors a single host for suspicious activity by analyzing events occurring within that host. HIPS solutions protect the host from the network layer all the way up to the application layer against known and unknown malicious attacks. Network intrusion detection/protection are network based, not host based.

74. **D.** When you have a HIDS/HIPS on an individual asset, you are monitoring and analyzing the internal workings of that system as well as network behavior. Based on how the system is configured, a HIDS/HIPS may discover what that program is accessing and if anyone or anything has altered the security policy on that machine.

75. **B.** This is incident detection and response (IDR). When you are able to learn about the different components of the attack life cycle, you become better at identifying, responding to, and remediating a threat before attackers can steal your data.

76. **A.** Voice over IP (VoIP) is more susceptible to power outages than the traditional plain old telephone system (POTS). Loss of power means the entire system fails.

77. **D.** In a business that encompasses hundreds of thousands of server units, hardware failures are difficult to detect at the software level due to their offline operation. Each failure poses a significant threat to stability. Dealing with these issues first of all involves the timely discovery of hardware failures, followed by effective service migration of failed machines. Automated self-healing hardware platforms simplify the response.

78. **B.** Using analytics to trigger a red flag to system administrators for a user behaving badly or outside the parameter of normal behavior is user and entity behavior analytics (UEBA). Using big data by taking a baseline over a certain period of time of any access outside of their normal baseline triggers an alert. This way, you're able to differentiate between legitimate activity and illegitimate activity.

79. **A.** The Mirai botnet known for a massive distributed denial-of-service (DDoS) attack in 2016 was composed primarily of Internet of Things (IoT) devices. A DDoS attack is an attempt to crash a web server or online system by overwhelming it with data. DDoS attacks can be simple mischief, revenge, or hacktivism, and can range from a minor annoyance to long-term downtime resulting in loss of business. The IoT is about interconnecting embedded systems. It brings together two evolving technologies: wireless connectivity and smart sensors. Combined with recent advances in low-power microcontrollers, these new "things" are being connected to the Internet easily and inexpensively, ushering in a second industrial revolution as well as a truckload of new security vulnerabilities.

80. **D.** Organizations today must reduce their IoT attack surface, increase the attack surfaces they monitor, and attempt to reduce false positive alerts that often affect IoT devices.

81. **D.** Smartphones today have very advanced technology, including system on a chip (SOC) embedded architecture. A SOC can include a primary CPR, graphics processor, flash memory, and voltage regulator. The cameras on modern smartphones are so sophisticated that they can pick up on infrared light and the illuminating light from IR cameras.

82. B. The application-specific integrated circuit (ASIC) can be premanufactured for a special application. It is a microchip designed for a particular kind of transmission protocol or a handheld computer. ASICs are used in a wide range of applications, including auto emission control, environmental monitoring, and personal digital assistants (PDAs), and most recently in bitcoin mining. The Trusted Platform Module (TPM) is a microcontroller that helps secure and assure integrity of a platform. The complex instruction set chip (CISC) is for single instructions executing multiple low-level operations or instructions. AAHA is the type of microchip you find in our furry best friends (dogs and cats).

83. A. The field-programmable gate array (FPGA) is an array of interconnected digital subcircuits that implement common functions while also offering extremely high levels of flexibility. Supervisory control and data acquisition (SCADA) is an architecture of systems of networked data communications for high-level management. Programmable logic controllers (PLCs) are computers that have been adapted for manufacturing processes like assembly lines or industrial manufacturing. A closed circuit is a complete electric circuit where a current can circulate.

84. D. A cold site has infrastructure only, perhaps four walls and heating, ventilation, and air conditioning (HVAC). A warm site is between two buildings—a building with HVAC, running water, and power, and after a backup, these assets are ready to be networked and have the business up and running in a reasonable amount of time. A PLC (programmable logic controller) is an industrial computer with a high degree of reliability capable of running a program without interruption in a 24/7/365 environment and can sometimes be found in HVAC. A Safety Instrumented System is used specifically on critical systems. It is made up of sensors, logic solvers, and control elements. The logic solver drives the control elements to the state required to provide a safe state if the inputs indicate an abnormal situation.

85. A. The SCADA historian is responsible for storing and logging all of the data that the SCADA system aggregates. It allows operators and stakeholders to look at historical data for the plant. A historian can also have reporting capability. It can generate manual or automated reports containing different sets of data and show what happened at the plant over specified periods of time. Ladder logic is a programming methodology used in SCADA and PLC for automation and relay logic controls, instructions, and commands. A human–machine interface (HMI) is a user interface or dashboard that connects a human to a system or device. A modbus is the industry standard for connecting industrial electronic devices.

86. C. The first step to managing/deleting old data is to decide how long it must be kept. Data retention is not just about sensitive data but about the different types of records such as logs, which should be kept, and then the data can be permanently deleted using a secure technique.

87. A. IT outsourcing is a phrase used to describe the practice of seeking resources or subcontracting outside of an organizational structure for all or part of the IT function. Most large organizations outsource a portion of any given IT function.

88. D. Easy deployment and lower cost for IT expertise are good things. Those who are attempting to weigh the advantages and disadvantages of using the cloud need to consider more factors than just initial price. They should consider return on investment (ROI). Once you're using the cloud, easy access to your company's data will save time and money in project startups. For those who are worried that they will end up paying for features that they do not need or want, most cloud-computing services are pay as you go.

89. A. Default to the highest control for multiple data points. In this case, PHI wins with a high confidentiality, integrity wins with a high, and availability is the same with a low.

90. D. A gap analysis assessment is a tool used to find the space between current performance and desired performance. It evaluates where you started and the actual performance and then identifies the necessary improvements to reach a goal by optimizing the allocation of resources and input.

91. D. The procedures already exist; they just are not being followed. Mandatory training is deemed essential for your organization to ensure its meeting policy, standards, guidelines, and procedures are being followed.

92. C. Zigbee is an IEEE 802.15.4–based specification used to create personal area networks. Zigbee is meant to be used for consumer and industrial equipment that needs wireless and low power and short range control. A controller area network (CAN) was developed by Bosch in 1985 for in-vehicle networks when manufacturers started using more electronic devices. Distributed Network Protocol (DNP3) is a set of standards-based operability between intelligent electronic devices and stations for electric companies. The Common Industrial Protocol (CIP) is a set of standards that is used for industrial automation applications such as control, motion, and synchronization.

93. D. Data Distribution Service (DDS) enables data, events, commands and other related communication between a message/data publisher and its associated subscribers. Typically, it is implemented in distributed computing applications (such as financial, trading, or big data) that rely on the timely and efficient delivery of communication between all participating nodes. DDS works by providing scalable, high-performance, and real-time interaction for publishers and subscribers. It totally eliminates the need for network programming that handles communications, since all connected nodes and applications rely on DDS, which automates their interaction.

94. C. Virtualization creates an abstract computing platform. Many servers can be replaced by one larger physical server to decrease the need for hardware. Many hosts enable the execution of complete operating systems, and access can be restricted for security, depending on the hardware access policy created by the host. In this scenario, the most secure option with a focus on confidentiality would be to assign virtual hosts to the client and physically partition storage. If confidentiality is in the question, look for encryption in the answer.

95. D. When you drag a file into the trash and empty the trash, it doesn't actually erase the file. It simply indicates to the filesystem that the file is deleted, but the data in the file remains on the hard drive until the filesystem eventually overwrites the file. We call this problem data remanence. Cloud computing complicates the data remanence issue. You have little or no visibility into the physical location of your data in the cloud, so overwriting the physical media is virtually impossible. The cloud infrastructure may distribute your storage or virtual machine instance across multiple physical drives. Deprovisioning that instance is similar to dragging it to the trash. The data that is written to various drives remains until the cloud provider reallocates the sectors you were using to other customers.

96. D. Creating an audit trail is vital. Security policy often specifies which data should be collected, how it should be stored, and how long it will be kept. An audit trail is often used to find unauthorized activity on a network.

97. D. Accountability is the task of reviewing logs for malicious activities. An administrator who regularly reviews server access to determine who is manipulating sensitive files is performing an accountability task.

98. A. Configuring NTP on all devices synchronizes the date/time on the devices, thereby synchronizing the timestamps on all logs and allowing for proper monitoring and alerting.

99. B. A virtual private network (VPN) is a tool used to protect privacy and security on the Internet. VPN securely connects two computers with an encrypted tunnel to transfer data between a remote user and a corporate network. Employees should use VPNs when accessing cloud storage services. By connecting to the cloud over an unsecured Internet connection, you risk exposing your data to attackers.

100. B. An alert from any one of these assets should trigger the security team to take a closer look at the cause of the alert. Monitoring and alerting are interrelated and have the ability to provide visibility into the health of your systems, help you understand trends in usage or behavior, and help you determine the impact of changes you make. If the metrics fall outside of your expected ranges, these systems can send notifications to prompt someone to take a look and can assist in surfacing information to help identify the possible causes.

101. A. VMs are easy to deploy, and many organizations do not follow proper procedures. This can lead to VM sprawl, which is the unplanned proliferation of VMs. Attackers can take advantage of poorly monitored resources, which results in failure points, so sprawl can cause problems even if no malice is involved.

102. C. The BIA is a process that identifies critical functions within a business and that predicts what the end results will be if there is a disruption. Potential effects include the loss of data or backups, equipment, and revenue, loss of staff, reputational damage, and other types of business losses. Business impact analysis is an important stage in developing a disaster recovery (DR) plan that will ensure operation of a company's infrastructure and applications in case of a major outage. A comprehensive disaster recovery BIA report is one the most crucial elements required to devise an emergency response strategy.

103. D. IP Security (IPSec) is a suite of protocols used across an IP network providing authentication, integrity, and confidentiality. This includes Authentication Header (AH), Encapsulating Security Payloads (ESP), and Security Associations (SAs), which provide the different configurations and keys used for those connections. Internet Security Association and Key Management Protocol (ISAKMP) is a component of SA and determines how the keys are managed and exchanged between the devices. An IPSec VPN will protect traffic being forwarded from client to server or from server to server.

104. A. A PKI token is a hardware device used to store digital certificates and private keys. The encryption and decryption are performed on the hardware device itself.

105. B. With an RTO or recovery time objective of 36 hours after an interruption, you can use a warm site to provide recovery within the stated time period and with the most reasonable cost. Some organizations are opting for warm sites in the cloud. A cold site would take much longer to build, and a hot site would offer instant recovery but is extremely expensive to maintain with all the administration and security costs.

106. C. A structured walk-through is a paper-only test where a group discusses the plan but takes no actions in the real world. You may also hear it called a round-table exercises or a dry run. Some organizations hire third-party organizations with BCDR experience to evaluate and make recommendations for their BCDR plans. Simulation, parallel, and full interruption tests are all real-world tests.

107. A. For these specific requirements, the ability to audit event logs that include source address and timestamps is most critical. If the systems are on premises, you have more physical control. Assets in the cloud require more technical controls.

108. B. A critical application would be externally facing and have customer information that needs protecting. These applications would need to be managed and tested first because they would be targeted by attackers. Serious applications may be internal or external and have sensitive information. Normal applications would be at the bottom of the list and would be included in tests only after critical and serious applications are fully tested.

109. C. Software-defined networking is a network architecture approach that enables the network to be centrally controlled using software applications. This helps manage the entire network consistently regardless of the underlying network technology. While evaluating such a large upgrade, contractual shifting of risk from one party to another is an example of transferring risk. Purchasing an insurance policy is an example of risk transference.

110. C. In computer networking, out-of-band data is the data transferred through a mechanism that is independent from the main in-band data stream. This type of configuration provides out-of-band management of the router should the primary management method fail.

111. D. Defining user access as well as devices and idle time are especially important to a network security policy. You should also decide what authentication methods are used, how authentication will be implemented, and what the standard operating procedures are should your organization be compromised.

112. B. Data dispersed and stored in multiple cloud pods is a key component of cloud storage architecture. The ability to have data replicated throughout a distributed storage infrastructure is critical. This allows a cloud service provider to offer storage services based on the level of the user's subscription or the popularity of the item. Bit splitting is another technique for securing data over a computer network that involves encrypting data, splitting the encrypted data into smaller data units, distributing those smaller units to different storage locations, and then further encrypting the data at its new location. Data is protected from security breaches, because even if an attacker is able to retrieve and decrypt one data unit, the information would be useless unless it can be combined with decrypted data units from the other locations.

113. A. The first priority should be to understand what data your organization has and to classify it through a data classification engine. Look for a comprehensive solution that locates and protects sensitive content on the assets uploaded to the cloud.

114. B. If you sign a message with your private key, the only key that can decrypt it is your public key. Successfully decrypting the signature with your public key proves that the message did come from you and was not altered in transit. Anyone who has your public key can also read the message. Signing the message does not protect the message contents.

115. C. Certificates are managed via their serial numbers. If a certificate is revoked, the certificate's serial number is placed on the revocation list.

116. D. You will provide the intermediate certificate authority with the public key so that it can be included in the digital certificate. Private keys always stay private and are never given out to others.

117. D. A digital signature is a mathematical process that verifies the authenticity of messages and documents. It enables a message to be received with a known sender and belief that it was not altered in transit. A digital signature is a hash value that is encrypted with the private key of a sender.

118. B. Online Certificate Status Protocol (OCSP) is a protocol designed to quickly check individual certificates with the issuing certificate authority in real time.

119. C. One of the biggest benefits of moving virtual hosts to the cloud is elasticity. Businesses adopting this cloud computing solution can enjoy the dynamic allocation of resources to projects and workflows. It makes using the cloud efficient and cost-effective.

120. A. A certificate revocation list (CRL) is a list of certificates that have been revoked before their expiration date by certificate authorities. There can be many reasons, according to the Internet Engineering Task Force (IETF) Request for Comments (RFC) 5280 as to why a certificate was revoked, such as key or CA compromise, cessation of operation, or the certificate was counterfeit.

121. D. A wildcard certificate is a public key certificate that can be used with multiple subdomains of a domain. A wildcard certificate can be cheaper and more convenient to manage than owning a certificate for every subdomain. The registration authority (RA) is the component of PKI that is responsible for accepting requests for digital certificates and authenticating a person or organization who is making the request. Once the validation is complete, the RA transmits the request to the CA, which passes it to the CS server. An extended validation (EV) certificate proves the legal entity of the owner. A multidomain certificate is used to secure many names across different domains and subdomains with the same certificate.

122. C. One of the most important email rules is to never, ever open attachments if you cannot verify the sender.

123. B. Kerberos is an authentication protocol for client-server applications. This protocol relies on a combination of private key encryption and access tickets to safely verify user identities. Kerberos is a single sign-on solution that uses a ticket-granting service to provide tickets to clients used to access specific network services.

124. A. It is a digital signature, which is a process that guarantees a message has not changed in transit. When you digitally sign a message, you hash the message and encrypt the hash using your private key. The receiver hashes the message and uses your public key to decrypt the hash sent. If they match, the message was not altered in transit and maintained integrity.

125. C. If the colleague's public key is used to encrypt the message, only the colleague's private key can decrypt it. As long as the colleague does not disclose their private key, only the colleague will be able to read the message.

126. D. If the colleague's public key is used to encrypt the message, only the colleague's private key can decrypt it. Because the colleague is the only one with their private key, it ensures that only the colleague can read the message.

127. A. A line-by-line code review and simulation uncovers vulnerabilities and enables behavior to be watched in a safe location with minimized risk. Code signing is the process of digitally signing executables and scripts to confirm the software author and guarantee that the code has not been altered or corrupted since it was signed. The process employs the use of a cryptographic hash to validate authenticity and integrity.

128. A. For securing websites, standard general-purpose SSL certificates provide SSL encryption plus traditional validation/vetting. These organizationally validated (OV) certificates include an organization's name and location on the certificate. For organizations looking to cost-effectively secure multiple websites with the highest levels of security, multidomain certificates expand the value by allowing businesses to secure up to 100 distinct domains on a single certificate. For e-commerce applications where sensitive information is exchanged, extended validation (EV) certificates deliver the highest level of trust to website visitors. For organizations hosting a single domain name but with different subdomains, the wildcard certificate is a cost-effective and efficient means of securing all subdomains without the need to manage multiple certificates.

129. A. The process will provide confidentiality via encryption, integrity of the file via the hashing process, and nonrepudiation because only the colleague's public key can decrypt the hash used for the digital signature.

130. B. Digital certificates are electronic credentials that bind the identity of the certificate owner to a pair of electronic encryption keys (one public and one private) that can be used to encrypt and sign information digitally. The main purpose of the digital certificate is to ensure that the public key contained in the certificate belongs to the entity to which the certificate was issued. Encryption techniques using public and private keys require a public-key infrastructure (PKI) to support the distribution and identification of public keys. Messages can be encrypted with either the public or the private key and then decrypted with the other key. A certificate authority (CA) then is a commonly trusted third party that is relied on to verify the matching of public keys to identity, email name, or other such information. Digital certificates can be used for a variety of electronic transactions, including email, e-commerce, groupware, and electronic funds transfers.

131. C. A trust anchor is a CA verification key used by the client application as the starting point for all certificate validation. If the user's trust anchor is not in the user's local CA, then the user's local CA is a subordinate CA. The user's trust anchor is the public key of the root CA of the hierarchy. All certificate validation by clients within a hierarchy starts with the root CA's public key.

132. A. The certificate authority (CA) profile defines every factor associated with a specific certificate to establish secure connection between two endpoints. The profiles specify which certificates to use, how to verify certificate revocation status, and how that status limits access. You can configure and assign a trusted CA group for authentication. When a peer tries to establish a connection with a client, only the certificate issued by that particular trusted CA of that entity gets validated.

133. B. Online Certificate Status Protocol (OCSP) is used to check to see if any certificates may have been revoked. This is a process that relies on the certificate authority. If you have too many devices that are needing to check in with the certificate authority, it becomes difficult to scale. Instead of using the central method to the CA, you can implement OCSP stapling. This means that the device that holds the certificate will also be the one to provide status of any revocation. This information is gathered directly from the device that holds the certificate rather than going all the way back to the certificate authority. The revocation status is stapled into the handshake that occurs initially for the SSL or TLS communication. Pinning is a security feature where a certain web server is linked with a public key to minimize the risk of forged certificates.

134. D. A certificate signing request (CSR) is one of the first steps toward getting your own SSL/TLS certificate. Generated on the same server you plan to install the certificate on, the CSR contains information (e.g., common name, organization, country) that the certificate authority (CA) will use to create your certificate. It also contains the public key that will be included in your certificate and is signed with the corresponding private key. You will need the fully qualified domain name (FQDN); legal name of the organization; the city, state, and country where the organization is located; and an email address. You will also need the public key that will be included in the certificate and the key size.

135. A. HTTP Strict Transport Security (HSTS) is a widely supported standard used to protect visitors by ensuring that their browsers always connect to a website over HTTPS. HSTS exists to remove the need for the common, insecure practice of redirecting users from http:// to https:// URLs. It removes the ability for users to click through warnings about invalid certificates and can protect websites against man-in-the-middle attacks.

136. A. Transport Layer Security (TLS) is a way of encrypting the data that users send across the web while interacting with your web applications. For pages where the end user is inputting data, logging in, purchasing something, and checking out, it is critical they be secured with TLS; this is indicated by the inclusion of HTTPS in the URL.

137. B. `Get-FileHash '.\Confidential.xls' -Algorithm SHA1` uses the `Get-FileHash` cmdlet to compute the hash value for the Confidential Excel file. When you press Enter and give the command a moment to compute, you will see the hash value.

138. A. The Data Encryption Standard (DES) is a symmetric-key method of data encryption, not a hash. DES works by using the same key to encrypt and decrypt a message, so both the sender and the receiver must know and use the same private key. SHA-1, MD5, and SHA-3 are all hashing functions where information is scrambled using an encryption key and unscrambled later using a decryption key. Hashing is a one-way function where a unique message digest is generated from an input file or a string of text.

139. A. HMAC is a keyed hash of data. HMAC stands for Keyed-Hashing for Message Authentication. It is a message authentication code created by running a cryptographic hash function (like MD5, SHA1, and SHA256) over the data (to be authenticated) and a shared secret key. HMACs are similar to digital signatures. They both enforce integrity and authenticity. They both use cryptographic keys, and they both employ hash functions. The main difference is that digital signatures use asymmetric keys, whereas HMACs use symmetric keys. An HMAC also provides collision resistance. In order to generate an HMAC, you require a key. If you only share this key with trusted parties, given an HMAC signature, you can be confident that only one of the trusted parties could have generated that signature.

140. D. When this command is entered, only SSH connections are allowed. Additional commands are required to configure SSH use on a router, but the answer is required under the `line vty 0 4` command to enable its use.

141. C. A VPN using IPSec in tunnel mode could be established via a border router or VPN appliance that has both LAN and Internet access. This solution is transparent to end users and does not require additional software on the host computers. Data is not secure while traversing each office's LAN. VPN via IPSec in transport mode is typically used to encrypt data from one computer to another and requires software installation on the host computers. VPN via SSL/TLS using a web browser is better suited for remote users. IPv4, unlike IPv6, does not include IPSec and is inherently unsecure.

142. B. Pretty Good Privacy (PGP) can be used to encrypt mail, files, and drives. It is used to provide confidentiality, integrity, and nonrepudiation. Confidentiality is created with encryption, integrity with a hash, and nonrepudiation with a digital signature. Elliptic Curve Cryptography (ECC) uses the mathematical properties of elliptic curves to produce public key cryptographic systems. Like all public-key cryptography, ECC is based on mathematical functions that are simple to compute in one direction but difficult to reverse. Secure/Multipurpose Internet Mail Extensions (S/MIME) is used for sending digitally signed and encrypted messages. S/MIME allows you to encrypt emails and digitally sign them. Extensible Authentication Protocol (EAP) is an authentication framework, not a specific authentication mechanism, frequently used in wireless networks and point-to-point connections.

143. C. The RFC system was invented in 1969 and has become the official documents of Internet specifications and communication protocols, procedures, and events. These static documents from the technology community are authored by engineers and computer scientists and shape the workings of the Internet and Internet-connected systems. Not all RFCs are standards, but they can also be classified at Informational, Best Practice, and Historic. For more information, you can visit `rfc-editor.org`.

144. A. Perfect Forward Secrecy is a way of protecting your asymmetric keys by only using these keys to generate temporary sessions keys based on your asymmetric keys. By doing this, your actual key pair is never used to encrypt and decrypt the data. Also, these temporary keys are periodically changed, so if any temporary key is compromised, only the data encrypted with the temporary key is exposed. All other sessions are still secure.

145. C. Integrity Measurement Architecture (IMA) maintains a runtime list of file hashes that are compared with the files executed on a system. The file hashes are stored in a TPM where they cannot be altered by malware. The comparison of hashes indicates if a file has been altered. If the file has been altered, it is a sign that malware may be active on a system.

146. B. Most developers will provide a hash (both SHA-1 and MD5) for files to be downloaded from their site to make sure that the file is not corrupted during download or tampered with.

147. B. A hash function returns a fixed output for variable input. There is a chance that different inputs can produce the same hash output. If this occurs, it is referred to as a collision. Separate chaining is a collision resolution technique by creating a linked list to the place where the collision occurred. The new key generated is inserted into the linked list.

148. D. Inline network encryptors (INEs) are used in pairs and provide a means of bulk encrypting data between two networks. INEs are a key enabling technology, ensuring communications security while preserving addressing information needed to route packets through the network. Present efforts to develop INE devices are focused primarily on asynchronous transfer mode (ATM) due to the higher capacity of these networks. For military use, an NSA-approved algorithm such as Advanced Encryption System (AES) must be used for encryption.

149. D. A hardware security module (HSM) is a hardware device designed specifically to manage cryptographic keys. By performing this process in hardware as opposed to software, the process is faster. Peripheral Component Interconnect (PCI) is a method of providing expansion slots in a computer. Bcrypt is a password hashing function based on the Blowfish cipher. It incorporates a salt to protect against rainbow table attacks. The bcrypt function is the default password hash algorithm for OpenBSD and other systems, including some Linux distributions such as SUSE Linux. RIPEMD (RACE Integrity Primitives Evaluation Message Digest) is a group of hash functions based on MD4, which in itself is a weak hash function. It is developed to work well with 32-bit processors. RIPEMD comes in 128, 160, 256, and 320 versions.

150. A. Standards define the technical aspects of a security program. Policies are high-level documents, while procedures are specific and include a great deal of detail. The Advanced Encryption Standard (AES) is a symmetric block cipher chosen by the U.S. government to protect classified information. AES is implemented in software and hardware throughout the world to encrypt sensitive data. It is essential for government cybersecurity and electronic data protection, including healthcare institutions.

151. A. Revoke! Of the choices you have listed, you should revoke the key to prevent unauthorized access. After the key has been revoked, you can then recover the data using a master decryption key or by recovering the revoked key. After data is recovered, encrypt with a new replacement key, and give the new key to the user.

152. C. Triple DES (aka 3DES, 3-DES, TDES) is a symmetric encryption algorithm and uses a single shared key. It is based on the DES (Data Encryption Standard) algorithm. It has the advantage of proven reliability and a longer key length that eliminates many of the attacks that can be used to reduce the amount of time it takes to break DES. However, even this more powerful version of DES may not be strong enough to protect data for very much longer because of block size. The DES algorithm itself has become obsolete and is no longer recommended. The National Institute of Standards and Technology (NIST) ratified the Advanced Encryption Standard (AES) as a replacement for DES. NIST had endorsed Triple DES as an interim standard to be used until AES was finished. Many security systems may support both Triple DES and AES, where AES is the default algorithm.

153. A. Developers face a number of challenges and pressures when creating an application and needing to meet release deadlines. Secure by design means combining security into your application as early in the process as possible. It involves considering security in the design state and adding security features into every aspect possible.

154. C. Virtual desktop infrastructure (VDI) is the practice of hosting a desktop environment within a virtual machine that is hosted on a centralized server. An AES-encrypted VDI keeps the vendor representatives out of the systems to which they should not have access.

155. B. RC4 is a symmetric streaming cipher that encrypts data bit by bit. It doesn't require as many hardware resources and can be used on legacy or hardware with few resources.

156. D. Authenticated Encryption with Additional Data (AEAD) is used by Google. Chrome has selected Poly1305 along with Bernstein's ChaCha20 symmetric cipher as a replacement for RC4 in TLS/SSL, which is used for Internet security. Google's initial implementation is used in securing HTTPS (TLS/SSL) traffic between the Chrome browser on Android phones and Google's websites. Advanced Encryption Standard (AES) is a modern symmetric block cipher ideal for encrypting large amounts of data. RC4 is a symmetric stream cipher used for Wired Equivalent Privacy (WEP) and Wi-Fi Protected Access (WPA). RIPEMD is a hashing function based on MD4.

157. D. By operating at the network layer, IPSec can protect data transmission in a variety of ways, giving users access to all IP-based applications. The VPN gateway and firewall are located at the perimeter of the network, and client software must be installed to use IPSec VPN if required.

158. B. An SSLVPN will encrypt; data remains in your data center, and users have the same programs on the virtual workstation image.

159. B. Encryption as a whole is used for confidentiality. Symmetric encryption is specifically used for privacy as well as authentication. The biggest issue with symmetric encryption is key distribution. Salsa20 is a cipher was created in 2008 and is considered to be a well-designed and efficient algorithm. There have been no known and effective attacks on the family of Salsa20 ciphers. Salsa20 works on data blocks of 64 bytes.

160. D. Created by Ron Rivest in 1987, RC4 is one of the most widely used streaming ciphers and is used in popular protocols like SSL. However, it is no longer considered secure, so take care if you use it. DES, 3DES, AES, and Blowfish are all block ciphers.

161. A. TLS is a hybrid protocol that uses asymmetric encryption for key exchange, such as Diffie–Hellman, and a symmetric algorithm like AES for data encryption.

162. C. An extended ACL allows you to permit or deny traffic from certain IP addresses to a specific destination IP address and port. With an extended access list, you can match information such as source and destination IP addresses, port numbers, and type of protocol. 3DES is an encryption algorithm, not a network-based protocol.

163. A. SNMP version 3 (SNMPv3) adds encryption and authentication, which can be used together or separately for enhanced security. SNMPv3 provides commercial-grade security and the ease of administration, which includes authentication, authorization, access control, and privacy. For authentication and privacy protocols, SNMPv3 uses MD5, SHA, and HMAC-SHA-2.

164. D. A centralized key management scheme does not grant the user full control over the private key. In fact, since the central CA generates both the public and private keys, the CA retains a copy of the private key in escrow. At any time, the authorities of the CA can use the private key to access any encrypted data without the cooperation of the end user. A centralized key management scheme generates both the public and private keys, provides a high level of control over the communications environment, and requires significant infrastructure to support the solution.

165. B. Digital signatures, which are private keys from an asymmetric cryptographic system, are the most obvious means of providing nonrepudiation. Only a single person is in possession of their private key. If a message is found with their digital signature, then they are the only user who could possibly have created and transmitted it. Public keys are useful for restricting delivery, such as using them as digital envelopes, but they do not provide for nonrepudiation. Hashing values protect integrity, and shared keys do not provide true nonrepudiation because two entities hold copies of the shared key.

166. B. Hashing of any sort at any time, including within a digital signature, provides data integrity. Signing the message with the private key provides nonrepudiation. A digital signature activity as a whole does not provide protection for confidentiality, because the original message is sent in clear form. No form of cryptography provides protection for availability.

167. A. RC5 is a block cipher that supports variable bit length keys and variable bit block sizes. RC4 is a stream cipher. RC2 is limited to 64-bit blocks. RSA is not a Rivest cipher; it is an asymmetric cryptography system developed by the same organization.

168. A. AES is the best option because it is a symmetric encryption algorithm. El-Gamal and Diffie–Hellman are both asymmetric algorithms, and SHA-1 is a hashing algorithm.

169. D. Electronic Code Book (ECB) repeatedly uses produced ciphertext to encipher a message consisting of blocks. The AES ECB can be used for a range of cryptographic functions like hash generation, digital signatures, and keystream generation for data encryption/decryption. The ECB encryption block supports 128-bit AES encryption (encryption only, not decryption).

170. B. Message authentication code (MAC), which is also referred to as message integrity code (MIC), ensures integrity of the messages. MAC adds authentication capability to a one-way hashing function. There are two basic types of MAC: Hash-MAC (HMAC) and Cipher Block Chaining (CBC) MAC. In HMAC, a symmetric key is appended to the message that is known only to the authorized recipient. HMAC provides data origin authentication and data integrity. In CBC-MAC, the message is encrypted with a symmetric block cipher. CBC-MAC provides message integrity, using a block cipher as the primitive, provided one of the following applies: the message is of fixed size or the key is not reused.

171. B. Keeping the key secure will be the biggest challenge. There is no certificate authority in private key encryption, only in public key encryption. The task was given to implement, not evaluate, so calculating the ROI would not be a challenge, and no user authentication is required for symmetric encryption.

172. D. During ciphertext-only attacks, the attacker has access only to a number of encrypted messages. They have no idea what the plaintext data or the secret key may be. The goal is to recover as much plaintext messages as possible or (preferably) to guess the secret key. Once the attacker discovers the encryption key, it will be possible to break all the other messages that have been encrypted by this key.

173. C. The advantage of Elliptic Curve Cryptography (ECC) over the Rivest, Shamir, and Adleman (RSA) algorithm is its improved efficiency and requirement of fewer resources than RSA. ECC has a higher strength per bit than an RSA. ECC is a method used to implement public-key (asymmetric) cryptography. ECC serves as an alternative to the RSA algorithm and provides similar functionalities. Wireless devices, smart cards, and cellphones have limited processing power, storage, power, memory, and bandwidth compared to other systems. To ensure efficient use of resources, ECC provides encryption by using shorter key lengths. Shorter key lengths do not imply less secure systems. Therefore, ECC provides the same level of security as RSA by using a shorter key that enables easier processing by the resource-constrained devices.

174. B. Diffie–Hellman is an example of asymmetric cryptography. Diffie–Hellman allows two computers to receive a symmetric key securely without requiring a previous relationship. It was the first public key algorithm. Asymmetric algorithms include Diffie–Hellman, RSA, and Elliptic Curve Cryptography (ECC). Symmetric algorithms include Data Encryption Standard (DES), Triple DES (3DES), Advanced Encryption Standard (AES), International Data Encryption Algorithm (IDEA), Blowfish, RC4, RC5, and RC6.

175. D. Message authentication code (MAC) prevents masquerading attacks. Masquerading or spoofing is a popular trick in which an attacker intercepts the network packet, replaces the source address of the packet header with the address of the authorized host, and reinserts information that is sent to the receiver. This type of attack involves modifying the content of the packets. MAC prevents the modification of the packet to ensure data integrity. A logic bomb implies a malicious program that remains dormant in a network until it is triggered following a specific action by the user, or after a certain time interval. In a SYN flood attack, the attacker floods the target with spoofed IP packets and causes it to either freeze or crash. A DoS attack floods the target system with unwanted requests, causing loss of service to users.

176. B. The asymmetric RSA encryption algorithm uses prime numbers to generate keys. A prime number is a number that has exactly two factors: 1 and the number itself. Encryption algorithms ensure the confidentiality of data. RSA is considered secure only if the prime numbers are large enough, so it is recommended that RSA keys be at least 2,048 bits long. Symmetric algorithms use identical keys for encryption and decryption. A composite number has more than two factors, which means apart from getting divided by number 1 and itself, it can also be divided by at least one integer or number.

177. D. The purpose of key escrow it to enable a trusted third party to access sensitive date if needed. The escrow agent would have the encryption keys and provide those keys to the investigating entity upon proof or rightful access to the encrypted data, such as a court order.

178. B. Up until early 2020, Zoom used 128-bit AES keys and with ECB (Electronic Code Book). ECB has been proven to be insecure. Zoom has upgraded to 256-bit AES with Galois/ Counter Mode (GCM). GCM is ideal for videoconferencing since it is a stream cipher rather than a block cipher.

179. A. The Counter (CTR) mode is a simple counter-based block cipher implementation. Every time a counter-initiated value is encrypted and given as input to XOR with plaintext, the result is a ciphertext block. The CTR mode is independent of feedback use and thus can be implemented in parallel. Electronic Code Book (ECB) is the easiest block cipher mode of functioning. It is easier because direct encryption of each block of input plaintext and output is in the form of blocks of encrypted ciphertext. It is also not very secure. Cipher block chaining (CBC) is an advancement made on ECB. In CBC, the previous cipher block is given as input to next encryption algorithm after an XOR with the original plaintext block. Cipher Feedback (CFB) mode produces a result using an initialization vector for the first encryption and then an XOR operation.

180. D. The output feedback (OFB) mode makes a block cipher into a synchronous stream cipher. OFB generates keystream blocks, which are then XORed with the plaintext blocks to get the ciphertext. Because of the balance of the XOR operation, encryption and decryption are exactly the same.

181. B. Elliptic Curve Cryptography (ECC) is a modern family of public-key cryptosystems based on the algebraic structures of the elliptic curves over finite fields. ECC cryptography is considered a successor of the RSA cryptosystem because ECC uses smaller keys and signatures than RSA for the same level of security and provides fast key generation, key agreement, and signatures. ECC crypto algorithms can use different underlying elliptic curves. Different curves provide different level of security, performance, and key length, and could involve different algorithms. The length of ECC keys directly depends on the underlying curve. In most applications (like OpenSSL, OpenSSH, and Bitcoin), the default key length for the ECC private keys is 256 bits.

182. C. Various elliptic curves used in ECC have different properties. P-384 is the elliptic curve that the NSA recommends everyone use until post-quantum methods have been standardized. It provides 192 bits of security, whereas more commonly used curves provide 128 bits. For anyone wanting to graph this, the equation of the P-384 curve is $y^2 = x^3 + ax + b$.

183. A. Forward secrecy (FS), also known as perfect forward secrecy (PFS), is a feature of specific key agreement protocols that gives assurances that session keys will not be compromised. FS encryption systems change the keys used to encrypt and decrypt information frequently and automatically. This ongoing process ensures that even if the most recent key is compromised, a minimal amount of sensitive data is exposed.

184. A. Authenticated Encryption with Associated Data (AEAD) provides both authenticated encryption (confidentiality and authentication) and the ability to check the integrity and authentication of additional authenticated data (AAD) sent in the clear. There is a built-in message authentication code for integrity checking both the ciphertext and authenticated but unencrypted data. The AEAD cipher suites in TLS v1.2 are using the AES-GCM and ChaCha20-Poly1305 algorithms. Going forward, these will be the only options supported for TLS v1.3, but for most enterprise systems currently, this is not a viable option.

185. C. Key-stretching techniques are used to make a possibly weak key or password more secure against a brute-force attack by increasing the work factor it takes to test each possible key. This works by inserting a random set of characters into the key to increase the size of the password hash, making things harder for the attacker.

186. B. Password-Based Key Derivation Function 2 (PBKDF2) is a simple cryptographic key derivation function that is resistant to dictionary attacks and rainbow table attacks. It is based on iteratively deriving HMAC many times with some padding. The components of a key built with PBKDF2 are `key = pbkdf2(password, salt, iterations-count, hash-function, derived-key-len)`. Today PBKDF2 is considered less secure than modern KDF functions, so it is recommended that you use bcrypt or Argon2 instead.

187. D. Bcrypt is a hash function that has built-in salt functionality. The MD5 function is now considered very insecure: it is easy to reverse with current processing power. SHA1, SHA256, and SHA512 functions are no longer considered secure. PBKDF2 is considered acceptable. The most secure current hash function listed here is bcrypt.

188. C. GNU Privacy Guard (GPG) is a free asymmetric encryption system in which the end users have to manage the keys and have to verify public key identities.

189. B. The Encrypting File System (EFS) is a Microsoft file encryption technology that enables a user to encrypt individual files.

190. A. GNU Privacy Guard (GPG) is a free software package that can run on Linux and that supports the encryption of data and communication using both symmetric and asymmetric encryption.

191. D. The Encrypting File System (EFS) is a component of the New Technology File System (NTFS). Other filesystems do not support EFS.

192. A. Although these are all good questions, the next question for mitigation should be "Can the attackers actually use what was stolen?" Attackers steal data all the time, but most of the time it is/should be unusable due to strong encryption. If the data stolen is in cleartext or with weak encryption, it changes the trajectory of your disaster recovery process.

193. A. HTTPS (Hypertext Transfer Protocol Secure) appears in the URL when a website is secured by a certificate. The details of the certificate, including the issuing authority and the corporate name of the website owner, can be viewed by clicking the lock symbol on the browser bar. In 2015, you could get an SSL/TLS certificate good for five years. In 2018, that was reduced to two years. In September 2020, it was announced that SSL/TLS certificates would no longer be issued for longer than 13 months or 397 days. An expired certificate is usually a management issue. The administrator of the website has not tracked and updated the digital certificate. An expired certificate will be treated as untrusted certificate.

194. A. By creating a unique session key for transactions instead of relying on an encrypted session, attackers cannot gain access to data for more than one single communication between a server and a user. The benefit is increased security for both the user and the server.

195. A. Attackers get creative and can piece together the name of your organization and randomly try different collaboration tools to try to find a way into your organization. Change the `mycompanyname.appname.com` to something more random to obfuscate the login portal.

196. A. Having an SSL/TLS certificate is particularly important. If your website does not have the proper certificate, your website will start displaying warnings like "Not Secure." If you have an SSL installed but it is not correct, it also shows warnings and error messages. These messages can negatively impact users—they might think your site is not safe and leave, which can lead to a loss in revenue.

197. C. The main reason for the occurrence of this error is when the SSL certificate (HTTPS security) of your site is revoked or nullified by the issuing authority—that is, the certificate authority (CA) who issues SSL certificate for your site. The `NET::ERR_CERT_REVOKED` error is displayed on your browser. The CA must have revoked the SSL certificate of the website you are visiting, due to keys being compromised or DNS issues, or perhaps the CA has found the certificate is issued to the wrong site.

198. D. Blockchain technology is inherently secure. By distributing data, or a ledger in most cases, across several computers, blockchains remove any single point of failure. Additionally, cryptographic proofs and game theory consensus mechanisms make a blockchain nearly impossible to hack. However, these fundamental safety features do not mean that blockchain security issues are nonexistent. Cryptojacking is the unauthorized use of someone else's computer to mine cryptocurrency. Attackers do this by getting the victim to click a malicious link in an email that loads cryptomining code on the computer.

199. A. Intermediate certificates are used as a stand-in for your root certificate. You use intermediate certificates as a proxy because you must keep your root certificate behind many layers of security, ensuring its keys are absolutely inaccessible. Because the root certificate itself signed the intermediate certificate, the intermediate certificate can be used to sign the SSLs your customers install and maintain the chain of trust.

200. B. A self-signed certificate is a security certificate that is not signed by a certificate authority (CA). These certificates are easy to make and do not cost money. Self-signed certificates can enable the same level of encryption as a $1,500 certificate signed by a trusted authority, but there are two major drawbacks: a visitor's connection could be hijacked, allowing an attacker to view all the data sent, and the certificate cannot be revoked like a trusted certificate can. The external user will most likely receive a prompt for an untrusted certificate, and since it cannot be verified, the user would have to manually trust the certificate for the errors to go away.

201. C. WPA2 is more advanced than the original WPA implementation and contains authentication, encryption (AES), and integrity (CCMP).

202. D. The next best step, if you do not want to lose this employee and their contribution to the company, is to limit what they can do. Reduce the risky behavior by removing their ability to perform the associated actions. For example, if you do not want administrators clicking links in emails, you can remove URLs in emails while signed into an administrators' account. Better yet, review if Colin even needs an administrator account.

203. B. An SSL certificate proves that your website is who it claims to be. The website name and the name on the certificate must match. The certificate should come from a trusted provider. There are a few reasons the names might not match, which can generate the error `ERR_SSL_VERSION_OR_CIPHER_MISMATCH`, such as when the domain does not use SSL but another domain with the same IP address uses SSL, or the site uses a CDN (content delivery network) that does not support SSL. Once you determine the source of the problem, you can resolve the issue easily.

204. A. Address Resolution Protocol (ARP) is a command used to review the ARP table that maps an IP address to a MAC address. It only sees the local area network segment connections and is used to discover which machines are connected to your host. It can be interesting to monitor for downgrade attacks or ARP poisoning, which is a common spoofing or man-in-the-middle (MiTM) attack. Downgrade attacks can be implemented as part of an MiTM and be used as a way of enabling a cryptographic attack that might not be possible otherwise. Downgrade attacks have been a consistent problem with the SSL/TLS family of protocols like the POODLE attack. ARP poisoning is a type of cyberattack carried out over a local area network (LAN) that involves sending malicious ARP packets to a default gateway in order to change the IP to a MAC address table.

205. D. The error `ERR_SSL_VERSION_OR_CIPHER_MISMATCH` occurs when a user's browser cannot establish a secure connection with a web server that uses HTTPS and SSL. The issue may lie in the server configuration or locally on the user's computer.

206. C. A common mistake is to put the keys for the server on the same server as the data itself. This means once the attacker has access to the server, they have access to keys as well as the data. Make sure there are enough degrees of separation between keys and data. This is like putting the backup of the server on the same server and, if the hard drive fails, you lose your data *and* your backup.

207. A. Using a keystore, as opposed to hard-coding keys, allows developers to set up passphrases for the keystore itself and for individual keys stored in the keystore. Some keystores come with a default password, and you must change these passwords. Use strong passphrases to protect the keystore, and use every method made available by your OS to put access controls against this file. This is to ensure that the keystore file is not accessible to the attacker.

208. B. Encryption key management is administering the full life cycle of cryptographic keys. According to NIST, this includes generating, using, storing, archiving, and deleting keys. Protection of the encryption keys includes limiting access to the keys physically, logically, and through user/role access. Encryption keys usually have a set expiration date so that data encryption can be renewed or "rotated" regularly, theoretically adding to the inherent protection encryption can provide. New, cryptographic key material is re-keyed, and a new expiration date is set.

209. C. Sometimes, despite best efforts, a private key may become compromised. A private key is said to be compromised if its value has been disclosed to an unauthorized person or an unauthorized person has had access to it. Although it can be difficult to know that a private key has been acquired by bad actors, if you identify a breach in your security, it's better to err on the side of safety and suspect that your key may have been compromised. If your private key is ever compromised, it should be considered an emergency, and your priority should be resolving the issue immediately.

210. A. With encryption per customer, crypto-shredding is the concept of destroying data through the destruction of the cryptographic keys protecting the data. Without the decryption keys, the encrypted data is unusable—like a safe without the combination. The relevance of crypto-shredding stems from advancements in technology and changes to the political and compliance environment. New regulations define specifics for data retention and consumers' rights over their personal information, and this incompatibility is what crypto-shredding tries to solve.

211. B. Obfuscation is used to prevent people from understanding the meaning of something and is often used with computer code to help prevent successful reverse engineering or theft of a product's functionality. Encoding is for maintaining data usability and can be reversed easily. Encryption is used for confidentiality, and hashing is done for integrity.

212. C. It is a best practice to rotate your root keys (that is, to create a new version of the key) on a regular basis. Regular rotations reduce what is known as the "crypto period" of the key and can also be used in specific cases such as personnel turnover, process malfunctions, or the detection of a security issue. This can be done automatically on a specific interval or manually if you want more control over the frequency of rotation.

213. D. A single compromised key could lead to a massive data breach with the consequential reputational damage, punitive regulatory fines, and loss of investor and customer confidence. With the increasing dependence on cryptography to protect digital assets and communications, the vulnerabilities in modern computing systems, and the growing sophistication of attacks, it has never been more important to keep your cryptographic keys safe and secure.

Chapter 4: Governance, Risk, and Compliance

1. A. The first step of integrating businesses/partnership is to develop an interconnection agreement and then perform a qualitative and quantitative risk assessment. You must set your goals and measure where you are from a security vantage point.

2. B. You could use Group Policy within Active Directory to configure lockout durations for unsuccessful login attempts. By locking out an account that is under attack for 10 minutes, you can greatly increase the time it takes for the attacker to be successful using a brute-force attack.

3. A. A DoS or DDoS attack occurs when legitimate users are unable to use devices or network resources. It affects availability.

4. A. Quantitative analysis is based on numbers and calculations, whereas qualitative research is based on written descriptions. Both should be in a BIA. If they are not included, you may not have a true picture on which to base your decisions.

5. A. An annualized rate of occurrence (ARO) is the average number of times that something specific is likely to be realized in a year. The annualized loss expectancy is calculated by multiplying the ARO by the single loss expectancy (SLE), which is the estimated per year loss. Simply put, ALE = ARO × SLE.

6. A. KRI identification measures how risky an activity is. To identify a KRI, you need to identify existing metrics, assess gaps, establish a control environment, and track changes in the risk profile.

7. C. The replacement cost is the actual cost to replace an asset and to restore to its previous state. It is not the cash value of the asset. The difference between replacement cost and cash value is the deduction taken for depreciation. Both are based on the cost today to replace the damaged asset.

8. A. With the evolution of adding wireless access (802.11x) to any network, you have increased capability due to its ease of use and movement. You also have an increased risk due to your data traveling over the airwaves, a higher total cost of ownership due to more security, an increased head count, and more assets being purchased and maintained on the network.

9. A. GRC stand for governance, risk, and compliance. A good GRC strategy leads to better decision-making, stronger return on investments, the elimination of silos, and reduced fragmentation. Governance ensures that activities align with business goals. Risk ensures that any risk associated with an activity supports the business goals. Compliance ensures that all activities meet laws and that regulations are used and secured properly. ITIL, PMI, and CRMA are certifications you can attain in GRC.

10. A. Mean time between failures = Total up time/number of breakdowns.
    Mean time to repair = Total downtime/number of breakdowns.
    Availability of device = MTBF / MTBF + MTTR.

11. A. The asset can be hardware, software or people. The value of the asset (AV) is assessed first—$100,000, for example. The single loss expectancy (SLE) contains information about the potential loss when a threat occurs. It is calculated as follows: SLE = AV × EF, where EF is exposure factor. Exposure factor describes the loss that will happen to the asset as a result of the threat which will be a percentage. SLE is $30,000 in our example, when EF is estimated to be 0.3. Annualized rate of occurrence (ARO) is described as an estimated frequency of the threat occurring in one year. ARO is used to calculate ALE (annualized loss expectancy). ALE is calculated as follows: ALE = SLE × ARO. ALE is $15,000 ($30,000 × 0.5), when ARO is estimated to be 0.5 (once in two years). The risk is about the impact of the vulnerability on the business and the probability of the vulnerability to be exploited. The valid equation in this list is ALE = ARO × EF × AV.

12. C. Gap analysis is the comparison of performance, actual versus potential. It helps identify areas for improvement and empowers an organization to quickly diagnose a problem.

13. A. The strategy of risk mitigation enables an organization to prepare and lessen the effects of threats facing them. Risk mitigation requires you to take steps to reduce the negative effects of threats and disasters and business continuity. You can avoid the risk by not handling the project. You can accept the risk and deal with the turbulence if something goes wrong, or you can transfer the risk by outsourcing so it becomes someone else's problem.

14. C. An enterprise risk management (ERM) team identifies risk and adopts risk management best practices to either avoid, accept, transfer, or limit risk. Insurance is an example of risk transference.

15. A. The risk has been evaluated, and management decided that the benefits outweigh the risk.

16. D. If a manager can fire an employee, they must understand the repercussions and risks of a hostile termination, and the former employee's accounts need to be disabled. If the employee has access to sensitive accounts, those passwords must be changed immediately.

17. A. Using qualitative methods of assessing means you gather information that cannot be readily translated into numbers. Often, feelings or actions can affect a situation and do not require technical expertise.

18. C. The official definition of this control is to actively manage, inventory, and track all hardware devices on the network so that only authorized devices are given access. Unauthorized and unmanaged devices should be prevented from gaining access.

19. D. The third-party organization should be contractually obligated to perform security activities noted in the business documents between the parties. Evidence of those contracts should be negotiated, investigated, and confirmed prior to beginning the project. Any agreement you enter into for recovery should include specific metrics such as time, cost, availability, response time, throughput, and bandwidth. These metrics fall under the category of service level agreements (SLAs) and include a number of different elements such as response time to initial request for services and guarantees.

Other important aspects to reviewing recovery service level agreements is to look at any existing SLAs you may have with external parties such as clients or customers. You may need to review your recovery options in light of those contractual agreements. It is good to take the opportunity to ensure your risk mitigation strategies address your contractual obligations.

20. D. The biggest threat to merging two disparate organizations is the security involved when both networks become one. With different physical assets, tactical standards, and operational processes and procedures combining with a productivity objective, the danger is high for overlooking the residual security risks and vulnerabilities in the merged network.

21. A. The first stage of any interaction with a third party is an RFI. After you receive the information, you can then request a quote (RFQ) so that you know approximately how much the service/asset will cost. After you have decided on a vendor, you can formally ask them for a request for proposal (RFP), which should supply a firm cost, an SLA, and other requirements.

22. A. Details and procedures should not be in the security policy. A security policy should be agile enough to change with technology and not have to be edited with every software update or hardware refresh. Exceptions, passwords, and access control should be in the technology policy.

23. B. A procedure consists of step-by-step instructions. It defines the technical aspects of your program, in addition to any hardware or software that is required. A baseline is a fixed point of reference so that you can make comparisons. Scope is the requirements and objectives of a project.

24. D. Due diligence is verifying that those responsible are doing the right thing. Due care is acting responsible. It is creating policies, procedures, and guidelines to protect information or assets in a way that is reasonable.

25. D. When users are made aware that their activities can be audited, it is a preventive control. It may help them take more thoughtful actions. Auditing is a detective control when logs are reviewed. Detective controls are designed to detect errors or irregularities that may have occurred. Corrective controls are designed to correct errors or irregularities that have been detected. Directive is not a control—it is an order.

26. A. Without an accurate inventory of systems, software, versions, locations, addresses, and data, it is nearly impossible to assess the priority of a real-time security alert.

27. A. There is no one-size-fits-all method for communicating up to stakeholders and down to staff. Independent review has proven successful. As someone tasked with communicating with upper management or department heads, you take your findings and share that information.

28. A. An external audit must have an independent certified authority and be performed against a recognized auditable standard. This is why an external audit can hold so much value for a company.

29. C. The ISO/IEC 27001 is a framework for internal auditing, involving a complete examination of 14 different domains, including security policy, access control, compliance, and asset management. SEC is the U.S. Securities and Exchange commission that enforces laws against market manipulation. Certified Information Security Manager (CISM) is an ISACA certification. The Center for Internet Security (CIS) is a nonprofit organization of volunteers who promote best practices for cyber-defense.

30. C. Every KPI has a measure, a target that matches your measure, and a time period, as well as a clearly defined data source so that you know how each is being measured and tracked. Examples of KPI are growth in revenue, percentage of market share, and time to market. A risk register is a document used as a risk management tool to fulfill regulatory compliance. It can act as a repository for all risks identified and includes additional information like the nature of the risk and mitigation measures.

31. D. Private cloud disadvantages include the expense and high total cost of ownership (TCO) as well as being difficult to scale to meet demand.

32. C. A standard operating environment (SOE) is a standardized base configuration of systems that normally consists of a basic operating system and software application installation. The SOE is installed on the computers, and additional features are added.

33. D. Working with storage-attached networks, multipathing is a technique that enables you to build different paths to transfer data between the asset and the storage device. For example, you can have two HBAs feeding one ESXi host. If one route fails, the data can be routed through another, providing availability.

34. A. The business impact analysis (BIA) is a systematic process to determine the potential effects of failure to processes and systems that are critical to business operations, whether the interruption is a natural disaster, an accident, or an upgrade.

35. A. A hurricane is a natural disaster that should be accounted for in a business impact analysis (BIA) document. The risk appetite or risk tolerance of an organization should be considered in a BIA. A BIA should provide a plan for resuming operations after a disaster and identify which events could impact the organization's operations.

36. A. A best practice provides as much security as possible, while it balances other factors such as cost, usability, and scalability.

37. B. The standard security practice of mandatory vacations prevents fraud. While an employee is on vacation with no access to the system, software, or network, you have ample opportunity to perform an audit. You should have a separation of duties policy set in place where one person writes the check and another signs the check.

38. B. The data owner has administrative control over the data and is accountable for who has access. A data custodian has technical control of that data.

39. D. The principle of least privilege is an important concept in IT security. It is the practice of limiting access rights for users to the bare minimum permission they need to get their job done. You may see this abbreviated as POLP.

40. A. Job rotation is vital to prevent a single point of failure. By rotating employees periodically, you have a backup in case of an emergency.

41. A. It is extremely important to have senior management fully accept and endorse the security policy. Otherwise, it can be difficult to implement disciplinary action against employees who violate the policy.

42. A. The best thing to do in this scenario is hold awareness sessions for everyone. Perhaps employees need reminding of what is appropriate. New awareness programs and training should reduce this activity. Reducing permission should happen only after retraining and auditing have no impact other than to inform you about the level of transgression. Termination should happen only after repeated attempts to train staff have occurred.

43. A. A cloud-based deployment solution will probably be entirely operated and maintained by a third-party vendor. You will pay a usage fee for access to that solution but will lose some control over hardware and software.

44. A. A thin client is economical because you do not have to purchase a lot of processing power; in addition, IT support costs are negligible because there is no PC to support. There is no storage, and the server is protected through cloud management features and settings.

45. A. A master service agreement (MSA) provides a strong foundation for future business. It typically specifies payment terms, warranties, geographic location, and intellectual property ownership.

46. A. Using a company's stuff to build more stuff is a platform as a service (PaaS). Using programming tools and languages to develop more applications is utilizing a platform, as opposed to infrastructure or software.

47. B. A private cloud is the cloud computing model where resources are located either on premise or at a vendor site, but where all resources are isolated, and no other customer can use them. Private clouds are customizable to meet the needs of your business. With greater visibility comes greater control.

48. A. A computer cluster is a set of connected computers that work together so they can be viewed as a single system. They are created to improve performance and availability while being cost-effective.

49. B. Job boards and social media are where most attackers start passive reconnaissance. With the information gained from job boards, they know what type of products you're using, as well as the level of expertise needed to attack your network. HR should make IT job advertisements as vague as possible to find the right person for the role.

50. B. This type of hacking is classic network spoofing. A rogue access point near a legitimate business that has a lot of human traffic is a perfect place for an attacker to require users to create an "account" complete with a username/password to use their free services.

51. B. The act of input validation is the proper testing of any input supplied by a user or application. It prevents invalid data from entering the database or information system.

52. D. BitLocker is a Microsoft file encryption technology that enables a user to encrypt an entire disk and/or partitions.

53. A. Many experts say that mobile payment methodologies offered by major providers are more secure than physical cards or cash. Mobile wallets use powerful encryption to mask credit card numbers, first when you enter them and again when you pay.

54. A. The major question that you should ask the vendor is what level of encryption they offer, and if the tools encryption is comprehensive. If not compliant with HIPAA or HITECH, you could be open to major regulatory compliance risk.

55. B. Secure Shell (SSH) encrypts the data sent to the network equipment. The other options send data in cleartext.

56. A. If a company has heavily invested in software and that company goes out of business, it would be beneficial to have access to the proprietary software code. Vendor lock-in, also known as proprietary lock-in or customer lock-in, makes a customer dependent on a vendor for products and services and thus unable to use another vendor without substantial switching costs.

57. A. In no event should any access of any kind be granted to any data that is classified as sensitive without the express permission of the data owner.

58. D. The need to preserve data begins when an organization anticipates litigation in the future. Care should be taken to ensure that due diligence is taken and that the data is not contaminated. Unlike hard-copy evidence, digital content can be voicemails, social media, websites, databases, and emails.

59. D. Fiscal responsibility is essential for budgets and decision-making when it comes to money spending. It is not fiscally responsible for any organization to spend money it does not have or to spend more money on an asset than that asset is worth.

60. C. Data retention is the amount of time that specific data is maintained in storage. Data stored for more time than is needed becomes a security risk to an organization. If you have a vendor managing your data archives, they need to know what type of compliance your organization falls under so they know how long to keep the data.

61. C. The success of a sustained FIM program is measured in how well it is integrated with change management. The whole purpose of FIM is to detect change, and it must hold up to the organizational needs without hampering performance.

62. D. Termination is not easy for the employer or the employee. When an employee is fired, often they are taken by HR into an exit interview, reminded of their NDA, and escorted from the premises. You must disable their network access and accounts and change the passwords to any device to which they might have had access. For example, if this employee had access to the vulnerability management program and you scan with credentials, that employee may have access to every single device on your network. These other options give that employee the ability to disrupt and cause damage to your network.

63. A. The command `ipconfig /all` displays more detailed information than `ipconfig` alone. The command `ipconfig /release` forces an asset to give up its lease by sending the DHCP server a notification. You can also use `ipconfig /renew` to request a new one.

64. B. VNC enables you to remotely access a computer and use the desktop over the Internet. Windows does have Remote Desktop, but it is available only on certain Window editions. Some use TeamViewer, but only VNC will enable you to install and manage your own servers and is available for all operating systems.

65. B. A preventive control would try to keep something from happening. If something did happen, then you would want to layer a detective control on top of the preventive one so that you'd have visibility that it happened, and you could quickly correct the problem. An example of a preventive control is a firewall or a fence. An example of a detective control is auditing or an intrusion detection system.

66. A. After an incident, the team should recommend technology, policy, governance, and training changes so that the incident does not happen again. Understanding the lessons learned will enable information to be shared across the company and added to existing security policy and procedures.

67. C. Code escrow is a storage facility hosted by a trusted third party that will ensure you have access to the code even if they go out of business.

68. B. The definition of attestation according to Merriam-Webster's dictionary is "an act or instance of proving the existence of something through evidence." The Payment Card Industry (PCI) is governed by the PCI Security Standards Council, which will certify an organization has completed and passed or failed an audit with an attestation of compliance.

69. A. You may be asked for your technical expertise to create policies that need updating or processes that need modifying. If any part of the security requirements is dependent on people, your organization must be aware of how security works and should not attempt to circumvent those controls.

70. A. A memory dump (i.e., crash dump) is the process of taking all information in RAM and writing it to a storage drive. A memory dump is most often caused by a registry's corrupted files. It can also be caused accidentally by overclocking or overheating. Most of the time, this shows up as a blue screen of death (BSOD).

71. A. Network access control (NAC) is a technology that enables IT staff to manage what devices can connect to a network. There are various means of authenticating a device via NAC, including using the device's MAC address and loading NAC software on the device.

72. D. I had to. Anyway, cookies are not always designed to store sensitive data. In fact, some cookies that are used with the checkbox Remember Me function may hold usernames and passwords in Base64, which can be reverse-engineered on several websites.

73. A. In an authenticated scan, the vulnerability manager logs in as a network user, and the scan shows vulnerabilities that are accessible to trusted insiders or an attacker who has gained access to the network and taken over a trusted user's account.

74. C. Standards define the technical aspects of a security program and include any hardware/software that is required by your organization. Like procedures, standards should be detailed enough so there is no question what hardware/software should be implemented. Standards ensure consistency.

75. B. Windows operating system that utilizes BitLocker on computers are dependent on having a Trusted Platform Module (TPM) chip on the motherboard for full-disk encryption. This chip generates and stores the actual encryption keys. It can automatically unlock your PC's drive when it boots so that you can sign in just by typing your Windows login password. The TPM chip is doing the hard work under the hood. If someone tampers with the PC or removes the drive from the computer and attempts to decrypt it, it cannot be accessed without the key stored in the TPM.

76. A. A white-box test requires the expertise of testers. These tests demand competences in programming and full knowledge of the code tested. Because of that knowledge and length of code, these tests can take a long time.

77. A. A global organization that collects data from customers must be concerned with data sovereignty. A learning management system (LMS) and a content management system (CMS) collect information on global students taking classes, viewing videos, and accessing files. This data is subject to the laws of the country where the data was collected. Many countries have passed various laws related to the control and storage of data.

78. C. A data owner has administrative control over a specific dataset. Some examples of a data owner are a treasurer who had administrative control and is accountable for financial data and a human resources director who has responsibility for employee data. In most enterprise organizations, the owner is not the custodian.

79. C. A system administrator is usually identified as the data custodian because of the technical expertise needed. This person has admin/sysadmin/root level of access. They have a critical role and work closely with the data owner to protect information important to the organization.

80. C. The primary purpose of data classification is to define necessary security protection. Data classification is based on the object's value rather than the opposite—being used to assign value. Data classification does not control user access. User classification or clearance controls user access.

81. D. Many local, state, federal, and international laws, as well as industry restrictions, require that data be kept for specific periods of time.

82. B. The data owner is an administrative function, whereas the data custodian administers the technical control.

83. C. Data users may come across a situation where they feel that information security is at risk. It should be reported to the appropriate authority, usually the data owner, as soon as possible.

84. D. Disgruntled employees can hide activity so that employers do not know how bad the damage is. Funds, trade secrets, intellectual property, and even access to your entire IT infrastructure can all be put in jeopardy by an unhappy employee.

85. C. Due diligence has the meaning of "required carefulness." Due diligence is exercising informed care that is expected of reasonable people. Performing this kind of process ensures that the proper information is systematically and deliberately protected.

86. B. The format for storing the data, who has access to that data, and how that data is eventually destroyed are important to a data retention policy.

87. B. A data custodian has technical control of data. The role is focused on types of data, especially data at rest and data in transit, not what the data is.

88. C. Large retailers are experimenting with location-sensing technologies by tracking a customer's location through their phone's GPS capability. Some organizations use this tool as a heat map and compare stores and department layouts, which can optimize the shopping experience for customers.

89. D. The initiation of work is not dependent on time. Health and human life are the primary concern, and you should not put that type of risk on your employees. You may return only when it has been deemed safe to do so by the appropriate parties in charge of the emergency.

90. A. A shadow copy allows for manual or automatic copies of computer files to a local or remote location.

91. C. Although the multitenancy cloud services would be less expensive because usage and resources are shared, they operate at maximum usage, making for best efficiency. They are easier to set up because of the high volume of customers with good experience onboarding. The limitations of multitenancy are multiple access points, less control, and if one tenant is affected, all tenants are affected, so it leaves some risk for vulnerabilities to be exposed.

92. C. A penetration test is one of the most intrusive types of vulnerability testing that will actively find and exploit weaknesses. A penetration test attempts to gain access physically and digitally without the proper authorization.

93. B. When the decision is made to outsource any IT function, process, or system, there is a risk to operations and process flows, confidentiality, continuity, and compliance. You cannot use the excuse "It wasn't me." Regulators and compliance auditors will still hold your organization accountable for performing the correct level of due diligence to confirm that a third-party service has the right people, processes, and technology in place to support your business need.

94. C. The primary purpose of penetration testing is to test the effectiveness of your security policies, procedures, and guidelines. It is important to obtain the proper approval before beginning a penetration test.

95. B. General Data Protection Regulation (GDPR) is a regulation in EU law on data protection and privacy for all citizens of the European Union and the European Economic Area. Adopted in April 2016, GDPR introduced requirements for data processors, controllers, and custodians, ensuring they gain explicit consent from individuals whose data is being used for specific purposes. In addition, it granted the right to individuals to request details of information and request that their data be deleted.

96. C. COBIT defines requirements for governance, management, and control of IT processes. Components of COBIT include process descriptions, objectives, maturity, and guidelines. ISO 27001 is the framework for security. ITIL is for enabling IT services and life cycles.

97. A. The National Institute of Standards and Technology (NIST) is part of the U.S. Department of Commerce. NIST promotes innovation and industrial competition by advancing science and supporting advanced technologies, including cybersecurity.

98. A. Most technical project managers know how important it is to capture lessons learned. The documentation reflects both the good and bad experiences of a project. It also provides future project teams with information that can make them more effective and efficient. Capability Maturity Model Integration is a process-level improvement training and appraisal program. Administered by the CMMI Institute, a subsidiary of ISACA, it was developed at Carnegie Mellon University. It is required by many U.S. government contracts, especially in software development.

99. C. Organizations still use Information Technology Security Evaluation Criteria (ITSEC). ITSEC uses the terminology target of evaluation (ToE) and has seven evaluation levels. Prior to ITSEC being developed in Europe, TCSEC was created by the U.S. Department of Defense; it is better known as the "orange book" and was more stringent than ITSEC. The Children's Online Privacy Protection Act (COPPA) imposes requirements on operators of websites or online services directed to children under 13 years of age, and on operators of other websites or online services that have actual knowledge that they are collecting personal information online from a child under 13 years of age. The Cloud Security Alliance (CSA) Security Trust and Risk (STAR) is a three-level, open source certification framework and is used for auditing and transparency. Common Criteria is the technical basis for an international agreement of use of secure IT products.

100. B. Due care is acting responsible. Due diligence is verifying those actions are sufficient. An organization that shows due care means they took every reasonable precaution to protect their assets and environment. If a breach occurs, the organization is not held negligent for losses but can still be held liable.

101. A. Laws and regulations differ from country to country. Opening offices in other countries will make those offices fall under different jurisdiction.

102. B. eDiscovery is the collection of intangible digital data. It is different than paper information because of volume, transience, and persistence. The six stages of eDiscovery are identification, preservation, collection, processing, review, and production.

103. D. Negotiating an SLA is in administrative contract guaranteeing service. It is created for, not deployed to, a cloud environment. You should absolutely have one that will protect the business and processes.

104. A. The only answer that works is threat reports and a trend analysis. An ISA, an MSA, and an RFI are business documents that come after management has approved the budget line item. An ISA is an agreement established between the organizations that own and operate connected IT systems to document the technical requirements of the interconnection. The ISA also supports a memorandum of understanding or agreement (MOU/A) between the organizations. An MSA is a contract made between two or more parties in which they both agree to most of the terms used to govern any future agreements or future transactions. This kind of an agreement has proven itself rather useful, because it allows parties to negotiate any future agreements and transactions rather quickly. An RFI is a common business process whose purpose is to collect written information about the capabilities of various suppliers for comparison.

105. C. A nondisclosure agreement (NDA) is a legal document that restricts what can be shared by either party. A service level agreement (SLA) is a document that defines the level of service between a customer and a vendor. A memorandum of understanding (MOU) is a formal agreement between two or more companies agreeing to official partnerships. A request for proposal (RFP) is a solicitation for a proposal from an organization.

106. B. A service level agreement offers precisely measured statements such as "There will be less than 50 lost labor hours per year due to computer maintenance." The operational level agreement (OLA) states what the functional IT group will need to do in relation to each other to support the SLA. For example, an OLA may state, "The server team will do patching of the servers every Friday at 5 p.m." A privacy level agreement (PLA) is a cloud-based document that contractually agrees that the information hosted will not be shared or seen by anyone with a conflict of interest. A nondisclosure agreement (NDA) establishes a confidential relationship. The party or parties signing the NDA agree that sensitive information they may obtain will not be made available to any others. Doing business as (DBA) refers to a company's operating name rather than its legal name.

107. D. A business impact analysis (BIA) is critical for survival of a business to identify processes, systems, and operations that are a priority. That is the focus of a BIA. The reason it is so important is that it determines how the interruption of your business operations may affect your organization. Areas to focus on include the loss of data, equipment, and revenue; loss of staff; reputational damage; and any other types of business losses. Business impact analysis is an important stage in developing a disaster recovery (DR) plan. A gap analysis is a method of assessing the differences in performance between a business's information systems or software applications to determine whether business requirements are being met and, if not, what steps should be taken to ensure they are met successfully. Disaster recovery is an area of security planning that aims to protect an organization from the effects of significant negative events. An intrusion detection system (IDS) is a device or software application that monitors a network for malicious activity or policy violations.

108. B. If your recovery point objective (RPO) is nine hours and the last available copy of backup is at midnight, you have until 9 a.m. to get that network backup server back up and running before it exceeds the RPO.

109. A. Senior management will initiate the BCP in the case of a disaster or emergency. The recovery team is responsible for performing the actual steps in the BCP. Security personnel may have a role in the BCP, but they will be informed by management or the recovery team.

110. C. The absolute way to know whether a disaster recovery plan (DRP) test works is to perform a full interrupt test. You must get senior management approval. Only through complete real-world implementation will you know if the plan is truly verified. The problem with a real-world full interrupt test is that it can be very costly and can interrupt normal business operations if the test fails. Operations are shut down at the primary site and shifted into recovery mode.

111. B. A warm site would be the best option. A cold site would take much longer than your maximum tolerable downtime (MTD) would allow, and a hot site is extremely expensive. A warm site usually has equipment and power but no data, but it could be operational within the MTD. A cold site usually has office or data center space without any server-related equipment installed. A hot site allows a business to continue computer and network operations in the event of a computer or equipment disaster. For example, if an enterprise's data center becomes inoperable, that enterprise can move all data processing operations to a hot site, although doing so is very expensive. Mobile disaster recovery sites often come in the form of trailers. They can be arranged in specific locations and fitted with the requisite technological infrastructure.

112. C. Most often, data is recovered from hard drives, flash drives, RAID drives, and other storage media. Data loss could be caused by physical damage or logical damage due to software updates.

113. B. A computer emergency response team (CERT) is an expert group that handles incidents. CERT is also a training organization for FEMA that trains volunteers for emergency preparedness. The name *computer emergency response team* comes from Carnegie Mellon University (CMU). CMU can certify organizations that are building a computer security incident response team (CSIRT).

114. D. You do not want to experience the same incident again. After you have completed all the steps in an incident response process, you bring all stakeholders together to list the lessons learned so that history does not repeat itself. This step in some organizations is called building the after-action report (AAR).

115. D. With written job descriptions, all responsibilities should be clearly defined. Job descriptions help ensure your expectations are established and met. A well-written job description will establish a solid set of expectations for employers to communicate to their employees as well as when evaluating performance.

116. D. The software is likely very different from a use standpoint. Policy documentation would state that vulnerability management would be done. Procedures would be a checklist of the step-by-step procedures and processes that you will take to run the new software.

117. A. A tabletop exercise is similar to a dry run. It enables you to talk through all aspects of policies and procedures without executing the business continuity plan. All stakeholders should be at this tabletop exercise so that multiple points of view of processes are examined.

118. C. A black-box penetration tester knows nothing about the environment they are testing, perhaps just a name and an address. The first thing a pentester does is perform reconnaissance, trying to find out as much about the organization as possible.

119. A. Anyone anywhere can log into a desktop sharing tool. A remote support session usually begins with an employee clicking a link and giving up control of a system. If this is a malicious person, you are in some serious trouble. Once they have control of the system, they can access other enterprise systems such as databases, supporting servers, and more.

120. C. The best example of fault tolerance for hardware would have an identical server running in parallel. Fault-tolerant systems use backup components that automatically take the place of failed components, ensuring no loss of service.

121. A. The three-tiered approach consists of a brainstorming session, evaluating the ideas that come out of the brainstorming session, and then deciding which solution is best. More than one solution can work in a situation, but you will want to take into account factors such as cost and complexity. Doing so will help you work these security controls into the budget and timeline.

122. D. Replacement cost is the cost to replace the property on the same premises with other assets of comparable material and quality for the same purpose.

123. C. Privileged users can compromise sensitive data. Evaluate how flexible the tool's levels of user access are and evaluate if there are security risks at each level. The right collaboration tool should permit administrators to set up controls for user visibility and to terminate access rights for an account that is suspected to be compromised.

124. B. There are three main types of controls: detective, preventive, and corrective. Controls are policies and procedures or technical safeguards that are implemented to prevent problems and protect the organization. A business continuity and incident response plan is a preventive control type. Preventive internal controls are those controls put in place to avoid a negative event from occurring. Corrective controls are typically those controls put in place after the detective internal controls discover a problem. These controls could include disciplinary action, software patches, or modifications.

Chapter 5: Practice Test 1

1. A. The ALE is the ARO × SLE. The SLE is EF × AV. In this question, you have two equations to solve. The SLE is 10% × $1,000, which is $100. The ALE is 2 × $100.

2. C. Threat and risk assessments are the best way to identify the risks this company is facing. Pentesting will come after the controls are in place.

3. B. Training is the first line of defense against security risks. You cannot protect what you do not know exists. You will need training for compliance with regulatory requirements as well as organizational objectives. Awareness is achieved through cultural attitudes combined with training.

4. D. A keylogger, by its very nature, is meant to steal the keystrokes that the victim makes on the keyboard. Using this information, the attacker can replay websites, usernames, and passwords typed in by the victim.

5. B. The data might not be in the same format and not be able to be restored to a different application.

6. C. HBA is a host bus adapter. It is a hardware device, like a circuit board, that provides connectivity between a server and storage-attached network used to improve performance. LUN storage is important to the configuration. A LUN is a unique identifier given to separate devices so that they can be accessed in a storage disk array.

7. D. The goal of the confidentiality model Bell–LaPadula is to keep secret data secret and share secret data when it is allowed to be shared.

8. C. The Biba model is a state transition system for computer security. Data is grouped into ordered levels of integrity. The model was created so that subjects cannot corrupt the data. Invocation properties mean that a process from below cannot even request a higher access. It can only work with the same or lower levels. (Think of it as the inverse of Bell–LaPadula, which deals with security and people.)

9. D. Least privilege is assigning permissions so that users can access only those resources required to do their job. Job rotation, need to know, and separation of duties are also important to security. Job rotation avoids single points of failure, need to know promotes confidentiality, and separation of duties gives clear and direct roles to employees.

10. B. A gray-box test is performed with limited knowledge. Gray-box testing is a good way of finding security flaws in programs. It can assist in discovering bugs or exploits due to incorrect code structure or incorrect use of applications. By combining white-box and black-box testing, gray-box testing tries to get the best out of the two techniques. A white-box test is performed with complete and full internal knowledge. Black-hat hackers have extensive knowledge about breaking into systems, which is usually for financial gain. Yes, there are blue-hat hackers. A blue-hat hacker is someone who typically tests systems before they launch, looking for bugs.

11. B. A standard is a kind of security policy that defines how to remain in compliance with best practices and industry standards. Procedures are the step-by-step instructions on how to implement those best practices. Guidelines are used to create the procedures. Policies are at the highest level and describe the mission and goals. Policies are usually nonspecific and goal-oriented.

12. C. The focus of ALE calculations is to prioritize countermeasures. A countermeasure is an action taken to counteract a danger or threat. The asset-risk pair with the largest ALE should be dealt with first.

13. A. A rollback is a change control process that makes it possible to roll back any change that has a negative effect.

14. D. Senior management is always responsible for security within an organization. They are responsible for following the recommendations of the auditor.

15. A. Accreditation is the action of officially recognizing a particular security status is qualified to perform a certain function. If a vulnerability is found during accreditation, the vulnerability must be fixed and the process started over from the beginning.

16. A. Bluetooth is a personal area network (PAN) that enables you to connect and even share data with assets that are in a close physical range. Risks include bluejacking, which is sending a text message to other Bluetooth users. Bluebugging is using someone else's phone to place calls or send texts without them knowing.

17. A. When providing choices to users, a meeting should be held to weigh the convenience of a security process against the level of security that is required to protect the asset. Ideas can vary from person to person. You should meet with all stakeholders to both educate them and learn from them what the best system would be in this scenario.

18. D. A list of root passwords is not a requirement. A vulnerability assessment is the testing of systems and access controls for weaknesses.

19. D. With the amount of information online today, data mining is a threat that involves taking large amounts of that information for aggregation. An attacker can use this technique to find patterns on how you conduct business and find critical times when systems are most vulnerable.

20. C. To quantitatively evaluate risk, you must assess threat, vulnerability, and impact. The equation is Risk = Threat × Vulnerability × Impact. In our scenario, the answer is $4 \times 2 \times 6 = 48$.

21. B. The MTTR is calculated by using the total maintenance time as the numerator and the total number of repairs as the denominator. The 3 hours divided by the two times it went down gives you an MTTR of 1.5.

22. D. Protocol decoding IDP tools can reassemble packets and look at higher-layer activity like protocols that operate at the application layer.

23. A. The content addressable memory (CAM) table is the table on a switch used to store MAC addresses. The CAM table maps MAC addresses to physical switch ports and is used in the forwarding of Ethernet frames from one port to another.

24. B. The commands in option B would enable a network engineer to remotely log into the router using the password "secret."

25. D. A unique device identifier (UDID) is used to identify a device for the purpose of app installation and registration. Most modern UDIDs consist of 8 characters, a hyphen, and 16 more characters—for example, 00000040-0084239fab923b3e. The first 8 characters indicate the chip/manufacturer, and the 16 end characters are hexadecimal.

26. D. Buffer overflow attacks are possible because programmers do not check the length and format of input data before processing. Web servers are notorious for being unprotected against buffer overflow vulnerabilities.

27. A. Object reuse is the process by which you use authentication credentials that an application or process may have in memory to authenticate a user or application.

28. A. Pretexting takes real knowledge of a victim and uses that to attempt to get even more information. This type of scenario will engage and increase the chance the victim will fall for the pretext.

29. A. Spear phishing is a term used to identify the process of attempting to acquire sensitive information by masquerading as a trustworthy organization to one specific individual. If the email was sent in bulk, then it's called plain phishing. Emails claiming to be from common banks, retail sites, or social media are commonly used to lure the victim.

30. D. Diversion is a social engineering campaign that targets vendor delivery or transport companies. The objective of this type of trick is to make the delivery of goods to another location rather than the original location.

31. D. With a hard time limit set on an external exploitation, after a system is compromised, you could use the compromised system to move laterally through the network. With the internal access, you can attempt to exfiltrate the data you have been able to acquire and exploit other machines in the environment.

32. B. WiGLE is a search engine that maps 802.11 wireless networks. This site is searchable and has vast amounts of statistics for network admins and compliance auditors. It is also freely available to attackers.

33. D. In this type of situation, the best protection is to hire an expert external red team to do a black-box test of the program/product/code. A peer review may not discover items, and if collusion was in play, this would not work.

34. A. A gray-box test is an intermediary-level test. Because testers have knowledge of the system, they give input to the systems, check if the result is what was expected, and then check what the result is. This test combines the white-box and black-box tests.

35. A. A red team can perform all the necessary steps that true attackers would use against you. By assuming that role, they indicate what your company is vulnerable to.

36. A. The Committee on National Security Systems (CNSS) Instruction defines a white team as a group that is responsible for refereeing an engagement of red team attackers versus the blue team, the actual defenders of information systems.

37. A. Rapid7 owns both Metasploit and Nexpose. Using these tools together enables you to find vulnerabilities and actively attempt to exploit those vulnerabilities to prioritize what needs to be fixed first.

38. B. Agent-based file integrity can leverage software agents installed on systems needing monitoring. Agentless FIM gets up and running quickly but does not have the depth of analysis that agent-based FIM does.

39. D. Basic RFID tags use no encryption and can be counterfeited easily. Attackers can write information and modify an existing tag or clone a tag to invalidate authenticity. By reading information from an RFID, an attacker can track the location or movement of a person or object. More advanced RFID readers send requests to the tags for identification. An attacker could use their own RFID reader and use the information for their own purposes.

40. C. Sometimes, damage is physical, and sometimes it's logical. If the machine will not boot up in its original state, follow standard procedures for removing a hard drive, and with the appropriate connection, plug it into a functioning computer to pull off files as soon as possible. If the platters inside the drive do not spin, you will need to send the hard drive to a professional company, unless you happen to have your own clean room.

41. D. A security policy is a high-level document. A set of procedures is the opposite. Procedures are specific and precise. For example, while working for the military, the security policy said we would use port security. Procedures were how we enforced that security policy with "sticky MAC."

42. D. A white-hat hacker has a passion for helping, whereas the black-hat hacker is usually after financial gain. Red team and blue team members have similar skill sets—the red team being the aggressor and the blue being the defender. A white-box engagement means you know the company processes and landscape intimately, whereas the black-box engagement is approaching the target from the outside.

43. D. Bollards are strong heavy posts placed in front of physical structures to prevent accidents or unauthorized entry of vehicles crashing into a secure facility.

44. B. Boundary testing is a specific form of testing where values that are known to be out of acceptable ranges are placed into the form to see how the application handles the errors.

45. C. Of these choices, 802.11n would provide the best speed for devices compatible with 802.11g with throughput up to 600 Mbps. Devices using the 802.11n standard transmit in both the 2.4 GHz and 5.0 GHz frequency ranges. WiMAX is based on IEEE 802.16.

46. D. Software as a service (SaaS) is a term used in cloud computing. SaaS providers use streaming services or web applications to enable users to interact with software.

47. A. Performing a risk analysis on merging two disparate organizations together is the first thing you do. The results will feed into the interconnection policy so that you can merge the two entities securely.

48. D. SPML is a standard used for federated identity and promotes the automation of user account management operations. It presents LDAP in an XML format. SAML is XML and is used for exchanging authentication/authorization, and it's also typically used in browsers for SSO.

49. A. CIS Top 20 controls is a prioritized set of best practices developed by leading security experts. The most important of these is knowing what hardware you have, what software is on it, and where it is.

50. A. After being hired as a subject-matter expert on network security, you must understand the business you're working with and what assets are most important to that business. For example, a bank will have different priorities than a healthcare facility.

51. C. Boundary control includes security services typically provided by devices focused on protecting a system's entry point. A firewall can be set to protect a network's border from threats originating from the Internet. You can also use routers and proxies for boundary control.

52. A. A Type 1 hypervisor is a hypervisor installed on a bare-metal server, meaning that the hypervisor is its own operating system. Type 1 hypervisors usually perform better due to the direct access to physical hardware.

53. C. Infrastructure as a service (IaaS) enables a company to use hardware resources provided by a third party, including processing and networking to host varied multiple hosts.

54. B. While difficult to perpetrate, VM escape is considered a serious threat to VM security. VM escape is committed against Type 2 hypervisors. If you escape a Type 1 hypervisor, it is called hyperjacking.

55. A. A denial of service (DoS) affects availability and can be perpetrated against on-premise assets and virtual assets as well as poorly configured cloud assets. These attacks exploit many hypervisor platforms by flooding the network with traffic and bringing operations to a halt.

56. C. Security as a service is known as SECaaS as well as SaaS. SaaS has traditionally been known as software as a service. SECaaS is applied to information security services and does not require hardware on premises, and companies will avoid a large capital outlay. Security services can include authentication, antivirus, and antimalware, as well as intrusion detection, incident response, and penetration testing.

57. A. Service Provisioning Markup Language (SPML) is an automated provisioning mechanism designed to automate identity management tasks.

58. C. A Federated Identity Management solution would allow employees from the various companies to log in once and access resources they are authenticated to access at all companies.

59. D. OAuth does not share password information at all. OAuth is a framework that provides access to a third-party application without providing the owner's credentials to the application.

60. B. The information could be hidden from the naked eye. One means of extracting information from an organization is to hide the information in unsuspecting files such as image, music, and video files.

61. B. Mobile devices typically have much less processing power than other computing devices, thereby requiring encryption technology that is not resource intensive.

62. A. After a thorough risk and needs assessment, make sure that the network security policy is part of the official company manual. In addition, ensure that all employees have security awareness training and a copy of the security policy.

63. B. SSL VPNs grant granular access to a corporate network. A remote user can access only those applications that are important to their work. An example is access to a mailbox on an Exchange Server instance or a specific subset of URLs on the intranet.

64. B. Using unified communications presents serious security challenges because it brings together disparate technologies. As technology becomes more complex and accessible from the public Internet, the threat increases. You must be diligent in protecting communications that are vital.

65. A. When a UC server is updated, it is important to follow the best practices for updating. Make sure you know what has changed and how the update impacts the rest of your environment, backing up the system first and performing the update during a proper maintenance window.

66. C. Social engineering is manipulating people to give up information. A social engineering attack can be an email from a friend or another trusted source using a compelling story or pretext. The danger of social engineering with collaboration tools is that an end user's guard is down because these are co-workers they can trust, which makes it easy to extract information.

67. C. The best programs today have some of the best in the security world working 24/7 to identify and prevent issues. Make sure that your vendor has the necessary support for your team to be successful and consider training to help minimize adoption problems.

68. D. In the implementation phase, the system is transferred from a development-and-testing environment to production.

69. A. You can configure various security-related settings under Group Policy within Active Directory, such as the ones mentioned in the question.

70. A. Identity proofing is the process of verifying someone's identity based on information provided by a trusted authority. A driver's license is a form of identification provided by a trusted authority, in this case, the government.

71. A. Using the classic technique of acquiring credentials, attackers gain access to the collaboration account and send legitimate-looking URLs to team members. We have social awareness training for employees regarding email, but we have to teach them that there are other ways that attackers can get into your network.

72. C. The padlock in the URL field indicates that TLS or SSL is used to encrypt the data.

73. D. Using a RADIUS solution would provide an authentication, authorization, and account (AAA) function that will allow credentials to be easily managed from a central location while also providing login tracking. Using common usernames and passwords would prevent tracking login activity per user. Having unique usernames and passwords on each device will be difficult to manage, since each device needs to be modified as credentials are changed.

74. C. While SSL does encrypt data, TLS is the latest and most secure means of securing web-based communications today.

75. B. A known vulnerability should always be managed by patching or installing compensating controls so that the vulnerability cannot be exploited.

76. D. Whitelisting programs will prevent the user from downloading and installing programs that were not on the whitelist. This prevents unknown and untested software programs from being installed on a system.

77. D. Of the options available, creating a corporate policy that specifies employees are not to divulge corporate information on social media sites and the consequences of doing so is a great first step. The next step is to train the employees on the policy and the importance of not divulging such information.

78. A. PCI DSS was collectively created in 2006 by American Express, Discover, Visa, Mastercard, and JDB International for *any* organization, regardless of size or number of transactions that accepts, transmits, or stores any cardholder data. These best practices improve the security posture of an organization and safeguard cardholder information. You can find PCI-DSS best practices at www.pcicomplianceguide.org.

79. B. All merchants fall into four levels based on transaction volume over a 12-month period. Transaction volume is based on the number of credit, debit, or prepaid cards from a business. Merchant level 1 processes more than 6 million transactions annually, whereas merchant level 4 is 20,000 or less. Any merchant that suffered a breach resulting in data compromise may be escalated to a higher level.

80. A. A method of authentication is utilizing hardware but in a new way. We used licensing and tokens in the past, but putting the authentication into hardware is especially important for the Internet of Things (IoT). Good authentication requires three things from users: what they know, who they are, and what they have. The device itself becomes what they have. This way, the network ensures the thing trying to gain access is something that should have access.

81. C. You need to know where this malicious behavior is coming from. Instead of looking at users, machine learning looks at the entity. With proper business analytics and developments in machine learning models, we know that a specific data center behaves a certain way. Any anomalous behavior should trigger an alert.

82. D. More approaches to security are being created in and for the cloud and are continuing to evolve. Some cloud-hosting organizations, like Amazon, have programs of certified data centers, including above-average data center security. The provider will be responsible for building physical security into their facility.

83. A. All four of these are threat models. However, spoofing identity, tampering with data, repudiation, information disclosure, denial of service, and elevation of privilege (STRIDE) was developed in 1999 by Microsoft. These help systematically determine how an attacker uses a threat against you. PASTA is a seven-step risk assessment model, and TRIKE is used for security auditing. VAST enables you to scale the threat model across an entire ecosystem and SDLC and gives actionable output.

84. B. An unintended flaw left in software or in an operating system where there is no patch or fix is called a zero-day vulnerability. These vulnerabilities open an organization up to exploitation should it be found by cybercriminals. The term *zero-day* refers to a software vulnerability without a fix. Once the vulnerability is made public, the vendor has to work quickly to fix the issue. If it is used against an organization before the fix or patch is made available, it is known as a zero-day attack.

85. A. As an organization, you should reserve your brand on all social media channels. This enables you to reach across different channels, making it easier to do business. However, do not ignore accounts that you stopped using or don't use often. Idle social media accounts can be used fraudulently against you and could send false information, damaging your business.

86. B. Even when you lock down your social media accounts, you must beware of third-party applications that integrate with big social networks. Attackers gained access to Forbes' Twitter account through a third-party app called Twitter Counter, which is used for analysis.

87. A. Your organization needs to think carefully about who needs to have posting permission as well as passwords to social media accounts. Limiting access is the best way to keep them secure.

88. D. The latest threats on social media would be in your social media training. Your social media policy should be easy to understand, and training will give employees a chance to engage, ask questions, and review latest threats on social media and discuss if the social media policy needs updating.

89. A. Social media companies update privacy settings regularly, which can impact your account and give you more control over how data is gathered and used. You should also perform a scan of who has access to your social media platforms as well as publishing rights. Any employee who does not work for your company needs their access suspended.

90. A. Cybercriminals can penetrate your systems and make your sensors show fake results. You can fail to notice alarms and miss an opportunity to solve a problem before irreversible damage happens. Attackers can fabricate data and use it against you. This attack is thwarted with fraud detection.

Chapter 6: Practice Test 2

1. B. The best security design methodology is to work on identifying mission-critical assets and protecting assets-out and then working outwardly from there. Outside-in is the opposite of assets-out.

2. A. Switches examine the destination MAC address of a frame entering a switch port and compare it to the MAC address and port number assignments in the CAM table. If a match is found, the frame is forwarded out the assigned port. If a match is not found, the frame is forwarded out all ports except the port it originated from.

3. D. Switches use Media Access Control (MAC) addresses to forward frames. A MAC address is 48 bits in length and consists of two parts: the organizationally unique identifier (OUI) that uniquely identifies the manufacturer of the network interface card (NIC) the MAC is assigned to and the device ID or vendor-assigned number created by the NIC manufacturer.

4. C. The predominant routable protocol used today is IP. Open Shortest Path First (OSPF) and Routing Information Protocol (RIP) are examples of routing protocols. Frames and segments are not routable or routing protocols.

5. A. The first rule in a firewall list to match the packet processed, and no further processing through the rules occurs. Therefore, rules 3, 4, and 5, as well as the implicit deny at the end of the list, are not evaluated because the packet matched rule 2 and was permitted through the firewall.

6. D. The command enables frames with a source MAC address of 00:0E:08:34:7C:9B to pass. If a frame is received on the port with a MAC address other than 00:0E:08:34:7C:9B, the port is shut down. Shutdown is the default violation action.

7. B. To recognize a distributed denial-of-service (DDoS) attack, you must understand the normal traffic patterns of an organization. If you can't tell what your normal traffic pattern looks like, you can't identify what the attack traffic pattern looks like.

8. A. A remotely triggered black hole is a technique where a triggering device (i.e., router) can recognize DDoS traffic and the device sends out a routing update to other network routers, thus setting up a black hole to drop traffic. Transport security involves securing data as it traverses a network. Trunking security involves securing trunk links used to propagate VLAN traffic. Port security is concerned with a mechanism to secure ports on an Ethernet switch.

9. C. Of all the answers available, only the IP address range 172.32.0.0/16 is a valid range of source IP addresses for traffic entering from the Internet. The other IP addresses are special addresses that cannot be routed over the Internet. Responses from this traffic cannot be returned to its sender and must be dropped at the border router. Because the sender can't be reached, it is a sign of malicious activity. The majority of IP traffic filtering should be performed by a firewall, but limited filtering can be performed by a router as long as the filtering doesn't adversely affect the routing function of the router.

10. C. Antispyware products detect and remove programs specifically designed to covertly collect information on the infected system. Antimalware products detect various types of malware, including viruses, Trojans, ransomware, spyware, adware, and similar malicious programs/code. Antivirus products recognize and remove viruses. Anti-adware products detect and remove programs designed to display advertisements on an infected user's screen.

11. C. Whitelisting programs is the technique of allowing only approved programs to be downloaded to an end user's computer. If the program is not on the whitelist, either it is blocked or it sends an alert to IT, notifying them of the action.

12. D. Blacklisting is the process of blocking known malicious things such as known malicious websites. The problem with blacklisting is that new malicious sites pop up constantly, and thus, blacklisting won't include all malicious sites.

13. A. There is an implicit deny at the end of an access control list, so if no statement matches the packet being examined, the packet is dropped.

14. A. It is an extended ACL that denies ICMP traffic inbound from the Internet and permits all other traffic.

15. D. Whether Wi-Fi is turned on or turned off on a device typically does not affect Bluetooth's functionality.

16. A. All Wi-Fi standards fall under the 802.11 umbrella standard.

17. B. App wrapping enables mobile application management admins to set up specific policies. Examples include whether user authentication is required for a specific application and whether data associated with that application is stored on the device or in the cloud.

18. D. USB On-the-Go is a standardized specification that enables a device to read data from a USB device. The device becomes a USB host. You will need an OTG cable or connector.

19. C. Your fingerprint is biometric. It is something you are, not something you know.

20. D. A major challenge is the process by which the data is captured and mapped to an identity. If the process is flawed and the data is inaccurate, a partial capture of data can lead to a system failure.

21. A. This attack could also be called whaling because a specific high-ranking employee was targeted. Email monitoring is critical. Never click on email links, especially on a mobile device where the screen can be tiny compared to a desktop computer. Always enter URLs manually.

22. A. A push notification is a way for apps to send you a message without opening the application where the notification is "pushed" to the application. The most common way to identify push notifications is to look for a red circle with a number inside it on the app. The number represents how many updates/messages are waiting for the device's owner.

23. D. Near-field communication (NFC) can be used to induce electric currents inside passive components. The passive devices do not need a power source, but rather receive power from the electromagnetic field produced by an NFC component when in range. Samsung, Android, and Apple Pay use NFC. Bluetooth works better for connecting devices for file transfers or sharing connections to speakers.

24. A. When a cyberattack occurs on a mobile device that is now a primary threat vector, an enterprise organization must move quickly. If data leaked, all affected users must be notified, because an average data breach can cost millions. It is a good idea to explore having an insurance policy.

25. D. You should give the end user a list of software that is vetted and approved by IT. If comparable software is not found on that list, then the end user can request that the software be tested.

26. A. SD3 is Microsoft's defense-in-depth strategy. SD3 stands for secure by design, secure by default, and secure in deployment. Design means designers use secure coding best practices. Default means that end users install applications without changing the defaults, and deployment means it can be securely maintained with patching and auditing.

27. B. Users do not often change default settings after installation. Some do not even change default passwords. Security settings should be set by default. If a feature is specifically wanted by a user, they can enable it in the future.

28. C. An application can be maintained securely after deployment with patch management and auditing. It should also involve a process for monitoring events at regular intervals or after any failure.

29. B. Forced browsing is a technique used by attackers while searching for content that is not linked together on a web server. This is oftentimes considered to be a type of brute-force attack. An attacker may type in a URL, such as www.sybex.com/1, and then change to www.sybex.com/2 to see what else they might find.

30. A. A cross-site request forgery (XSRF) is an attack that takes advantage of a software vulnerability and redirects static content from a trusted site. An example might be stealing online banking credentials and account information from a user who logs into a legitimate banking site. CAPTCHA forms require solving some type of puzzle to validate that the user is human, revalidating the authenticity of the user.

31. D. When a web user accesses a decoy website or clicks a button to download a file or win a prize, they were tricked into clicking a hidden button that may result in payment of some sort on another site. It is not a CSRF, which depends on forging the entire request without the user's knowledge or input.

32. A. When developing any application, you must assume that all users are bad actors. Developers forget to properly handle error messages, which can be leveraged for the information they contain.

33. D. Depending on your security policy and compliance, the use of cookies could be a violation of privacy. Cookies can be used to record data, web-surfing habits, and so forth. Secure environments and organizations concerned about privacy should restrict the use of cookies. Cookies could possibly aid an attacker in spoofing a user's identity or contain connection and session management information.

34. A. When a computer functions normally, RAM gets used dynamically, and resources are allocated as needed. When software no longer needs the RAM, it is reallocated to the next program when necessary. In certain situations, RAM gets allocated but not freed up when no longer needed.

35. D. Encapsulation is a characteristic of object-oriented programming (OOP). OOP uses objects and instances of classes. Data that is defined for a specific class relates only to that specific class. The end result is that an object cannot accidentally read data from other objects.

36. C. Pseudonymization uses aliases or other fake identifiers to represent data that should be protected.

37. A. When managing a graphical user interface with text fields and radio buttons that can trigger other text or input fields, one input state can influence another input state.

38. C. JavaScript vulnerabilities are common in web applications. Insecure JavaScript and bad coding can cost time and money. Several tools, like ZAP and Grabber, can help examine those web applications, scanning a site for vulnerabilities.

39. A. You must target specific areas to identify the maximum number of high-severity vulnerabilities within the time you have to deploy the new assets.

40. C. Runtime debugging is useful to examine the state of a program during runtime. Setting breakpoints and executing small pieces of code at a time helps find why a theoretically correct piece of code does not execute the way you expect.

41. D. A technique used by attackers takes advantage of websites that people regularly visit and trust. The attacker gathers information about group of people visiting specific websites and tests those websites for vulnerabilities. Over time, the odds of that target group visiting that site and getting infected increases and then the attacker has access.

42. D. It is no coincidence this is called baiting. What do you do to a "phish" hook? Baiting means that you dangle something interesting in front of your victim like a movie file or something labeled "confidential." Once the malicious file is downloaded and installed, the victim is infected, enabling the attacker to pivot and own the network.

43. C. Quid pro quo is Latin for "something for something." In this case, someone from "IT support" calls you to say they have something for you if you do something for them. This is a good way to get malware/ransomware installed on a machine.

44. D. Passive recon is when you use tools like social media to find out all you can about an organization and who works for them. Social engineering can be used to find email addresses, the types of available jobs, and the tools used in that environment.

45. A. Whois is a protocol used to query databases that store registered users of a domain name or IP address.

46. A. A routing table is a dataset used to determine where packets are directed on a network. Routing table poisoning occurs when unwanted or malicious changes are made in the table.

47. B. Shodan is a search engine that helps you locate devices connected to the Internet, their location, and how they are used. It is free and helps with digital footprinting. Shodan also offers a public API that enables other tools to access all Shodan's data.

48. B. A black-box penetration test occurs when the penetration tester has no knowledge of the organization.

49. A. The black-box penetration test done by a small firm that has signed an NDA gives you a true external perspective of the environment that the CTO requires.

50. A. The Common Vulnerability Scoring System (CVSS) is a generic mathematical algorithm that scores a vulnerability based on the CIA triad, as well as attack vector, authentication, and complexity. The concern is how these vulnerabilities affect your specific environment, and for that you need a black-box test so that vulnerabilities can be prioritized based on local impact.

51. D. An anomaly detection–based IDS is best at detecting the newest security threats. An anomaly detection device finds the oddities in network traffic behavior by taking a baseline first of what normal patterns look like. Once you have a baseline, it will compare current traffic to detect abnormal traffic.

52. B. KillDisk is a tool that enables you to overwrite hard drives numerous times. Hard drives contain sectors, and groups of sectors are called *clusters*. When data is written to a sector, the OS can allocate the entire cluster to that data. Deleting data by using the OS does not remove the data from clusters. It removes the filename from the file allocation table and makes the space available for writing again. The data is still there, even when you delete the contents of the recycle bin.

53. D. You should check the DNS because the FTP server is mapped to an IP address. The DNS server is used to resolved hostnames or fully qualified domain names (FQDNs) to an IP.

54. B. A vulnerability scan should be used as an intruder would, without trusted credentials on a network. This type of scan can show vulnerabilities that can be accessed without logging into the network.

55. A. An application scanner can help ensure that software applications are free from the flaws and weaknesses that attackers often use to exploit and exfiltrate data. Backdoors, malicious code, and threats are flaws present in both commercial and open source software.

56. B. Option B is the only answer that is a legitimate process. Scan the client-facing web portal to identify any ports that are exposed and services running on those ports; then determine if they are vulnerable.

57. C. Acunetix WVS (i.e., web vulnerability scanner) is used specifically for web vulnerabilities. It includes a login sequence recorder giving you access to password-protected areas of a website. Also, you can scan any WordPress site for more than 1,200 vulnerabilities.

58. C. Metasploit is an open source collection of exploit tools that can be customized with your own tools. It is one of the most popular tools backed by hundreds of thousands of users. As a pentester, this tool enables you to pinpoint vulnerabilities as well as integrate with Nexpose, one of the best vulnerability management tools.

59. C. Maltego is an open source platform that can be used as a forensics platform to show the complexity in your infrastructure. With Maltego, you can find individuals, email structure, websites, domains, IP addresses, DNS, and even documents and passwords. It has a GUI interface that can be customized.

60. B. After running md5 "C:printer_driver.dll", the program returns a series of characters that you check against the checksum on the file's original download page.

61. D. ping is one of the most basic network commands. It helps determine connectivity and can be used to measure speed or latency.

62. C. traceroute is a diagnostic network command and tells us where the packet is going. This will show the route a packet takes to the destination and can show if the network is working properly.

63. B. With file integrity monitoring (FIM), the standard or regulation states that data must be monitored or managed so as to ensure integrity. FIM software is among the most critical PCI DSS compliance requirements for the health of a security program. As configurations and networks change, it's possible to become noncompliant with PCI standards quickly. FIM works by detecting changes to files and configurations. When FIM is installed, it creates a baseline to determine your current status. It is stored in a database as cryptographic hashes that cannot be edited, deleted, or altered.

64. D. Locks secure and fasten something with the goal that the only one with a key should have access. Lock picks or skeleton keys are tools used to unlock a lock by manipulating the tumblers inside.

65. B. Infrared (IR) cameras see at night by using light with wavelengths that are invisible to the human eye. If you need to monitor property at night, choose an IR camera.

66. A. RFID is a tracking system that uses radio frequency. Placing tags on equipment enables you to trace who checks out the tools. And, if you have a portal type entrance/exit reader, you'll know where these tools are, should someone need a specific tool and it's checked out to another user.

67. A. RFID is prone to virus attacks, with the backend database being the main target. An RFID virus can disclose the tag data or destroy what is in the database, disrupting the service.

68. A. Do not save any program files or documents, because doing so makes your computer write data to the hard drive, which increases the possibility that the data you are trying to rescue will be overwritten. You should not move files or folders or reboot the machine.

69. A. With storage, you need strong enough security systems that a break would cost potential attackers more time and effort (i.e., work factor) than the data is worth. Cost and value of data is most important—no one wants to end up with systems that are more expensive than the data's value.

70. D. Network topology and subnets are not a concern to be addressed with data-at-rest policies and procedures.

71. C. A direct-attached storage (DAS) system is often the cheapest option. The first problem with DAS is limited disk space, and depending on size, some servers have only two or three disk slots. This space can be consumed quickly, depending on the type of RAID deployed. The other problems with DAS are that they need to be backed up often, and they cannot share data with other servers on the network. DAS is best used for operating systems.

72. C. A storage area network (SAN) is a data network composed of servers that connect to a centralized storage space. Storage can be easily expanded to increase data recovery. And, if the server's boot from the SAN rather than DAS, a failover server can boot from the original SAN disk, reducing downtime. It costs more, but you get more.

73. D. Patch management is expected, but unexpected software installs are not. Know your network, including what is normal and what is abnormal, and always assume you are under attack.

74. D. Although every company is unique, you must ensure that technical, legal, and public relations are all on the same page. Technical teams obviously are in charge of incident handling, legal assures compliance with the law, and public relations needs a clear corporate position to communicate to the media and the rest of the company. For example, sales will need to know what to say to customers regarding the incident but will likely get that from PR.

75. A. Mapping regulations to security metrics enables hunt team members to prove compliance quickly. If not, they have to gather, organize, and store the necessary metrics each time they need to prove compliance, which is time spent better elsewhere.

76. B. Heuristics and behavior analysis supplement the rules with subtle and detailed interpretations of patterns of events, which are based on experience instead of a binary rule set.

77. D. When a Windows machine blue-screens, it creates a memory dump or a crash dump. This file has all the computer's memory at the time of the crash. It can help diagnose problems that led to the crash in the first place.

78. D. Most organizations orchestrate their own incident classification framework and base severity on the same categories as the NIST CVE. Those categories are Critical, High, Moderate, and Low.

79. C. You need to determine what types of records were compromised. Was it personal information with credit card information or personal information with healthcare data? Not only are each type valued differently on the dark web, but you will be fined differently based on your compliance requirements.

80. C. If the hard disk fails due to a mechanical issue, then repeated access to the drive can result in losing more data or corrupting what still exists. You should minimize access to the drive.

81. A. With vulnerabilities, patch management is crucial for reducing risk. Some vulnerabilities require compensating controls, whereas others require removal from the organization. Either way, a reevaluation of response times, head count acquisition, and process improvement can all come from an AAR.

82. A. TCP port 20 is used to transfer data, and TCP port 21 is used for control commands. The FTP server listens for a client to initiate a session on port 21 and then initiates the data connection over port 20.

83. D. Security best practices and policies should be short—a maximum of two to three pages. Shorter policies are elaborated on with procedures, standards, and guidelines. Shorter policies are more easily understood and easier for an organization to comply with.

84. D. The situation described has a security risk of data remanence. Remanence is the residual information that remains on a disk after it has been erased. The VM is unavailable, but that doesn't mean the data has been destroyed.

85. D. Security marking uses human-readable labels. Security labeling is the use of security attributes for internal data structure inside information systems. Security marking enables organizational process-based enforcement of security policies, whereas labeling enables information system–based enforcement of security policies.

86. C. A covert channel is a type of computer attack that enables information to be leaked through existing information channels or networks using the existing structure. It has been used to steal sensitive data by using some of the space available within network packets, enabling the attacker to receive the data without leaving a data trail. A packet may have only a single bit of the covert data, making it nearly impossible to detect. A primary way of defending against covert channels is to examine source code and monitor resource usage by critical systems.

87. D. Software developers often leave a backdoor in tools but should remove them before the software goes to market. If the backdoor is left in a product by accident, it is called a maintenance hook. A security patch is often used to remove the maintenance hook.

88. A. A workgroup is a prime example of privilege management where the user accounts are decentralized. The other options are all centralized privilege management solutions.

89. C. NIST recommends that data storage media be physically destroyed at the final stage of media life. It is also considered the best method of sanitizing data.

90. D. A hazard of machine learning is model drift. Machines learn for themselves, and it is impossible to figure out how they learned and why decisions were made. It is, therefore, difficult to prevent undesirable outcomes in advance or to trace them to correct them afterward.

Index

A

access control/access control lists (ACLs),
24, 29, 51, 78, 99, 163, 204, 253, 264,
266, 272, 282, 295, 326, 345
account lockout, 48, 270
accountability, 53, 151, 274, 319
accreditation, 210, 347
Active Directory (AD), 221, 273, 351
active reconnaissance, 87, 280, 288
active scanning, 82, 285
Acunetix WVS, 239, 358
Address Resolution Protocol (ARP), 16,
171, 251, 332
address space layout randomization
(ASLR), 142, 314
Advanced Encryption Standard
(AES), 161, 165–167, 310, 325,
326, 327, 329
after-action report (AAR), 79,
102, 283, 297
agent-based file integrity, 215, 349
agentless NAC, 23, 255
agents, 14, 82, 249, 284
Agile, 40, 265
Aircrack-ng, 115, 303
alerts, monitoring, 152, 319
Android ROM, 35, 261
annual loss expectancy (ALE), 183,
208, 334, 346
annualized rate of occurrence
(ARO), 181, 334
anomaly devices, 238, 358
anti-adware products, 254, 315, 354

antimalware products, 146, 254, 315, 354
antispyware products, 230, 315, 354
antivirus products, 21, 254, 315, 354
Apache log, 78, 282
app wrapping, 33, 232, 260, 355
application programming interface (API),
33, 92, 260, 290
application scanner, 239, 252, 358
application-specific integrated circuit
(ASIC), 148, 317
approval, 78, 282
ARP cache, 250
asset management, 36, 262
Asset Reporting Format (ARF), 285
assets-out, 228, 353
asymmetric encryption algorithm, 58,
277
Asynchronous JavaScript and XML
(Ajax), 18, 93, 252, 291
asynchronous transfer mode (ATM), 325
attack surface, 42, 147, 266, 316
attestation, 145, 194, 274, 315, 340
attribute-based access control (ABAC),
52, 272–273
audit logs, 105, 153, 298, 320
audit trail, 77, 143, 151, 282, 314, 318
Authenticated Encryption with Additional
Data (AEAD), 162, 168, 326, 329
authenticated scan, 195, 340
authentication, 15, 163, 204, 250,
266, 326, 345
authorization, 52, 266, 272
automation, 259
autoscaling, 30, 259

N

S

W

warm site, 153, 203, 317, 319, 344
waterfall method, 41, 265
watering hole, 236, 357
weaponization, 286–287
wearables, 59, 277–278
web application firewall (WAF),
    14, 249, 251
white team, 214, 349
white-box testing, 34, 86, 196, 261, 262,
    264, 287, 340, 346, 349
white-hat hacker, 215–216, 349
whitelisting, 222, 230, 352, 354
Whois, 26, 237, 256, 357
Wi-Fi, 133, 231, 250, 309, 355
Wi-Fi Protected Access (WPA),
    171, 326, 331
WiGLE, 214, 348

wildcard certificate, 156, 321
Wired Equivalent Privacy (WEP), 326
Wireless Equivalent Protection
    (WEP), 134, 309
wireless intrusion detection system
    (WIDS), 13, 248
wireless LAN (WLAN), 309
Wireshark, 44, 77, 110, 111, 119, 121,
    268, 282, 301, 306, 307
workgroup, 37, 246, 263, 361

Z

zero trust, 24, 256
zero-day vulnerability, 83, 224,
    285–286, 353
Zigbee, 150, 318
zip command, 305

Online Test Bank

Register to gain one year of FREE access after activation to the online interactive test bank to help you study for your CASP+ certification exam—included with your purchase of this book! All of the chapter review questions and the practice tests in this book are included in the online test bank so you can practice in a timed and graded setting.

Register and Access the Online Test Bank

To register your book and get access to the online test bank, follow these steps:

1. Go to www.wiley.com/go/sybextestprep.
2. Select your book from the list.
3. Complete the required registration information, including answering the security verification to prove book ownership. You will be emailed a pin code.
4. Follow the directions in the email or go to www.wiley.com/go/sybextestprep.
5. Find your book on that page and click the "Register or Login" link with it. Then enter the pin code you received and click the "Activate PIN" button.
6. On the Create an Account or Login page, enter your username and password, and click Login or, if you don't have an account already, create a new account.
7. At this point, you should be in the test bank site with your new test bank listed at the top of the page. If you do not see it there, please refresh the page or log out and log back in.

SYBEX®
A Wiley Brand